APPLIED

FOODSERVICE SANITATION

APPLIED
FOODSERVICE SANITATION
Third Edition

National Restaurant Association
THE EDUCATIONAL FOUNDATION

A Foundation Textbook

WILEY

John Wiley & Sons
in cooperation with the
Educational Foundation of the National Restaurant Association
(Formerly the National Institute for the Foodservice Industry)

Developed in collaboration with the
National Sanitation Foundation

APPLIED
FOODSERVICE SANITATION
Third Edition

WITHDRAWN

National Restaurant Association
THE EDUCATIONAL FOUNDATION
A Foundation Textbook

WILEY

John Wiley & Sons
in cooperation with the
Educational Foundation of the National Restaurant Association
(Formerly the National Institute for the Foodservice Industry)

Developed in collaboration with the
National Sanitation Foundation

On behalf of the
people in the foodservice industry
who will benefit, the Educational Foundation
is pleased to thank

NORTH AMERICAN FOODSERVICE COMPANIES, INC.
and
NABISCO BRANDS USA

for the financial support
which has made possible
the development of this book.

Contents

Foreword

The number of outbreaks of foodborne disease reported to the **Centers for Disease Control** has not declined substantially during the past two decades. The majority of these outbreaks have originated from foods that were mishandled or subject to time-and-temperature abuse in *foodservice establishments*. In addition, food spoilage and deterioration cause an unneeded economic burden to the foodservice industry. These situations have developed despite continuous improvements in foodservice facilities and equipment because some workers and some supervisors were either unaware of or indifferent to measures for controlling food safety.

Appropriate training is the best way for foodservice personnel, especially managers and supervisors, to learn about the hazards that are associated with their particular operation and with the foods they prepare for patrons. Furthermore, training can stimulate them to control and monitor critical phases of their operations.

Early educational approaches, usually conducted by officials from health agencies, commenced in the early 1940s and concentrated on training foodservice workers. Frustration with this approach evolved during the next decade or two because of the tremendous turnover of foodservice personnel and the lack of involvement of managers of establishments from which the trainees came. In the 1970s, renewed interest in training emerged, but this time the emphasis was on training managers of foodservice operations.

The **National Institute for the Foodservice Industry (NIFI)*** was *and is* a leader in the movement for training and certifying foodservice managers in sanitation. This began, in part, when NIFI first developed a certification course in foodservice sanitation built around the text, *Applied Foodservice Sanitation,* prepared other training aids in food safety, and established a protocol for training reciprocity. As a result, many of the foodservice industry's leading chains and institutions have trained their managers and set up intensive programs to ensure that foods are prepared in a manner that protects their quality and prevents food-borne disease. NIFI leadership in foodservice sanitation training continues and is demonstrated in the third edition of this text.

Foodservice industry professionals, regulatory agencies, and instructors in academic institutions who either apply or teach others to apply the principles and practices presented in *Applied Foodservice Sanitation, Third Edition,* will contribute to the reduction of food-borne disease and the improvement of food quality. This text, therefore, serves as a cohesive force to help these groups work together for these two important, common goals.

Frank L. Bryan, Ph.D.
Scientist Director
Centers for Disease Control
U.S. Public Health Service

On January 1, 1987, the National Institute for the Foodservice Industry was consolidated with the educational services of the National Restaurant Association to form the Educational Foundation of the National Restaurant Association.

A Message from the Educational Foundation

THE EDUCATIONAL FOUNDATION OF THE NATIONAL RESTAURANT ASSOCIATION is proud to present *Applied Foodservice Sanitation, Third Edition,* a book for foodservice managers, supervisors, workers, and those aspiring to management jobs in the foodservice industry. The third edition of this widely used text increases its focus on meeting the everyday concerns of foodservice managers and also includes new, vital information on foodservice sanitation.

Sanitation is an important concern of patrons. We've always known that. However, the practice of foodservice sanitation is another challenge to management amid a number of challenges. *Applied Foodservice Sanitation* provides information and methods to help the foodservice manager *apply* sanitation procedures to foodhandling functions from purchasing, storing, to preparing and serving it to patrons. Only by implementing a complete sanitation program can the operator be assured that food is safe right up to the time it is served.

Applied Foodservice Sanitation, Third Edition reflects the growing awareness in the industry that good foodservice sanitation is essential to the bottom line. Sanitation helps preserve the good image of an establishment, keeps patrons happy, and helps the operation stay on the right side of state and local health requirements. *Whatever the setting or type of operation, it is good business to run a clean and sanitary establishment.*

This update incorporates changes in the FDA standards, new information on equipment, and new material on cleaning and sanitizing operations. It also includes vital information on how to *work through people* to maintain a sanitary operation, such as training workers, working with a pest control operator, and dealing with local health officers.

Applied Foodservice Sanitation is the central text for a management course designed to reach the greatest possible number of people entrusted with serving food to the general public. As with other management courses in the series, the sanitation course is arranged for administration in a variety of ways. Individuals may undertake it as a home study project in direct correspondence with the Educational Foundation. Foodservice personnel may take the course in a format tailored for in-service group-training programs sponsored by foodservice companies, trade associations, and other industry organizations. The text and related course materials will, of course, be available to college and community college students of hotel, restaurant, and institutional management as part of the regular academic curriculum.

All who complete the course—through home study, in industry groups, or in the college classroom—will be eligible for an Educational Foundation certificate upon satisfactory completion of a certification examination administered under Institute auspices.

The development of this book was greatly aided by members of the industry and educator representatives who served on the *Applied Foodservice Sanitation* Review Board. They include Joel Simpson, Director of Quality Assurance, Dobbs House; Michael Farnsworth, Program Manager, Chief Foodservice Sanitation Section of the Michigan Department of Health; Professor Charles Eshbach, Department of Hotel, Restaurant, and Travel Administration, the University of Massachusetts; Ron McKinley, Instructor of Managerial Skills, Marriott; Sam Jones, Supervisor of Operations Training, Red Lobster Inns of America; Paul F. Martin, Director of Educational Programs, the Educational Foundation; Gary Sherlaw, Director of Standards and Development, and Tom Gable, Executive Vice President, both of the National Sanitation Foundation. Special recognition is due Marlene R. Chamberlain, the Foundation's Managing Editor, who managed this project and whose expertise resulted in the smooth integration of new FDA code interpretations and reviewer comments in this edition.

We also appreciate the technical review and information received from Robert Ulm, Instructor, Culinary Division, Johnson & Wales College; Charles Phillips, Regional Retail Food Specialist, The Food and Drug Administration; Jerome P. O'Hara, Research and Training, Anderson Pest Control; and Nancy O'Connell, Quality Assurance Manager, formerly with Creative Dining Inc.

We would like to thank the National Sanitation Foundation for cooperation in the development of *Applied Foodservice Sanitation, Third Edition.*

THE EDUCATIONAL FOUNDATION OF THE NATIONAL RESTAURANT ASSOCIATION IS THE FOODSERVICE INDUSTRY'S *EDUCATIONAL FOUNDATION.* The Educational Foundation is dedicated to the advancement of professionalism in the foodservice industry, fostering and nurturing it through education. The Foundation provides vital services to the industry through the development of educational programs and materials and the administration of scholarships and work-study grants, and by promoting industry careers.

Education contributes to both the growth of the industry and to the professional and personal growth of the individual who enjoys the rewards. *Applied Foodservice Sanitation, Third Edition,* is one way we can contribute to your professional growth.

Richard J. Hauer
Executive Director
The Educational Foundation of the National Restaurant Association

Part I
Sanitation and Health

1
Providing Safe Food

Eating out is fun. Having meals away from home is a national pastime that aggressively rivals other social activities such as attending the theater, watching sports games, and other forms of recreation. It is also an important part of these activities.

Eating out helps us meet social as well as physical needs. People love to get together over food. Friends meet for lunch, for cocktails after work, or go to dinner after an evening at the theater.

Eating out also helps us take care of business. Meeting over food is often conducive to negotiating and planning. The business lunch is the key to success for many full-service restaurants in metropolitan areas. In addition, conferences are often arranged around a schedule that includes at least one, and possibly three meals.

As enjoyable as eating out is, it is also true that many of us simply must eat away from home at one time or another. Passengers on transportation systems, guests in hotels, patients in hospitals, residents of nursing homes or other institutions, students in schools and universities, and the men and women serving in the military all need food provided for them. Through choice or necessity the average person eats out at least three times a week.

WHAT PEOPLE EXPECT

Diners walking into a commercial facility for the first time bring with them a number of expectations. They expect good, safe food, clean surroundings, and pleasant service. These things taken together make up a pleasant dining experience. Subtract any one of these factors and customers of a commercial operation can take their business elsewhere.

Patrons of noncommercial or semicommercial operations such as patients in hospitals and other health institutions, students in schools and colleges, and prisoners incarcerated in various local, state, and federal facilities also have a number of expectations. They expect good, safe food, clean surroundings, and pleasant service. Sound familiar? It should. *People dining anywhere outside the home assume that they will receive all these things.*

It is a challenge to managers of commercial and noncommercial establishments to direct a number of activities at once, including employee training, the purchasing, preparation, and service of food, all to provide the customer or patron with good, safe food and pleasant dining. This is the bottom line—giving people what they expect.

Foodservice managers in both commercial and noncommercial operations generally expect that they will meet the diner's expectations. They *assume* that they are going to provide good, safe food in clean surroundings, and preferably, friendly service. This assumption, especially regarding safe food and clean surroundings, too often is based on a foundation of goodwill and good intentions rather than a sound background in sanitary procedures.

It is critical that foodservice operators and employees have a solid foundation in procedures that will—at minimum—ensure that diners receive safe food. *Safe food* is hot food that is hot, cold food that is cold, and food that is not contaminated by disease-causing organisms, or physical or chemical contaminants. The last thing any foodservice operator wants to do is serve food that makes someone ill. Yet this is a very real possibility.

In this chapter we will

- Learn the reasons for managing a sanitary foodservice operation
- Examine the terms *foodborne illness* and *outbreak*
- Define sanitation
- Review the hazards to sanitary food
- Consider the role of the foodservice manager in sanitation

FOODBORNE ILLNESS

We all know that people sometimes get sick from what they eat. It doesn't happen very often to any one of us, and when it does we may not get very sick or be sick for very long. Moreover, in many cases we are inclined to shrug it off with the thought that maybe we ate too much.

But we are also aware that sometimes large numbers of people become ill in public eating places and at community gatherings with *serious* results. These events are much more likely to be reported, as are, of course, sensational incidents in which death or grave illness is caused by contaminated food.

What usually happens, however, is that people who get sick in public places go to different doctors, different hospitals, or do nothing. Still, the bottom line is that if the illness comes after a visit to a particular facility, most people will be *understandably reluctant to visit it again*. The reason for this is simply that eating unsafe food just isn't what people expect.

A *foodborne illness* is a disease that is carried or transmitted to human beings by food. Any kind of food can be the vehicle for foodborne illness. Some of the foods implicated in foodborne illnesses are poisonous by nature, for example, mushrooms or certain types of fish. However, it is mostly high-protein foods we eat regularly—poultry, beef, fish, dairy products, and pork—that are responsible for most foodborne illnesses. Such foods are receptive hosts to certain forms of bacteria and other disease agents. This problem is made worse by poor storage, preparation, and service. These high-protein foods are classified as *potentially hazardous* by the U.S. Public Health Service.

The U.S. Public Health Service identifies potentially hazardous food as *any food that consists in whole or in part of milk or milk products, eggs, meat, poultry, fish, shellfish, edible crustacea, baked or boiled potatoes, tofu, and other soy-protein foods, or other ingredients, including synthetic ingredients, in a form capable of supporting rapid and progressive growth of infectious or toxigenic micro-organisms. In addition, recent research has indicated that cooked rice, and beans, can support bacterial growth and should also be considered potentially hazardous. The term does not include clean, whole, uncracked, odor-free shell eggs, nor foods that have a pH level of 4.6 or below or a water activity of 0.85 or less under standard conditions, nor food products in hermetically sealed containers.* (*Water activity* is the amount of moisture available to aid in bacterial growth.)

Outbreaks of Foodborne Illness

"It was probably just something I ate." "It was just a touch of the flu." These common expressions are often used to mask the problem of foodborne illness. Most victims of foodborne illnesses do not readily identify the source of their ailment, and are understandably more concerned with obtaining relief. However, there are increasing signs that the public is becoming more aware of the connection between food and illness. Newspapers report outbreaks connected to schools and other public gatherings. Other newspapers such as the *New York Times* regularly report closings of restaurants due to sanitation violations. Mostly, though, it is up to the various government bodies and the state and local equivalents of the U.S. Public Health Service to obtain information on foodborne illnesses.

Since 1938 the U.S. Public Health Service's Centers for Disease Control (CDC) have published annual summaries on outbreaks of foodborne illness. An *outbreak* is defined as an incidence of foodborne illness that involves two or more persons who eat a common food, with the food confirmed as the source of the illness by a laboratory analysis. (One exception: A single incidence of botulism qualifies as an

Exhibit 1.1   Cost of foodborne illness to the foodservice industry

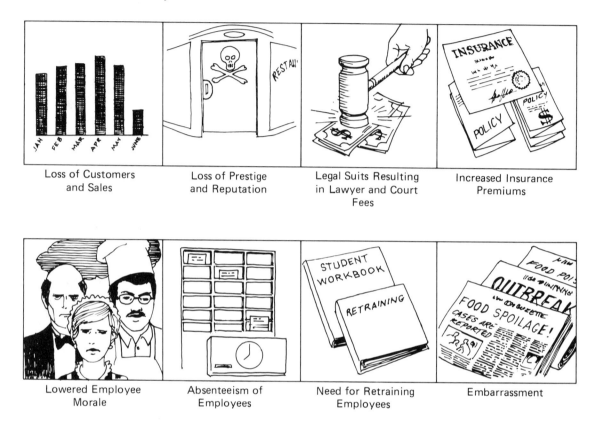

Loss of Customers and Sales   Loss of Prestige and Reputation   Legal Suits Resulting in Lawyer and Court Fees   Increased Insurance Premiums

Lowered Employee Morale   Absenteeism of Employees   Need for Retraining Employees   Embarrassment

outbreak.) Public Health Service reports are based on summaries of foodborne illnesses reported by individual states.

The Public Health Service has three objectives in gathering information on foodborne illnesses: (1) disease prevention and control, including correction of faulty food preparation practices in foodservice establishments; (2) knowledge of the disease and the causing element (To control foodborne diseases it is important to zero in on the source, so that remedies can be found and control measures adopted.); (3) administrative guides. The U.S. Public Health Service provides information on outbreaks to help guide local public health departments in reviewing their programs in order that they may come up with more effective inspection procedures.

WHY FOODSERVICE MANAGERS SHOULD PROTECT CUSTOMERS (DOLLARS AND SENSE)

Why should the foodservice manager be interested in protecting customers and patrons from foodborne illness? Because it makes good sense, it helps maintain patronage, it preserves goodwill, it prevents legal liability, and

Exhibit 1.2   How people decide where to eat

	Frequent Patrons	Heaviest Spenders	Adventurers	Business Diners	Total Sample
Friend's recommendation	73.3%	76.1%	69.4%	73.7%	65.0%
Reputation of restaurant	45.5	52.7	45.4	51.5	39.8
Family member recommendation	39.1	35.3	39.3	38.7	39.0
Review in newspaper	26.9	28.4	23.8	26.5	19.9
Price discount	28.8	23.9	25.8	25.5	24.6
Coupons	28.2	20.9	24.6	23.9	23.9
Newspaper ad	23.2	22.4	24.6	21.8	21.3
Restaurant guide	8.5	13.4	10.0	11.1	5.9
Television ad	11.2	10.0	8.9	10.3	10.3
Radio ad	7.7	6.5	6.6	9.3	6.7

Reprinted by permission from *Restaurants & Institutions*, Volume 94, Number 24, December 5, 1984.

when all these things are taken into account, it helps save dollars. The costs of foodborne illness can be high (see Exhibit 1.1).

Patrons and Goodwill

The best form of advertising is the type that generates *goodwill*. Goodwill is one of those intangibles that is measured by the recognition of patrons that the foodservice operator means well and wants them to return.

Without regular patrons foodservice operations would close their doors. Without a steady, regular patronage commercial operations would not survive lean times and might barely make a profit during good times. Continued, repeat patronage or the kind that can reflect a steady profit margin is not an automatic right of anyone entering the foodservice business. It is earned. Further, good customers are the best form of advertising. They tell other customers (see Exhibit 1.2). They can also warn people away (see Exhibit 1.3).

Exhibit 1.3   People tell potential customers negative as well as positive views

Potential Customer   Former Potential Customer

The chicken soup was good and hot, and the restroom was clean.

There was a fly in my cold soup, and the restroom was filthy.

Regulation

One powerful motive for protecting customers and patrons is the law. Simply put, it is illegal to be unsanitary. State laws, county or regional health codes, and municipal ordinances with provision for fines or closure for violations, outlaw unsafe foodhandling practices for local food services. These laws are aimed at protecting the public. Many local health services also serve as consultants on safe foodhandling practices as well as employee training and advise operators on meeting requirements for sanitary facilities. Federal regulations, which cover food produced and processed for interstate commerce, may or may not directly affect foodservice operations.

Liability

The law provides yet another incentive. Today, consumers are increasingly willing to use the law to seek compensation for products that have caused them harm. This is true for items from cars to baby cribs and is certainly true for unsafe food products. The *Uniform Commercial Code* provides an option to people who want compensation for illness or injury from unsafe food products. People suing only need prove that the food was unfit, that it caused them harm, and that in serving them unfit food the operator violated the warranty of sale.

Operators of noncommercial facilities share similar concerns regarding the law, and in some cases liability. However, particular establishments have an additional reason for wanting to protect patrons. For example, most people go to hospitals because they are already ill. The last thing hospital patients need is a foodborne illness. The results could be serious, even deadly. Residents of nursing homes have especially low resistance and such an illness could worsen an already weak condition. Many deaths that result from foodborne illnesses occur among the elderly. The very young and the very old are especially susceptible to serious problems from foodborne illness; the former because they have not built up adequate immune systems to cope with such diseases and the latter simply because they have less immunity and resistance as they age.

The Bottom Line

If these aren't incentives enough, consider the bad publicity that can follow an outbreak of foodborne illness. Even if only one person gets ill, he or she may be willing to warn others to stay away from an operation.

The bottom line is that sanitary procedures will prevent outbreaks of foodborne illness, maintain goodwill, and keep the financial bottom line from bottoming out.

IT CAN HAPPEN ANYWHERE

All foodservice operations have the potential to cause foodborne illness through errors in purchasing, receiving, storing, preparing, and serving food. Of the many types of operations that exist (see Exhibit 1.4), none are exempt from causing foodborne illness in the absence of adequate precautions.

Illness can result from eating in virtually any type of operation where foods are served. Consider the following:

- A once popular restaurant in the Midwest is forced into bankruptcy after a botulism outbreak caused by tainted onions. Lawsuits lodged against the restaurant reach well into millions of dollars.
- A major food chain in the Southwest is sued by parents of children who were served food prepared too far in advance, not reheated, and contaminated with *Bacillus cereus* bacteria.
- At a hospital in the East, 34 patients, including two in traction and with their mouths wired shut, are stricken with the foodborne illness salmonellosis. The culprit is traced to eggnog prepared in the hospital kitchen.

Exhibit 1.4   Classification of foodservice operations

Group I Commercial Feeding

Eating and Drinking Places

Restaurants, lunchrooms

Limited-menu restaurants, refreshment places

Commercial cafeterias

Social caterers

Ice cream, frozen custard stands

Bars and taverns

Food Contractors

Manufacturing and industrial plants

Commercial and office buildings

Hospitals and nursing homes

Colleges and universities

Primary and secondary schools

In-transit feeding (airlines)

Recreation and sports centers

Lodging Places

Hotel restaurants

Motor hotel restaurants

Motel restaurants

Miscellaneous

Retail host restaurants

Recreation and sports
—Includes drive-in movies, bowling lanes, recreation and sport centers

Mobile caterers

Vending and non-store retailers
—Includes sales of hot foods, sandwiches, pastries, coffee, and other hot beverages

Group II Institutional Feeding

Business, Education, Government, or Institutional Organizations That Operate Their Own Foodservices

Employee feeding
—Includes industrial and commercial organizations, seagoing ships, and inland-waterway vessels

Public and parochial elementary and secondary schools

Colleges and universities

Transportation

Hospitals
—Includes sanatoriums, voluntary and proprietary hospitals, long-term general and mental hospitals, and sales, or commercial equivalent, to employees in state and local short-term hospitals and federal hospitals

Nursing homes, homes for aged, blind, orphans, mentally and physically handicapped
—Includes sales (commercial equivalent) calculated for nursing homes and homes for aged only. All others in this category make no charge for food served either in cash or in kind

Clubs, sporting and recreational camps

Community centers

Group III Military Feeding

In Continental U.S. Only

Officers and NCO clubs ("Open Mess")

Foodservice—military exchanges

Adapted from "The Foodservice Industry—Food and Drink Sales Projected to 1984," NRA Forecast 1984, *NRA News,* December 1983. Reprinted by permission.

- At a school in the East, more than 400 children suddenly become ill from staphylococcal foodborne illness. The bacteria is traced to egg salad sandwiches.
- At a school in the South a number of students develop a violent gastrointestinal illness from an orange drink prepared in the school's milk shake machine. The machine contained copper tubing in the mixing chamber.

HAZARDS TO SAFE FOOD

Hazards to safe food are of three types. These are *biological, chemical,* and *physical* hazards.

Biological hazards consist of tiny creatures called *micro-organisms* and their waste products, which can cause illness when transmitted to humans through food. Biological hazards also include foods that are in themselves poisonous to humans, such as certain forms of fish and mushrooms.

Biological hazards are not the only threat to the safeness of food. As society becomes more complex, so too it seems, do the hazards to which we are exposed. Toxic *chemical hazards,* such as cleaning agents or pesticides, can also find their way into food and make people ill. *Physical contaminants,* pebbles, slivers of metal, chips of glass—all of these items can also contaminate food and injure people.

Contamination and Spoilage

We have used the word *contamination* a great deal in the previous pages, and we will be using it a great deal more in chapters to come. It is time now to stop and define this word, and to distinguish it from a related concept, "spoilage."

Contamination is the presence of harmful substances in food. If a food contains any substance that can cause injury or disease to a person who eats or tastes it, that food is contaminated. The contaminants may be biological, chemical, or physical, and may be tasteless or odorless.

Spoilage is damage to the edible quality of a food. Food that has acquired an unacceptable taste, appearance, or aroma can be said to be spoiled. Spoiled food may also be contaminated, but this is not necessarily the case. Sour milk, for example, is spoiled for such uses as drinking, but it may still be perfectly wholesome and suited for the making of cheese.

In many cases, however, the micro-organisms that cause disease will also spoil food. The conditions that lead to the spoilage of food are frequently the same ones that allow pathogenic micro-organisms to flourish. So the presence of spoilage is a strong indication that food has become unsafe to eat. It must always be remembered, however, that food *can* be contaminated with dangerous micro-organisms or toxins without betraying this condition in its outward appearance at all. Some contaminants cannot be detected by smell or even taste. So do not assume that every food that looks unspoiled is actually safe.

In our analysis of the problem of safe food, it is clear that the condition of the food itself has to be brought into central focus. We must make it our objective to serve only safe, healthful food; that is, food that is clean, uncontaminated, and unspoiled. Chapters 4, 5, and 6 discuss the methods for protecting the healthfulness of food in purchasing, storing, preparation, and serving.

WHAT IS SANITATION?

Contamination of food is preventable if proper precautions are taken to keep the disease-causing agents from the food in the first place or to keep these agents from growing if they do get on the food. The existence of a case of foodborne illness usually means that some unsanitary condition exists that must be identified and eliminated.

How does a foodservice manager realize the important objective of protecting people against illness from food contamination? The most powerful tool in this effort is a sanitation program geared to the needs of an individual facility. This is the challenge.

Sanitation is the creation and maintenance of healthful, or hygienic, conditions. "Sanitation" comes from the Latin word *sanitas* meaning "health." In a foodservice situation, sanitation means wholesome food, handled in a hygienic environment by healthy foodhandlers in a way that the food is not contaminated with illness-causing, harmful agents. In other words, sanitation is what helps safe food stay safe. There is a direct relationship between sanitation and safe food. Conversely, there is usually a direct relationship between a lack of sanitation and illness caused by food.

But does "sanitary" simply mean "clean"? Not necessarily. That which appears to be clean may not always be sanitary.

Clean means free of visible soil. *Sanitary* means free of disease-causing organisms and other harmful contaminants. Clean refers to aesthetics and concerns outward appearance—a face without a smudge, a glass that sparkles, a shelf wiped clear of dust. However, these objects, though clean on the surface, can in fact harbor invisible disease-causing agents or harmful chemicals. On the other hand, baby bottles boiled in water for ten minutes may be splotched and water-marked. They may not be clean on the surface, but they *are* free of disease-causing agents and can accurately be termed sanitary.

A sanitation-conscious foodservice manager will keep both of these concepts in mind, and operate his or her establishment by the rule: *Look Clean—Be Sanitary.*

In sorting out the subject of sanitation and a sanitation program in foodservice establishments, it is useful not only to define our terms and set our goals, but also to look at the factors involved in keeping food safe, as well as the inherent risks. They generally fall into three categories.

- Food—its safe condition initially and its protection in preparation and service
- People—those involved in handling food both as employees and as customers
- Facilities—the sanitary condition of the physical plant and the equipment used in a foodservice operation

The Food Itself

Case. Several outbreaks of foodborne illness were attributed to pre-cooked roast beef obtained commercially for foodservice use. Two of the outbreaks were traced to the same processing plant. The outbreaks were caused by failure to achieve minimum temperature during processing.

Not all food is safe when it arrives in the operation. Food products such as fresh poultry and frozen fish may already be contaminated by the time the items are received. The foodservice manager must work with reputable suppliers and implement tight receiving procedures to help ensure safe food.

Once the food arrives it must be stored, prepared, and served using methods that maintain its safety. This is the everyday challenge to the foodservice manager.

People

Case. More than half of the 150 women attending a restaurant luncheon became ill with nausea, vomiting, and diarrhea. Laboratory tests on four of the foods eaten implicated the chicken salad, which contained a large number of disease-causing micro-organisms. Investigations showed that the chef, who had prepared the salad by hand, had an infected finger cut. The salad was allowed to sit out for several hours before refrigeration. In addition, the refrigerator, where the salad was stored for 24 hours, had temperatures reaching 52°F (11.1°C).

From the above example it is clear that the safeness of food depends to a great extent on *people*—those who produce and process it, those who transport and deliver it, and finally the foodhandlers who prepare it for the ultimate consumer. In a most fundamental way the success of a foodservice manager in dealing with the foodborne-illness problem depends on how the human factor is handled—how workers are trained and how the manager follows up and reinforces that training.

The foodservice manager often finds that he or she is concentrating on elementary sanitation precepts and basic rules of personal hygiene. Sometimes the manager will be fighting plain ignorance, as with the cook who just doesn't understand the danger in using the hand that has a minor, but infected, cut or burn; or a salad maker who reaches for a knife previously used in cutting up raw chicken and not subsequently washed and sanitized.

People pose the number one risk to safe food. Employees and customers both pose the biggest threat to food safety. Of course, the foodservice manager has the most control over the former. Hiring healthy foodservice workers, training them in sanitary procedures, and supervising and motivating them on the job—all will help prevent safe food from becoming contaminated.

Sometimes the manager will be faced simply with careless habits, as when the bussing attendant puts down the scrub mop to add an extra place-setting without washing his or her hands; or when the short-order server, working hard to keep up, serves food, handles money,

clears away soiled tableware, makes a new set-up, catches a cigarette, and serves more food—all without proper handwashing.

By long-standing custom, many restaurant personnel are hired off the street. The hard-pressed manager—indeed, the entire industry—faces a hard task in surmounting the obstacles posed by the poor personal hygiene and unsanitary habits of foodservice employees.

What the manager can do about the unsanitary customer is a problem unto itself. The people who "hate to see food wasted" and put their handled but uneaten roll back into the breadbasket, and the customer with an uncontrolled and unshielded cough, are not easy to cope with.

In terms of the "people" problem, chapters 7 and 13 of this text cover in detail the elements of personal hygiene and sanitary food practices, as well as employee training and motivation in regard to these practices.

Facilities and Equipment

Case. Complaints of foodborne illness involved a drive-in restaurant whose specialty was ice-box pies. A check of the refrigerators revealed temperatures ranging from 52° to 60°F (11.1° to 15.6°C). Laboratory analysis of the ice-box pies showed disease-causing bacteria in large numbers in the pies. Investigation revealed other sanitation breakdowns as well.

Faulty or inadequate equipment is one major threat to safe food. Food should never be allowed to stay in the *temperature danger zone* for any length of *time* (see Exhibit 1.5). The temperature danger zone includes those temperatures in the range where bacterial contaminants multiply most rapidly.

Hard-to-clean work areas, faulty or overloaded refrigerators or other equipment, dirty surroundings, and conditions attractive to pest infestation make up the third focus of our analysis—the facilities and equipment problem.

Exhibit 1.5 The shaded part of the thermometer represents the temperature danger zone for food

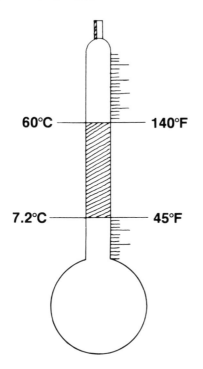

Of course, sometimes equipment is improperly used. Using a steam table to reheat food or putting too much food in a refrigerator unit already loaded to capacity are examples. Using equipment only for the purpose for which it was designed, and continually maintaining it, will ensure food safety in most operations.

From the time when the foodservice establishment exists only as an architect's blueprint, sanitation must be a major consideration in design. Sanitation must also be the first concern when choosing foodservice equipment. Ease of cleaning and *regular* cleaning of equipment can eliminate this source of food contamination. All features of a facility's physical plant should be constructed with "cleanability" in mind. With forethought given to these matters, the stage is at least set for a safe operation.

Chapter 8 of this text treats the subject of "built-in" sanitation in terms of materials, design, construction, and installation and layout of equipment—all with a view to facilitating cleaning and maintenance and eliminating entryways and breeding places for insects and rodents. Adequacy of utilities and services, as well as other environmental factors in safeguarding people and food products, are also covered.

Chapters 9 and 10 present procedures for, and the scheduling of, the cleaning and sanitizing of equipment, utensils, and food preparation areas. Chapter 11 gives some practical information on pest control.

OPPORTUNITIES FOR CONTAMINATION

Complex food systems increase the chances of contamination. By the time the food reaches the final consumer, the foodservice customer, it has had several opportunities to become contaminated. Multiple handling of food products from grower or supplier to buyer multiplies the chances of food contamination.

First, the food could have been contaminated at the source—the grower, processor, canner, or packer—through mishandling or poor control methods. Many food products go through middlemen such as distributors and storage companies, so there is a second opportunity for the food to become contaminated.

Finally, the food reaches the foodservice operation. Here is where the foodservice manager has the greatest control, and the greatest challenge, to protect food from receiving, through storage and preparation, and right up to service to the customer.

We are concerned in this book with food protection in the last part of the food chain—the prevention of foodborne illness in foodservice operations. The goal of this book is to provide the foodservice manager or prospective manager with the proper guidelines for effective foodservice sanitation. With this knowledge the manager can take steps to protect customers and ensure continued patronage.

In any type of foodservice facility, there are four steps taken before the food reaches the customer or patron. These steps are purchase, storage, preparation, and service. Each of these steps offers opportunities for contamination if they are performed improperly. The challenge to foodservice operators is to develop procedures or controls for each of these steps that will ensure that food is safe right up to the time it is eaten.

Before these steps are taken, however, the manager must look at the menu and ask the central question: "Considering the staff, equipment, and facilities, can these menu items be stored, prepared, and served in a sanitary manner?" Once that question is answered in the affirmative, planning sanitation procedures at each stage of the foodservice operation can take place.

As we look at the four steps, let's take an item that is commonly served in a foodservice facility—roast beef—and see how it fares.

Purchase

Purchasing safe food is the first step in keeping it safe. Purchasing food from reputable suppliers, never allowing home-canned foods in the facility, and proper checking during receiving are all important requirements. Checking all types of food items, including canned goods, is essential. Of course, developing good receiving procedures not only aids in sanitation, but also helps the foodservice operator guarantee that what is received is what was ordered.

When it comes from the (reputable) supplier, our roast beef must be checked. The packaging should be unopened, the raw beef should be bright red, and there should not be

any excess liquid. A metal-stemmed thermometer must be used to check for safe temperatures. (A safe temperature for raw roast beef would be under 45°F or 7.2°C—under the temperature danger zone.)

Storage

Food that is not going to be prepared right away must be stored—safely. Storage is where many breakdowns in sanitation occur. Cramming a large roast into an overcrowded refrigerator with high temperatures is one way disease-causing organisms already present will multiply, resulting in serious contamination. Of course, storage equipment should be clean to promote food safety.

Planning ahead for storage space and usage will help protect foods. For instance, fresh roast beef should be used within five days. After that, contamination and spoilage may have already started.

Preparation

Up to this point our roast beef hasn't been handled that much, and it has been packaged. Now we must take it out of the package and give it to the cook to prepare. Here the possibilities for contamination really multiply.

Say that the cook has a sore throat and a slight cough. He clears his throat and is careful to cover up his mouth with his hands. Unfortunately he doesn't wash his hands before handling the roast and contaminates it with bacteria.

To compound the problem, the cook has other foods to prepare for the noon meal. The roast is for dinner. It can wait, but in case he has a chance to work with it, he leaves it out on the table—for three hours. The bacteria, in the temperature danger zone for too long, multiply.

Now the cook is ready to cook the roast beef, which he does, but cooking will not destroy the toxins already present. Finally, with a knife he had used to cut up raw chicken, he cuts up the roast beef on a cutting board scored with old knife cuts. Pity the customer who orders the roast beef!

If this sounds extreme, bear in mind that such breakdowns do occur *and that any one of them can contaminate foods*.

Preparation procedures must be tightly controlled to ensure that

1. Food is not held in the temperature danger zone longer than necessary before, during, and after preparation (see Exhibit 1.5)
2. Foodservice workers do not harbor disease or expose food to contamination through careless personal habits
3. Food is not contaminated by unclean utensils or equipment or by contact with raw foods

Service

Let's say that the roast made it through all three previous steps without being contaminated. There is still one more opportunity for safe food to be made unsafe: serving the food is the final step.

While the opportunities are not as great for contamination during serving as during preparation, they do exist. Such unsanitary practices as handling clean knives and forks after wiping off a dirty table, failing to provide sneeze guards or food shields over self-service areas, and allowing handling of food by a sick server can make this final step the one that contaminates otherwise safe food. Procedures for serving food should be checked to see that they meet sanitation standards. It is pointless to implement sanitary procedures at each preceding step only to expose safe food to contamination during service.

FOOD QUALITY

Food safety and *food quality* are critical to the bottom line. Food that has off flavors, is dry, or appears stale is not likely to impress customers. Preserving food quality is another objective of sanitation. It would be oversimplifying it to say that if sanitary procedures are used food quality would take care of itself, but it is not too far off the mark.

Sanitary handling is a major factor in both food quality and safety. Food that is stored, prepared, and served properly is more likely to retain its quality. The standards of a food's quality include its safety, appearance, chemical properties, texture, consistency, palatability, and nutritional values, and of course, flavor. Any one of these can be destroyed by unsanitary procedures from purchase to service. Proper foodhandling is the key to preserving food quality.

THE SANITATION CHALLENGE

In most operations it is management that decides how important sanitation is. Managers not only must establish sanitation procedures, but train workers in them, and supervise each employee to be sure the procedures are followed. This is the sanitation challenge.

Providing safe food is a necessary challenge of running a foodservice operation—not an impossible barrier. Recognizing the importance of sanitation is the first step. Developing procedures to keep the facility sanitary and protect people from illness is the second step.

How does a foodservice manager realize the important objective of protecting people against illness from food contamination? The most powerful tool in this effort is a sanitation program geared to the needs of an individual facility.

Goals of a Sanitation Program

The primary goal of a foodservice sanitation program is to protect the customer from food-borne illness. This is not easy, but it can be done. The most effective strategy is a two-pronged attack: (1) protect food from contamination, and (2) reduce the effect of contamination that does occur.

Protecting Food Against Contamination

This goal is a difficult one to reach because of one fact: pathogenic micro-organisms capable of contaminating food are practically everywhere—in soil, dust, and air; on rodents and insects; on unsanitary equipment and utensils; and, most importantly, in approximately 50 percent of the people who handle food. These people harbor food-contaminating micro-organisms in their intestinal tracts, noses, throats, and mouths, as well as on their hands.

In addition, most raw food, no matter how reliable its source, is contaminated to a certain extent before it arrives at the foodservice establishment. It is estimated that as much as 30 percent of raw market poultry contains bacteria that can cause disease in humans. Beef, even when freshly slaughtered, is seldom free of bacteria. By the time the beef is ready for cooking, it may contain thousands, if not millions, of harmful organisms per gram.

But if all of this food is already contaminated when it reaches the food service, what is the use of trying to serve uncontaminated food? The answer is that proper cleaning and cooking will help reduce the disease-causing organisms mentioned. The job of the foodservice manager is to prevent raw foods from contaminating cooked ones, to reduce the opportunities for further contamination of foods by unhygienic workers and facilities, and in short, to create a controlled environment in which additional contaminating micro-organisms and other hazards are not introduced into the food.

How does food become contaminated with harmful agents and other poisonous substances? The principal offenders are

- Infected foodhandlers
- Contaminated food supplies
- Unsafe foodhandlers
- Unsanitary equipment
- Hazardous chemicals

Exhibits 1.6 and 1.7 show routes of food contamination.

Reducing the Effect of Contamination

As previously mentioned, some foods are contaminated before they enter the foodservice establishment; others will be exposed to harmful organisms during preparation and service. Fortunately for the foodservice industry, there are very effective ways of counteracting this contamination.

From ancient times, human beings have apparently had some good ideas about how to protect themselves from contaminated food. Game was sun-dried, salted, smoked, or chilled, if possible, to preserve it. Perhaps even the most primitive people knew of the purifying effects of fire as they cooked their food to improve its texture and flavor. We now know, a bit more scientifically, the value of temperature control in keeping food and rendering it safe.

Micro-organisms require a moist, warm, nutritious environment to prosper. Their growth can be slowed or stopped by refrigeration, and they can be destroyed by sufficient heat. But at temperatures between 45° and 140°F (7.2° and 60°C), micro-organisms flourish and multiply to enormous numbers in a very short time.

It is that temperature middle ground that we have to look out for. Food should be kept out of this temperature danger zone whenever possible. The sanitation-conscious manager will always keep in mind the danger zone on the thermometer.

Exhibit 1.6   Transmission of a foodborne
illness from infected human beings to food
and back to other human beings

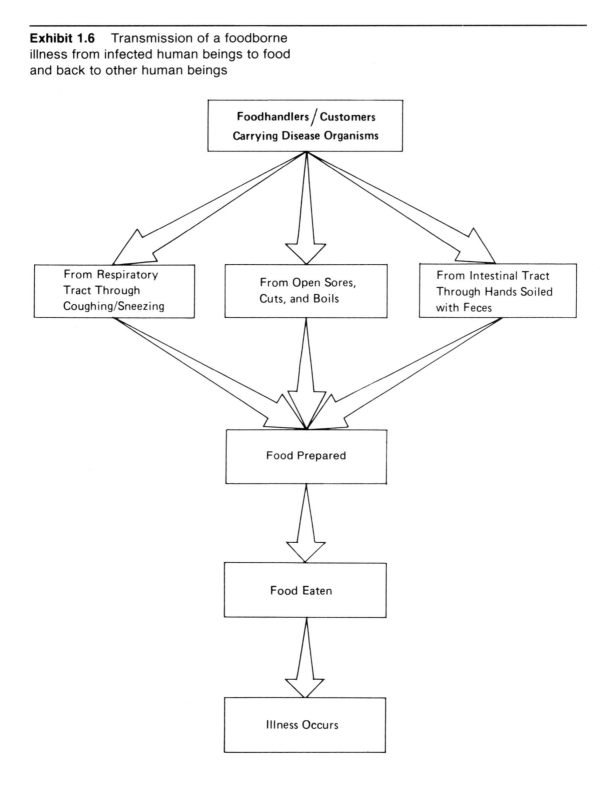

Exhibit 1.7   Transmission of a foodborne illness from an intermediate source to food and on to human beings

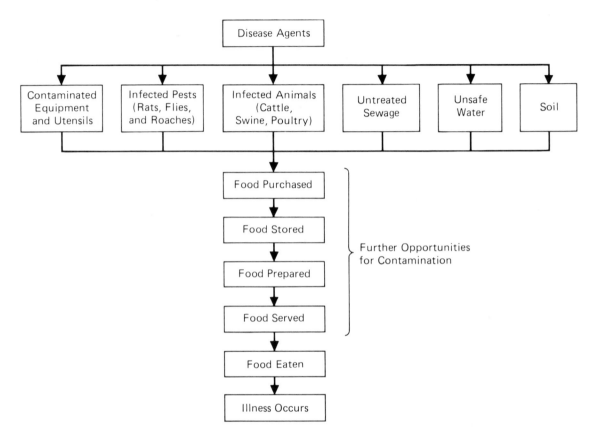

THE EIGHT CAPITAL OFFENSES

Guideposts, marking the way for a foodservice manager who seeks to eliminate the causes of foodborne illness, vary. Here is a list of the eight *most frequently cited factors* involved in outbreaks of foodborne illness.

1. Failure to properly refrigerate food
2. Failure to thoroughly heat or cook food
3. Infected employees who practice poor personal hygiene
4. Foods prepared a day or more before they are served
5. Raw, contaminated ingredients incorporated into foods that receive no further cooking
6. Foods allowed to remain at bacteria-incubating temperatures
7. Failure to reheat cooked foods to temperatures that kill vegetative bacteria
8. Cross-contamination of cooked foods with raw items either by workers who mishandle foods or through improperly cleaned equipment

THE ROLE OF THE FOODSERVICE MANAGER IN SANITATION

The typical foodservice operator probably thinks of his or her role as that of business manager, providing a vital service to owner and customer alike. It is unlikely that typical managers envision themselves as sanitarians. But in catering to the fundamental needs of customers, foodservice managers hold the health of these customers in their hands. A knowledge of sanitation, and an appreciation of its importance, can transform the sanitation aspect of a manager's job into a manageable task, even an interesting one.

Ask a sanitation-conscious manager how he or she goes about the problem, and you may get a surprisingly brief reply, like, "Trained people and plenty of hot water." A typical food sanitarian lecturing to a group of foodhandlers may sum up the situation with this advice: "Serve hot food hot and keep cold food cold, wash your hands, and don't sneeze."

Reduced to the simplest terms, protecting people from illness due to contaminated food does appear to be a pretty straightforward matter. It is. The stumbling block is awakening people to the existence of the problem and getting them to do something about it.

Adding the role of sanitarian to an already many-faceted job is necessary. As you embark on this phase of your education in foodservice management, your own attitude toward the subject is of the utmost importance. This attitude must be based on a knowledge of the industry and an appreciation of the dimensions of the foodborne illness problem, and your professional and legal position in relation to it. In short, sanitation "goes with the territory."

The following are the major tasks required of the foodservice sanitarian/manager:

1. Making sanitation a top priority and communicating this to workers.
2. Purchasing food from safe sources.
3. Implementing sanitary procedures in the storage, preparation, and service of food.
4. Training, motivating, and supervising workers in order to maintain a sanitary facility serving safe food.
5. Regularly inspecting the facility and workers to assure that sanitation standards are being met.
6. Cooperating with local public health officials during inspections and in developing a sanitation program, including worker training.

The goal of this book is to set before the manager or prospective manager the specific guidelines for effective foodservice sanitation for the purpose of enabling that person to protect foodservice customers and ensure their patronage.

SUMMARY

More people are eating out than ever before. When people eat out they have a number of expectations: good, safe food, clean surroundings, and pleasant service. Foodservice managers need to recognize the customer's desire for safe food and implement procedures to ensure food safety.

A foodborne illness is a disease or injury caused by ingestion of contaminated food. The most common source of foodborne illness outbreaks is the foodservice establishment.

Sanitation is the creation and maintenance of healthful conditions to prevent food contamination and meet customers' expectations. The sanitation program is directed at the elimination of foodborne illness through the reduction of opportunities for food contamination and the remedying of contamination that does occur. This task is complicated by the fact that food contaminants—particularly disease-causing micro-organisms—are everywhere. But difficult or not, the foodservice manager has a legal and a moral responsibility to see that this job is done. In addition, sanitary practices help maintain the bottom line in profits and a balanced budget.

Since any type of foodservice can be responsible for an outbreak of foodborne illness, sanitary procedures are necessary in every type of facility.

The three hazards to food safety are biological, chemical, and physical. Of these, biological hazards are the major concern of the foodservice manager.

This textbook will analyze the solution to the problem of safe food in three parts. First is the food itself—how to obtain safe food and how to keep it safe through application of proper temperature control and other measures. Second, we will look at the people factor—how to train and motivate employees to learn and apply hygienic foodhandling practices—and the problem of the facility itself—how to build in sanitation. Third, we will discuss how to manage the operation so that the foodservice environment does not hinder the sanitation effort.

The objective of a sanitation program is to keep food safe from contamination and to reduce the effects of contamination. There are four steps during which sanitation breakdowns can occur. These steps are purchase, storage, preparation, and service.

No matter how we analyze the problem, in the end it is the foodservice manager's attitude that will make or break the sanitation program. Only if the foodservice manager is convinced of the importance of sanitation, well informed on the subject of food protection, and actively interested in preventing foodborne illness, can this effort possibly succeed. Fortunately the manager is not at the mercy of uncontrollable factors. Most of the opportunities for contamination are controllable by an alert management with trained employees, using a planned and thorough sanitation program.

A CASE IN POINT

Nearly 200 passengers who had been on an excursion train that traveled through the South experienced gastrointestinal illness on June 14 and 15. At least 55 required hospitalization. The 200 were among 627 passengers who had stopped for box lunches prepared by a restaurant in Tennessee. An analysis of food histories implicated ham served in the lunches; a bacterial contaminant was found to be the culprit.

Investigation revealed that the restaurant's walk-in refrigerator was above the maximum recommended holding temperature of 45°F (7.2°C) and that the boxed lunches had been held unrefrigerated for up to three hours before distribution to passengers.

By 1:00 A.M. on the day after eating the meal, an estimated 200 persons had become ill. All of the ill passengers had eaten lunches containing ham, baked beans, potato salad, rolls, pickled eggs, and coffee or tea.

Three persons who had eaten ham on June 15 at the restaurant that prepared the box lunches also became ill.

Ham was implicated as the vehicle of transmission. A refrigerated sample of ham eaten by the passengers was tested and had bacteria in sufficient numbers to cause the illness. A fingernail culture of a foodhandler yielded *Staphylococcus aureus* of a type identical to that found in the implicated ham.

Investigation revealed that on June 11, three days before the lunches were served, 40 hams were delivered to the restaurant and stored in a walk-in refrigerator that, on June 14, registered 57°F (13.9°C). The next day, the hams were cooked at 400°F (204.4°C) for 2½ hours, re-refrigerated for 1½ hours, and then deboned and separated. They were then re-refrigerated in stainless steel pans until June 13, when they were sliced and then returned to the walk-in refrigerator. On June 14, the sliced hams were preheated in ovens at 350°F (176.6°C) for 1½ to 2 hours, and placed over a chafing dish with flame. Portions of the ham were then boxed with other food items. The boxes were closed with tape, delivered to the railroad station at 12:15 P.M., and distributed between 12:50 and 2:15 P.M. Ham not used for the box lunches was reheated and served in the restaurant the next day.

Guess! What do you think happened here?

STUDY QUESTIONS

1. What is a foodborne illness?
2. What is an outbreak?
3. Describe the route by which foodhandlers may contaminate food.
4. What are the legal reasons foodservice managers should provide safe food?
5. Name the foodservice steps during which food may become contaminated.
6. What is the difference in meaning between the terms "clean" and "sanitary"?
7. Differentiate between "food contamination" and "food spoilage."
8. What are the two goals of a sound sanitation program?
9. Which federal agency records and summarizes information on foodborne illness outbreaks?
10. Describe how food, people, and facilities can contribute to the problem of foodborne illness.

MORE ON THE SUBJECT

GUTHRIE, RUFUS K. *Food Sanitation.* Westport, Conn.: AVI Publishing Company, 1980. 326 pages. This reference text presents an overview of food sanitation, covering common diseases and their modes of transmission. Representative sanitation laws and ordinances and recommended health codes are included. The purpose of the book is to give the food industry worker an understanding of the biological principles involved in air, land, and water pollution control.

LONGREE, KARLA, and GERTRUDE G. BLAKER. *Sanitary Techniques in Food Service, 2d ed.* New York: Wiley, 1982. 271 pages. This text provides practical guidance in culinary sanitation for the foodhandler. Designed as a teaching aid for vocational training, the book contains many charts and tables depicting safe operating procedures. It includes new material on foods prepared away from the serving permises, new equipment, changes in the food supply, and changes in micro-biological problems.

U.S. PUBLIC HEALTH SERVICE. *Food Service Sanitation Manual.* Washington, D.C.: U.S. Government Printing Office, 1976. These official federal guidelines contain the 1976 Public Health Service recommendations for "A Model Food Service Sanitation Ordinance and Code" presented for adoption by state and local jurisdictions or for incorporation into their laws and regulations. The manual is annotated with descriptive matter concerning reasons for the code's provisions and compliance criteria.

ANSWER TO A CASE IN POINT

This is a classic case of whatever can go wrong will. An infected foodhandler, a warm refrigerator, no real cooking time before the hams were placed in the refrigerator, and possibly too many hams for initial storage were some of the factors.

However, things don't just "go" wrong. People contributed to this outbreak, and people could have *prevented* it. In most operations the person who must contribute the most to prevention is the foodservice manager.

2
The Microworld

Of the three hazards to safe food mentioned in the last chapter—biological, chemical, and physical—the biological hazard is of the most concern to the foodservice manager. Most outbreaks of foodborne illness are caused by biological hazards. These hazards are a challenge to control, because they mainly consist of tiny living creatures that are all around us. These creatures are called *micro-organisms,* a word from the Greek meaning "small" and "living beings." They are so small that they can only be seen with the aid of a microscope, as the name implies.

If you could look for a long enough time through a powerful enough microscope at, say, a scraping from the inside of a freshly dressed chicken just delivered to your restaurant, you would see tiny beings, wriggling and turning, and—this is significant—increasing in number. These are micro-organisms. They are very much alive—taking in nourishment, discharging wastes, and reproducing.

The existence of this invisible world was first discovered in about 1693 by the Dutch merchant, Anton van Leeuwenhoek. However, it was another 200 years before the Frenchman Louis Pasteur and a small number of his associates tried to convince the medical profession that certain types of these micro-organisms cause disease.

The work of these pioneers encouraged further study of micro-organisms, and since that time much has been learned about the control of micro-organisms responsible for the spread of infectious diseases such as smallpox, diphtheria, typhoid fever, and tuberculosis. Further study eventually led to the connection between the contamination of food or water and disease.

Why should foodservice managers learn about micro-organisms? The answer is obvious. One of the primary responsibilities of a foodservice manager is to protect the consumer by serving safe and wholesome food.

One way to do this is to keep dangerous levels of micro-organisms out of food. The fact is, micro-organisms are responsible for *more than 90 percent of the diseases transmitted by food.* These tiny, but dangerous creatures are the number one concern of foodservice managers wishing to protect customers and patrons from foodborne illness.

It is hardly surprising that food ready for our consumption is a very desirable nutritional medium for other life forms as well—micro-organisms included. Unfortunately, some micro-organisms are not content to simply join us for dinner; they have an irritating habit of wearing out their welcome and making us ill.

To protect the consumer from the injurious effects of micro-organisms from food products, foodservice managers must know what micro-organisms are, how they thrive, and how they can be controlled. Equipped with this background, the foodservice manager will have no difficulty in applying suitable measures to control harmful micro-organisms.

This chapter follows the adage, "Know thine enemy," and looks at the principal forms of microbiological life that concern the foodservice manager in the storage, preparation, holding, and serving of food. The micro-organisms of interest to the foodservice manager are *bacteria, viruses, yeasts,* and *molds.* In this chapter, we will

- Review the size and shape of bacteria, and the ways in which they multiply
- Examine what kind of environment bacteria thrive in and how nourishment, moisture, temperatures, and time affect their survival and growth
- Consider the conditions of growth for viruses, yeasts, and molds
- Learn that micro-organisms are both harmful and helpful to humans

Exhibit 2.1 *From left to right:* cocci in single cells (mono-), in pairs (diplo-), in chains (strepto-), and in clusters (staphylo-)

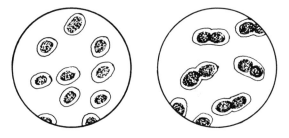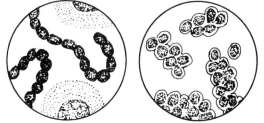

BACTERIA

Of all micro-organisms, *bacteria* should be of greatest concern to the foodservice manager. They are more commonly involved in cases of foodborne illness than are other biological forms of life such as viruses, yeasts, and molds. Knowing what bacteria are, and particularly, knowing the environment they flourish in is a first step in controlling them. Some of the factors that cause growth of harmful numbers of bacteria are the very ones the manager can control.

A *bacterium* is a living organism made up of a single cell. Like all living things, bacteria need nutrients to maintain their function. They take in these nutrients through their cell walls. Bacteria in food cause illness in two ways. Some bacteria are infectious disease germs, which feed on nutrients in certain foods, primarily proteins, and multiply very rapidly at favorable temperatures. These organisms are using the food as a medium for growth and also as transportation to the human body, where they cause foodborne infection. Other bacteria are not infectious in themselves, but discharge toxic wastes that poison us. A *foodborne intoxication* is the resulting illness.

Size of Bacteria

Bacteria are extremely small. It would take 2000 typical bacteria to reach across the head of a pin at its widest point.

Some bacteria are larger than this typical example, some are smaller. The actual size of a bacterium will vary with the species, with the stage of its development, and with the medium in which it lives.

Shapes of Bacteria

A mental picture of sorts will help to distinguish bacteria in a general way. Bacteria occur in three basic shapes.

Cocci (meaning "berry") are spherically shaped bacteria. Various kinds of cocci arrange themselves in different patterns. Some occur as single cells; other arrange themselves in groups of two called *diplococci* (*diplo-* meaning "two"). Other coccal bacteria are arranged in chains and are called *streptococci* (*strepto-* meaning "twisted"), and still others, *staphylococci*, occur in clusters (*staphylo-* from a Greek word meaning "bunch of grapes"). You almost certainly have had some of the diseases caused by bacteria, and now you know where they got their names like "strep" or "staph" (see Exhibit 2.1).

Exhibit 2.2   Bacilli: *left,* vegetative; *right,* with spores

The second major group of bacteria in terms of shape are the *bacilli,* or rod-shaped bacteria. Somewhat like the cocci, the bacilli may be found singly, in pairs, or in chains like links of sausage (see Exhibit 2.2).

The third shape used to classify bacteria is the spiral or comma shape. Such bacteria are called *spirilla.* These bacteria are found only as single cells (see Exhibit 2.3).

Of these three shapes, the cocci and bacilli groups are responsible for most foodborne illness.

Spore-Forming and Vegetative Stages

Some of the rod-shaped bacteria, or bacilli, have the ability to produce a special structure called a *spore* as a means of protection against an unfavorable environment. A spore is a thick-walled formation within the bacterial cell and is capable of becoming a vegetative organism when conditions again become favorable. The thick wall of the spore makes it much more resistant to heat, cold, and chemicals than is the usual bacterial cell (see Exhibit 2.2). Thus, it may survive some cooking temperatures.

A spore may survive boiling water for an hour or more. It also holds up well under freezing and may resist some sanitizing solutions. The fact that spores are so difficult to

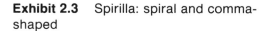

Exhibit 2.3   Spirilla: spiral and comma-shaped

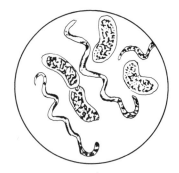

destroy is one of the reasons for careful procedures to keep harmful levels of bacteria out of the food in the first place.

A bacterium in a developing, nonspore stage is said to be *vegetative.* Unlike spores, vegetative cells are capable of reproducing. Vegetative bacteria may be killed by high temperatures but are more resistant to low temperatures, and some may even survive freezing.

Reproduction of Bacteria

Given the right conditions, bacteria reproduce in a very simple manner. The vegetative cell enlarges and then divides into two (Exhibit 2.4). Each of these two bacteria may divide into two

Exhibit 2.4   Bacteria reproduce by dividing. Under ideal conditions, bacteria multiply at an explosive rate, a single cell becoming billions in 10 to 12 hours.

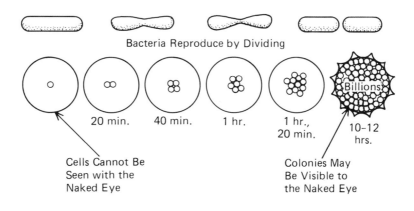

Bacteria Reproduce by Dividing

20 min.   40 min.   1 hr.   1 hr., 20 min.   10–12 hrs.

Cells Cannot Be Seen with the Naked Eye

Colonies May Be Visible to the Naked Eye

more cells, and so on. This doubling process is known as *fission* and may occur several times in an hour.

The result of this kind of growth is a *tremendous increase in the numbers of bacteria.* The offspring of a single bacterium will double with each division—2, 4, 8, 16, 32, and so on—producing billions in a matter of hours (see Exhibit 2.4). All this reproduction increases the odds of producing sufficient bacteria to cause a foodborne illness. The conditions important to the reproductive process are food, moisture, and mainly, favorable temperature.

Groups of bacteria cluster together to form *colonies.* Colonies of bacteria may be visible to the naked eye, but do not always have a distinctive appearance that could make it possible to identify them.

Growth Pattern of Bacteria

Under ideal conditions, the growth rate for a typical colony of bacteria follows a distinct pattern.

If you touched a slice of ham with your thumb, you would probably plant several thousand bacteria on its surface. Some of these organisms probably would not survive the change in environment, so for a time there would be fewer organisms, or no marked increase in number. This period of adaptation to a new environment is called the *lag phase* of bacterial growth.

After a longer period of time—from an hour to several days, depending on conditions—the bacteria would start to multiply very rapidly. This accelerated growth phase is designated the *log phase.*

When the bacteria have increased to such large numbers that they compete for space and nourishment, they no longer multiply so rapidly and some may start dying. The period of competition is called the *stationary phase.* The last phase, when bacterial cells begin to die more quickly because of a lack of nutrients or because of their own waste products, is called the *decline phase* (see Exhibit 2.5).

The time it takes for bacterial cells to develop and decline depends on temperature, food supply, the species of the bacteria, and the age of the organisms (see Exhibit 2.6).

Bacteria should not be allowed to grow past the lag phase. Here is where the foodservice manager has *the most control.* Providing conditions favorable for growth can allow bacteria

Exhibit 2.5   Bacterial growth curve

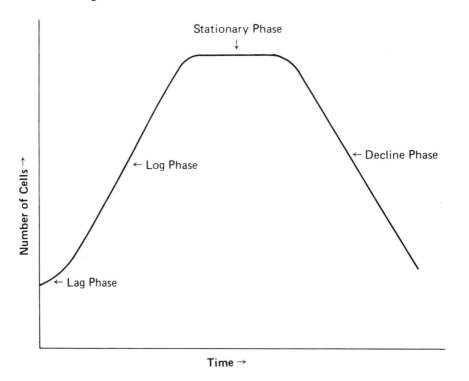

Exhibit 2.6   Effect of temperature in
Salmonella growth

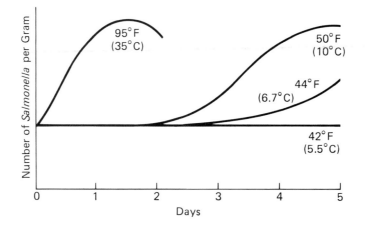

to expand in sufficient number to cause illness. *Temperature control* is the key factor in preventing bacterial growth.

Toxins

As chemical changes occur in living human cells, so too do changes take place in bacteria. Like humans, bacteria throw off waste matter and decompose when they die. The results of this decomposition in bacteria are *toxins*. Toxins, as the name implies, are poisonous to humans and may come into existence during the *decline phase* of bacterial growth. While some bacteria are dying they are producing toxins, *which can themselves cause foodborne illness*. So even though the disease-causing bacteria may be dead, they have the last word by leaving behind their deadly toxins to make people ill.

Mobility

Some bacterial cells are able to move about by themselves by means of whiplike appendages known as *flagella*. Some of the bacilli and all of the known forms of spirilla move about by means of flagella (see Exhibit 2.7).

The use of flagella is not a practical means of locomotion for longer distances, so most bacteria depend on someone or something to move them from place to place: water, wind, food, insects, rodents or other animals, and human beings—especially human beings. Bacteria are notorious hitchikers of rides from human hosts. They occur in the hair, on the skin, and in the clothing of human beings. They are found in the mucus membranes in the mouth, nose, and throat, and on scabs or scars from skin wounds or lesions.

Environmental Needs of Bacteria

Bacteria can live anywhere a human being can. In fact, they survive hotter and colder temperatures within a wider range of atmospheric conditions than do humans. Generally

Exhibit 2.7   Bacilli: vegetative with flagella

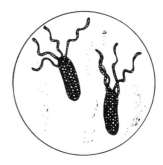

speaking, they thrive in a warm, moist environment that is neutral or slightly acid. Some species, however, tolerate—and even prefer—extremes of heat or cold; and a few can even survive in a dry medium or one of high acid or salt content.

The following sections examine the need of bacteria for a life-sustaining medium that provides a suitable temperature, food, moisture, pH (level of acidity or alkalinity), and in some cases, oxygen.

Temperature Requirements

In general, bacteria survive a wide range of temperatures. The majority, however, fare best between 60° and 110°F (15.6° and 43.3°C). The bacteria that grow well in this temperature range are called *mesophiles*. Note these temperature limits—they coincide closely with the range between normal room temperature and normal body temperature for humans. Thus, many of the bacteria that invade human beings find an ideal temperature for growth.

Some bacteria live and multiply readily between 110° and 130°F (43.3° and 54.4°C). These varieties are referred to as *thermophiles*, from the Greek words for "heat" and "love." Thermophilic bacteria are found in nature in such places as hot springs and compost heaps.

Both of these types, the mesophiles and the thermophiles, find much comfort within the *temperature danger zone* for foods, between 45° and 140°F (7.2° and 60°C) (see Exhibit 2.8). Here bacteria thrive, and given the right environment—moist, high-protein food and enough time—they will multiply rapidly.

Other bacteria seem to prosper between 32° and 45°F (0° and 7.2°C), but can grow at temperatures as low as 19°F (−7.2°C). These bacteria are known as *psychrophiles,* from the Greek words for "cold" and "love." Such organisms can continue to multiply even at refrigerator temperatures. This fact is worth remembering because placing food in a refrigerator will not provide absolute insurance against microbial growth.

Knowledge of the effects of temperature on bacteria can be a valuable tool in keeping food safe. Bacteria grow very slowly at lower temperatures. They are not killed by freezing, but their growth stops. They grow most readily between room temperature and a little above our body temperature. Potentially hazardous foods that spend too much time in the temperature danger zone provide a good growth medium for bacteria. In order to grow most rapidly bacteria need both time and temperature.

About 110°F (43.3°C) many bacteria will start dying, and by the time the temperature reaches 140°F (60°C), most will be killed. Spores are not always killed by high temperatures—they can even survive boiling—but vegetative cells are destroyed by high heat.

Food and Moisture Requirements

Bacteria are extremely diverse in the kinds of environments in which they can find nourishment. One species or another can find a "home" in almost every possible kind of food eaten by humans. Some bacteria thrive on meats but only just survive on vegetables, and in other instances the reverse may be true. Bacteria are especially partial to the high-protein foods identified in the previous chapter as

Exhibit 2.8   Temperature and bacterial growth

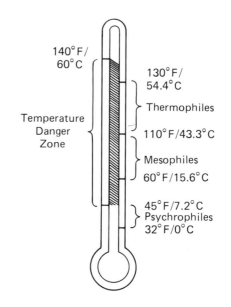

"potentially hazardous." Milk, meat, poultry, and fish provide food and a moist, favorable environment.

Bacteria need water as well as food for growth and development. Since bacteria cannot take their food in solid form, they must receive their nutrients in some kind of water solution. This solution is described as "water activity" (expressed as a_w) which means the amount of water available for favorable growth. A solution favorable for bacterial growth usually measures $0.85a_w$ or more. Therefore, foods with a water activity of 0.85 or higher will support bacterial growth—if other conditions are right—and this is why they are defined as potentially hazardous by the FDA.

Other conditions affect whether or not the water in a food item is available for the growth of bacteria. For example, peanut butter is a moist, high protein food. However, the sugar and salt included in its chemical composition tie up or bond the available moisture, thereby limiting bacterial growth. This is why, though

Exhibit 2.9   Effect of pH on bacterial growth

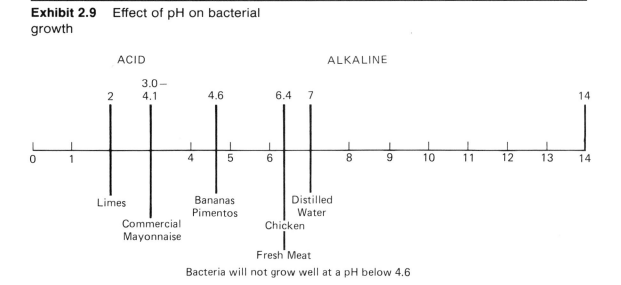

Bacteria will not grow well at a pH below 4.6

most peanut butters held too long become rancid and spoil in quality and flavor, their bacterial levels may still be low. Available moisture is also closely related to pH. A food that is moist may not necessarily be favorable for bacterial growth, especially if the moisture is acidic, as in the case of pickles soaked in vinegar.

Bacterial growth is halted in human foods that are very low in moisture content, although the bacteria remain alive. This fact is a key to food preservation. Many food products are handled dry, such as sugar, flour, some meats, and some fruits. So long as they are kept dry, these supplies will store safely, even though some bacteria are present. Once the food becomes wet, however, the organisms start multiplying.

pH Requirements

Bacteria grow best in media that are neutral or slightly acidic. The growth of most bacteria is greatly inhibited in very acidic media. Thus, acidic foods such as vinegar and most fresh fruits, especially citrus fruits and tomatoes, are very seldom vehicles for disease-causing bacteria.

The pH of a medium is a measure of its acidity or alkalinity. pH is measured on a scale from 0 to 14. A medium with a pH of 7 is exactly neutral, being neither acidic nor alkaline. A medium with a pH below 7 is acid, and one with a pH above 7 is alkaline. Most bacteria will not grow well at pH levels below 4.6. They grow best in a range between 4.6 and 9, one that is more alkaline. Unfortunately, many foods, especially meats, have a pH factor that is very favorable for the growth of bacteria (see Exhibit 2.9).

A common fallacy is to assume that adding an acidic substance to a food item is a protection against bacterial growth. For instance, mayonnaise has a pH below 4.6; however, adding it to a ham salad is not going to stop the growth of bacteria already in the ham. Instead, the alkaline and moisture present in the ham will only "mix" the pH level of the mayonnaise, producing an alkaline solution favorable to the bacteria.

Oxygen Requirements

Bacteria vary in their requirements for oxygen. Some bacteria will grow only when supplied with free oxygen; these are called *aerobes*.

Other bacteria will grow only when free oxygen is excluded—in a vacuum-sealed jar or can, or in the center of a large pot of food, for example—these are called *anaerobes*. Most of the bacteria that cause foodborne illness, however, are very adaptable. They can grow with or without the presence of free oxygen. These are called the *facultative* forms of bacteria.

PARASITES

Parasites are small or microscopic creatures that need a host to feed off of and live inside of or on. *Trichinella spiralis* is the best known of the parasites that contaminate food. This parasite is actually a worm. It prefers mammals, including humans, pigs, rats, and even bears. The larvae from this worm cause a disease called *trichinosis*. Heating food at high temperatures or freezing it before preparation will usually kill the larvae (see Exhibit 2.10).

VIRUSES

Another type of micro-organism of concern to the foodservice manager is the virus (from the Latin word for "poison"). Viruses are the smallest and perhaps the simplest form of life known—there is some doubt as to whether they are alive at all.

Unlike bacteria, viruses are not complete cells. They contain no nucleus or cell wall. Viruses are very simple organisms consisting of a slug of genetic material in a protein wrapper or overcoat.

Because of their simple structure, viruses lack certain essentials for their own reproduction. Instead they must depend on a living host to supply these missing factors in order to reproduce. Once viruses gain entrance to a cell within a host, they order its life processes to stop and force the cell to assist in producing

Exhibit 2.10   *Trichinella spiralis*

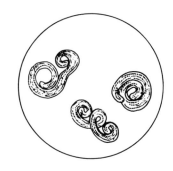

more viruses. Because of this relationship with a living host, viruses can also be categorized as *parasites*. Different kinds of viruses require different hosts, ranging from bacteria and larger plants to insects, higher animals, and humans.

Viruses vary in size. The size of a virus may range from $\frac{1}{100}$ to $\frac{1}{3}$ the size of the average bacterium. Because of their small size, they cannot be seen with a standard optical microscope. Viruses can be viewed through an electron microscope, but because the process of preparing a specimen for electron microscopy necessarily kills it, no one has ever been able to see a functioning virus. It is known that viruses occur in a variety of shapes—spherical, rectangular, brick-shaped, and bullet-shaped, among others.

Viruses seem to vary in their reaction to heat and cold. The influenza virus is very sensitive to heat, while another type of virus has been shown to survive in food even at temperatures as high as 176°F (80°C). This same virus, which is so resistant to heat, can also remain active after storage in a refrigerator for over a year.

Although the relationship between viruses and foodborne disease is not clearly understood by scientists, one fact about this relationship should be noted. Viruses do not *increase* in number while they are in food. The

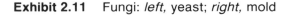

Exhibit 2.11   Fungi: *left,* yeast; *right,* mold

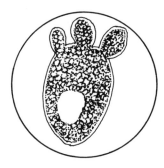 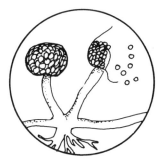

food merely serves to transport the viruses, which then may lodge themselves in the human host and reproduce abundantly.

It takes fewer viruses than bacteria to cause illness. Because of this *they must not be allowed to contaminate food in the first place.* Viruses do not require potentially hazardous foods to survive. Outbreaks of viral diseases are often attributed to poor personal hygiene and a contaminated water supply.

A variety of viral diseases can be transferred through food, including the hepatitis virus. Viruses are most often found, however, in water that has not been chemically treated. (Methods of preventing contaminated water from coming into contact with usable water in the foodservice facility are discussed in a later chapter.) Fish and shellfish from tainted water are often found to be the culprits in a foodborne viral illness.

FUNGI

Fungi range in size from microscopic, single-celled creatures to giant mushrooms. They are found naturally in air, soil, plants, animals, water, and some food. The members of this group of organisms that are of most concern to the foodservice manager are molds and yeasts (see Exhibit 2.11).

Molds

The furry-looking stuff you see growing on bread and cheese is probably mold. So is the blue or green powdery covering on citrus fruits.

Molds are fungi composed of tubular elements called *hyphae.* Hyphae are made up of cells joined together end-to-end. The cells that make up the hyphae vary in size. Some are approximately the same size as bacteria and some are larger. Molds grow quickly, and the tangled, cottony mass can easily be seen as a kind of fuzzy growth. It should be remembered, though, that individual mold plants can usually only be seen with a microscope; patches of mold that are visible to the naked eye consist of large numbers of plants.

Hyphae produce enzymes used to store food, and they also form spores. These spores are not survival devices, as with bacteria, but are for the purpose of reproduction. In molds, a spore is similar to a seed—a seed that is capable of developing into a new plant.

In common with some of the other microorganisms, some molds are useful (as sources of antibiotics such as penicillin, and in the ripening of some cheeses), and some are harmful (in imparting a musty odor and flavor to foods). It was once thought that food molds were not dangerous to humans, but we now know that certain molds produce toxins that have been shown to cause cancer in animals, though the question remains open concerning human cancer. These same toxins have been linked to rare, isolated incidents of foodborne illness, known as *mycotoxicoses* poisoning. Also, certain other types of molds can cause serious infections and allergies involving such body areas as the sinuses (often contracted by sniffing mold in spices and other foods), eyes, ears, and the respiratory tract.

Mostly, molds spoil foods. One characteristic that makes molds a nuisance is their great adaptability. They can grow on almost any food, at almost any storage temperature, under almost any conditions—moist or dry, acidic or low-acid, salty or sweet.

Virtually all foods are susceptible to mold. Molds commonly grow on fruit where they may be pink, purple, yellow, and sometimes other colors. They also grow on vegetables, refrigerated meats, and cheese that has been exposed to the air. Even dried foods such as spices, nuts, and popcorn can carry the fungus.

Although the cells and spores of most molds can be killed by heating them to 140°F (60°C) for 10 minutes, the toxins are heat-stable and are not destroyed by normal cooking methods. Therefore, foods with molds that are not a natural part of the items should be discarded. This will ensure quality control as well as food safety. Freezing prevents the growth of molds but will not kill those already present in the food.

Yeasts

Yeasts are fungi, usually spherical or oval in shape. Each yeast organism is composed of one cell and is slightly larger than the average bacterium. Yeasts reproduce by a process called *budding*.

Many of the beneficial uses of yeasts are well known: they aid in leavening bread and in fermenting beer, sauerkraut, and other products. Nonetheless, yeasts can cause damage to food. Since they require sugar and moisture

for survival, they often consume these ingredients from food products such as jellies and honey and spoil the food in the process.

Though yeast contamination is often not visible, it does sometimes create a visible slime on beer, pickle brine, or fruit juices. In addition, the pink discoloration in cottage cheese may be due to the presence of yeasts. In general, yeast spoilage is most readily recognizable by the presence of bubbles and an alcoholic smell or taste.

Yeast organisms can be killed by heating to 136°F (57.8°C) for 15 minutes.

While yeasts are responsible for a few diseases in human beings, no evidence suggests that these diseases are transmitted by food or that the yeasts occurring naturally in foods are harmful to human beings. However, since yeasts do spoil food they still need to be controlled.

BENEFITS FROM MICRO-ORGANISMS

Up to this point we have treated micro-organisms primarily as hazards for humans, and in fact, it is the harmful side of micro-organisms that is of crucial importance to the foodservice manager. Nevertheless, we would be wrong to think of micro-organisms strictly as causes of disease. Actually, only about 1 percent of all micro-organisms are harmful to human beings. Certain micro-organisms are native to our skin, our mouths, and our digestive tracts. They are in our food and water. They are, quite literally, everywhere life can exist.

Bacteria aid in the digestion of food and help to break down wastes in our bodies. Micro-organisms are active in the biochemical changes that convert our sewage, break down (biodegrade) our garbage, and decompose our grass cuttings and other rubbish, turning these wastes back to the life-giving soil.

Can you imagine what our environment would be like if the debris of modern society did not revert to the soil? Or if leaves and dead wood continued to accumulate on the forest floor? Micro-organisms are part of nature's eternal recycling process. This is what ecology—the balance of life—is all about.

Micro-organisms are also essential to the development of certain kinds of foods. They help make cheese and they serve in the fermentation process which lets bread dough rise, turns grape juice into wine, converts cereal mash into beer, and turns apple cider into vinegar.

We are concerned in this book with the 1 percent that cause illness—the 1 percent that is responsible for 90 percent of foodborne illnesses.

SUMMARY

There are five main classes of micro-organisms with which the foodservice manager is concerned. The greatest menace to food comes from *bacteria*. Except in large colonies, bacteria can only be seen under the microscope. While bacteria can survive a wider range of environmental conditions than human beings can, they flourish at temperatures that very nearly coincide with those most favorable to human life. High temperatures, for the most part, kill bacteria; low temperatures and stable dry conditions slow their growth.

Parasites are also dangerous to humans, particularly the larvae of the *Trichinella spiralis* worm. These larvae usually are transported to humans via undercooked meat, mainly pork.

The smallest of the micro-organisms, *viruses*, which are a type of parasite, can multiply only in living cells. For these tiny predators, foodstuffs serve largely as a means of transportation to the potential disease victim.

Mold and *yeast* growth occurs commonly on certain foods. Molds are highly adaptable organisms that are of value in medicine and cheese-making, but some varieties contribute to disease. Although yeasts are helpful to us as agents in fermentation and leavening, they detract from the flavor of some foods.

Micro-organisms are everywhere—in our bodies, in the soil, in water, and in the air. They perform useful functions—as instruments in decomposing debris and in producing certain foods—but their effects are obviously harmful when they serve as agents of foodborne disease and food spoilage.

A CASE IN POINT 2.1

It was 10:45 A.M. Mike, the cook at Frisky-Fried, looked at the empty space on the steam table. The store would open at 11:00 A.M. and the gravy wasn't ready. He had deep-fried the chicken, baked the rolls, cooked and mashed the potatoes, and prepared the coleslaw. The chicken, the rolls, and the potatoes were placed in the steam table right after cooking at 10:40 A.M. The coleslaw was placed in the cold display case. Mike double-checked the temperature. He then looked at the table and noticed that he had not heated the gravy left over from the day before. He had taken the gravy out of the refrigerator and forgotten it. No problem. The steam table would eventually reheat it. He placed the gravy in the steam table. Alicia, the foodservice manager, came through and checked the temperature of the steam table and the cold display case. All the food was there. She went to unlock the front door.

At 1:15 P.M. Mr. Skinner came in and took out five chicken dinners, including gravy and coleslaw, to take home to his family for lunch. By 3:00 A.M. the next day they were all ill. Their physician found *Clostridium perfringens* bacteria in stool specimens from two of the family members. A health department official isolated the same species of bacteria from one of the food items.

What food item do you think contained the bacteria?
How did the sanitation breakdown occur?
What do you think the cook should have done to prevent this outbreak?

A CASE IN POINT 2.2

The Department of Health in a midwestern state began an investigation when it received reports June 4–7 that three unrelated patients hospitalized with abdominal cramps and diarrhea had stool cultures positive for *Salmonella* bacteria. Investigation revealed that one of these patients worked at a suburban restaurant and that the other two had eaten at the same restaurant four days apart. Seven more cases of gastrointestinal illness in restaurant customers were found. The management voluntarily closed the restaurant on June 10.

Forty-seven restaurant patrons were interviewed. Twenty-five of them were found to be ill. The foods implicated as the vehicles of transmission were the ham, the roast beef, and the prime rib. When questioned, the employees identified several breaks in foodhandling techniques, including inadequate refrigeration. *Salmonella* was isolated from the cooked prime rib, the cooked roast beef, the cooked ham, the lettuce, and the coleslaw, as well as from the surface of a wooden cutting board. The health department mandated an extensive education program conducted for the restaurant employees, and all employees also had to have three, consecutive, negative, stool cultures before resuming work. The restaurant was reopened on July 21.

What do you think happened here?

STUDY QUESTIONS

1. Why are micro-organisms of concern to foodservice managers?
2. Which type of micro-organism is most associated with foodborne illness?
3. What name is given to bacteria that grow both in the presence and absence of free oxygen?
4. What is the shape of staphylococcal bacteria?
5. Describe a bacterial spore.
6. Name four environmental needs for the growth of bacteria.
7. What is the name given to bacteria that grow well at refrigerator temperatures?
8. Describe the four phases in the growth of bacteria.

9. Why is pH an important factor in the control of bacteria?
10. How are viruses different from bacteria?
11. What are some of the beneficial uses of yeasts?
12. What conditions in food indicate yeast spoilage?
13. How can *Trichinella spiralis* larvae be killed?
14. Name two ways in which molds may harm human beings.

MORE ON THE SUBJECT

BANWART, GEORGE J. *Basic Food Microbiology.* Westport, Conn.: AVI, 1981. 519 pages. Chapters 1–4 on micro-organisms associated with food provide a very useful source on factors influencing microbial growth. The book presumes some background in biology and chemistry.

LONGREE, KARLA. *Quantity Food Sanitation.* New York: Wiley Interscience, 1980. 456 pages. The introduction to bacteria, yeasts, molds, and viruses in chapter 2, "Some Basic Facts on Micro-organisms Important in Food Sanitation," is complete and is especially useful for the drawings it presents. This book is written for students with some knowledge of elementary biology and chemistry.

ANSWER TO A CASE IN POINT 2.1

The bacteria had everything they needed to survive and grow in the gravy: food, moisture, and because the gravy was placed in the steam table without being reheated, proper temperature. They multiplied into more than enough numbers to cause illness.

The cook should have reheated the food to a sufficient temperature (165°F, 73.9°C) to kill the bacteria. Only then should it have been placed in the steam table.

ANSWER TO A CASE IN POINT 2.2

Inadequate refrigeration, an unsanitary piece of equipment (the cutting board), an ill employee, and poor foodhandling techniques were factors in this outbreak. This outbreak too could have been prevented. To find out how—keep reading!

3
Contamination and Foodborne Illness

With the scientific advances of recent decades, one might think that the biological, chemical, and physical agents that invade our food and menace our health would long since have been conquered. It is true that advances have resulted in safer foods, better methods of preservation, and improved storage practices. However, these advances should not lull the foodservice manager into complacency. It is still important to guard against the hazards that result in foodborne illness. Some advances in our food production system can even have an adverse as well as a positive effect. Remember that *multiple* handling of food items *increases* the chances of contamination. Preventing contamination of safe food by biological, chemical, or physical hazards should be a prime objective of every foodservice manager. Knowing the steps in prevention is the major weapon in the operator's arsenal.

This chapter, then, will cover the following three hazards responsible for outbreaks of foodborne illness:

- Biological hazards—for example, harmful bacteria that contaminate food
- Chemical hazards—for example, the accidental contamination of food with pesticides
- Physical hazards—for example, the contamination of food with glass or metal particles

The biological hazard represents the most widespread problem, but contamination of food by chemical and physical hazards is on the increase and is no less dangerous.

THE BIOLOGICAL HAZARD

Biological hazards arise from pathogenic microorganisms, such as bacteria, viruses, and parasites, as well as from poisonous plants and fish. When biological hazards result in foodborne illnesses, these illnesses are generally classified as either infections or intoxications.

Infection and Intoxication

A *foodborne infection* is a disease that results from eating food that contains harmful microorganisms. These micro-organisms must be alive for the infection to occur.

A *foodborne intoxication* results when poisons or toxins, which are present in ingested food, cause illness in the host (that is, the human body). Toxins may be present in foods naturally, as in the case of certain plants such as mushrooms and certain animals such as puffer fish. When a human being mistakenly consumes these plants and animals, illness may result. Toxins may also be present in food contaminated by micro-organisms that give off poisonous wastes as they die. These toxins are generally odorless and tasteless.

In contrast to foodborne infection, food intoxication is not caused directly by living organisms, but by their toxins. In the case of food contaminated with toxin-producing micro-organisms, the toxins may be capable of causing disease even after the offending micro-organisms have been killed.

The term "food poisoning" is still commonly used to lump together various illnesses caused by food. This term is somewhat imprecise. However, there is enough disagreement about the correct classification of several foodborne illnesses to warrant using "food poisoning" to classify them.

Foodborne Intoxications and Poisonings of Bacterial Origin

We will discuss in some detail the principal bacterial offenders and the diseases they cause. The measures necessary for controlling these offenders will also serve to safeguard consumers from the effects of other less threatening biological life-forms (see Exhibit 3.1).

Exhibit 3.1   Major foodborne diseases of bacterial origin

	Staphylococcal Intoxication	Clostridium Perfringens Infection/ Intoxication	Bacillus Cereus Intoxication
Bacteria	Staphylococcus aureus	Clostridium perfringens	Bacillus cereus
Incubation period	1–6 hours	8–22 hours	8–16 hours
Duration of illness	24–48 hours	24 hours	12 hours or less
Symptoms	Abdominal pain, nausea, vomiting, diarrhea	Abdominal pain, diarrhea	Diarrhea, abdominal pain, nausea, vomiting
Reservoir	Human beings: skin, mucous membranes of nose, throat; infected sores; also animals	Intestinal tract of human beings and animals; also soil	Soil, dust
Foods implicated	Improperly prepared custards, cream-filled pastries, dairy products, bread pudding, potato and other salads, hollandaise sauce, warmed-over foods, meat, poultry, and many other protein foods	Meat that has been boiled, steamed, braised, stewed, or insufficiently roasted and allowed to cool slowly and served the next day, either cold or reheated	Rice and rice dishes, meat, meat products, seasoning, mixes, spices, dry-mix food items (potatoes, soups, gravy)
Spore-former	No	Yes	Yes
Prevention	Cleanliness, sanitary habits, proper heating and refrigeration, exclusion of infected foodhandlers	Careful time-and-temperature control, quick-chilling of cooked meat dishes to be eaten later, isolation of raw components that may contaminate cooked menu items	Careful time-and-temperature control; quick-chilling. Avoidance of cross-contamination

	Botulism Intoxication	Salmonellosis Infection	Shigellosis Infection
Bacteria	Clostridium botulinum	Salmonella	Shigella
Incubation period	12–36 hours	6–48 hours	1–7 days
Duration of illness	Several days to a year	2–3 days	Indefinite, depending on treatment
Symptoms	Fatigue, headache, dizziness, visual disturbances, inability to swallow	Abdominal pain, headache, nausea, vomiting, fever, diarrhea	Diarrhea, fever, cramps, chills, lassitude, dehydration
Reservoir	Soil, water, some animals and fish	Domestic and wild animals, also human beings—especially carriers	Human feces
Foods implicated	Improperly processed canned food such as green beans, corn, beets, chili peppers, mushrooms, spinach, figs, tuna	Meat, meat products, meat and poultry salads, egg custards, and other protein foods	Beans, potatoes, tuna, shrimp, turkey and macaroni salads, apple cider, moist, mixed foods
Spore-former	Yes	No	No
Prevention	Pressure-cooking food at high temperatures in canning. Boiling and stirring home-canned food for 20 minutes	Strict personal hygiene. Avoidance of fecal contamination from unclean foodhandlers and unsafe practices	Personal hygiene. Safe foodhandling. Sanitary food and water sources. Insect and vermin control

Staphylococcal Food Intoxication

Staphylococcal food intoxication is one of the most common types of foodborne illness reported in the United States. The foodservice operator who understands the characteristics of this disease and its causative bacteria can readily understand the control measures needed for its prevention.

Symptoms.   The symptoms of staphylococcal food intoxication are nausea, vomiting, cramps, and diarrhea. These signs appear suddenly, usually within 1 to 6 hours after the contaminated food is eaten, and they last for 24 to 48 hours. Most affected individuals recover from this foodborne illness without any complications.

Exhibit 3.2   *Staphylococcus aureus*

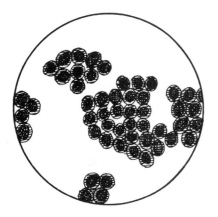

Causative Agent.   The cause of staphylococcal food intoxication is a round or oval bacterium known as *Staphylococcus aureus* (Exhibit 3.2). As they grow these bacteria secrete their toxins into food, contaminating it. Even after the bacteria are killed or die off, the toxins stay behind to cause illness. Staph organisms thrive in the presence of atmospheric oxygen; however, they can also grow in its absence. They also seem to survive over a rather wide temperature range. Staphlococci do not form spores.

Source of Bacteria.   Though this pathogen is sometimes found in meat and poultry, human beings are considered to be the most important source, or reservoir, of *Staphylococcus aureus* in foods. It is estimated that at any given time, 40 to 50 percent of all healthy human adults are carriers of staph organisms. (A *carrier* is a person who harbors disease-causing micro-organisms in his or her body without being noticeably affected by them.) Staphylococcus bacteria are commonly found in the nasal passages and throat, on the hands and skin, and especially in infected cuts, abrasions, burns, boils, and pimples.

Foods Involved.   Food products frequently involved in staph intoxications include cooked meat products (especially ham, stews, and gravies), custards, pastry fillings, cheeses, potato salads, and other moist, high-protein foods. Foods contaminated with staph bacteria have no particular odor or taste that might make the contamination obvious.

A Typical Case.   Consider how a staph problem could arise in your food-preparation area. Assume that a chef has a skin infection on his neck. When it itches, he naturally scratches it.

Let's say that one of his assignments is to prepare ham for use in ham salad, an item usually held for some time before being served. Once the ham is ready, it will not be cooked further. Fresh from the pot, the ham is carved by the chef, who plants staph bacteria from his neck everywhere he touches the ham with his hands. The sliced ham should have been quickly chilled, which would have stopped or slowed bacterial growth. Instead, it is put aside on a work table at bacteria-incubating room temperatures. Next stop is the salad pantry where the ham is chopped or diced and mixed into the salad base, which was prepared separately and held at room temperature. All the while—from slicing to mixing—the population of staph bacteria not only is growing at an astounding rate but also is producing harmful toxins. The completed mixture—staphylococci, toxins, and all—is once more set aside, unrefrigerated, to await the customer's call for a ham salad sandwich. (If you study Exhibit 3.3, you can see the effect of temperature on the growth patterns of most bacteria.)

Even if the chef had not been infected, staphylococcal organisms could have entered the salad at any stage in its preparation. The knife used to dice the ham could have been contaminated through prior use on raw foods in which staphylococci are sometimes present.

Exhibit 3.3   Temperature of food for the
control of bacteria

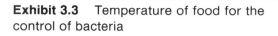

°F		°C
250	Canning temperatures for low-acid vegetables, meat, and poultry in pressure canner.	121.1
240		115.5
	Canning temperatures for fruits, tomatoes, and pickles in water-bath canner.	
212		100.0
	Cooking temperatures destroy most bacteria. Time required to kill bacteria decreases as temperature is increased.	
165		73.8
	Warming temperatures prevent growth but allow survival of some bacteria.	
140		60
	Some bacterial growth may occur. Many bacteria survive.	
120		48.8
	Temperatures in this zone allow rapid growth of bacteria and production of toxins by some bacteria.	
60		15.5
	Some growth of food-poisoning bacteria may occur.	
45		7.2
40		4.4
	Cold temperatures permit slow growth of some bacteria that cause spoilage.	
32		0
	Freezing temperatures stop growth of bacteria, but may allow bacteria to survive.	
0		−17.7

Exhibit 3.4   Typical events that lead to outbreaks of staphylococcal intoxication. ("In Survey of Contemporary Toxicology, Volume 1," A. T. Tu, Editor. Copyright © 1980 by John Wiley & Sons, Inc. Reprinted by permission.)

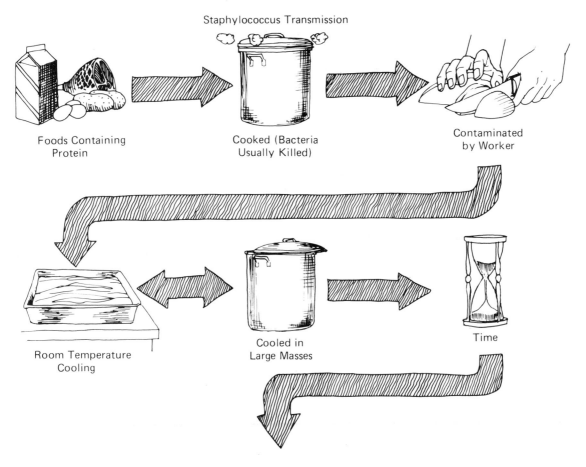

Staphylococcus Transmission

Foods Containing Protein   Cooked (Bacteria Usually Killed)   Contaminated by Worker

Room Temperature Cooling   Cooled in Large Masses   Time

Staphylococcal Intoxication

Another worker entering the kitchen could have coughed or sneezed over the food. The ham could have been sliced on a chopping block so worn from use that it had plenty of crevices in which bacteria could lurk. Some of the ingredients of the salad base might not be ideal media for bacterial growth, but they could have carried the organisms to the ham, where conditions were highly favorable.

The rest of the story is sad and unpleasant to relate. Several hours after eating this ham salad, the customer suffers a sudden onset of nausea, vomiting, diarrhea, and abdominal cramps—the typical symptoms of staphylococcal poisoning. This description is not merely a dramatic representation of what *might* have happened. The very incidents described are typical of cases actually reported to the U.S. Centers for Disease Control (see Exhibit 3.4).

Control Measures. Staph bacteria will be killed under proper cooking conditions, but some of the toxins produced by the bacteria are very resistant to heat. For this reason, the foodservice manager cannot rely on proper cooking alone to prevent staph contamination. Proper procedures in storage and handling are also important.

Control measures in the prevention of staphylococcal intoxication are

- Prompt refrigeration of food (especially of sliced and chopped meats, custards, and cream fillings) at 45°F (7.2°C) or below
- Exclusion from foodhandling of workers with respiratory infections, pimples, boils, and infected cuts and burns
- Avoidance of hand contact with food, or proper use of disposable gloves
- Careful handling of leftovers—either by disposing of them or reheating them thoroughly to 165°F (73.9°C) or above

Clostridium Perfringens Food Poisoning

Clostridium perfringens food poisoning was first identified in the 1890s. By the 1950s, outbreaks of this foodborne illness were being reported with considerable frequency. The disease is not easily classified as it has characteristics of both an intoxication and an infection. Clostridium perfringens poisoning is sometimes classed as an infection because of the length of time it takes for symptoms to appear (8 to 22 hours). It is sometimes classed as an intoxication because of the toxic substances given off by *C. perfringens* bacteria after they enter the human body. Clostridium perfringens poisoning is thought to account for many of the mild—and unreported—cases of foodborne illness.

Symptoms. The symptoms of clostridium perfringens poisoning are usually milder than those of staphylococcal intoxication and clear up within 24 hours of their first appearance.

Exhibit 3.5 *Clostridium perfringens*

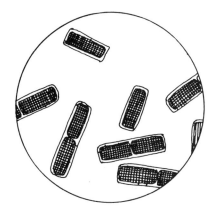

This illness is marked by abdominal pain, diarrhea, nausea, and occasionally vomiting and fever. These signs show up from 8 to 22 hours after the bacteria-laden food has been eaten.

Causative Agent. The bacterium *Clostridium perfringens* (Exhibit 3.5) is the cause of the poisoning. These bacteria are rod-shaped, spore-forming organisms that thrive in the *absence* of oxygen. The vegetative cells of *C. perfringens* are killed by normal cooking temperatures, but surviving heat-stable spores may withstand temperatures as high as 212°F (100°C). Some spores may also resist freezing.

Source of Bacteria. *C. perfringens* bacteria are found in soil, dust, and the intestinal tracts of humans and animals. These pathogens are therefore likely to accompany any raw food products brought into a foodservice establishment.

Foods Involved. Occurrences of clostridium perfringens poisoning are associated with cooked meat (frequently beef), poultry (frequently turkey), and even beans that have remained at room temperature for several hours or have been permitted to pass slowly through the temperature danger zone as a result of gradual heating, reheating, or cooling. Inadequate heating or cooling is a particular problem in the interiors of large food masses.

A Typical Case.   Consider a typical situation. Let's say that we are preparing a large pot of vegetable soup and that it will contain fresh carrots. The soup is boiled in a 20-gallon stockpot on Wednesday evening for serving at lunch on Thursday. After cooking, it is placed on a side table at room temperature, until it is cool enough to be refrigerated. The soup is removed from the refrigerator at 10:30 A.M. on Thursday and brought to the steam table on the serving line.

Let us investigate what has happened. Carrots are grown in soil, of course, where they very probably have been contaminated with *C. perfringens* bacteria and spores, which may collect on the carrots. It is impossible, using normal methods, to remove all these bacteria and spores by washing and scraping.

The process of heating the soup would have halted the growth of the *C. perfringens* bacteria for a while, but it would not have succeeded in killing the spores.

To compound the problem, the soup was allowed to cool at room temperature—well within the danger zone—for several hours. The bacteria thus had plenty of time to multiply and poison the soup. Later the soup was brought directly from the refrigerator to the steam table. A steam table is designed to hold food that is already hot—it cannot always heat large amounts of cold soup to temperatures high enough to halt bacterial growth. So the *C. perfringens* bacteria had another chance to multiply unhindered during the entire time that the soup was in the steam table.

Control Measures.   Since *C. perfringens* bacteria are present naturally in so many of the supplies available to the foodservice operator, he or she cannot expect to prevent totally their entry into the establishment. And since the spores of these bacteria are so heat-stable, the operator cannot expect to kill all of the spores.

Effective control of *C. perfringens* bacteria can be achieved through the following measures:

- Serve meat and poultry dishes hot or as soon as they are cooked; avoid preparing food a day in advance.
- Quick-chill meat dishes that will be eaten later; foods should not be allowed to cool at room temperature.
- Do not allow frozen foods to thaw at room temperature.
- Isolate raw foods from cooked items to prevent cross-contamination.
- Reheating should not merely warm the food but should heat it thoroughly to 165°F (73.9°C) or higher.
- Divide large batches of food into small lots for rapid refrigeration.
- Exercise extreme caution when holding foods on a steam table or on other hot-holding devices; take steps to ensure proper time and temperature control.

Bacillus Cereus Food Poisoning

Bacillus cereus food poisoning is of growing concern to foodservice managers. The disease is generally classified as an intoxication. The bacteria, which cause the illness, can be found in a wide variety of foods.

Symptoms.   The symptoms of bacillus cereus food poisoning are mild compared to staphylococcal intoxication. The symptoms are diarrhea, abdominal pain, nausea, and occasionally, vomiting. They appear usually 8 to 16 hours after ingestion of the contaminated food and usually last not more than 12 hours.

Causative Agent.   The *Bacillus cereus* bacterium is a large, rod-shaped, spore-forming organism. It is facultative.

Source of Bacteria. *Bacillus cereus* are found in soil, water, and dust.

Foods Involved. The bacteria are frequently found in grains, including rice, flour, and in starch, and in dry-mix products such as for soups, gravies, puddings, and dried potatoes. They have also been found in meats and milk. Cooked rice that has been allowed to sit at room temperature has been implicated in a number of outbreaks.

Control Measures. As with other types of bacteria, time and temperature violations are causes of the rapid increase in the organisms and the spores. Since these bacteria are found all around us there is little the foodservice manager can do to keep them out of food, but they must be prevented from growing once they get in food. The following measures should prevent *Bacillus cereus* from contaminating food:

- Do not hold foods at room temperature for any period of time.
- Chill foods quickly after preparation.
- Store food in the refrigerator in shallow, smaller pans rather than in large, deep pots.
- Use up food items as quickly as possible after preparation.
- Keep dry foods and mixes dry.

Botulism: A Food Intoxication

Botulism is a foodborne illness of bacterial origin, which is probably the most familiar of these to the general public because of its high mortality rate and the sensational publicity surrounding any outbreak. This disease is truly a scourge when it strikes and can be fatal. Fortunately, botulism outbreaks originating in commercial foodservice establishments are rare.

Symptoms. The symptoms of botulism are vomiting, abdominal pain, headache, double vision, and progressive respiratory paralysis. Symptoms usually appear within 12 to 36 hours after the ingestion of contaminated food. Unlike most foodborne illnesses of bacterial origin, botulism attacks the nervous system. Paralysis may result. In some severe cases the respiratory system may be paralyzed, resulting in death. Depending on the age and the condition of the individual and the promptness of treatment, the botulism victim may face either a long convalescence or death.

Causative Agent. The bacterium that causes botulism is *Clostridium botulinum,* a rod-shaped, spore-forming organism that can grow only in the absence of oxygen—for example, in a sealed container—but is vulnerable to high temperatures. The toxin *botulin,* which is given off by *C. botulinum,* is deadly.

Source of Bacteria. *Clostridium botulinum* bacteria are found in soil, water, and the intestinal tracts of animals, including fish.

Foods Involved. Foods implicated in botulism outbreaks are improperly processed, usually home-canned, low-acid foods (green beans, mushrooms, corn, beets, spinach, figs, tuna, for example) and smoked vacuum-packed fish.

Control Measures. Preventive measures include adherence to the following two rules:

- Never use home-canned foods at any time in a commercial foodservice establishment.
- Never accept canned goods if the cans are swollen or show signs of internal pressure or if the contents are foamy, foul-smelling, or give some other indication of being spoiled. Do not even *taste* suspect goods. Death can result from a single taste of botulinum-contaminated food.

Foodborne Infections of Bacterial Origin

Salmonellosis: A Food Infection

Another disease of major concern to foodservice managers is salmonellosis. Since salmonellosis results from the consumption of food contaminated with pathogenic bacteria, it is classified as an infection.

Symptoms.   The symptoms of salmonellosis are slower to appear than those of a staph intoxication. The illness is marked by headache followed by vomiting, diarrhea, abdominal pain, and fever. These symptoms show themselves within 6 to 48 hours after ingestion of contaminated food. Milder cases of salmonellosis usually last two to three days, while severe infections may last longer and can, in rare cases, be fatal.

Causative Agent.   Salmonellosis is caused by members of the *Salmonella* genus of bacteria. There are more than 400 types of *Salmonella* bacteria that cause illness in human beings. One type of *Salmonella*, the *Salmonella typhi*, causes typhoid fever (see Exhibit 3.6).

    Salmonella are rod-shaped bacteria that will grow with or without the presence of oxygen. They do not form spores. *Salmonella* grow best at human body temperature (98.6°F or 37°C) but will survive somewhat higher and lower temperatures. *Salmonella* will be killed by temperatures of 140°F (60°C) and higher.

Source of Bacteria.   *Salmonella* bacteria are found in domestic and wild animals, including pets such as turtles and ducklings, as well as in human beings. Persons who eat food contaminated by *Salmonella* may not necessarily become ill but may become carriers of the bacteria and transmit them back to food.

Foods Involved.   A multitude of foods are implicated in outbreaks of salmonellosis. They include meat and poultry, especially fine-cut components such as sausage; lightly cooked

Exhibit 3.6   A species of *Salmonella*

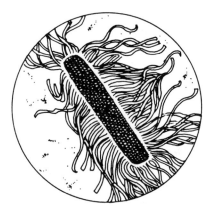

foods containing eggs and egg products; shellfish, especially oysters and clams; fish from polluted waters; and unpasteurized milk or dairy products.

A Typical Case.   Consider how *Salmonella* bacteria can enter your food products uninvited—and stay long enough to make people sick. Let's say that a cook takes raw chicken out of the freezer and raw beef out of the refrigerator. She sets the chicken out to thaw at room temperature and begins to prepare and cook the beef. Meanwhile, the chicken is thawing, with some parts thawing faster than others, and *Salmonella* bacteria already present are multiplying at an alarming rate.

    A few hours later, when the beef is done cooking, it is placed on top of the range to cool before preparation.

    The cook now begins to prepare the thawed and contaminated chicken. She cuts it up for cooking and places it in the oven. Using the same knife she cuts the now cooled beef, placing *Salmonella* from the chicken onto the roast beef. The roast beef is cut up to await orders for sandwiches. When the chicken is taken out of the oven, the chances are that not all parts have been cooked sufficiently to kill all the bacteria present. The chicken is cut up

Exhibit 3.7 Typical events that lead to outbreaks of salmonellosis

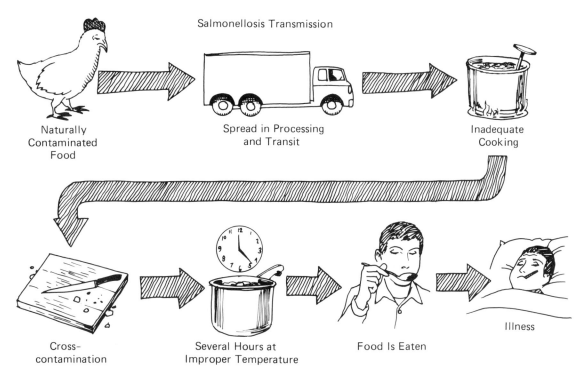

Salmonellosis Transmission

Naturally
Contaminated
Food

Spread in Processing
and Transit

Inadequate
Cooking

Cross-
contamination

Several Hours at
Improper Temperature

Food Is Eaten

Illness

with the same unwashed knife used on the beef and is re-contaminated—the cycle starts again.

Cross-contamination or *re-contamination* of cooked foods with raw foods is a *frequent* factor in salmonellosis outbreaks (see Exhibit 3.7).

Control Measures. Since food processors have found it difficult to eliminate *Salmonella* contamination from all the food available to the public, it is up to the foodservice manager to guarantee that these bacteria do not infect the customer. The following steps will help in achieving that goal:

■ Guard against cross-contamination— the transfer of harmful micro- organisms from one item of food to another by means of a nonfood medium such as equipment, utensils, or human hands. *Salmonella* bacteria are frequently present in raw poultry, so do not use the same utensils for both raw and cooked poultry without cleaning and sanitizing the utensils between uses. Separate cutting boards should be maintained for raw and cooked products.

■ Beware of contaminated supplies. Dry milk and dry eggs should be pasteurized. Never use eggs that have dirty, cracked, or broken shells; in addition, only whole eggs—not dry or frozen eggs—should be used in products that do not receive thorough additional cooking, such as meringues and custards.

- Make sure that all foodhandlers follow the rules of personal hygiene, particularly handwashing after use of the toilet. Persons contaminated with *Salmonella* may carry the bacteria in their fecal matter long after they are first contaminated.
- Be sure to cook foods adequately to a minimum internal temperature appropriate for each item (see chapter 6). Chill foods promptly to 45°F (7.2°C) or below.

Shigellosis: A Food Infection

Another foodborne illness of bacterial origin is shigellosis, sometimes called *bacillary dysentery.*

Symptoms.   Shigellosis is an infection characterized by diarrhea, cramps, and chills, often accompanied by fever. The bacteria responsible for shigellosis belong to the *Shigella* genus.

Source of Bacteria.   Humans themselves are the prime reservoir for the dysentery bacillus. Many people become carriers of this pathogen for periods lasting for several weeks. Carriers excrete *Shigella* bacteria in their feces, subsequently fail to wash their hands properly, and then transmit the bacteria to food. Roaches, flies, and rodents are also thought to be responsible for the transmission of this bacteria.

Foods Involved.   Although contaminated water has been indicted more frequently than food in the transmission of shigellosis, suspect foods include moist prepared foods (such as potato, tuna, turkey, and macaroni salads), gravies, and milk and dairy products.

Control Measures.   Sanitary sewage disposal, purification of water supplies, attention to rules of personal hygiene, and adequate pest control are important weapons against shigellosis.

Infectious Hepatitis: A Viral Disease

Infectious hepatitis is a viral disease that is often the result of poor personal hygiene on the part of foodhandlers.

Symptoms.   Infectious hepatitis symptoms—jaundice, nausea, abdominal pain, and malaise—appear 10 to 50 days after infection. A mild case may last several weeks, whereas a severe infection may linger for several months.

Source of Virus.   Infectious hepatitis is caused by a virus found in the feces and urine of infected persons and in raw shellfish harvested from polluted waters.

This disease is most often transmitted from person to person by direct contact and indirectly through contaminated water. Some occurrences have been reported involving person-to-food-to-person transmission. When food is involved, infectious hepatitis has been transmitted most frequently through raw oysters and clams from sewage-contaminated waters; on occasion, however, such foods as milk, orange juice, strawberry sauce, and glazed doughnuts have been implicated.

Control Measures.   Outbreaks can be controlled by obtaining shellfish from safe sources, by cooking the shellfish to destroy the virus, by using safe water supplies, and by making sure that foodhandlers practice good personal hygiene.

Trichinosis: A Parasitic Disease

Another biological hazard of concern to foodservice managers is the presence in food of parasites—tiny organisms that depend on a living host to provide certain requirements for growth. Trichinosis is a foodborne illness caused by such parasites.

Trichinosis involves delicate, coiled roundworms called *Trichinella spiralis.* A person eats food—primarily meat—infested with the larvae of this parasitic organism. After the food is eaten, the larvae mature into adult worms. The female worm then invades the lining of the host's small intestine and discharges new larvae there. These tiny larvae are carried by the blood to muscle tissue where they imbed themselves and cause illness.

Symptoms. The initial symptoms of trichinosis, which appear between 2 to 28 days after eating the contaminated food, are like those of other foodborne illnesses: vomiting, nausea, and abdominal pain. Later, muscular stiffness, fever, and perhaps rashes develop.

Foods Involved. The most common reservoir of this parasite in the United States is undercooked pork. Despite improvements in methods of raising pork for food in the past 20 years, the foodservice manager can still expect that some raw pork, including government-inspected pork, is infected. Trichinae also infest bear meat and certain other game animals. Cross-contamination is a problem. Raw pork should not come in contact with other foods.

Control Measures. The only sure safeguard against trichinosis is the cooking of pork until it reaches an internal temperature of 150°F (65.6°C) or until the pork turns gray (170°F or 76.7°C if cooked in a microwave oven). Freezing will also kill the larvae if pork is stored at 5°F (−15°C) for 30 days, −10°F (−23.3°C) for 20 days, or −30°F (−34.4°C) for 12 days.

Other Illnesses Transmitted by Food

There are a number of other diseases that can be transmitted by food. Human plague or dengue has been associated with eating raw wild game. In addition, raw milk has been linked to campylobacteriosis, caused by the *Campylobacter jejuni* bacteria.

Such illnesses are rare, and a combined management strategy of hiring healthy workers and keeping food from unapproved sources out of the facility should eliminate such problems.

Poisonous Plants and Fish

Certain plants and animals, which are themselves poisonous, can be classed as biological hazards. These plants and animals occasionally have been used as food—either accidentally or through ignorance. Cooking these poisonous plants and animals does not usually destroy the toxins that produce illness.

Plants that have been implicated in outbreaks of foodborne illness include fava beans, rhubarb leaves, jimson weed, and water hemlock. Honey from bees that have gathered nectar from the mountain laurel, milk from cows that have eaten snakeroot, and jelly made from apricot kernels have also poisoned human beings.

Of the hundreds of poisonous plants, one merits special mention—the fungus known as the mushroom. Poisonous and nonpoisonous mushrooms often look so much alike that the untrained eye cannot tell the difference. To avoid the problem, avoid using any mushroom not secured from an approved and reliable source. *There is no sure method that the amateur can use to detect poisonous varieties of mushrooms.*

Fish may be designated as poisonous for one of two reasons: either because toxins are always present in the fish or because certain circumstances encourage toxin production. Some poisonous fish are the puffer, blowfish, moray eel, fresh-water minnow, and some fish belonging to the scombroid group. Other fish may become poisonous in certain seasons, or in certain waters; for example, swordfish has occasionally become contaminated with mercury in mercury-polluted water.

Ciguatera is a painful illness caused by marine fish, which eat fish that had in turn eaten toxic algae. Scientists have linked some outbreaks to offshore construction projects, which may cause fish food to become contaminated. This illness can be fatal and is characterized by vomiting, intense nausea, hot and cold flashes, and in some cases, hallucinations.

There are no guarantees against receiving contaminated fish, but there are steps that can be taken to help prevent illness.

- Buy fish only from reputable sources.
- Clean all fish promptly and thoroughly.

Foodservice managers should scrupulously follow the rule of using only safe and approved food sources.

THE CHEMICAL HAZARD

Chemical contamination of food is a matter of concern all along the food supply chain. The danger has been increased by the industrialization of agriculture and the trend toward mass manufacture and pre-processing of food products. The more chemicals in the environment, the greater the chance they have to get into our food. Three kinds of chemical hazards are of special concern to the foodservice manager: (1) contamination of food with pesticides, (2) use of excessive quantities of additives and preservatives, and (3) contamination of food with toxic metals.

Pesticides

Of the chemical agents causing foodborne illness, those receiving the most attention have been the pesticides. These agents can enter the food supply by several routes.

- Pesticides and fungicides may be applied directly to the growing plant or animal to protect it from insects, fungus, and microbial attack.
- Food animals and plants may take up pesticidal agents during the growing process and incorporate them in living cells.

- Food can be contaminated by chemical agents during processing and at the foodservice facility.

Obviously the foodservice manager has very little control over the first two routes of contamination. The federal government regulates the use of pesticides in food for interstate commerce, but often food grown and sold within the same state has not been strictly regulated. The best that the average foodservice operator can do is to purchase food only from reputable, legally approved sources and to wash *all* fresh fruits and vegetables, no matter what the source.

The foodservice operator can and must prevent contamination of food by chemical agents within the foodservice establishment. Pesticides and germicides should not be used in the facility, except by professionals. If they are stored in the operation they must be labeled properly, kept in their original containers, and stored separately from food and food-contact materials. Pesticides have caused poisoning when they were accidentally mixed into flour, sprayed onto oatmeal, and mistaken for baking soda.

Many other chemicals commonly found in food services are poisonous to humans. Detergents, polishes, caustics, cleaning and drying agents, and other products of this type should never come into contact with food. Great care must be exercised to follow label directions for use and to store these chemicals under safe conditions away from food. Food poisonings have occurred when drain cleaner, paint remover, and silver polish accidentally contaminated food.

Additives and Preservatives

Additives, like some pesticides, are a subject of debate among scientists and legislators. Although the effects of long-term use of additives are not yet known, it cannot be denied that certain food preservatives and additives, when used in excessive amounts, have caused illness. Additives include emulsifiers, firming agents, flavorings, non-nutritive sweeteners, nutrient supplements, oxidizers and antioxidizers, stabilizers, thickeners, and anticaking agents. Color additives also fall under this general category. Nitrites, for example, used as coloring agents and preservatives in meat, are toxic in large concentrations. Cobalt used to stabilize the foam in beer has caused cardiac failure among heavy beer drinkers in two cities.

Another foodborne illness results from the use of too much monosodium glutamate (MSG). Symptoms of MSG poisoning in susceptible consumers are flushing of the face, dizziness, headache, and nausea.

Agents used to preserve the flavor, safety, and consistency of foods are increasingly linked to food contamination.

Sulfiting agents are preservatives that are used to maintain the freshness and color of fresh fruits and vegetables, particularly lettuce, but also of potatoes and coleslaw. Some of them have been linked to a number of lethal allergic reactions among sensitive individuals, particularly asthmatics. The reactions include nausea, diarrhea, asthma attacks, and in some cases, loss of consciousness.

Foodservice operators should read labels on all processed foods to determine whether sulfiting agents are present. These include sulfur dioxide, potassium bisulfite, potassium metabisulfite, sodium bisulfite, sodium metabisulfite, or sodium sulfite. When preserving lettuce and other vegetables in the operation it is best to use alternative fresheners such as citric acid juices or else prepare smaller quantities in advance. The FDA has established rules forbidding the addition of sulfites to foods in the foodservice operation.

Nitrites are another preservative of concern to foodservice managers. Nitrites are used by the meat industry to prevent growth of certain bacteria and also as flavor enhancers. Scientists have established a direct link between cancer and nitrites. The risk may increase by the over-browning or burning of foods treated with nitrites. Some manufacturers have added vitamin C and vitamin E to nitrite-treated foods to prevent the formation of tumor-causing nitrosamines. For the foodservice manager's part, unless the consumer insists, foods should never be burned or over-browned.

To control the possibility of poisoning from the overzealous use of food additives and preservatives, the foodservice manager should see to it that these products are never used to cover up spoilage in foods and that only approved additives and preservatives are used in limited amounts. Manufacturer's instructions should be carefully read and followed to the letter.

One invisible, but very real, hazard is radiation emitted from microwave ovens. Although the safety standards and acceptable radiation emission levels are specified by the federal government, it is up to the foodservice manager to see to it that proper maintenance procedures are followed. If the instruction manual indicates that the oven should be inspected by a trained technician at regular intervals, the manager should make sure such inspection takes place.

The use of radiation in food processing to eliminate micro-organisms from food materials and to lengthen storage life is also controlled by regulatory agencies. Food irradiation is regulated by the federal Food and Drug Administration, and the process of irradiation is classified as an additive. This means that the FDA must approve each food item proposed for irradiation.

Foodservice managers should be familiar with chemicals used in their operations. The federal government regularly publishes a list of chemicals classified as hazardous and local health departments may provide this information. Chemicals are being used to improve and maintain the quality and safety of foods. However, becoming aware of which chemicals are *potential hazards* is a safety step an astute manager can take to avoid chemical contamination.

Poisonous Metals

Some metals, like iron, are necessary components of the human diet in at least trace quantities. As is true with almost any substance, however, they become toxic in excessive amounts. In addition, when metals come into contact with certain foods, contamination results and illness occurs when the foods are eaten.

Poisoning can result when high-acid foods are stored or prepared in copper or brass containers, in galvanized (zinc-coated) containers, or in containers of gray enamelware, which may be plated with antimony or cadmium. Foods implicated in metal poisonings are sauerkraut, tomatoes, fruit gelatins, lemonade, and fruit punches. To prevent such accidental poisonings, use containers only for the purposes for which they are intended.

Enamelware coated with lead glaze and tin milk cans used to store fruit juices have been linked to contamination. Enamelware should not be used in foodservice operations since it may chip and become a physical contaminant. It also is a chemical contaminant. Chipping exposes the underlying metal which may cause problems with acid food items.

Copper water lines accidentally exposed to carbonated beverages in dispensing machines have also figured in chemical food poisoning incidents. Copper poisoning is characterized by the rapid and violent onset of symptoms. Foodservice managers should check *or have checked* soft drink post-mix systems to be sure no backflow of gas from the carbonator is occurring or that the beverage is not exposed to the copper tubing.

Uncovered meats can become poisoned through contact with refrigerator shelves containing *cadmium.*

Management must be sure that hazardous metals are not used in foodservice preparation, storage, and service equipment. It goes without saying that no lead or lead-based product should ever be used in foodservice areas.

THE PHYSICAL HAZARD

Physical contaminants such as chips of glass from broken light fixtures or glassware and metal fragments from kitchenware and tableware are obvious dangers. The foodservice manager must be on the alert to minimize these hazards.

A worn can opener, for example, is not just an annoyance. It may, as often happens, shower metal curls on the food in the can being opened. The common—but inexcusable—practice of scooping up ice with a glass is definitely hazardous, since glass chips may find their way into beverage servings. Good facilities planning and the training of personnel in safe operating procedures can eliminate these physical hazards.

Dangers caused by physical contaminants are on the rise, some the result of nasty pranks with soft-packaged food items. Such items arriving at the foodservice facility should not be accepted if there is evidence of tampering.

If items such as glass, nails, or other objects are found in foods and appear to have been intentionally placed there, the manager should alert the supplier. It may just be an isolated incident. However, a series of such incidents obliges the manager to contact both the public health department and the police. The foodservice facility's own storage procedures should be checked to ensure that they are not part of the problem.

SUMMARY

Foodborne illness poses a potentially serious threat to public health in this country. The foodservice manager plays an important role in preventing contamination of food.

The most serious hazards associated with food are *biological* in nature. The diseases arising from *Staphylococcus aureus, Clostridium perfringens, Salmonella, Clostridium botulinum,* and *Shigella* bacteria all have serious consequences. The basic measures to be taken against biological hazards are as follows: use food from only approved sources; prevent contamination; kill harmful organisms; and prevent bacterial growth. It should always be remembered that *people*—in one way or another—are the primary cause of food contamination.

Chemical hazards arise from the improper use of pesticides, additives, preservatives, and poisonous metals. Chemicals and metal products should be used only for their intended purposes. The foodservice manager must also guard against *physical* dangers that may arise from faulty equipment or improper design, or from improperly inspected incoming food items in the foodservice establishment.

A CASE IN POINT

On February 2, 1975, the passengers and one crew member aboard a chartered aircraft flying from Tokyo to Copenhagen, with an interim stop in Anchorage, developed an illness characterized by diarrhea, vomiting, abdominal cramps, and nausea.

Breakfast was served 5½ hours after the plane left Anchorage and the 196 passengers began getting ill approximately 2 hours after this meal was served. Breakfast consisted of an omelette, ham slices, yogurt, bread, butter, and cheese.

Except for the one crew member who had eaten the ham, none of the plane's crew became ill. They had been served a steak dinner instead of breakfast since it was suppertime for them.

Breakfast was prepared in Anchorage by a catering company. Three cooks were involved in preparation of the ham and omelettes. The ham had been prepared the night before and refrigerated. The next day, as the omelettes were being prepared, one of the cooks placed ham slices on top. The food was stored at room temperature during the 6 hours required for the preparation of all of the omelettes.

Following preparation, this food was placed for 14½ hours in a holding room where the temperature was measured at 50°F (10°C). Beginning about 7:30 A.M., the breakfast food was loaded onto the plane. The food was again stored at room temperature in the galley ovens until it was heated just prior to serving.

This large foodborne outbreak resulted from ham that had been handled by a cook who had an inflamed finger lesion from which *Staphylococcus aureus* was later cultured.

What else went wrong that contributed to the outbreak?

STUDY QUESTIONS

1. Give examples of the biological, chemical, and physical hazards connected with contamination and foodborne illness.
2. Which of the hazards in question 1 is most common in terms of foodborne illness?
3. What is the difference between an infection and an intoxication?
4. What are some factors in controlling clostridium perfringens food contamination?
5. What is meant by the term "cross-contamination"? Give an example.

6.   Describe how staphylococcal food intoxication might be transmitted.

7.   What is the primary reservoir, or source, of the *Staphylococcus aureus* bacteria?

8.   List two control measures for preventing staph intoxications in a foodservice establishment.

9.   What is meant by the term "disease carrier"?

10. What foods are associated with cases of clostridium perfringens poisoning?

11. What are the symptoms of salmonellosis?

12. What two rules should always be followed by the foodservice manager who wishes to prevent occurrences of botulism?

13. Name an effective method of controlling trichinosis.

14. What are two common sources of the infectious hepatitis virus?

15. How can metals cause poisoning in a foodservice operation?

MORE ON THE SUBJECT

CENTERS FOR DISEASE CONTROL. *Foodborne Disease Surveillance.* Annual Summary. U.S. Department of Health and Human Services, Public Health Service. These summaries, published annually, are the authoritative surveys of foodborne illness and infection in the United States. They contain statistical information on incidence of disease, cite places in which food was mishandled in such a way as to cause a disease outbreak, and identify the kinds of food implicated in the outbreaks. Details on every reported outbreak and analysis of all statistical information are also provided.

RICHARDSON, TREVA M. and WADE R. NICODEMUS. *Sanitation for Foodservice Workers.* New York: CBI/Van Nostrand Reinhold Co., 1981. 275 pages. This book concentrates on the major foodborne diseases and their bacteriology. It also provides information on sanitary dishwashing, effective pest control, and the dimensions of liability.

ZOTOLLA, EDMUND A. University of Minnesota, Agricultural Extension Service, Communication Resources Distribution. Extension Bulletins. *Salmonellosis* (1980, #AG–DU–0477), *Staphylococcus Food Poisoning* (1981, #AG–BU–0483), *Clostridium Perfringens* (1979, #AG–BU–0487), *Botulism* (1976, #AG–BU–0490).

ANSWER TO A CASE IN POINT

The ham was held at room temperature for more than a sufficient amount of time to allow the growth of the staphylococcal bacteria and the production of toxins. A total of 20½ hours at temperature ranges dangerous to food, between 50° and 70°F (10° and 21.1°C), made this ham the source of one of the largest foodborne illness outbreaks ever recorded.

Staphylococcal toxin is not easily destroyed by ordinary cooking temperatures, so the best control measure is the prevention of entry of the bacteria into the food in the first place. The risk of storing food at room temperatures for long periods of time and of allowing infected foodhandlers to prepare food is once more emphasized.

Part II
Serving Sanitary Food

4

Purchasing and Receiving Safe Food

To paraphrase an old saying, it would be easier to make a silk purse from a sow's ear than to prepare a wholesome meal with contaminated or deteriorated ingredients. It is essential that completely safe materials be used in a food service. It follows, then, that food supplies must be in excellent condition when they arrive in the receiving area and that they must be examined for signs of spoilage and contamination before being used.

In previous chapters we have explored the fundamental role of micro-organisms in food contamination. Now we are prepared to consider the importance of safe procurement and proper inspection in protecting food.

Government regulation of food processors helps prevent the distribution of unsafe products, but the final responsibility for product safety in a foodservice establishment rests with the manager—for several reasons. In the first place, government inspectors are unable to inspect all food production, and they cannot check the products at every point in the distribution network. In addition, the recent tendency to employ mass production and to create a variety of processed foods, though improving efficiency and economy in foodservice operations, has brought new hazards to the consumer. The additional processing steps and longer lines of supply have increased the number of events that can cause contamination or spoilage. For example, a frozen food product, which is perfectly safe when it leaves the manufacturer's plant, may be damaged by thawing in the railroad car or truck that carries it to the wholesaler, and again, in the van that carries it to the point of use.

In this chapter, then, we will consider the following:

■ Government programs to ensure a safe food supply

■ General rules for inspection of food as it arrives at a foodservice establishment

■ Specific signs of spoilage in food products

SOURCES OF SAFE FOOD

To a great extent the foodservice manager must rely on assurances from suppliers that the food coming into the establishment is of sanitary quality. It would be impossible for the manager to control or inspect every step of the production and processing of the countless food items used in the average restaurant, commissary, or kitchen.

At the very least, then, the foodservice operator should investigate suppliers from time to time and ask to inspect their facilites. For example, many multi-unit foodservice companies have resident inspectors in the processing plants and supplier operations from which they make purchases.

A foodservice operator inspecting a supplier might ask these questions: What are the standards of sanitation used here? Does the supply company follow approved practices in handling products? If it handles refrigerated or frozen foods, is it equipped to do the job? Is there enough warehouse space? Are delivery trucks adequately refrigerated? Are employees cooperative and are they trained in sanitary practices? Is the supplier willing to make deliveries when the personnel are not rushed so that food can be handled quickly and properly? Is the product quality consistent? Are the products packaged safely? Are minimal bacterial requirements for specific products met? (See Exhibit 4.1)

Exhibit 4.1   A typical food product, fresh or frozen, runs the risk of passing many times through the temperature danger zone.

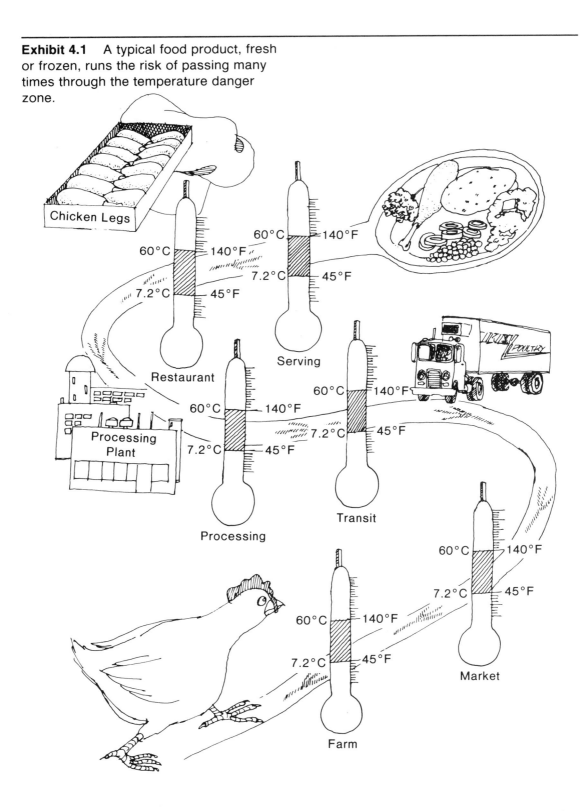

Chicken Legs

60°C — 140°F
7.2°C — 45°F
Restaurant

60°C — 140°F
7.2°C — 45°F
Serving

Processing Plant

60°C — 140°F
7.2°C — 45°F
Processing

60°C — 140°F
7.2°C — 45°F
Transit

60°C — 140°F
7.2°C — 45°F
Farm

60°C — 140°F
7.2°C — 45°F
Market

The selection of suppliers who meet minimum sanitary requirements should be an ongoing process. With foodservice supply houses constantly coming into or leaving the marketplace and with continuing innovations (such as prepared frozen entrees, mechanically tenderized meats, microwave ovens, and onsite packaging of produce), a foodservice operation's inventory of suppliers must be constantly updated—and upgraded.

GOVERNMENT CONTROL

Fortunately for the foodservice operator there is tremendous assistance available in the form of government programs for the inspection and evaluation of many kinds of foods. Regulations for the processing or shipping of food have been developed over the years by local, state, and federal governments. Without a doubt, these regulations have contributed much to improvement in the quality of food available to foodservice operators and to the average consumer in this country. Now managers responsible for purchasing food supplies can use government guidelines as aids in buying safe foods. The government also goes a step further and provides *grading* services, which can be used as guides to the quality of some products.

Many regulations regarding food processing work in favor of the foodservice manager. U.S. government inspection programs now cover meat, dairy products, shellfish, poultry, and eggs—in the production and processing stages. U.S. government agencies also inspect canned and frozen food processing plants. These various federal agencies have established regulations and standards for food shipped in *interstate* commerce. In turn, many state and local agencies have adopted these federally developed criteria—or have imposed even more stringent ones—and also monitor the production and processing of food for *intrastate* commerce.

The foodservice manager responsible for purchasing should have an understanding of the extent of these inspection services and their significance. Local public health officials may be consulted for information on food inspection regulations.

Of direct significance to foodservice establishments are the two departments of the federal government most concerned with food protection standards: The Department of Health and Human Services (HHS) and the Department of Agriculture (USDA). Within HHS, the Food and Drug Administration exercises inspection control over food processing and provides guidance for state and local regulation of foodservice operations. Through its Food Safety and Quality Service, the USDA is largely engaged in the grading and inspection of meat, poultry, and dairy products.

The discussion that follows covers food inspection activities as they pertain to meat, poultry, eggs, seafood, milk and dairy products, and processed foods.

Meat

All meat (beef, pork, veal, and lamb) and meat products that are prepared in plants selling their products across state lines must be inspected for wholesomeness by the U.S. Department of Agriculture. For this reason, and because many states have adopted laws requiring the inspection of meat prepared and sold within a state, virtually all meat available in the United States has been inspected by some government agency.

It is advisable that the foodservice operator purchase only meat that has been inspected by the USDA. Such meat is stamped with a circle containing the abbreviations for "inspected and passed" and the number identifying the processing plant (see Exhibit 4.2). The stamp will not appear on every cut of meat, but it should be present on every inspected carcass. The foodservice operator can determine from the supplier whether cuts of meat are from

Exhibit 4.2   Inspection and grade stamps for meats: *left,* wholesomeness; *right,* quality

Exhibit 4.3   Inspection and grade stamps for poultry: *left,* wholesomeness; *right,* quality

inspected carcasses. It is generally advisable to ask suppliers for written verification of USDA inspection of meats.

The *inspection service* of the USDA should not be confused with its *grading service.* Grading is a voluntary service provided by the USDA to meat packers and others. Grades refer to the quality and palatability of the meat, not to its sanitary or wholesome condition. "U.S. High Prime" beef is not necessarily any more sanitary or wholesome than "U.S. Low Choice." The USDA grade information is printed in a shield-shaped symbol (see Exhibit 4.2).

Poultry

All poultry (chickens, ducks, turkeys, and so on) to be sold for human consumption must be inspected either by the federal or the state government. Inspection covers the fitness of the live and slaughtered fowl. Before slaughter, the fowl are inspected for disease. After slaughter, the carcasses are checked for disease, contamination, and drug or chemical residue. The sanitary conditions of poultry-processing methods and poultry plant operations are also a major part of the inspection procedure.

The USDA, through its Food Safety and Quality Service, inspects poultry for wholesomeness. Federal legislation passed in 1968 also provides for involvement by the states in poultry inspection. Some states have their own inspection programs, which in most cases must be equal to the federal system. Federal inspection is required in states without inspection systems. Plants that engage in interstate or foreign commerce must have federal inspections.

Processed poultry products may or may not be inspected—this is a voluntary program that the processors request. It is wise to ask suppliers of processed poultry if their plants have been approved by federal inspectors.

There is a grading system for poultry quality, performed by the USDA for the individuals or firms who desire, on a voluntary basis, to use this service. The shield with the grade stamp may appear on any kind of chilled or frozen, ready-to-cook poultry or poultry parts, either on a section of the carcass or the packaging. Grading may also be done in cooperation with a state, in which case the official grade shield may include the words "Federal-State Graded." Exhibit 4.3 depicts the USDA inspection and grade stamps.

Eggs and Egg Products

Not all shell eggs that reach the marketplace are inspected or graded. Whereas inspection and grading of meat and poultry represent two separate processes, grading for shell eggs

Exhibit 4.4   Egg quality by grade

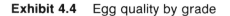

	Grade AA	Grade A	Grade B
Break out appearance	Covers a small area.	Covers a moderate area.	Covers a wide area.
Albumen appearance	White is thick and stands high; chalaza prominent.	White is reasonably thick, stands fairly high; chalaza prominent.	Small amount of thick white; chalaza small or absent. Appears weak and watery.
Yolk appearance	Yolk is firm, round and high.	Yolk is firm and stands fairly high.	Yolk is somewhat flattened and enlarged.
Shell appearance	Approximates usual shape; generally clean,* unbroken; ridges/rough spots that do not affect the shell strength permitted.		Abnormal shape; some slight stained areas permitted; unbroken; pronounced ridges/ thin spots permitted.
Usage	Ideal for any use, but are especially desirable for poaching, frying, and cooking in shell.		Good for scrambling, baking, and use as an ingredient in other foods.

*An egg may be considered clean if it has only very small specks, stains, or cage marks.

Source: United States Department of Agriculture

Exhibit 4.5   Inspection and grade stamps for eggs: *left,* wholesomeness; *right,* quality

covers standards for *both* wholesomeness and quality (see Exhibit 4.4). The federal grade mark—U.S. Grade AA, A, or B—is the consumer's assurance that these shell eggs met certain size and quality standards and were, at least initially, free from cracks, checks, excessive dirt, blood spots, and various types of rot (see Exhibit 4.5).

Shell egg inspection is a voluntary program conducted under the auspices of the USDA's Food Safety and Quality Service. Inspection under this program is available to firms or individuals who request it.

Particular states may also have their own egg-inspection programs, though if state-inspected eggs are destined for interstate commerce, the state standards may not differ from the federal requirements for size and grade.

The Federal Egg Products Inspection Act of 1970 set up a program to further ensure the wholesomeness of shell eggs in the marketplace. It provides for the safe disposition of dirty, cracked, or otherwise unsuitable shell eggs and requires that all businesses selling shell eggs to retail stores, restaurants, institutions, and food manufacturers be registered with the USDA and undergo periodic inspection.

This same legislation also concerns itself with egg products, providing for continuous inspection of plants that process liquid, frozen, or dried egg products. Processed egg products must bear the USDA inspection mark. This law requires pasteurization of all egg products and further stipulates that all users of processed egg products must obtain such products from plants operating under continuous inspection.

The FDA requires that only whole eggs be used in items that are not going to receive further cooking. Therefore, liquid, frozen, or dried eggs should be purchased only for use in recipes that call for further cooking.

Seafood

The National Shellfish Safety Program—a cooperative undertaking involving the Food and Drug Administration, state governments, and the shellfish industry—is instrumental in ensuring a sanitary shellfish product. The National Shellfish Safety Program covers oysters, clams, and mussels, but not shrimp, crabs, and other crustacea. The FDA oversees the shipping of shellfish in interstate commerce. This agency also enforces the sections of the Food, Drug, and Cosmetic Act requiring that shellfish be prepared, packed, and held under sanitary conditions, and be honestly and informatively labeled. Shellfish shipped interstate are therefore subject to fairly stringent conditions. Even so, the supplier should be verified as a safe source. Each state supervises the harvesting, handling, shipping, and marketing of shellfish within its own boundaries.

A principal problem with shellfish purchased intrastate has been the lack of uniformity of state regulations. The Interstate Shellfish Sanitation Conference formed in 1982 has the FDA working in conjunction with regulatory agencies of a number of states to establish uniform guidelines for shellfish sanitation. Foodservice managers in those states will therefore have an additional resource to use when determining safe shellfish sources. The states determine the quality of the waters from which safe shellfish can be taken and certify firms or individuals who comply with sanitary measures. Only shellfish (clams, mussels, and oysters) from approved waters can be legally sold.

If the Food and Drug Administration approves the state-controlled program, the name of the individual or the firm is placed on the monthly list of approved shellfish sources, and the individual or the firm can list an interstate certification number on the package in which the shellfish is placed. The FDA listing of approved sources is available from local health agencies and can be used by the foodservice operator to verify the sanitary source of shellfish that have been transferred from the original package to a new container. As a safety measure, the FDA requires that foodservice operators keep shell-stock identification tags for 90 days after receipt of shellfish. Upon receipt, the foodservice operator writes the date on the tag (see Exhibit 4.6).

Exhibit 4.6   Facsimile of shell-stock
identification tag (Source: Alabama State
Board of Health)

CONSISTS OF
OYSTERS

THIS PACKAGE   Gals.   Bu.

THIS TAG IS REQUIRED TO BE KEPT ON
CONTAINER UNTIL EMPTY AND THEREAFTER
KEPT ON FILE FOR 90 DAYS.

Packed by

Address: Bon Secour, Ala.

Distributed By

Address

Date Reshipped

SHELLFISH DREDGED FROM
BAY GARDENE

LOCAL AREA OR
BED NO.   LA 51

DATE
                01/10/84

TO BE RETAINED BY RECEIVER FOR 90
DAYS.

TO:

OYSTERS

ALABAMA STATE
BOARD OF HEALTH
BUREAU OF
SANITATION

DIVISION OF INSPECTION
MONTGOMERY, ALA.

No.   00576

SHIPPER'S NAME AND ADDRESS

FROM:
                Bon Secour, AL 36511

Certificate No. Ala 49

BELOW TO BE FILLED IN BY RECEIVER

DATE
REC'D

LOT. NO. | LOT CONSISTS OF

There are no general regulations for seafood other than shellfish. The Department of Commerce, through its National Marine Fisheries Service, will inspect and grade the products of fish producers who request such services. If such U.S.-inspected fish is unavailable, the foodservice operation's purchasing agent must rely on the advice of a dependable local dealer. A "dependable" dealer means one who supplies fish from or fishes only in safe, unpolluted waters and whose equipment and procedures are designed to ensure seafood safety.

Milk and Dairy Products

The milk surveillance program in the United States is one of the most successful food-protection programs ever instituted. The milk surveillance program stemmed from early recognition that milk and milk products were major potential sources of foodborne illnesses, and of such contagious diseases as *tuberculosis*. It was also realized that standards of sanitation had a direct bearing on the keeping quality of milk.

Government inspectors oversee virtually all dairy production areas. They check the health of dairy animals, as well as the manner in which milk and milk products are processed and transported. The FDA requires that all milk purchased for use in foodservice establishments be pasteurized.

Processed Food

Processed foods are foods that are taken from the fresh state and are either prepared further by cooking or made into another form before they are marketed. Food additives, preservatives, and flavor enhancers may be added during the process.

The agency most responsible for the regulation of canning plants, frozen-food preparation plants, and other such food processors is the federal Food and Drug Administration, though this varies according to the nature of the food item. No inspection mark is placed on individual products.

The USDA is responsible for overseeing the processing of meat and poultry products. Manufacturers of processed meat and poultry products must use cooking, cooling, and mixing methods that are approved by the USDA. The foodservice manager must see to it that all processed products are purchased from reliable suppliers who handle items processed by reputable food processors.

RECEIVING AND INSPECTING FOOD

A foodservice manager, remodeling a plush dining room, would never accept tables or chairs that were scratched, chipped, or broken. The same manager should be even more particular about the food products coming into the establishment.

The following rules should help the foodservice operator guarantee the high sanitary quality of foods entering the establishment:

- Inspect foods immediately upon their receipt. Not only will this prompt inspection facilitate returns or credits from the supplier but it will also make certain that perishable foods are not kept out of proper storage conditions for more than the briefest time. It is hardly necessary to open every can in a shipment or handle every tomato. Nevertheless, an attentive inspection is necessary since the possibility always exists that any food—even government-inspected and -approved supplies—may have been mishandled in transit.
- Try to arrange for delivery during off-peak hours. This arrangement will make it easier for employees to examine foods properly.

- Plan ahead for the arrival of shipments. Make sure that sufficient refrigerator/freezer space is available. In some well-equipped operations, there is a refrigerator and a freezer in the receiving area for quick and temporary storage. Many operations also provide for the preliminary washing of produce to prevent insects and excessive soil from being brought into the operation.

- Make certain that employees are trained properly in inspection functions. Receiving personnel should be able to judge quality; check temperatures of frozen foods, dairy products, fresh meat, fish and poultry products; detect damage; spot insect infestations; and so on.

The remaining sections of this chapter give some pointers on the inspection of specific food items. Keep in mind that if the foodservice establishment is to be a fortress against enemy vermin and micro-organisms, its receiving area must be the first line of defense.

Meat

When meat arrives at a foodservice facility, it should be inspected on the basis of several factors: color, odor, texture, temperature, and packaging.

Beef should be a bright, cherry red, though deliberately aged beef may be darker. A purplish tinge may simply mean that the beef has not been exposed to the air for a long enough period of time, though it can also be a sign of deterioration. Do not accept beef that is turning brown or greenish. Beef usually spoils first at or near the surface of the cut. A whitish or bleached surface on frozen beef indicates that the beef was frozen too quickly and may be dehydrated. Be particularly careful of ground beef, especially when packaged in bulk, since it is the meat most subject to spoilage.

Fresh, unfrozen *lamb* is red in color if it has been properly exposed to air. It should be rejected when—in its unfrozen state—it is brown in color or if there is a whitish surface on the cut.

The fat portions of *pork* should be white and firm, the lean portions light pink. Deterioration is usually evidenced by darkening of lean meat and discoloration and rancidity of the rind. Like beef, pork spoilage is first evidenced near the surface of the cut. In a few cases, pork has been reported to spoil in the interior near the bone. Test for this condition by pushing a knife into the flesh and then sniffing the knife tip. A sour odor is cause for rejection.

Sausage should be free of slime and mold, which indicate decomposition. External mold is common on dry sausages such as salami, but it can be washed off and is considered harmless if it is confined to the casing.

With all meats, discoloration is a cause for concern. Brown, green, or purple blotches are all signs of a microbial attack. Black, white, and green spots indicate molds.

Fresh meat can also be inspected on the basis of smell. A sour smell is grounds for rejection, except in the case of deliberately aged beef.

Some raw, cooked, and cured meats, and smoked and raw fish, are purchased chilled or frozen and vacuum-packaged in clear plastic or shrink-wrapped packages. Meat that is vacuum-aged in a bag by a process called *Cryo-vac aging,* or by any other method, should be checked for temperature and to ensure that the bag is not torn or too loose. Foodservice managers should request processors' instructions on handling and storing vacuum-packed meats and follow them closely.

Unfrozen meat should be firm and elastic to the touch. No meat should feel slimy, sticky, or dry. Generally, the appearance of slime, caused by microbic growth on meats stored under conditions of high temperature and humidity, is the very first indication of deterioration in meat.

Fresh meat should be checked for its temperature before it is put in storage. Upon arrival, chilled meat should have a maximum internal temperature of 40°F (4.4°C) or below. Frozen meat should be below a temperature of 0°F (−17.7°C) and show *no* sign of thawing. (See chapter 5 for information on storing meat).

The packaging in which the meat arrives should be inspected for broken cartons, dirty meat wrappers, and torn packaging—all indicators of poor sanitary practices and possible contamination. These products should be rejected.

Poultry

Indications of spoiled or inferior poultry are readily observable. Soft, flabby flesh and dull, sunken eyes usually mean an inferior product. A purplish or greenish overall cast, or a greenish discoloration around the neck and vent may mean staleness, improper bleeding after killing, or improper handling. Other signs of spoilage include an abnormal odor, stickiness under the wings and around the joints, and darkened wing tips.

Poultry should be graded A, surrounded by crushed ice, and delivered at a temperature below 40°F (4.4°C). Temperatures below 28°F (−2.2°C) may significantly extend shelf life.

Eggs

Fresh eggs should not be more than two weeks old when received from the vendor. Only the quantity of eggs that will be used within one to two weeks should be purchased. The eggs should be delivered in refrigerated trucks. The shells should not be cracked, checked, or dirty, because of the danger of contamination with *Salmonella* bacteria.

To test the freshness of a shipment of eggs, break one open. If the white clings to the yolk, and the yolk is firm, high, and does not break

easily, the egg is acceptable. In a very fresh egg of top quality, the white will stand up well on its own. Sniff the egg. There should not be any real odor to a fresh egg.

Check to make sure that frozen or dehydrated eggs are pasteurized.

Seafood

Few food items suffer from improper handling as much as do fresh and frozen fish. Fish that has been thawed and refrozen before it reaches the foodservice establishment should not be used. Refrozen fish will have soft, flabby flesh, a sour odor, and an off-color. The paper in which it was wrapped will be moist, slimy, and discolored. The bottom of the shipping carton may have ice formations, indicating that refreezing has taken place; and the container itself may be deformed by internal pressure. Brown coloring at the edges of a fillet is also an indication of refreezing.

Fresh fish should be checked for temperature. Fish should be packed in self-draining ice. Upon arrival seafood should be between 32° and 40°F (0° and 4.4°C).

Fresh fish can be distinguished from stale fish by marked differences in appearance. Fresh fish have bright red, moist gills. The eyes are bulging and clear. The flesh and belly areas are firm and elastic. Fresh fish also do not have a noticeably strong, fishy odor. The flesh should not pull away from the bones easily, and the scales should stick to the flesh. The skin should be vibrant and bright.

An unacceptably stale fish presents a complete contrast. The gill slits are gray, or gray-green, and dry. The eyes are cloudy, red-bordered, and sunken. The flesh is soft and yielding. If finger pressure is applied, the impression will remain. If fish or shellfish have an ammonia odor, the deterioration is advanced.

Exhibit 4.7   Signs of acceptable and unacceptable quality in fresh fruits

	Signs of Good Quality	Signs of Bad Quality, Spoilage
Apples	Firmness; crispness; bright color	Softness; bruises. (Irregularly shaped brown or tan areas do not usually affect quality)
Apricots	Bright, uniform color; plumpness	Dull color; shriveled appearance
Bananas	Firmness; brightness of color	Grayish or dull appearance (indicates exposure to cold and inability to ripen properly)
Blueberries	Dark blue color with silvery bloom	Moist berries
Cantaloupes (Muskmelons)	Stem should be gone; netting or veining should be coarse; skin should be yellow-gray or pale yellow	Bright yellow color; mold; large bruises
Cherries	Very dark color; plumpness	Dry stems; soft flesh; gray mold
Cranberries	Plumpness; firmness. Ripe cranberries should bounce	Leaky berries
Grapefruit	Should be heavy for its size	Soft areas; dull color
Grapes	Should be firmly attached to stems. Bright color and plumpness are good signs	Drying stems; leaking berries
Honeydew melon	Soft skin; faint aroma; yellowish white to creamy rind color	White or greenish color; bruises or watersoaked areas; cuts or punctures in rind

In addition to surface indications, unacceptable fish may exhibit internal signs of decay. Freshwater varieties may show signs of parasites and diseases, tumors, abscesses, and cysts.

Shellfish

Fresh lobster and other shellfish shipped in the shell should be alive on delivery. If lobsters or shellfish give off a strong odor, they are about to die on their own and should be rejected. The shell of a live lobster should be hard and heavy. The shells of clams and oysters will be closed in the living state, partly open if dead. The edible portions of frozen lobsters should have firm flesh. Frozen lobsters are acceptable for use as long as there is no evidence of shrinkage or a change in the normal contours of the unshelled lobsters.

Fruits and Vegetables

For fruits, taste is the best test of quality. Many foodservice operators rely on appearance as an indication of quality, but this criterion may not, in all respects, be dependable. Blemishes can be present even though the flavor and quality are unimpaired.

	Signs of Good Quality	Signs of Bad Quality, Spoilage
Lemons	Firmness; heaviness. Should have rich yellow color	Dull color; shriveled skin
Limes	Glossy skin; heavy weight	Dry skin; molds
Oranges	Firmness; heaviness; bright color	Dry skin; spongy texture; blue mold
Peaches	Slightly soft flesh	A pale tan spot (indicates beginning of decay); very hard or very soft flesh
Pears	Firmness	Dull skin; shriveling; spots on the sides
Pineapples	"Spike" at top should separate easily from flesh	Mold; large bruises; unpleasant odor; brown leaves
Plums	Fairly firm to slightly soft flesh	Leaking; brownish discoloration
Raspberries, boysenberries	Stem caps should be absent; flesh should be plump and tender	Mushiness; wet spots on containers (sign of possible decay of berries)
Strawberries	Stem cap should be attached; berries should have rich red color	Gray mold; large uncolored areas
Tangerines	Bright orange or deep yellow color; loose skin	Punctured skin; mold
Watermelon	Smooth surface; creamy underside; bright red flesh	Stringy or mealy flesh (spoilage difficult to see on outside)

Fresh fruits and vegetables must be handled with extreme care because of their perishability. Pinching, squeezing, or unnecessary handling upon receipt will bruise them, leading to decay and premature spoilage. Upon receipt, produce cartons should be checked for signs of insect infestation and for insect eggs.

Fruits and vegetables show spoilage in a variety of ways. The foodservice operator should be able to identify not only produce that is obviously spoiled but also produce that will spoil under storage in a very short time. Exhibits 4.7 and 4.8 list signs of freshness and signs of spoilage, or incipient spoilage, in common fruits and vegetables.

Dairy Products

Unpasteurized milk is a potential source of diseases ranging from salmonellosis and shigellosis to undulant fever and diphtheria. Thus all cartons and bulk containers that enter a foodservice establishment should carry the pasteurization label. Cream and dried milk must be pasteurized; cottage cheese, Neufchatel cheese, and cream cheese should all be made from pasteurized milk.

The pasteurization process, which consists of heating milk to the prescribed temperature for the proper amount of time—usually 145°F (62.8°C) for 30 minutes, or 161°F (71.7°C) for

Exhibit 4.8   Signs of acceptable and unacceptable quality in fresh vegetables

	Signs of Good Quality	Signs of Poor Quality, Spoilage
Artichokes	Plumpness; green scales; clinging leaves	Brown scales; grayish-black discoloration; mold
Asparagus	Closed tips; round spears	Spread-out tips; spears with ridges; spears that are not round
Beans (snap)	Firm, crisp pods	Extensive discoloration; tough pods
Beets	Firmness; roundness; deep red color	Gray mold; wilting; flabbiness
Brussels sprouts	Bright color; tight-fitting leaves	Loose, yellow-green outer leaves; ragged leaves (may indicate worm damage)
Cabbage	Firmness; heaviness for size	Wilted or decayed outer leaves (Leaves should not separate easily from base)
Carrots	Smoothness; firmness	Soft spots
Cauliflower	Clean, white curd; bright green leaves	Speckled curd; severe wilting; loose flower clusters
Celery	Firmness; crispness; smooth stems	Flabby leaves; brown-black interior discoloration
Cucumber	Green color; firmness	Yellowish color; softness
Eggplant	Uniform, dark purple color	Softness; irregular dark brown spots
Greens	Tender leaves free of blemishes	Yellow-green leaves; evidence of insect decay
Lettuce	Crisp leaves; bright color	Tipburn on edges of leaves (slight discoloration of outer leaves is not harmful)
Mushrooms	White, creamy, or tan color on tops of caps	Dark color on underside of cap; withering veil
Onions	Hardness; firmness; small necks; papery outer scales	Wet or soft necks
Onions (green)	Crisp, green tops; white portion two to three inches in length	Yellowing; wilting
Peppers (green)	Glossy appearance; dark green color	Thin walls; cuts, punctures
Potatoes	Firmness; relative smoothness	Green rot or mold; large cuts; sprouts

	Signs of Good Quality	Signs of Poor Quality, Spoilage
Radishes	Plumpness; roundness; red color	Yellowing of tops (sign of aging); softness
Squash (summer)	Glossy skin	Dull appearance; tough surface
Squash (winter)	Hard rind	Mold; softness
Sweet potatoes	Bright skins	Wetness; shriveling; sunken and discolored areas on sides of potato (Sweet potatoes are extremely susceptible to decay.)
Tomatoes	Smoothness; redness. (Tomatoes that are pink or slightly green will ripen in a warm place.)	Bruises; deep cracks around the stem scar
Watercress	Crispness; bright green color	Yellowing, wilting, decaying of leaves

at least 15 seconds—destroys, with minimal chemical change, significant pathogenic organisms.

Milk does not need to be marked "Grade A" to be acceptable. All market milk is in fact Grade-A quality. Even without this designation, local, state, and federal milk-control programs combine to assure the consumer that the milk is unadulterated, taken from safe cows, and processed in a sanitary manner.

Generally, milk intended for use as a beverage must be packaged in individual containers. In some localities, regulations permit the serving of beverage milk from refrigerated dispensers. Dried milk or milk in bulk containers (5 to 10 gallons) may be used for cooking purposes if local regulations permit.

Fresh, clean milk has a sweetish taste. Sour, bitter, or moldy-tasting milk should be rejected. In many states, the health departments require that milk be dated with a stamp. Milk that is delivered after the expiration date marked on the container should be rejected. Milk with a temperature above 45°F (7.2°C) on delivery should likewise be rejected. Milk with off flavors—possibly from odor absorption or from abnormal conditions in the cows—may still be wholesome but nonetheless should routinely be rejected. It will not taste good to customers.

Butter should have a sweet, fresh flavor, uniform color, and firm texture. It should be free of mold, specks, and other foreign substances and should be received in clean, unbroken containers. Butter that is rancid or that has absorbed foreign odors should not be accepted.

In the United States, the composition of cheese is regulated by a government standard of identity specifying the ingredients that may be used, the maximum moisture content, the minimum fat content, and the requirements for pasteurization or holding of the milk to remove harmful bacteria. Cheese ought to be checked to see that each type has its characteristic flavor and texture, as well as a uniform color. If the cheese has a rind, the rind should be clean and unbroken. Cheese that is dried out or has uncharacteristic mold should be rejected.

Frozen Foods

Frozen foods should be inspected for signs of thawing and refreezing as well as for other signs of deterioration. Obvious signs of thawing include fluid or frozen liquids in the food carton. Large ice crystals in the product itself indicate that it has been thawed and then refrozen.

To check the temperature of incoming frozen goods, insert a clean and sanitized stainless steel thermometer under the top layer of goods inside the package or through a hole punched in an unopened case. An accurate reading depends on firm contact between the thermometer and the product. Leave the thermometer in place for five minutes. The temperature of frozen foods, including meat, should not be above 0°F (-17.7°C). Ice cream, however, may be delivered and stored at a temperature of 6° to 10°F (-14.4° to -12.2°C).

Canned Foods

Illnesses that may result from contaminated canned foods are so dangerous that all shipments of canned goods should be checked (see Exhibit 4.9). External indications that cans should be rejected are the following (see Exhibit 4.10):

1. *Swelled top or bottom.* One or both ends of a can may bulge outward as a result of gas produced by bacterial or chemical action. Whether the ends spring back when touched by a finger or not, discard the can. Sometimes both ends of a can

will appear flat, though one will bulge outward when the other is pressed. Such cans are also not acceptable.

2. *Leakage.* Any can leaking a product should be rejected.

3. *Flawed seals.* Improper sealing at the top or side of the can is cause for rejection.

4. *Rust.* Badly rusted cans should be rejected. They're either too old to use or the contents may be contaminated. Rust may conceal pinholes, which lead to contamination.

5. *Dents.* Dents along the side seams of a can, or dents that make it impossible to open the can with a manual can opener, are cause for rejection. The seams have probably been broken.

A can that seems undamaged on the outside may still contain contaminated food. Any canned goods that appear abnormal in odor, color, or texture; that are foamy; or that have a milky-colored liquid should be rejected. *Such goods should not even be taste-tested.* People have died from botulism poisoning contracted from tasting *and spitting out* contaminated food.

Dry Foods

Cartons of cereals, sugars, dried fruits and vegetables, and flour should be dry and undamaged. Punctures, tears, or slashes in the package may indicate insect or rodent entry. If the outside of a container is damp or moldy, the condition may extend to the contents, raising the possibility of advanced microbial contamination. Most dry foods are poor media for bacteria, but a touch of moisture can radically change this situation. *Dry foods must be kept dry!*

goods may develop defects through improper handling; a temporary power shortage may cause defrosting and refreezing of fish. To put it simply, the foodservice operator must see to it that the same standards that are applied to products when they are received are applied to them once they are inside the back door.

It should also be noted at this point that we have used the terms "spoilage" and "contamination" almost interchangeably throughout this chapter. In chapter 1, however, "spoilage" refers to the breakdown in the edible quality of a product, while "contamination" refers to the ability of the food to carry disease to humans. The fact of the matter is that when it comes to evaluating specific items of food, it is often difficult to tell the difference between spoilage and contamination. Spoiled sausage, for example, may very well contain dangerous *Salmonella* organisms. Brown, wilted lettuce, on the other hand, is unappetizing, but probably not dangerous. Yet in many cases, only an expert using advanced methods of scientific analysis can tell whether a spoiled product is or is not contaminated. In other words, for the foodservice manager the best rule to follow is *when in doubt, throw it out.*

SUMMARY

Procuring safe supplies is an important aspect of foodservice sanitation. Although various government agencies regulate the production and processing of foods, including meat, shellfish, poultry, canned goods, and eggs, it is still the responsibility of the foodservice manager to check the sanitary quality of foods used in the establishment.

A complete inspection should be made of all incoming supplies. Plans must be made so that deliveries can be handled promptly and correctly.

Workers responsible for inspecting incoming supplies should be able to identify damaged, contaminated, and spoiled products. Frozen goods must be checked for temperature, canned goods for indications of damage, and meats, poultry, fish, and dairy goods should be checked for temperature and freshness. Eggs, fruits, and vegetables must be wholesome and fresh. On the receiving dock and within the establishment, products of suspect quality should be rejected.

A CASE IN POINT

The food orders all came in at once during the lunch hour. While the expense account crowd was coming in the front door of Nickerson's Steak and Suds, the food order was coming in the back door. The problem was that the food products were all different— cases of steaks, both frozen and fresh; canned vegetables; fresh tomatoes; fresh chicken for the special on Tuesday; frozen shrimp for the Friday fish special; and finally, a case of potatoes. Juanita Nickerson thought that the best thing to do was to put everything away and check it later. She had the storeroom attendant put the frozen steaks and shrimps in the freezer and the chicken and fresh steaks in the refrigerator. Finally, the cases of potatoes and tomatoes went into dry storage, and she herself moved the canned vegetables also into dry storage. "Whew," she said when she was finished. "I'm glad that's over." Then she went back to the front of the house.

What is wrong here?
What could be the possible result?

STUDY QUESTIONS

1. Give examples of questions that ought to be asked when a foodservice manager investigates the sanitary practices of a supplier.

2. Why are government regulations for inspections and evaluation of food products good for foodservice managers who are responsible for purchasing?

3. What is the difference between the grading and inspection processes for meat?

4. How does the Egg Products Inspection Act affect the manufacture of egg products?

5. How does the FDA oversee the interstate handling and shipping of shellfish? What service does it provide that foodservice operators may use?

6. List at least three general rules for the safe receipt of food products.

7. Describe some signs of meat spoilage.

8. Describe indications of spoiled poultry.

9. Differentiate between the appearance of fresh and stale fish.

10. Give a reason to reject a shipment of milk.

11. What are the signs of spoilage for grapefruit, pineapples, and lettuce?

12. Describe a method for checking the temperature of frozen foods.

13. Name five external signs that indicate a canned food item ought to be rejected.

14. What is the inspection procedure for dry food items?

MORE ON THE SUBJECT

Code of Recommended Practices for the Handling and Merchandising of Frozen Foods. Washington, D.C.: Frozen Food Coordinating Committee, 1982. This publication supplies a set of specific recommendations for the handling of frozen foods.

Guidelines for Evaluation and Disposition of Damaged Canned Food Containers. Washington, D.C.: National Food Processors Association, 1979. In addition to information on how to evaluate the external conditions of canned goods, the publication provides 21 pictures and drawings showing acceptable and unacceptable damage to cans.

Meat in the Foodservice Industry. Chicago: National Livestock and Meat Board, 1977. 80 pages. The section on meat grades and the purchasing of meat provides valuable information and illustrations.

U.S. DEPARTMENT OF AGRICULTURE. Agricultural Marketing Service. *How to Buy Fresh Fruits and Vegetables.* Washington, D.C., 1971. Home and Garden Bulletins 141 and 143. These short pamphlets describing signs of freshness and signs of deterioration in fruits and vegetables are available from the Agricultural Marketing Service, USDA.

ANSWER TO A CASE IN POINT

Usually, "later" never comes, so we have to assume that food items may go unchecked until they are ready to be used. Even then, the cook or the preparer may be in such a hurry that the "inspection" may be cursory or nonexistent. As to what was wrong in this case, consider the following:

1. Juanita should have arranged with the suppliers to bring the foods at a different time so that she and her employees would have had more time to inspect them.
2. At the minimum, food items such as these should have gone into storage marked with the date of arrival.
3. The canned goods were not inspected, nor were the fresh vegetables.
4. The tomatoes probably should have been put in a produce refrigerator.
5. The frozen foods may or may not have been delivered at the proper temperature. The shrimp, in particular, should have been checked to be sure no thawing and refreezing had taken place.
6. The poultry and beef should have been checked for proper color and correct temperatures. The chicken, especially, may have been mishandled in transit and could have been delivered at a temperature favorable to the growth of *Salmonella* bacteria. Prompt, proper refrigeration may have been too late to keep the chicken from causing illness.

All in all the failure to inspect the delivered food could have proved disastrous for the operation. Not only the quality might have been off but the safety of these food items might have been uncertain, forcing the Nickerson operation to take a financial loss. A good purchasing/receiving program is a check of the quality and the sanitation of food products.

5

Keeping Food Safe in Storage

Outline

Keeping food safe in storage is a matter of purchasing foods that will be used as soon as possible, placing them in properly maintained storage equipment or areas, and using them up quickly. The problems that can be caused by poor storage practices of food are numerous, but contamination tops the list. Loss of quality and loss of inventory are others.

With the exception of most fine wines, some cheeses, and a few other such speciality items, food does not improve in quality while in storage. In fact, no one really wants to keep food in storage. Most customers prefer the taste of fresh products, and the foodservice manager knows all too well the costs of keeping food in storage and of purchasing and maintaining storage equipment.

In the best of all possible worlds, storage would not be necessary. Deliveries would be made just as the chef set out to prepare a dish. All foods would be available at all times of the year. A manager would be able to predict the exact amount of food needed for any given day.

In real life, storage is necessary, and incorrect storage has the potential for causing serious and costly problems. For example, when insects infest dry stores, or a sewer pipe floods a storage area, or a freezer breaks down completely, the damage is severe and the danger of contamination is widespread.

Problems occasioned by improper storage can be of a particularly disastrous sort. Imagine what would happen if garbage were mixed with food or pesticides confused with spices. Cases such as these make for gruesome—but true—reading.

There is a direct relationship between cost control and the need to maintain good storage practices. In addition, proper storage of food items is another line of defense against spoilage and contamination. Preserving food quality and keeping it sanitary can prevent both inventory loss and liability. However, the bottom line is *safe food,* and poor storage practices are a major cause of bacterial contamination of food.

This chapter will discuss methods for preventing the contamination and spoilage of foods in storage. We will cover the following main topics:

- Fundamental principles of storage in foodservice facilities
- Elementary rules for the use of refrigerators, freezers, and dry-storage facilities
- Appropriate storage procedures and recommended storage times for most common foods

STORAGE PRINCIPLES

Despite the wide variety of products usually inventoried in a foodservice facility, a few general storage principles can be successfully applied to most storage situations. The rules that follow cover storage of all types of foods:

1. Unfailingly follow the golden rule of "First In, First Out"—sometimes abbreviated FIFO. Adherence to this principle means that goods should be used in the order in which they are received. For example, do not stack new deliveries of canned fruit on top of the cans already in storage. Do not put today's frozen beef roasts into the freezer in front of those delivered last month. Create some system—such as the dating of goods upon receipt and the placement of new deliveries in the rear of storage areas—that will guarantee the "First In, First Out" is followed in the establishment.

2. Perishable, potentially hazardous foods must be kept out of the temperature danger zone, which is 45° to 140°F (7.2° to 60°C). Foods should be prepared as quickly as possible to reduce the time spent in the temperature danger zone.

3. Store food only in areas designed for storage. There is no excuse for storing food products in toilet areas, under stairways, or in vestibules. Such procedures are dangerous and are usually prohibited by local health codes.

4. All goods should be kept in clean wrappers or containers. A dirty wrapper can attract pests or contaminate food as it is being opened. Packaging should not be reused. Unless special conditions apply, wrap products in material that is moisture-proof and airtight.

5. Keep storage areas clean. This rule applies to dry storage, refrigerators, and freezers.

6. Keep vehicles for transporting food within the establishment clean. It is senseless, for example, to wrap meat properly, refrigerate it at the optimum temperature, keep the refrigerator clean, and then carry the meat to the kitchen on a cart that has just been used to transport garbage.

TYPES OF STORAGE

The story of storage can be told in three parts. It revolves around the three keeping-areas of major importance: (1) refrigerated storage for short-term holding of perishable and potentially hazardous food items; (2) freezer storage for longer-term keeping; and (3) dry storage for the somewhat longer holding of less perishable items. Each storage area has its own particular sanitation requirements.

Refrigeration

Refrigeration retards the growth of bacteria in foods; it cannot, however, correct damage already done. Perishable and potentially hazardous items can be held in a refrigerator only on a short-term basis.

Exhibit 5.1   The commercial-type walk-in refrigerator (Source: U.S. Department of Agriculture)

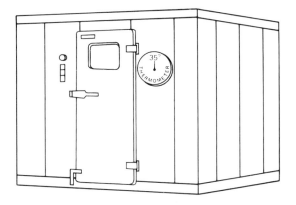

There are two types of foodservice refrigeration units: the walk-in type and the reach-in or upright units (see Exhibits 5.1 and 5.2).

Walk-in and upright refrigerators are best when made of stainless steel or a combination of stainless steel and aluminum. The doors should withstand heavy use. They should close with a slight nudge. Walk-in units should include an inside unlocked latch to prevent employees from locking themselves in. The door gaskets should be easily replaceable. Condensate vapors and defrost water are unsanitary hazards and a system provided to drain excess water should be *outside* the unit. An optional device for both types is a warning alarm that signals the manager if the power is interrupted. Walk-in refrigerators should have windows for observation of food items. This saves opening the door if the item isn't there. The unit should be sealed to the floor and offer no access to moisture or vermin. The floor panels should be of heavy duty material.

All refrigeration units—and all other food-service equipment for that matter—purchased for a food service should have the

Exhibit 5.2 The commercial-type reach-in refrigerator (Source: U.S. Department of Agriculture)

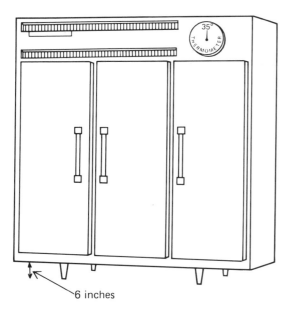

6 inches

Exhibit 5.3 Look for NSF and UL labels (facsimiles shown) for sanitary and safe equipment (Source: National Sanitation Foundation and Underwriters Laboratories)

approval of the National Sanitation Foundation, as meeting sanitary requirements, and of Underwriters Laboratories, as meeting safety requirements (see Exhibit 5.3).

Sanitary Features

When purchasing a refrigeration unit, consider the following features important to sanitation:

- Refrigerators used in a foodservice facility must be commercial *foodservice* equipment. Refrigerators for homes are not designed to hold the volume of food that can be stored in a foodservice refrigerator. The mechanical capacity of home-type refrigerators is usually lower than that of foodservice refrigerators. Also, most foodservice refrigerators must have

forced-air cooling fans to keep the compressor working. Few home models have this feature.

- The total capacity of refrigeration units must be adequate for the needs of the foodservice operation. Lack of sufficient refrigerated storage space promotes improper practices. It discourages frequent cleaning, slows cooling of foods, and allows moisture buildup. Breakdowns are more frequent with overloaded equipment.

- Refrigerators must meet the minimum temperature requirements for the foods they are expected to hold. If temperature varies in different parts of the refrigerator, only foods to be held within the temperature range of the part should be stored there. Meat should be stored in the coldest part of the refrigerator and eggs in a slightly warmer part. Ideally, separate refrigerators should be available for different food types.

- All surfaces of the unit should be made of easily cleanable materials.

- All shelves inside the cabinet should be removable without tools so that the unit may be easily cleaned on a regular basis.

- Interiors should be free of sharp edges and tight corners—places where harmful micro-organisms may lurk.
- Surfaces should resist corrosion, chipping, and cracking. Otherwise, loose particles may end up in stored food.
- Coils should not be in such a location that condensation might collect and drip into food. They should also be located so food-contact surfaces are protected.
- Drains, except those for condensates, should not be located inside the refrigerator cabinet.
- Reach-in refrigerators should be sealed to the floor or elevated six inches off it so as not to harbor vermin or allow dirt to accumulate. Units mounted on a masonry or curb base designed for that purpose are also acceptable, as are units with casters, as long as the unit itself is six inches off the floor.
- Walk-in units should be sealed to the floor and offer no access to moisture or vermin. The floor panels should be of heavy-duty material. Floor materials should be chosen to withstand heavy impact if that is a frequent concern. Walk-in units mounted on a specially designed base are acceptable as long as the bottom of the refrigeration unit is six inches off the floor.

Operating Practices

The most efficient refrigerator can become a hazard or can fail to hold foods at the proper temperature if workers do not follow standard operating practices.

Refrigerators should not be filled beyond their capacity. This practice not only makes cleaning difficult but it prevents air circulation necessary for maintenance of proper temperatures.

Ideally, separate refrigerators should be maintained for each food category. Where this flexibility does not exist, meats and dairy products should be stored in the coldest part of the unit. Dairy items in particular should be tightly covered to prevent odor absorption. Where it is not feasible to store ready-to-serve food separately, prepared foods ought to be stored *above,* not below, raw foods to prevent cross-contamination. Raw foods also tend to drip more than cooked foods.

Refrigerator Temperatures

A maximum refrigerator air temperature of 40°F (4.4°C) or lower should be maintained and regularly checked with a reliable thermometer. Ideally, foods should be kept at the coldest temperature possible to maintain safety and quality. Many food services find it useful to have separate refrigerators for different foods. When such is the case, temperatures and humidity factors should be as follows:

Meat and Poultry
32° to 36°F (0° to 2.2°C)
75 to 85 percent relative humidity

Fish
30° to 34°F (−1.1° to 1.1°C)
75 to 85 percent relative humidity

Eggs
38° to 40°F (3.3° to 4.4°C)

Dairy Products
38° to 40°F (3.3° to 4.4°C)
75 to 85 percent relative humidity

Most Fruits and Vegetables
40° to 45°F (4.4° to 7.2°C)
85 to 95 percent relative humidity

Sometimes an additional refrigeration unit with a temperature of 32° to 35°F (0° to 1.7°C) and humidity of about 90 percent is used for storage of some fruits and vegetables.

When one refrigerator is used for more than one kind of food, be sure to put meat, fish, and

Exhibit 5.4   Refrigerator-freezer thermometer (Photograph courtesy of Tel-Tru Manufacturing Company, Rochester, N.Y.)

dairy products in the colder parts of the refrigerator. Each refrigeration unit must be checked to ascertain the location of these colder spots.

Temperatures should be checked regularly in all refrigerators. There should be a thermometer for each temperature zone of the refrigerator. One should be in the warmest part of the unit and one in the coolest part to ensure that the proper minimum temperatures are maintained. Refrigerator thermometers should be easily readable and be accurate to ±3°F (±1°C). Keep the thermometer there, and check the temperature regularly. The accuracy of any thermometer should also be checked frequently (see Exhibit 5.4). With good air circulation the temperature should be consistent. It is important that food product temperatures be frequently checked with a metal-stemmed thermometer.

An externally mounted or built-in thermometer may also be used. Many commercial food-service refrigerators are equipped with these. This enables the foodservice manager or anyone else to check the temperature at any time without opening the door. The inside temperature must still be checked regularly.

Cleaning Refrigerators

Although refrigerators prevent the growth of most micro-organisms, they may become homes for certain kinds of bacteria and fungi unless cleaned properly. All interior parts should be cleaned and sanitized on a regular basis—as often as once a day or once a week, depending on use. Shelves should be removed as part of this cleaning process. The presence of debris, mold, or objectionable odors is a sign of poor cleaning and demands immediate remedy.

Foods—whether raw or prepared—that have been removed from their original package for storage in a refrigerator should be placed in clean, nonabsorbent, covered containers. Food cartons should not be stored in such a way as to interfere with the circulation of cold air. For the same reason, shelving should be of the open, slatted type. Lining the shelves—with aluminum foil, for example—may make them look neater, but it drastically reduces refrigeration efficiency.

In walk-in coolers, food should be stored away from the walls—to prevent insect or rodent nesting—and off the floors to avoid contamination from cleaning and possible spillage. This storage procedure also encourages air circulation through the unit.

Care should be taken not to disturb the temperature of the unit through the storage of large amounts of warmer foods. Most commercial refrigerators are designed to keep cold foods cold. They may not have the capacity to bring warm food items down to the proper temperature quickly enough to prevent possible damage. Small quantities of warm, or even hot, food can, however, be accommodated without harm. Large quantities should be divided into small containers and shallow, rectangular pans and, if necessary to encourage cooling, stirred periodically.

Too much traffic, allowing warm kitchen air to flood the interior of a refrigeration unit, can also have an unfavorable effect on temperature. Open-door periods should be kept to a minimum. The time to open a refrigerator is after you have decided on the products you want to remove, not before.

Freezer Storage

Freezers have their limitations. They are not substitutes for good advance planning of menus and food purchases. If you make an error and buy too much food for your needs, it is not enough merely to store the surplus until some distant date when it can be used up. Lengthy freezer storage means increased opportunities for contamination and spoilage.

Freezing will not improve the culinary quality of foods; with some products, the reverse may be true. Among items that may deteriorate in freezer storage are hamburger, fatty fish (mackerel, salmon, swordfish), turkey, pork, creamed foods, custards, gravies, sauces, and puddings. Storage freezers should not be used for freezing chilled foods. They are not designed for that. Storage freezers *are* designed to receive and keep frozen foods at 0°F (−17.7°C) or below.

Guidelines

All of the limitations of freezers impose a responsibility on the manager to make certain that both freezer and frozen food are handled with care. The following recommended guidelines should be put into practice:

1. Freezers must be maintained at an air temperature of 0°F (−17.7°C) or lower. Many experts recommend that the freezer temperature be kept between −10° and 0°F (−23.3° and −17.7°C). Even slight variations above the 0°F mark can be destructive, especially for meat. It has been found, for example, that food deteriorates several times faster at 15°F (about −9°C) than at zero. Defrost damage is cumulative. Each incident of thawing adds to the damage, and cannot be corrected by refreezing. Note that partial thawing of food may occur in a self-defrosting freezer that goes through a warm-up phase one or more times a day.

2. Products should be placed in storage facilities of approved design promptly after delivery and removed from storage only in quantities that can be used immediately.

    The rule on immediate storage of frozen foods does not strictly apply if the delivered items are going to be used soon. The amount of time meant by ''soon'' will depend on the type of food, but in every case the products should be kept refrigerated and not held at room temperature under any circumstances. For frozen vegetables and preportioned meats, ''soon'' means right away; for average-sized roasts, it is the next day; and for turkeys, two days.

3. Frozen food inventories should be rotated on a ''First In, First Out'' basis. Labeling each product with its description and date of entry can make this process easy.

4. Reach-in freezers should be defrosted as frequently as necessary to maintain efficiency. The operator's manual for the freezer should give some indication of the proper frequency. To maintain food safety and quality, frozen food items should be moved to another freezer during defrosting or used up first. Foods should not be allowed to thaw. Frost-free

freezers may go through higher temperature cycles during defrosting, and temperatures must be checked periodically.

5. An easily visible thermometer or other mechanism to record temperature should be present in each freezer unit. It may be useful to have more than one thermometer in order to check for "hot spots" and temperature variations.

6. Foods should be placed in a freezer in a way that will allow circulation of cold air among them. Foods that are packed in too tightly may begin to defrost.

Sanitary Features

Freezers should be purchased with some of the same factors in mind as when buying a refrigerator. The units must be designed for cleanability and protection of food-contact surfaces. They should have the capacity to meet the needs of the operation. Sufficient temperatures must be maintained to keep foods from thawing. When purchasing equipment for frozen-food storage, consider the following points:

■ The equipment should be constructed of easily cleanable materials, and the unit should be properly sealed.

■ Interior corners of the freezer cabinet should be rounded and smooth.

■ Exterior and interior materials should be rust- and corrosion-resistant.

■ The unit should be adequately insulated to prevent development of undue surface condensation.

■ Doors should be well-constructed, fitted with proper gaskets, and easily opened. Hinges should be easily cleanable.

■ Lighting should be adequate.

■ Shelves should be easy to adjust and clean.

■ The compressor should have sufficient horsepower.

Operating Practices

For food-protection purposes, standard operating procedures should be followed in storing products in a freezer. Foods earmarked for frozen-food storage should be wrapped or packaged in moisture-proof material or containers. This practice prevents loss of flavor, discoloration, dehydration, and odor absorption.

Whenever circumstances permit, frozen-food products should be stored in the original cartons in which they were shipped. If the carton is broken or the original cartons take up too much space, food items should be properly repackaged for storage.

Workers should be trained to open freezer doors only when necessary and to remove as many items as possible at one time. Freezer "cold curtains" can be used to guard against cold loss.

One last warning: Most freezers used in foodservice operations are designed *only* to hold already-frozen foods. Freezers that can be used to process unfrozen foods are called *blast freezers* or *plate freezers* and are usually capable of producing temperatures below $-20°F$ ($-28.8°C$).

Deep Chilling

Deep Chilling is a fairly recent concept to foodservice storage. Deep chilling can be used to safely hold foods for periods of time without damaging quality. Deep chilling differs from regular freezing and refrigeration in the temperatures in the unit. It has been found that bacterial growth can be sufficiently decreased by storing certain foods at temperatures between 26°F and 32°F ($-4°C$ and $0°C$) for three days or less. These temperatures are lower than those of regular refrigerators and higher than the temperatures for freezers.

Exhibit 5.5   An acceptable dry storage facility

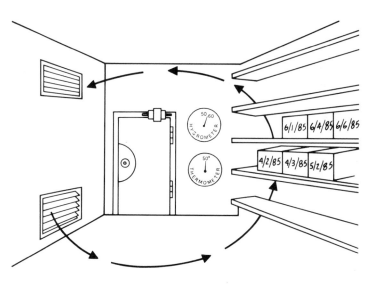

Foods such as poultry, meat, seafood, and a few other protein items may be held at these temperatures without forming ice crystals or otherwise losing quality. This method has been shown to increase the shelf life of food products. Further, it usually does so without the compromise of quality that hard freezing may cause in foods. Specially designed units may be used for this purpose, or refrigerators kept at deep-chill temperature ranges may be used if they have the compressor capacity. These deep-chilling units must meet all other sanitation criteria.

Dry Storage

The storage of dry food items should be given careful attention. The amount of storage space required varies with the type of operation, the menu, the number of customers served, the purchasing policies, the delivery frequency, and so on. Whatever the dimensions of the space allotted, the area should be well-ventilated, well-lighted, clean, and protected from pests and excessive moisture (see Exhibit 5.5).

Environmental Control

Temperatures of 60° to 70°F (15.6° to 21.1°C) are adequate for most goods placed in dry storage. A temperature of 50°F (10°C), however, is ideal and increases the shelf life—the time a product can be stored without serious change in quality—of virtually all dry products. A relative humidity of 50 to 60 percent is satisfactory for the storage of most goods; adequate ventilation ensures preservation of dry products and prevents infestation by certain insects. A thermometer, and possibly a hygrometer, should be prominently displayed in all storage locations. The accuracy of these devices should be verified from time to time and, of course, the temperature and humidity checked often.

Design Factors

Easy-to-clean materials should be used in the construction of dry storerooms. Floors should be of painted or sealed concrete or should have a covering of quarry tile. Wood floors are too difficult to clean and to keep free of vermin; improperly installed asphalt tile floors may crack under heavy loads, opening up hiding places for insects. The ideal storeroom has walls that are covered with epoxy or enamel paint or glazed tile. Shelving and tabletops are of corrosion-resistant metals. Bins for flour, cereals, grains, and dried vegetables are also of corrosion-resistant metals and are covered to keep out moisture and vermin. These items should be labeled.

Using slatted shelves and avoiding overcrowding will help to improve air circulation. Food should be kept away from walls and at least six inches above the floor. Keeping food above the floor eliminates hiding places for pests, makes cleaning easier, protects food from dampness, and keeps food containers clean.

Windows in storerooms should have frosted glass or shades, since direct sunlight can increase the temperature of the room and thus affect food quality. Exposure to bright light can even change the colors of spices and chocolate and help turn cooking oils and fats rancid.

Steam pipes, ventilation ducts, water lines, and other conduits have no place in a well-designed storeroom. Dripping condensation or leaks in overhead pipes can promote bacterial growth in such normally stable items as crackers, flour, and baking powder. Leaking overhead sewer lines are obviously a highly dangerous source of contamination for any food. Hot water pipes and machinery could increase the temperature of the storeroom to harmful levels. Equipment that requires the attention of an engineer or maintenance worker should never be placed in a storage area.

It should be emphasized that dry goods are especially susceptible to attack by insects and rodents. Cracks and crevices in the floor or walls should be filled in so that they cannot harbor dirt or vermin or allow the entry of ro-

dents. Doorways to the storage area should be closed off with solid or screened, self-closing doors to stop flying insects. As a guard against rodents, there should be no openings around pipes passing through the walls.

Cleaning

Easy-to-clean or not, the storeroom must be swept and scrubbed regularly. Walls, ceiling, floor, shelves, light fixtures, and racks all require cleaning on a routine basis.

Operating Practices

Two rules should be observed in relation to dry-storage areas. First, garbage must never be kept in the same room as food. Second, smoking should *not* be permitted in dry storage areas.

STORAGE OF SPECIFIC ITEMS

Up to this point we have considered the general rules for refrigerator, freezer, and dry storage. Now let's take a look at some of the correct storage procedures for specific items of food. Exhibit 5.6 lists the recommended storage times, temperatures, and procedures for food stored on a short-term basis. Exhibit 5.7 suggests maximum freezer storage times. Exhibit 5.8 gives recommended maximum storage periods for foods kept in dry storage. Refer to these charts for details on the food products discussed in the following sections of this chapter. Keep in mind, however, that not all experts agree on storage periods: the times given in these charts should be taken as general guides only. In addition, the times suggested are *maximum* storage times. The manager should see to it that supplies are usually stored for shorter periods.

Exhibit 5.6   Refrigerated storage of foods

Food	Recommended Temperatures (°F/°C)	Maximum Storage Periods	Comments
Meat			
Roasts, steaks, chops	32–36/0–2.2	3 to 5 days	Wrap loosely
Ground and stewing	32–36/0–2.2	1 to 2 days	Wrap loosely
Variety meats	32–36/0–2.2	1 to 2 days	Wrap loosely
Whole ham	32–36/0–2.2	7 days	May wrap tightly
Half ham	32–36/0–2.2	3 to 5 days	May wrap tightly
Ham slices	32–36/0–2.2	3 to 5 days	May wrap tightly
Canned ham	32–36/0–2.2	1 year	Keep in can
Frankfurters	32–36/0–2.2	1 week	Original wrapping
Bacon	32–36/0–2.2	1 week	May wrap tightly
Luncheon meats	32–36/0–2.2	3 to 5 days	Wrap tightly when opened
Leftover Cooked Meats	32–36/0–2.2	1 to 2 days	Wrap or cover tightly
Gravy, Broth	32–36/0–2.2	1 to 2 days	Highly perishable
Poultry			
Whole chicken, turkey, duck, goose	32–36/0–2.2	1 to 2 days	Wrap loosely
Giblets	32–36/0–2.2	1 to 2 days	Wrap separate from bird
Stuffing	32–36/0–2.2	1 to 2 days	Covered container separate from bird
Cut-up cooked poultry	32–36/0–2.2	1 to 2 days	Cover
Fish			
Fatty fish	30–34/–1.1–1.1	1 to 2 days	Wrap loosely
Fish—not iced	30–34/–1.1–1.1	1 to 2 days	Wrap loosely
Fish—iced	32/0	3 days	Don't bruise with ice
Shellfish	30–34/–1.1–1.1	1 to 2 days	Covered container
Eggs			
Eggs in shell	40–45/4.4–7.2	1 week	Do not wash. Remove from container
Leftover yolks/whites	40–45/4.4–7.2	2 days	Cover yolks with water
Dried eggs	40–45/4.4–7.2	1 year	Cover tightly
Reconstituted eggs	40–45/4.4–7.2	1 week	Same treatment as eggs in shell
Cooked Dishes with Eggs, Meat, Milk, Fish, Poultry	32–36/0–2.2	Serve day prepared.	Highly perishable

Food	Recommended Temperatures (°F/°C)	Maximum Storage Periods	Comments
Cream-Filled Pastries	32–36/0–2.2	Serve day prepared.	Highly perishable
Dairy Products			
Fluid milk	38–39/3.3–3.9	5 to 7 days after date on carton	Keep covered and in original container
Butter	38–40/3.3–4.4	2 weeks	Waxed cartons
Hard cheese (cheddar, parmesan, romano)	38–40/3.3–4.4	6 months	Cover tightly to preserve moisture
Soft cheese			
Cottage cheese	38–40/3.3–4.4	3 days	Cover tightly
Other soft cheeses	38–40/3.3–4.4	7 days	Cover tightly
Evaporated milk	50–70/10–21.1	1 year unopened	Refrigerate after opening
Dry milk (nonfat)	50–70/10–21.1	1 year unopened	Refrigerate after opening
Reconstituted dry milk	38–40/3.3–4.4	1 week	Treat as fluid milk
Fruit			
Apples	40–45/4.4–7.2	2 weeks	Room temperature till ripe
Avocados	40–45/4.4–7.2	3 to 5 days	Room temperature till ripe
Bananas	40–45/4.4–7.2	3 to 5 days	Room temperature till ripe
Berries, cherries	40–45/4.4–7.2	2 to 5 days	Do not wash before refrigerating
Citrus	40–45/4.4–7.2	1 month	Original container
Cranberries	40–45/4.4–7.2	1 week	
Grapes	40–45/4.4–7.2	3 to 5 days	Room temperature till ripe
Pears	40–45/4.4–7.2	3 to 5 days	Room temperature till ripe
Pineapples	40–45/4.4–7.2	3 to 5 days	Refrigerate (lightly covered) after cutting
Plums	40–45/4.4–7.2	1 week	Do not wash before refrigerating
Vegetables			
Sweet potatoes, mature onions, hard-rind squashes, rutabagas	60/15.6	1 to 2 weeks at room temp. 3 months at 60°F	Ventilated containers for onions
Potatoes	45–50/7.2–10	30 days	Ventilated containers
All other vegetables	40–45/4.4–7.2	5 days maximum for most; 2 weeks for cabbage, root vegetables	Unwashed for storage

Exhibit 5.7   Storage of frozen foods

Food	Maximum Storage Period at −10° to 0°F (−23.3° to −17.7°C)
Meat	
Beef, roasts and steaks	6 months
Beef, ground and stewing	3 to 4 months
Pork, roasts and chops	4 to 8 months
Pork, ground	1 to 3 months
Lamb, roasts and chops	6 to 8 months
Lamb, ground	3 to 5 months
Veal	8 to 12 months
Variety meats (liver, tongue)	3 to 4 months
Ham, frankfurters, bacon, luncheon meats	2 weeks (freezing not generally recommended.)
Leftover cooked meats	2 to 3 months
Gravy, broth	2 to 3 months
Sandwiches with meat filling	1 to 2 months
Poultry	
Whole chicken, turkey, duck, goose	12 months
Giblets	3 months
Cut-up cooked poultry	4 months

Meat

Meats should be placed in storage as soon as possible after delivery to the foodservice operation. For meat placed under refrigeration, 32° to 36°F (0° to 2.2°C) is the recommended temperature range, and 75 to 85 percent is the recommended relative humidity.

Raw meat should be wrapped loosely to allow for air circulation; leftover cooked meat should be wrapped tightly. Quarters and sides of beef may be hung in refrigerated storage without a covering, provided that nothing is stored under them and that the hook on which they are hung is cleaned and sanitized.

Frozen meats must be held at a temperature of 0°F (−17.7°C) or below. They should be wrapped and sealed in moisture-proof paper or containers before being placed in the freezer. Faulty wrapping or overly long storage may result in brownish freezer burn.

Unless processed meats are delivered in the frozen state, they should not generally be frozen. Such products as ham, bacon, and luncheon meats deteriorate quickly when frozen.

Food	Maximum Storage Period at −10° to 0°F (−23.3° to −17.7°C)
Fish	
Fatty fish (mackerel, salmon)	3 months
Other fish	6 months
Shellfish	3 to 4 months
Ice Cream	3 months. Original container. Quality maintained better at 10°F (−12.2°C)
Fruit	8 to 12 months
Fruit Juice	8 to 12 months
Vegetables	8 months
French-Fried Potatoes	2 to 6 months
Precooked Combination Dishes	2 to 6 months
Baked Goods	
Cakes, prebaked	4 to 9 months
Cake batters	3 to 4 months
Fruit pies, baked or unbaked	3 to 4 months
Pie shells, baked or unbaked	1½ to 2 months
Cookies	6 to 12 months
Yeast breads and rolls, prebaked	3 to 9 months
Yeast breads and rolls, dough	1 to 1½ months

Poultry and Eggs

In general, poultry is more perishable than meat. Whole birds should be wrapped loosely, refrigerated at 32° to 36°F (0° to 2.2°C) with a relative humidity of 75 to 85 percent. Refrigerated poultry should be used within three days of receipt. Giblets and cooked, cut-up pieces of poultry should be kept no more than one or two days in the refrigerator.

Fresh eggs should be refrigerated. Temperatures of 40° to 45°F (4.4° to 7.2°C) are adequate for eggs, though somewhat lower temperatures will not harm them. Washing eggs before refrigeration reduces their quality and safeness.

Reconstituted eggs should be treated just as eggs in liquid form. Powdered dry eggs are semiperishable. In their reconstituted form they are perishable products.

Exhibit 5.8 Recommended maximum storage periods for goods in dry storage

Food	Recommended Maximum Storage Period if Unopened
Baking Materials	
Baking powder	8 to 12 months
Chocolate, baking	6 to 12 months
Chocolate, sweetened	2 years
Cornstarch	2 to 3 years
Tapioca	1 year
Yeast, dry	18 months
Baking soda	8 to 12 months
Beverages	
Coffee, ground, vacuum packed	7 to 12 months
Coffee, ground, not vacuum packed	2 weeks
Coffee, instant	8 to 12 months
Tea, leaves	12 to 18 months
Tea, instant	8 to 12 months
Carbonated beverages	Indefinitely
Canned Goods	
Fruits (in general)	1 year
Fruits, acidic (citrus, berries, sour cherries)	6 to 12 months
Fruit juices	6 to 9 months
Seafood (in general)	1 year
Pickled fish	4 months
Soups	1 year
Vegetables (in general)	1 year
Vegetables, acidic (tomatoes, sauerkraut)	7 to 12 months
Dairy Foods	
Cream, powdered	4 months
Milk, condensed	1 year
Milk, evaporated	1 year
Fats and Oils	
Mayonnaise	2 months
Salad dressings	2 months
Salad oil	6 to 9 months
Vegetable shortenings	2 to 4 months

Food	Recommended Maximum Storage Period if Unopened
Grains and Grain Products	
Cereal grains for cooked cereal	8 months
Cereals, ready-to-eat	6 months
Flour, bleached	9 to 12 months
Macaroni, spaghetti, and other noodles	3 months
Prepared mixes	6 months
Rice, parboiled	9 to 12 months
Rice, brown or wild	Should be refrigerated
Seasonings	
Flavoring extracts	Indefinite
Monosodium glutamate	Indefinite
Mustard, prepared	2 to 6 months
Salt	Indefinite
Sauces (steak, soy, etc.)	2 years
Spices and herbs (whole)	2 years to indefinite
Paprika, chili powder, cayenne	1 year
Seasoning salts	1 year
Vinegar	2 years
Sweeteners	
Sugar, granulated	Indefinite
Sugar, confectioners	Indefinite
Sugar, brown	Should be refrigerated
Syrups, corn, honey, molasses, sugar	1 year
Miscellaneous	
Dried beans	1 to 2 years
Cookies, crackers	1 to 6 months
Dried fruits	6 to 8 months
Gelatin	2 to 3 years
Dried prunes	Should be refrigerated
Jams, jellies	1 year
Nuts	1 year
Pickles, relishes	1 year
Potato chips	1 month

Seafood

If refrigerated at 32°F (0°C) and covered with self-draining ice, fresh fish may be stored up to three days. Only crushed ice should be used in icing fish. Cubes or large pieces of ice can bruise the fish, thus encouraging spoilage. If stored at all, fish should always be wrapped in order to prevent possible damage from waterlogging. If kept at 32°F (0°C) but not iced, the fish should be used within 24 hours. Ideally, fish should be kept at 75 to 85 percent humidity.

Dairy Products

Most dairy foods readily absorb strong odors, including flavors from other foods kept in the vicinity. For this reason these products ought to be kept tightly covered and stored away from sources of strong odor, such as fish, peaches, onions, or cabbage. A storage temperature below 40°F (4.4°C) is necessary, and a humidity level of about 75 to 85 percent is desirable.

Cottage cheese should be used within three days of receipt; milk and cream keep their good quality about five to seven days after the date marked on the carton or delivery container.

Dairy products should never be left out at room temperature except when they are being used in cooking or actually being served. Milk that has been held at room temperature should never be poured back into a refrigerated carton.

Fruits

Most fruits keep best in the refrigerator, though apples, avocados, bananas, and pears ripen best at room temperature. Berries, cherries, and plums should *not* be washed before refrigeration, since moisture increases the likelihood that mold will grow. Contrary to common opinion, citrus fruits are best stored at a cool room temperature. The USDA recommends that citrus fruits be stored at temperatures of 60° to 70°F (15.6° to 21.1°C). For fruits that *are* refrigerated, a humidity of 85 to 95 percent is ideal.

Vegetables

Most fresh vegetables are best kept under refrigeration. The temperature range should be about 40° to 45°F (4.4° to 7.2°C) with the relative humidity at 85 to 95 percent.

Vegetables that quickly spoil or lose flavor include lima beans, cauliflower, and cucumbers. Vegetables need some exposure to air, but too much air will cause them to lose necessary moisture. Onions should not be stored with potatoes or other moist vegetables.

The best way to store potatoes is at a temperature of 45° to 50°F (7.2° to 10°C) in ventilated containers in a dry, dark place. Potatoes will, however, keep for two weeks at 70°F (21.1°C). Sweet potatoes, mature onions, hard-rind squashes, eggplants, and rutabagas should not be refrigerated and should be held at temperatures of about 60°F (15.6°C).

Vacuum-Packaged Foods

Packaging innovations such as vacuum-packaging can help extend the shelf life and quality under *proper storage* conditions. However, these special processes do not eliminate the need for proper storage of foods. Vacuum packaging will not stop the growth of bacteria when the foods are held in the temperature danger zone. Avoiding these temperatures is especially critical when storing cooked meats and cured fish that are often served without additional cooking. The foodservice manager must store these foods in the freezer or refrigerator according to package directions.

Canned Goods

Storage of canned goods should meet all the general requirements for dry storage. It is important to remember that canned goods are semiperishable. In other words, they are subject to spoilage and deterioration in quality over long periods of time.

The most critical requirements for storage of canned goods is a temperature of 50° to 70°F (10.0° to 21.1°C) and a relative humidity of 50 to 60 percent. Higher temperatures are likely to accelerate bacterial action and food deterioration, and too much moisture may cause rusting of the cans.

The storage times listed in Exhibit 5.8 are based on ideal conditions. Note that acidic foods such as tomatoes and berries keep for a shorter period of time than nonacidic foods. Acidic canned goods also can cause pinholing of containers.

Canned goods should always be wiped with a clean cloth before opening to prevent external dirt from getting into the contents.

Baking Supplies and Grain Products

Salt and sugar are virtually the only foodstuffs that can be stored indefinitely. Other dry goods deteriorate over time, with cereals and noodles being especially subject to loss of quality.

Many cereal and grain products are favorite targets of vermin and can easily become moldy or musty.

SUMMARY

Improper storage of food is a potential source of contamination and spoilage within the foodservice establishment. Although different kinds of food have different storage requirements, all should be kept in areas that are clean and used only for the storage of food. In addition, all food stocks should be rotated on the "First In, First Out" principle.

Refrigerators are used for short-term storage of potentially hazardous and some perishable foods. There are two types: walk-ins and reach-ins. Ideally, separate refrigerators should be used—one each for meat and poultry, fish, dairy products and eggs, and fruits and vegetables. Refrigerators should be cleaned and defrosted regularly. A close watch should be kept on the temperatures of all refrigerated storage areas and food products.

Freezers are useful for long-term storage of many food items. The foodservice manager should be aware that some foods deteriorate quickly when frozen. Normal foodservice freezers should not be used to freeze volumes of food, only to hold already frozen foods.

Temperature, ventilation, absence of insects and rodents, dryness, and cleanliness are all important factors in evaluating a dry storage area.

The recommendations for maximum storage periods in refrigerators and freezers should be followed carefully. Although dry goods generally have a longer shelf life (keeping period) than goods that are refrigerated or frozen, it should be remembered that they, too, eventually lose quality, even if kept under proper conditions.

A CASE IN POINT

At 7 A.M. on Monday, the bakery chef took the coconut cream and the pecan pies from the oven. They were for the faculty lunch the next day. The pies were the most popular selections at the faculty dining room of this large Eastern university, and they were made from scratch entirely on the premises.

The chef decided to let the pies cool. So he put them on a table near the oven. An hour later he put all 24 of them in a reach-in refrigerator, which was running at higher than normal temperatures.

By noon on Tuesday the faculty started to come in and the chef took the pies out and cut slices in anticipation of orders. Since the pies were only offered once a week the slices went quickly. By 2:30 P.M., only part of a coconut cream remained.

On Wednesday the faculty dean received a number of phone calls from various professors canceling their student advisement sessions for the day. One thing the callers seemed to have in common was that they had all eaten in the faculty cafeteria. She called the foodservice director.

The public health inspector came to check the food items remaining and the food-service facilities. Among the food items taken back to the lab was the remaining part of the coconut cream pie. *Staphylococcus aureus* bacteria were found in an abundance of numbers sufficient to cause illness. It was also found that the refrigerator had as its lowest temperature 58°F (14.4°C).

What sanitation breakdowns happened here?
What are your recommendations to the foodservice director to avoid such breakdowns in the future?

STUDY QUESTIONS

1. Why is proper storage so important in a foodservice operation?
2. What is meant by the "First In, First Out" principle?
3. List five general rules that apply to refrigerated-, frozen-, and dry-food storage.
4. If separate refrigerators are used, what is the recommended temperature for the storage of dairy products?
5. From a sanitation viewpoint, what features should be present in a well-designed refrigeration unit?
6. Why should shelves in a refrigerator be of the slatted type?
7. Name several foods that cannot be successfully frozen.
8. What is the correct air temperature that should be maintained in a frozen-food storage unit?

9. List at least three points that should be considered when purchasing equipment for frozen-food storage.

10. What are the desirable characteristics of a dry-storage area?

11. Raw meat should be properly wrapped for storage in a refrigerator. What is the exception to the "wrapping" rule?

12. Describe the conditions for the sanitary storage of fresh fish.

13. Why should berries, cherries, and plums *not* be washed prior to refrigeration?

14. What is the ideal storage temperature for fresh potatoes?

MORE ON THE SUBJECT

LEY, SANDRA J. *Foodservice Refrigeration*. New York: CBI, 1980. 354 pages. This book offers a fairly complete discussion of all aspects of the refrigeration of foods. Chapter 5 is most useful in the selection of refrigerators.

NATIONAL SANITATION FOUNDATION. *Standard Number 7, Food Service Refrigerators and Storage Freezers*. Revised November 1983. NSF standards for approval of these items is rigorous. Managers should use these standards as guides for buying.

ANSWER TO A CASE IN POINT

First, the pies should not have been cooled at room temperature—especially since foodservice kitchens can be warmer than other rooms. Cooling the pies under refrigeration would have been more appropriate.

Second, refrigerator temperatures should have been checked periodically to ensure that food temperatures were under 45°F (7.2°C). Also, even if the refrigerator had been at the proper temperature, it might have needed adjustment to accommodate all the pies at safe temperatures.

To prevent a similar occurrence, the foodservice director should institute procedures (1) for cooling off large volumes of food safely before refrigeration, and (2) for regularly checking equipment and logging refrigerator temperatures.

A number of things could also have happened to cause such an outbreak of food illness. There could have been a power breakdown, the refrigerator could have been too crowded, poor personal hygiene on the part of the workers could have contributed to the problem, etc.

Nevertheless, all the sanitary procedures in preparation may come to naught if storage or holding equipment is not proper for food service or if the proper equipment is not functioning correctly.

6
Protecting Food in Preparation and Serving

You're the manager of a large four-star restaurant in midtown Manhattan. It's late afternoon and your big ticket items are being prepared in the back-of-the-house. So far everything is going right. The food items came in on schedule, were carefully checked, and stored promptly in equipment especially designed for each item. Temperatures were checked. Now the foods are ready to be prepared and cooked, held for orders, and served to customers.

Let's assume that the preparers and servers are in good health, with no infections that could contaminate food beyond the redemptive powers of proper cooking. We will further assume that from the beginning, you as the manager have followed the script for a safe food service, adhering to the familiar rule: "Start with the menu."

This means that you selected a menu compatible with the facilities, trained the staff not to alter the menu in any way that would compromise food safety, and designed the menu to match anticipated customer demands. You have, in short, tried to head off all the problems associated with the flow of food, from menu-planning to serving the customer.

Even so, the following may jeopardize food safety:

- Mistakes in preparing food and combining ingredients
- Failure to control temperatures properly in the processing and holding of food
- Unsanitary methods of displaying and serving food

The path to a safe food service may seem to be strewn with booby traps, but it is fairly well lighted and there are markers along the way for those who will read them. Providing such markers for the safe preparation of food is the concern of this chapter.

TIME-AND-TEMPERATURE PRINCIPLE

Virtually all bacteria are capable of rapid multiplication at temperatures from 45° to 140°F (7.2° to 60°C). This range of temperatures is the *temperature danger zone.* Although the thermometer depicted in Exhibit 6.1 may seem to be a minor element in food preparation, the image of a thermometer with the temperature danger zone clearly marked should serve to remind everyone who plays a part in a food-service establishment of the cardinal rule of food protection.

The rule—called the *time-and-temperature principle*—requires that all potentially hazardous food be kept at an internal temperature *below* 45°F (7.2°C) or at an internal temperature *above* 140°F (60°C) during display and service. If, during periods of preparation, potentially hazardous foods must be exposed to temperatures between 45° and 140°F (7.2° and 60°C), this exposure time must be kept to an absolute minimum. The importance of this time-and-temperature principle *cannot* be overestimated. (Note that some health codes specify 40°F and/or 145°F (4.4° and/or 62.8°C) as the lower and upper limits of the temperature danger zone for potentially hazardous foods.)

It is always easy to state a rule; providing mechanisms for implementing a rule is another matter. Adherence to the time-and-temperature rule is the most critical line of defense in keeping safe food safe. The examples that follow will illustrate the dangers involved in violating the time-and-temperature principle and the techniques that can be used to guarantee that this principle, and others, are observed in a foodservice operation.

Exhibit 6.1   The temperature danger
zone for food: 45° to 140°F (7.2° to 60°C)

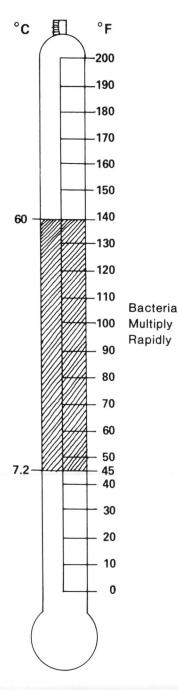

The Untimely Turkey

As a first example of the application (or misapplication) of the time-and-temperature principle, suppose a cook is preparing a 20-pound
frozen turkey. The bird must be thawed prior
to preparation because it requires additional
cleaning and trimming. It would take two days
to defrost the turkey in the refrigerator, and the
cook is in a hurry. He or she lays the gobbler
out on a work table in the kitchen to thaw overnight. The air temperature is about 75°F
(23.9°C). The skin and outer layers of flesh
thaw rather rapidly, but this outer thawing
slows down heat transfer to the inside of the
bird. As a result, the inner parts thaw very
slowly, while the skin and outer layers rapidly
reach temperatures favorable for the growth of
micro-organisms. In the overnight thawing period, these organisms increase to enormous
numbers.

Actually, several problems develop because of this overnight-thawing procedure:

■   A veritable hotbed of bacteria has
been produced that will contaminate
everything in the vicinity: the worker's
hands, the work table, the cutting
board, knives, cutters, and other
utensils. If these utensils are used on
other products without first being
cleaned and sanitized, the
contamination will be passed along.
Such a transfer of micro-organisms
represents a classic example of *cross-
contamination.*

■   Harmful micro-organisms have
multiplied to extensive numbers. If
subsequent cleaning, cooking, and
further preparation are not done with
extreme care, a dangerous dose of
disease agents will be served to the
customer.

■   The microbial population has run wild,
diminishing the culinary quality of the
turkey, introducing rancid taste or
other off-flavors.

Thawing Foods Properly

Some of the problems of the untimely turkey can occur with almost any frozen product that is improperly thawed. Freezing only keeps most bacteria from multiplying—it does not kill them. Micro-organisms that are present on a product before it is frozen can multiply once the product begins to thaw. For this reason, frozen foods—like all potentially hazardous foods—must be kept out of the temperature danger zone.

To guarantee the culinary and sanitary quality of frozen foods, always defrost them in one of the following ways:

1. *Under refrigeration, at temperatures below 45°F (7.2°C).* This method often requires much time and space, but sanitation must take precedence over convenience. Many facilities maintain special refrigerators exclusively for the thawing of frozen foods. Pre-planning is important if this system is used.

2. *Under potable running water at a temperature of 70°F (21.1°C) or below.* When this method is used the water must have sufficient velocity to shake any loose food particles into the overflow. There should be a time limit of two hours in using this procedure.

3. *As part of the conventional cooking process.* Frozen vegetables, with the exception of corn on the cob, are usually put on the stove directly from the freezer. Roasts, too, can be put in the oven directly from the freezer, although in such instances, the cooking time must be increased.

4. *In a microwave oven.* This method is acceptable only if the food will be transferred immediately to conventional cooking facilities as part of a continuous cooking process or if the entire, uninterrupted cooking process takes place in the microwave oven.

The "Cooked" Goose

Improper thawing of frozen foods is not the only hazardous practice contributing to food contamination. Other practices in preparation and cooking will increase a food's vulnerability, as this example illustrates.

Assume that a goose is to be prepared for cooking. The chef will clean and trim it, stuff it, and take other steps to get it ready for the oven. At this stage of preparation, the possibility of new contamination problems arises.

- Heat transfer may be as slow during the cooking process of the goose as it was during the thawing process of the turkey, so that parts of the food remain in the temperature danger zone, allowing micro-organisms to multiply rapidly.

- Parts of the bird may be cooked tender without having reached temperatures high enough to destroy all micro-organisms and spores. This situation is especially likely to occur if the fowl was grossly contaminated to begin with.

- The chef may use bare hands to stuff the cavity of the goose, ignoring the plastic gloves and utensils provided. Such hand contact may contaminate the bird.

- Any added ingredient, such as dressing in and around the bird, will compound the insulation problem, helping to keep parts of the goose in the temperature danger zone during the cooking process. In fact, stuffing must always be treated with special care. Very often the poultry or meat is cooked to a desirable state from both a culinary and sanitary standpoint, while the stuffing has not reached an adequate internal temperature to destroy micro-organisms. It is advisable, therefore, that all stuffings be cooked separately from the meat or poultry with which they are served.

Correct Cooking Temperature

All of these factors can keep the internal temperature of the goose from reaching the safe temperature needed to kill micro-organisms that may be present in the bird. Although a final temperature of 140°F (60°C) is considered adequate to prevent further growth of micro-organisms, certain foods—including our goose—have different temperature requirements.

Poultry, stuffed meat, and all stuffing should be cooked to an internal temperature of 165°F (73.9°C). This temperature should be reached *without* any interruption of the cooking process.

Pork and any food containing pork—such as sausage or bacon—should be cooked until all parts are heated to at least 150°F (65.6°C). The proper final temperature for pork is a matter of some dispute. Most cookbooks recommend cooking pork until it is gray. Since pork does not usually turn gray until it reaches an internal temperature of 170°F (76.7°C), it has become common practice to recommend cooking pork to an internal temperature of 170°F (76.7°C). A temperature of 150°F (65.6°C), however, is considered adequate to kill any trichinella larvae that may have infested the pork. Exception: pork cooked in a microwave oven must be heated to an internal temperature of 170°F (76.7°C). Microwaves tend to cook food unevenly, and to ensure that all parts of the pork reach the minimum temperature of 150°F (65.6°C), it must be brought up to 170°F (76.7°C).

When cooking an entire beef roast the factors of weight and mass should be evaluated to ensure that all parts of the meat are cooked to a minimum temperature of 130°F (54.4°C). Managers who offer rare roast beef to patrons must follow additional roasting and holding procedures.

The type of oven used will be a factor. If a beef roast weighs under ten pounds, the setting on a dry-heat oven should be at least 350°F (176.7°C). The oven should be held at that temperature for the entire cooking process. If the meat is cooked in a convection oven, the oven should be preheated and held at an air temperature of 325°F (162.8°C). When beef roasts ten pounds or over are cooked in a dry-heat oven, the oven should be preheated to and held at an air temperature of at least 250°F (121.1°C). Foodservice managers who hold beef roasts at less than 140°F (60°C) must utilize equipment designed for that purpose and follow the manufacturer's directions. Rare beef steaks should be cooked to a temperature of 130°F (54.4°C) or as the customer requests. Rolled roasts must be cooked to a minimum of 140°F (60°C). Beef roasts cooked in a microwave oven must be cooked to an internal temperature of 145°F (62.8°C).

The temperatures just described are all minimum temperatures. If it is possible to cook food to 165°F (73.9°C) without loss of culinary quality, this temperature is preferable. Any product that can be cooked to an internal temperature of 165°F (73.9°C) should receive the "extra" insurance that this higher temperature provides.

Competent as the cook may be, his or her judgment is never an adequate basis for determining the temperature of a product. *Thermometers should always be at hand for the cooks and their helpers and should be used to check the temperature of products before the cooking process is ended.* These thermometers should be metal-stemmed, numerically scaled, and accurate to ±2°F (±1°C). The internal temperatures should be checked in several places in a product: in at least one case on record, turkey thighs had reached an internal temperature of 200°F (93.3°C) while the stuffing was still at 90°F (32.2°C).

The Unstirred Beef Stew

Poultry products are not alone in requiring care in preparation and cooking. Let's consider typical problems that may arise in the preparation of a beef stew.

In addition to beef, the stew will contain various chopped vegetables, bases, and condiments, and the beef itself is likely to have been trimmed from larger cuts. In approaching these many small tasks, the preparer will be tempted to say, "I'll go ahead and leave this out of the refrigerator because I'm going to use it before long." The "before long" may become hours. The potential growth time for organisms, added to the possibility of contamination at each step of the preparation, becomes very significant. The vegetables, regardless of their source, must also be thoroughly cleaned since they may be contaminated with *C. perfringens* organisms.

Prudence and good planning in making this stew can avoid an accumulation of hazards. If the meat portions are not to be used immediately after being cut up, they should be placed in covered, shallow containers and held under refrigeration. Vegetable components should also remain under refrigeration until the last minute. Perhaps the meat stock could be cooking, and the vegetables added to the stock as they are cleaned and cut.

Heat Distribution

In working with menu items such as stew, the cook often has to deal with large volumes. Lack of thorough heat penetration can be a problem in this case. Interior parts may never reach temperatures sufficient to destroy bacteria. It is important to recognize that heat-transfer factors associated with the insulation properties of a mixture may create a temperature condition in which bacteria can flourish. The best remedy for this is *frequent stirring* so that every particle of the mixture is completely cooked. Also, potentially hazardous foods in a liquid mixture must be reheated to an internal product temperature within 90 minutes.

Bacteria and Breading

Chicken, steak, and oysters to be breaded or similarly prepared can present special problems. If different food items are combined, they all must be safe when mixed together. In this example, assume that the item has been cleaned, refrigerated, and otherwise readied for breading. At this point, food ingredients prepared separately are added—a batter made primarily of milk and eggs, we'll say. A cook on the alert for food-contamination accidents would think about the following questions: When was this batter prepared? Has it been under refrigeration since that time? How much use has it had? The same questions would apply to the crumbs, flour, or meal with which the dipped item is to be coated. The reasons behind these questions are simple enough.

- The batter, even though it had a low microbic population when mixed, may have become contaminated through handling and contact with the dipped meat or seafood.

- The breading itself, though a relatively lean microbic medium in the dry state, may become a rich medium after exposure to drippings or carryover from the batter.

- The breading operation is normally accomplished in a general work area, and under these circumstances the ingredients will be exposed to temperatures favorable for bacterial growth. (Remember that a kitchen is 20° to 30° warmer than other rooms.)

■ Breadings and similar coatings are efficient heat insulators and may inhibit heat transfer in the cooking process.

Store It or Throw It Away

All ingredients involved in a breading operation must be considered potentially hazardous and should therefore be refrigerated when not actually in use or else discarded. Old breading should not be used again and again, nor should the same breading be used for different food items, such as chicken and fish. Extreme caution must be taken by the person preparing the food to minimize its exposure to unfavorable temperatures or contaminating conditions. If the food is not to be cooked immediately, it should be returned to the refrigerator.

Always remember this fundamental point: *Conventional cooking procedures cannot destroy all bacteria and their spores or inhibit their toxins.* Food must be handled with care at every stage of preparation.

The Contaminated Custard

At times a contamination problem arises when raw foods are added to, or combined with, cooked products. This problem is especially significant when foods with a high-protein content, such as fish, meat, poultry, eggs, or dairy products, are involved.

The preparation of a hollandaise sauce, for example, may involve the addition of raw eggs to a product that is not usually cooked at high temperatures. The temptation in this case is to cook the combined product only slightly. Succumbing to this temptation provides no guarantee that the *Salmonella* or other microorganisms that might be present in the eggs have been killed.

Using Proper Ingredients

Whenever eggs are *not* going to be cooked to at least 140°F (60°C), only clean, whole-shell eggs should be used. Frozen, liquid, or reconstituted dry eggs are not acceptable for use in

foods that are not going to be cooked further. Although the procedures used by processors of these items are usually sanitary, merely cracking open an egg greatly increases the risk of contamination. This precaution applies to all other dishes in which eggs are not heated thoroughly to 140°F (60°C). Meringues, eggnog, cream-filled pastries, and sometimes even scrambled eggs, may all fall into this category. Ideally, all such dishes should be prepared in some way that allows the eggs to reach a temperature of 140°F (60°C).

Blending raw and cooked ingredients also occurs in the preparation of salads and sandwich spreads. All sandwiches and salads containing egg, meat, or poultry should be refrigerated immediately after preparation. Sandwiches are particularly dangerous because they are often prepared in large quantities and are held for long periods of time. Even when the sandwiches are refrigerated, the bread may act as a heat insulator.

HOLDING HOT FOODS

It should be apparent from the examples in the previous sections of this chapter that certain foods have to be cooked to certain temperatures to destroy contaminants. It should also be fairly clear that cooking will serve to counteract cross-contamination and re-contamination that may occur during extensive preparation and handling. What is *not* readily apparent is the hazard involved in allowing already cooked food to remain in the temperature danger zone for prolonged periods as it sits on the steam table, in a double-boiler, bain-marie, chafing dish, or the like.

It may be tempting to keep food just hot enough to serve, but not at a hot enough temperature to kill bacteria or destroy their toxins. A delicate problem arises when, for example, the chef says to hold the prime ribs at a warming temperature below 120°F (48.9°C) to keep them rare or directs that the soup be kept well below boiling to preserve its flavor. Any such conflict between culinary and sanitary quality *must always be resolved in favor of food safety*. However, this policy can mean lost time and wasted food if re-refrigeration and re-heating or premature disposal is involved. The answer lies in good timing and proper pre-planning.

"Hot" foods *must* be held at 140°F (60°C) or higher. If a product is removed from the range and placed immediately on a heated steam table, there will probably be no major problem, provided adequate equipment is available and is used properly. But the manager should be alert to the following requirements:

■ In order to guarantee that food kept in hot-holding equipment is at a temperature of 140°F (60°C) or above, thermometers must be used to check the temperature of the food product. It is not enough to rely on the thermostat of the warming or holding equipment.

■ All parts of the food must be exposed to a safe holding temperature. If a deep vessel is used, while the lower parts are being sufficiently heated, the upper surfaces are being cooled by the surrounding air and the heat may not be penetrating all parts of the food. The food should be stirred at reasonable intervals.

■ Containers must be covered, or otherwise protected, to guard against splash and spillage and also to retain heat.

■ Proper utensils must be used for portioning or serving. Cups, bowls, and other utensils with short handles should be avoided. Use a long-handled ladle, dipper, or the like, that keeps the server's hand away from the food. The serving utensil should be stored properly when not in use. If left in the pot, its handle may contaminate the food. If set down carelessly, it may become contaminated.

■ Food should not be prepared further in advance than necessary. Even under the best conditions, extended hot-holding of foods will not improve their culinary quality, and excessive handling always increases the risk of promoting bacterial action.

■ Most hot-holding equipment is intended for just that—to receive foods already heated to the desired temperature of 140°F (60°C) or higher, and to hold them at that temperature. The equipment is usually not designed to receive cold or cool food and heat it to temperatures that are lethal for micro-organisms. Products to be reheated must be brought rapidly to 165°F (73.9°C) before being transferred to hot-holding equipment.

Holding breaded, fried, and baked dishes can also present problems. Holding temperatures of 140°F (60°C) or above will tend to dry out or overcook the food. The inclination, therefore, is to hold these items at lower than approved temperatures. If it is necessary to keep food below 140°F (60°C) to preserve its flavor, the food should be prepared as needed and served right away.

PROTECTING LEFTOVERS

Concern for the sanitary quality of food cannot stop once the food has been served. Unless the menu has been sold out, the manager must make some decisions about leftover food. Highly vulnerable foods, such as custards, puddings, and creamed casseroles, should not be retained for service. Many other foods can be kept for a period of 24 hours if proper methods of holding and reheating are used.

Exhibit 6.2   Safe procedures for cooling hot foods

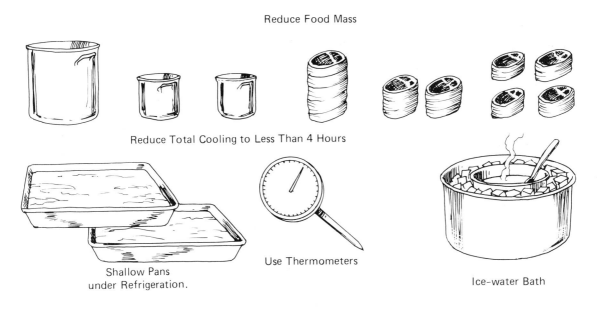

Reduce Food Mass

Reduce Total Cooling to Less Than 4 Hours

Shallow Pans
under Refrigeration.

Use Thermometers

Ice-water Bath

Regardless of the care exerted during preparation and serving, leftover foods have undoubtedly been exposed to contamination. For this reason, the amount of leftover food should always be kept to a minimum, and leftovers should be handled with special care.

All cooked, potentially hazardous leftovers should be chilled to an internal temperature of 45°F (7.2°C) or less within two to four hours. It should be kept in mind, however, that the allowable time for chilling must be reduced if food has already spent time in the temperature danger zone.

Adequate chilling of food does not occur automatically when a hot item is taken from the stove or warming table and placed in the refrigerator. Many variables influence the rate of cooling for a food product. Among these variables are the type of food, the material of the storage container, the dimensions of the container, the temperature of the refrigeration unit,

and the kind of covering put on the food. The manager should experiment with various techniques of cooling to determine the amount of time needed to cool products to temperatures below 45°F (7.2°C) (see Exhibit 6.2).

It is time to recall the beef stew prepared in an earlier example. Suppose that 16 gallons of stew had been prepared and that 4 gallons were served, leaving 12 gallons to be held over until the next day. Too much time, effort, and expense were expended on this stew to discard it. The leftover stew must be held above 140°F (60°C) or be chilled below 45°F (7.2°C) as soon as possible. Since it is seldom practical to hold the stew above 140°F (60°C) for an extended period, the most practical solution is to hold it in the refrigerator. However, because commercial refrigeration equipment is not intended to receive large quantities of hot food, the stew must be cooled beforehand.

Twelve gallons of stew will weigh about 93 pounds. If this stew is placed in a stockpot with a diameter of 16 inches, the stew will be about 13 inches deep. If this pot of stew were placed in a refrigerator that has an air temperature of 40°F (4.4°C), it would require well over 36 hours to cool the center portion below 50°F (10°C). *That's too long.* There would be more than enough time for dangerous bacterial growth, so it is obvious that a better cooling procedure must be used.

Water is a much better heat conductor than air. One way to achieve proper cooling would be to divide the stew into two six-gallon pots and put them both in an ice-water bath to chill. To chill the stew uniformly, it must be stirred frequently. The pots of stew must be covered as soon as it is practical and be protected from additional contamination. By using the ice-water bath and frequent stirring, the temperature of the stew can be brought down from 140°F (60°C) to around 75°F (23.9°C) in an hour or so. The refrigerator can accommodate it much better now.

To expedite further cooling in the refrigerator, the stew should be placed in *shallow* containers and should be stirred frequently under refrigeration until the product temperature reaches 45°F (7.2°C) or below.

Large quantities of soup, gravy, or other highly liquid foods can be cooled quickly in a steam-jacketed kettle by introducing cold water, instead of steam, into the jacket. The cooling can be further accelerated with a mechanical agitator.

The following guidelines are of special importance in the care and use of leftovers:

■ Use thermometers to determine the internal temperature of foods. Remember, the internal temperature of the food is not necessarily identical to the air temperature of the refrigerator.

■ Store leftovers in containers with the greatest surface area possible. Food such as casseroles and stews should be spread in shallow pans three to four inches in depth instead of being placed in large, deep kettles. Turkey, chicken, and roasts should also be cut into smaller pieces and placed in shallow pans.

■ Keep in mind that large quantities of food can raise the temperature of the refrigeration unit to such a point that adequate cooling is no longer possible. Studies in one establishment showed that the temperature of the main refrigeration unit regularly rose from 39° to 55°F (3.9° to 12.8°C) whenever leftovers from supper were placed in the unit. The temperature-rise problem can be overcome by rapidly pre-cooling the food in special low-temperature, quick-chilling refrigerators. Quick-chilling refrigerator systems are designed to hold shallow pans and smaller units of foods for fast chilling before removal to regular refrigeration units. They should be used as interim cooling systems and *not* as regular refrigerators.

Other acceptable methods of chilling include placing food in shallow pans in regular refrigerators or placing pots of food in ice baths and frequently stirring the food. Chilling of foods should take *no longer* than four hours. *Never* cool foods at room temperatures.

■ Always cover leftovers tightly. Before being reused, they should be heated quickly to 165°F (73.9°C). Do not mix leftovers with fresh food portions. *Never* use steam tables, bun warmers, bains marie, and other hot food holding equipment to reheat potentially hazardous foods.

Exhibit 6.3 Thermometer for checking internal temperatures of food (Photograph courtesy of Tel-Tru Manufacturing Company, Rochester, N.Y.)

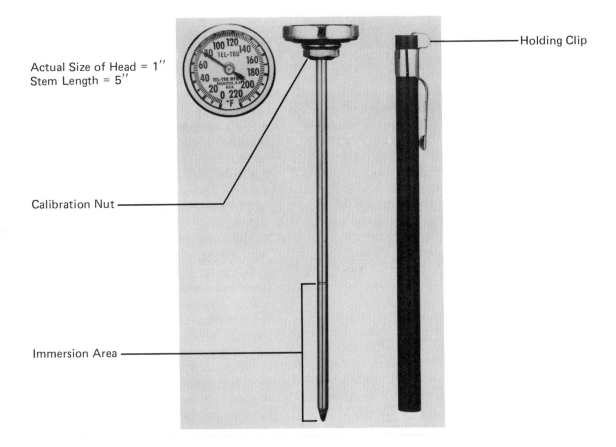

Actual Size of Head = 1″
Stem Length = 5″

Calibration Nut

Immersion Area

Holding Clip

CHOOSING THE RIGHT FOOD THERMOMETER

A number of thermometers are used in the foodservice facility. Some are used to check temperatures of equipment and storage areas. Built-in or hang-type thermometers are usually required in refrigerator and freezer units. Thermometers are also built into hot-holding equipment and machine dishwashers. Others are used to check the temperatures of food. Since temperature control is such an integral part of food sanitation, choosing the appropriate food thermometer and using it properly are of critical importance.

The most versatile type of thermometer for checking *food temperature* is the bi-metallic thermometer (see Exhibit 6.3). These thermometers must be numerically scaled, easily readable, and accurate to ±2°F (±1°C). The metal stem should be at least five inches long with the lower two inches being the sensing area for immersion into foods. Most thermometers of this type have a calibration nut so that the device can be adjusted to maintain maximum accuracy. Thermometers with a scale ranging from 0°F (−17.7°C) to 220°F (104.4°C) can be used to check the temperatures of incoming shipments of frozen and refrigerated food products; final cooking temperatures; food temperatures in refrigerators, freezers, and hot holder units; and the temperatures of sanitizing solutions. Bi-metallic thermometers with a plastic lens cover should not be left in food during cooking. A glass or mercury-filled thermometer should *never* be used to measure food temperatures.

Using Food Thermometers

After selecting an appropriate thermometer, the sanitation-conscious manager must be sure that each device is used properly and that it performs as an instrument of sanitation and is not a contributing factor in contamination. A few simple rules will ensure this.

- Sanitize the thermometer *before each use* to eliminate any contamination. A sanitizing solution appropriate to other food-contact surfaces may be used (see chapter 9). Alcohol swabs are also recommended because they are inexpensive, readily available from medical supply houses, and portable.

- Take the temperature in the thermal center of the food. This is usually the center of the thickest part, although composition of the food being tested may alter the heat distribution. Allow 15 seconds after the indicator stops moving, and record the reading.

- Recalibrate or adjust the accuracy of the thermometer periodically, and especially after an extreme temperature change or if the thermometer has been dropped. This can be done by inserting the sensing area of the thermometer into an ice water slush until the indicator stabilizes, and then adjusting the calibration nut so the indicator reads 32°F (0°C).

SANITARY SERVICE OF FOOD

A variety of diseases can be transmitted as a result of unsanitary practices in the serving of food. These illnesses include both those that are technically referred to as foodborne illnesses and those that are commonly termed "colds" and "flu." Steps taken to prevent the spread of such diseases are more often based on common sense and simple courtesy than on any sophisticated, scientific knowledge.

Milk and milk products presented to the customer for drinking purposes should be supplied in commercially filled, unopened packages that are one pint in volume or smaller. Milk may also be drawn from commercially filled, mechanically refrigerated, bulk dispensers. When bulk dispensers are not available, and portions of less than a half pint are required, milk products may be poured from a commercially filled container of not more than a half gallon in capacity. Cream or half-and-half should be provided in individual, unopened containers or in covered pitchers or should be drawn from a refrigerated dispenser. These precautions are designed to prevent contamination of dairy products by airborne micro-organisms.

Serving personnel should learn to handle dishes and utensils in a sanitary manner. Parts of dishes and utensils that will make contact with the customer's mouth should never be touched by a server. Plates should be held by the bottom or at the edge; cups by handles or the bottoms; silverware by the handles. Storing silverware with the handles up should make the last-mentioned practice easy to observe. Personnel should also observe the practice of using tongs to dispense rolls and bread (see Exhibit 6.4).

Exhibit 6.4   Sanitary manner of carrying
utensils and serving food

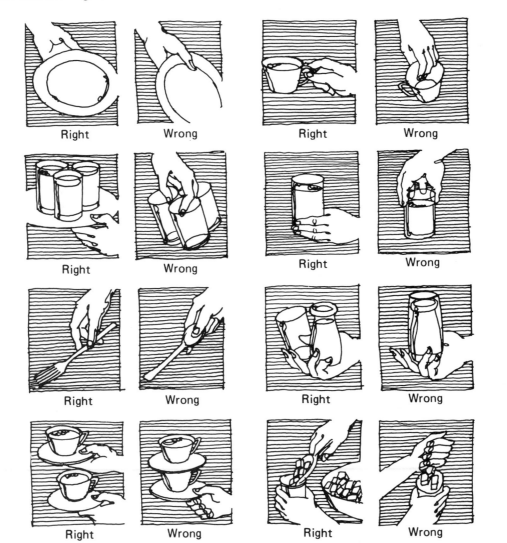

In some operations, soups, stews, or salads are portioned at the table by a server or by the customer. These situations increase the risk of contamination unless strict attention is given to the workability of this procedure, and to the careful monitoring of its use. It should become instinctive for those who serve food to make a visual check of serving dishes and tableware for apparent soil or improper cleaning. Supervisors should spot-check from time to time to encourage safe practices.

Another aspect of serving requires constant vigilance: the inclination on the part of servers, bussing personnel, and others to

Exhibit 6.5   Food shield for buffet-style service (Source: Ohio Department of Health)

handle clean place settings and to serve food without washing their hands after wiping tables and bussing soiled dishes. The potential for contamination in these practices is extremely high, and workers must be made keenly aware of the hazards. Planning and scheduling of tasks can eliminate a large part of this problem, and supervisors must see to it that such conduct does not go unchallenged.

Self-Service

Self-service areas and display areas should be designed to protect customers from one another's germs. Sneeze guards, or food shields, are absolutely essential over display counters and salad bars. These guards should be placed so as to intercept a direct line between the mouth of the average-height customer and the food being displayed (see Exhibit 6.5).

Devices dispensing single-service items such as cups and utensils should allow a customer to remove one item at a time without touching those awaiting other customers. Dispensing utensils should be either stored in the food with the handle extended out of the food, stored on a clean and dry surface in a properly designed holder, or stored in potable running water.

As a further safeguard, customers should not be allowed to refill soiled salad or buffet plates. Either a sign should be posted to that effect or an employee should be on hand to take the soiled plates.

The proper temperatures for foods held in self-service units should be maintained, and the temperatures of potentially hazardous foods should be checked frequently. Hot foods should be kept hot and cold foods cold.

Refrigerated pans for buffet-type self-service equipment are generally designed to hold ice, *not* to hold the foods directly. Packaged food items such as sandwiches and the like should not be placed directly on ice.

PROTECTING FOOD IN CENTRAL KITCHENS AND IN MOBILE, TEMPORARY, AND VENDING UNITS

It is one of the curious paradoxes of modern life that though we are always on the go, we never want to go very far to meet basic necessities. Branch banks and bookmobiles bring their services into countless neighborhoods. Television allows us to keep track of news around the world without ever leaving our living rooms. Shopping centers follow the spread of residential developments.

The foodservice industry has kept pace with this modern phenomenon. One of the primary ways in which it has done so is through the development of fast-food outlets. But there are other, less obvious parts of the industry that help to bring food and beverages to consumers. Caterers bring parties to private homes and supply food for company picnics. Temporary food stands supply the needs of audiences at sporting events and outdoor theaters. Pushcart operations peddle frankfurters and soda to crowds in city streets. Vending machines offer a wide variety of foods in numerous locations.

The primary rules of sanitation are applicable to all such mobile, temporary, and mechanical units. Facilities must be designed with sanitation and ease of cleaning in mind, operators must follow rules of personal hygiene, and food must be protected from contamination. Special recommendations, however, are in order for each type of facility.

Central-Kitchen Food Preparation

Unless special precautions are taken, food that is prepared in central kitchens or commissaries to be distributed to satellite feeding units or private houses is in danger of contamination. Even if safe conditions are maintained in storage and preparation, breakdowns that occur during distribution of the food can contaminate it at the final stage. Also, if any contamination occurs in the earlier stage, the problem is worsened by unsafe conditions in transporting the food.

Central kitchens are usually used for feeding large groups of people such as elementary and secondary school students or for providing food for shut-ins such as "meals-on-wheels" programs for senior citizens. Either way, the proper handling of food and use of appropriate food-holding equipment are the keys to safe food. Equipment that is used in transportation must be designed to hold food and keep hot foods hot and cold foods cold (see Exhibit 6.6). Makeshift supplies such as cardboard boxes are not designed to hold food for any period of

Exhibit 6.6   Specially designed carriers for transporting hot foods (Photograph courtesy of Cambro Manufacturing Company, Huntington Beach, Calif.)

time. Delays caused by traffic, scattered stop sites, and weather conditions add to the time problem. Food temperatures must be maintained regardless of these conditions. Containers and vehicles specifically designed for the purpose are the best options.

Hot-food containers for transporting food should be (1) firm and sectioned so that food items do not mix; (2) capable of being tightly closed to retain heat; (3) non-porous so that there is no seepage; (4) easy to clean or disposable; and (5) built to be stacked for transporting.

Mobile Units

If a mobile unit serves only frozen dessert novelties, soft drinks, popcorn, candy, wrapped crackers or cookies, and similar confections, it will need to meet only basic sanitation requirements. However, if a mobile unit prepares and packages food and serves such packaged food directly to customers, it will need to meet more extensive sanitation regulations—ones similar to those that apply to permanent food-service operations.

These mobile units will need provisions for handling potentially hazardous foods, such as adequate cooking devices, hot-holding units, and mechanical refrigeration units (not ice). In addition, adequate facilities for cleaning, sanitizing, and hand washing are necessary. Such facilities will need potable hot and cold water under pressure.

Consideration must be given to providing adequate refuse storage and disposal, insect control, satisfactory ventilation, and proper food storage. Mobile units should be returned daily to a central commissary for cleaning, maintenance, repairs, and waste disposal. Such tasks should be performed in areas separate from the food preparation and loading areas of the commissary.

Temporary Units

A temporary foodservice installation or unit is generally considered to be one that operates in one location for a period of time of not more than 14 consecutive days and in conjunction with a single event or celebration. This definition also refers to restricted operations, where the units may be set up for a longer period of time; for example, during the summer near a beach area. Definitions of, and requirements for, temporary units vary from location to location. For that reason, information on the requirements for temporary units should be obtained from the local public health authority.

In general it is not advisable for restricted operations to serve any potentially hazardous foods other than those that require limited preparation, such as hamburgers and frankfurters, or foods that are pre-prepared and prepackaged. Cream-filled pastries and sandwiches containing poultry, fish, eggs, or meat

should not be *prepared* in a temporary installation. If such dishes, and other potentially hazardous foods, are allowed by local laws and are *served* in a temporary installation, the following precautions should be observed:

- The foods must be prepared in a nontemporary facility in accordance with rules of sanitation.
- Such foods must be prepackaged for individual service.
- Such foods must be transported to and held in temporary installations at temperatures below 45°F (7.2°C) or above 140°F (60°C). No potentially hazardous foods, no matter how carefully wrapped, should be stored in direct contact with water or ice.
- Potable water must be available for preparation, cleaning and sanitizing, and hand washing. If cleaning and sanitizing of utensils is impossible, only single-service articles may be used.

Since temporary installations are often set up at fairs or picnic grounds, control of insects can pose special problems. In this regard, it is essential to keep food covered at all times, and where practical, prepackaged products should be used. Ideally, all counter service areas should be enclosed with tight-fitting solid or screened doors. Openings should be kept closed except when in actual use for service. Walls and ceilings should be made of materials that protect the interior from the weather.

Vending Machines

The coin-operated machine for vending of various types of food and beverages is a common sight. It is estimated that about 1.7 million people get at least one meal per day from automatic vending machines.

Foods dispensed by these machines are usually prepared and packaged in commissaries that are inspected and controlled under the same sanitation regulations applied to foodservice operations. It is important to prevent contamination of vended foods during delivery, storage in the machines, and during dispensing.

Potentially hazardous foods must be dispensed in the original container into which the items were placed at the plant. Fresh fruits should be washed before being placed in the unit.

The basic principles of sanitation apply to automatic food-dispensing machines. Temperature controls are required in machines to maintain potentially hazardous foods below 45°F (7.2°C) or above 140°F (60°C). Thermostatic controls that are checked regularly are a must. Food to be used in vending machines should be from commissaries that use sanitary procedures in its preparation.

Proper cleaning, sanitizing, vermin prevention, easily cleanable location, storage and disposal of wastes, and safe water supplies are important considerations where vending machines are used. Good personal hygiene of workers loading machines or otherwise handling the foods is a must. Hand-washing facilities must be available nearby to both service attendants and customers.

The food-contact surfaces of the machine should be of cleanable, corrosion-resistant, and nonabsorbent materials. The machine should be cleaned regularly. Dirty vending units are attractive to vermin.

Restaurant and foodservice operators may set up and stock vending machines as one form of service in their operation. Under such circumstances, responsibility for protection of the food in the vending machines rests with the restaurant operator. The foodservice operator must also make certain that the machines are not placed directly under pipes, that sufficient trash containers are provided, and that sewage maintenance schedules are observed.

THE TEN COMMANDMENTS OF SAFE FOOD SERVICE

We began our investigation of contamination within the foodservice establishment with a presentation in chapter 1 of the Eight Capital Offenses. The following list takes the positive approach. It reviews the ten most important rules of safe foodhandling or the Ten Commandments of Safe Food Service.

1. Before refrigerating potentially hazardous foods, make certain an internal product temperature of 45°F (7.2°C) or less will be maintained. Cooked food should be chilled rapidly in shallow pans either by refrigeration or in a quick-chilling unit, or in an ice water bath and stirred or agitated frequently during the chilling.

2. Use extreme care in storing and handling food prepared in advance of service.

3. Cook or heat-process food to recommended temperatures.

4. Relieve infected employees of food-handling duties and require strict personal hygiene on the part of all employees.

5. Make certain that hot-holding devices maintain food at temperatures of 140°F (60°C) or higher.

6. Give special attention to the inspection and the cleaning of raw ingredients that will be used in foods that will require little or no cooking.

7. Heat leftovers quickly to an internal temperature of 165°F (73.9°C).

8. Avoid carrying contamination from raw to cooked and ready-to-serve foods via hands, equipment, and utensils.

9. Clean and sanitize food-contact surfaces of equipment after every use.

10. Obtain foods from approved sources.

SUMMARY

Food must be protected at every step in the process of preparation and serving. The most important guideline for protecting food in the kitchen and in the dining room is the time-and-temperature principle.

In the first stages of preparation, raw foods must be cleaned thoroughly and frozen foods must be defrosted according to accepted procedures. Special care must be exercised in the mixing of raw and cooked ingredients, especially if the product will not be cooked again.

Cooking can kill many, but not all, of the bacteria present in food if proper internal temperatures are reached. Hot foods must always be held at temperatures above 140°F (60°C); cold foods at temperatures below 45°F (7.2°C). Leftovers and any other cooked foods that are to be refrigerated must be chilled immediately. Leftovers must be thoroughly reheated before they are served again.

Thermometers should be used throughout the processes of cooking, chilling, holding, and reheating.

Food is subject to contamination in display and service. Display-cabinet temperatures that are too high or too low, arrangements that allow customers to contaminate food, and sloppy habits on the part of serving personnel can all contribute to the transmission of disease.

Special precautions to be observed by operators of mobile units, temporary installations, satellite feeding systems, and vending machines include regulations covering maintenance, construction, waste disposal, and supplies, as well as restrictions on the types of food that can be kept safely in such facilities.

The Ten Commandments of Safe Food Service present positive guidelines for achieving and maintaining high standards of sanitation in the foodservice industry.

A CASE IN POINT

Consider the following incident adapted from a research report on a recent outbreak of foodborne illness. See if you can identify all the unsanitary practices that led to the outbreak.

Chicken salad was prepared at a central commissary to be delivered to 16 elementary schools in a Texas school system. On the afternoon before the salad was to be served, frozen chickens were placed in pots of boiling water and boiled for three hours. When the chickens were cool enough to handle, they were deboned. At least one of the employees doing the deboning, who was later found to be harboring *Staphylococcus aureus* bacteria in his throat, had coughed frequently while handling the chicken.

After deboning, the chicken was further cooled—this time to room temperature—with electric fans. It was then cut into pieces, placed in 12-inch deep pans, and stored overnight in a walk-in refrigerator with a temperature of 42° to 45°F (5.6° to 7.2°C). The following morning the remaining ingredients were added to the chicken, and the mixture was blended with an electric mixer.

The chicken salad was then delivered to the schools in thermal containers. Some schools received shipments at 9:15 A.M., and others at 10:30 A.M. Once in the schools, the containers were kept in warm classrooms until lunch was served around noon.

Chicken salad was the main dish served where 5,824 children ate lunch; 1,364 of the children eventually showed symptoms of staph food poisoning, including nausea, vomiting, diarrhea, and cramps. The immediate cause of the outbreak was the infected foodhandler who coughed on the chicken. But other factors contributed to the severity of the outbreak.

What were the other factors?

STUDY QUESTIONS

1. What is the time-and-temperature principle? Give one example of its application.
2. As described in this text, what are the upper and lower limits of the temperature danger zone?
3. Name four permissible methods of thawing frozen foods.
4. Why should the factor of heat transfer be considered important in the sanitary cooking of food?
5. What is the minimum, required, final cooking temperature for poultry? Stuffing? Pork? Bacon?
6. Why is stirring a necessary activity in the cooking and cooling of large volumes of food?
7. Describe precautions that should take place in the preparation of breaded food items.
8. Is it true or false that cooking will destroy all bacteria and their spores?
9. What rules should apply to the use of eggs added to foods that will receive little or no additional heat treatment?
10. What precautions should be exercised in the preparation of salads and of sandwiches containing potentially hazardous ingredients?
11. If the chef requests that a food be held in the warming oven at 120°F (48.9°C), what response should be made?
12. Describe two methods of cooling cooked items before they are to be held over in a refrigerator.
13. What rules govern the sanitary service of milk and cream?
14. Under what conditions may potentially hazardous food be served in a temporary foodservice unit?

MORE ON THE SUBJECT

LONGREE, KARLA. *Quantity Food Sanitation*. New York: Wiley, 1980. 456 pages. Chapter 11 on "Multiplication of Bacterial Contaminants in Ingredients and Menu Items" and chapter 13 on "Time-Temperature Control" provide many hints for implementing the rules for protecting food in preparation and service, as well as much discussion of the scientific evidence on which the rules are based.

NATIONAL SANITATION FOUNDATION. *Vending Machines for Food and Beverages. Foodservice Standard Number 25*. Ann Arbor, Michigan, 1980. This publication covers the basic construction of vending machines.

U.S. DEPARTMENT OF HEALTH AND HUMAN SERVICES, PUBLIC HEALTH SERVICES, FOOD AND DRUG ADMINISTRATION, DIVISION OF RETAIL FOOD PROTECTION. *The Vending of Food and Beverages, Including a Model Sanitation Ordinance*. DHEW Publication No. (FDA) 78–2091. 1978. The publication provides a recommended model sanitation ordinance regulating the sale of food and beverages through vending machines.

ANSWER TO A CASE IN POINT

Placing the ground chicken in deep pans kept it from cooling properly. Shallow pans should have been used.

Just because the *refrigerator* temperatures were 42° to 45°F (5.6° to 7.2°C) did not mean that the product quickly reached that temperature range. Thermometers should have been used to ascertain the temperature of the chicken itself. The temperature of the refrigerator should have been no higher than 40°F (4.4°C), which is the maximum temperature for storing potentially hazardous foods.

Keeping the chicken in warm classrooms obviously gave the bacteria an additional opportunity to multiply. Personal hygiene and observance of the time-and-temperature principle could have prevented this unfortunate occurrence.

7

The Safe Foodhandler

Human beings are the single most common source of food contamination. However they touch their environment—with their hands, perspiration, breath—they spread bacteria and other micro-organisms. Every unguarded cough or sneeze transmits a wave of invisible life forms capable of causing disease. Human as well as animal excrement is also a significant factor in the distribution of pathogens that invade the food supply.

It is ironic that people are the culprits as well as the victims in food poisoning incidents. We do it to ourselves. The foodservice manager intent on providing safe and wholesome food is confronted with a seeming paradox; somehow he or she must erect a sanitary barrier between the product and the people who prepare, serve, and consume it. To do this requires, first of all, a trained staff of safe foodhandlers. Thus the manager must be primarily concerned with the following:

- Hiring suitable workers who are in reasonably good health
- Training new and present personnel in clean personal habits and safe food practices
- Setting high standards regarding sanitary food procedures
- Conducting a continuous audit of sanitary practices

These concerns form the scope of this chapter.

THE DANGER IN AND AROUND US

An apparently healthy individual may harbor sizeable numbers of micro-organisms. Staphylococci may be found on the hair and skin and in the person's mouth, throat, and nose. The lower intestinal tract is a common habitat for *Salmonella* and *Clostridium perfringens* organisms. According to one estimate, up to 50 percent of all foodhandlers are bearers of disease agents transmissible by food. Another study indicates that more than half of the general public carries highly toxic strains of staphylococci. Once the individual becomes visibly ill, the bacterial count increases dramatically his or her potential as a food contaminator.

A sore throat, a nagging cough, sinus pains, and other symptoms of the "common cold" are signs that micro-organisms are taking over, with possibly dangerous consequences for the foodservice operation. The same may be said of symptoms of gastrointestinal ailments—a touch of diarrhea, an upset stomach.

Even when the illness passes, some of the organisms that caused it may remain as a source of re-contamination. *Salmonella* may remain in a person's system for months after the patient has recovered, and the hepatitis virus has been found in the intestinal tract up to five years after the disappearance of disease symptoms.

Respiratory-tract infections are especially difficult to control because they are spread so easily to large groups. An uncontrolled sneeze expels numerous water droplets, each of which contains innumerable bacteria. "Strep throat" is one of the more common ailments spread in this manner. Influenza and tuberculosis are other respiratory infections spread by careless sneezing and coughing.

A person's skin is a prime location for the growth of bacteria. The temperature is ideal for bacterial growth, and skin secretions provide nutrients for such growth. Staph bacteria abound in and around boils, pimples, carbuncles, inflamed cuts, and infected eyes and ears. Because of these factors, foodservice workers' hands are possibly the most dangerous "serving equipment" in the operation. Simple acts that, in another setting, would at worst be considered uncouth behavior—picking the nose, rubbing the ear, scratching the scalp, fingering a pimple or other open sore, running fingers through the hair, and so on—are transportation for micro-organisms.

BUILDING THE SANITARY BARRIER

The sanitary barrier that the manager must establish is simple to describe but not always easy to maintain. It is built on (1) proper methods of employee selection; (2) high standards of personal cleanliness among workers; (3) provision by management of the necessary equipment for maintaining personal cleanliness and sanitary practices; (4) adequate training of employees; and (5) constant supervision to ensure that only healthy workers come into contact with food. Each of these topics will be taken up, in turn, in the following sections of this chapter.

Hiring the New Worker

The foodservice manager is obligated to protect customers and employees from workers who have health problems that can affect the sanitary quality of food. Professional ethics, good business sense, and the law all require such protective behavior. In most communities, the health code prohibits persons having communicable diseases and persons who are carriers of such diseases from engaging in work activity that may result in contamination of food or food-contact surfaces. Care in hiring is the manager's first step in fulfilling the obligation to provide healthy workers.

Obviously, the best time to discover if a worker is a poor sanitation risk is *before* that worker starts on the job—at the hiring interview. But how is the foodservice manager, a nonmedical person, to judge the health of an applicant? There are three guides to making a hiring decision.

First, use the application form. In addition to the routine questions on work experience, training, and other relevant information, the application form should require information on past illnesses, injuries, and current health. The answers may not be wholly reliable because an applicant may be tempted to omit ailments that would be disqualifying, but the answers are one indicator.

Second, the manager should *carefully* observe the applicant, applying the following mental checklist:

1. *Is the applicant neatly groomed and dressed?* If not, it is reasonable to expect that this person's work habits may be questionable. Dirty clothing, dirty or unkempt hair, ragged and unclean fingernails, and an unpleasant body odor should all flash danger signals to the alert manager.

2. *Does the applicant show evidence of skin infections, pimples, acne, or open sores?* If so, this person presents an obvious sanitary hazard, especially if the manager observes the applicant fingering the sores.

3. *Does the applicant cough or sneeze repeatedly? Is sniffling exhibited?* These are signs of possible throat, sinus, or respiratory infections.

4. *Does the applicant pick at his or her face, scalp, or neck, or exhibit other unsanitary habits?* Such behavior may be a nervous habit or a sign of infection—in either case an undesirable condition for a foodhandler.

Third, the manager can and should seek a medical opinion in doubtful cases. Many operations routinely schedule or require a medical examination for new employees as a matter of policy, and some communities require health certificates for foodservice personnel.

The problem of excluding infectious personnel does not end with the hiring process, however careful and efficient it is. In fact, the person who becomes a carrier of contamination *after* he or she is on the job is far more likely to be the source of food-poisoning incidents. Frequently, food contamination originates with an established employee whose illness or infection comes and goes in a week.

The truly safe foodhandler is a product of continuing vigilance on the part of management. Every workday the conscientious manager must observe workers and be on the lookout for disease symptoms and unsafe personal habits—the telltale signs forecasting events that might defeat the most ambitious program of foodservice sanitation.

Rules for Personal Hygiene

After the manager has ensured that new workers are not disease carriers, it is imperative that they be taught the rules of personal hygiene, which must be followed and enforced in the foodservice facility. All the screening in the world will not guarantee safe foodhandling unless new employees clearly understand what is expected of them.

Management must establish definite "house rules" that are easily understood and uniformly enforced. Workers should learn the rules either from the manager in person or from a highly dependable supervisor. Policies should be written in simple language and available for all employees to read—in employee manuals and posted in employee restrooms, over washstands, and on bulletin boards. The rules and their wording may vary, depending on the size and complexity of the foodservice operation, but they should cover these areas: personal cleanliness, smoking and use of tobacco; proper working attire; acceptable foodhandling practices; and prohibited actions and habits.

Personal Cleanliness

Emphasis on personal hygiene is a fundamental responsibility of the foodservice manager. To pursue the subject of personal cleanliness with mature people may be an awkward and embarrassing task for the manager, but the alternatives are, at the least, an unfavorable impact on patrons, which will hurt the rate of return patronage, or at the worst, an outbreak of foodborne illness, which can ruin a business.

Dirty people are dangerous, for the obvious reason that they compound the natural contamination found even in clean and healthy people. They also are a poor advertisement for the house. One worker with a slovenly and unclean appearance can offend customers and, in their eyes, condemn the entire operation. Rules for personal cleanliness should cover the following:

Hair Washing. Oily, dirty hair is attractive to bacteria, and dandruff can fall into food.

Bathing. Touchy as the subject may seem, the manager is bound to insist that workers bathe daily or more often if their jobs require it. Body odor is offensive to patrons and to other workers, and the skin is a prime breeding ground for bacteria. The written rules should state the acceptable standards in this regard and the rules should be applied consistently.

Hand Washing. The most important aspect of personal cleanliness is frequent and thorough hand washing. Body odor may offend, and lack of bathing may accelerate bacterial growth, but most often it will be dirty hands that transmit contaminants to the food product. Hand washing should follow any act that offers even a remote possibility that the hands have picked up contaminants. One of the most notorious incidents of food poisoning on record involved a single worker who scratched a facial infection and then handled a large amount of sliced meats.

The following oft-repeated activities, among others, should always be followed by thorough hand washing:

- Touching areas of the body such as ears, mouth, nose, or hair, or scratching anywhere
- Intimate contact with infected or otherwise unsanitary areas of the body

- Use of a handkerchief or tissue
- Hand contact with unclean equipment and work surfaces, soiled clothing, wash rags, and so on
- Handling raw food—particularly meat and poultry
- Handling money
- Smoking a cigarette
- Clearing away and scraping dishes and utensils; scullery operations
- Eating
- Use of restroom

Every one of these everyday actions, and numerous others, involve use of the foodservice worker's hands. Frequent hand washing is the way to make each action safe.

It may seem elementary, but clean hands are so critically important that employees should be instructed in proper hand-washing procedures if there is any possibility that they do not know them. Proper hand washing is more complicated than just running water, even soapy water, over the hands. All personnel should use the following techniques when washing their hands (see Exhibit 7.1):

1. Turn the water to a temperature as warm as the hands can comfortably stand.

2. Moisten the hands and apply a disinfectant soap to them, lathering well beyond the wrists and up the arms to the elbows to remove soil and dirt.

3. Pay particular attention to the area between the fingers and around the nails; a brush should be used for cleaning under the nails.

4. Rub one hand against the other in a rotating motion, using friction for about 20 seconds.

5. Rinse thoroughly under running water, allowing the water to flow from the elbows down to the fingertips. This action will rinse away contaminants.

6. Dry hands thoroughly with a sanitary, single-service towel or a hot air dryer.

7. Be careful not to touch anything that re-contaminates the hands before returning to work. Drying hands on aprons, using a handkerchief, or handling dirty dishes will undo the process.

8. Repeat this procedure as often as necessary to keep hands immaculately clean at all times.

Fingernails. Fingernails should be trimmed and clean. Ragged nails harbor bacteria and are very difficult to keep sanitary. Long fingernails have the same disadvantage. Hangnails should be clipped and treated.

In maintaining a house policy on hand care, as with other hygienic routines, it is not enough merely to set up rigid rules. The reason behind a rule should be clearly explained. Rather than warning employees to keep their fingernails trimmed (or else!), the manager should tell them: "Fingernails that are long or ragged are very difficult to keep clean, and they can carry a tremendous number of infectious bacteria."

Cuts and Abrasions. Exposed cuts or abrasions disturb the worker, the patrons, and the operation's public image, and they are sources of bacteria. Wounds and open sores should be antiseptically bandaged and the bandage covered with a waterproof protector. In some cases, the worker may need to be moved to another job station, where food need not be handled, until the injury heals.

Smoking and Gum-Chewing. Employees should not smoke or use tobacco in any form while engaged in food preparation or service and while in areas used for equipment or utensil washing or food preparation. Employees should be allowed to smoke only in designated areas where the use of tobacco will not result in food contamination, such as in employee rest areas.

Exhibit 7.1   Proper hand-washing
techniques

1. Use water as hot as the
hands can comfortably stand.

2. Moisten hands, soap
thoroughly, and lather
to elbow.

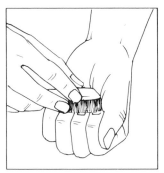

3. Scrub thoroughly, using
brush for nails.

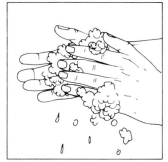

4. Rub hands together, using
friction for 20 seconds.

5. Rinse thoroughly under
running water.

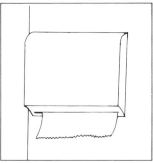

6. Dry hands, using single-
service towels or hot-air
dryer.

Smoking can endanger the health of both the worker and the customer. It is virtually impossible to smoke without exposing the fingers to droplets of saliva. However small and unnoticed, these droplets may contain thousands of bacteria, which can contaminate anything the fingers touch. Exhaled smoke will launch the same saliva droplets into the air. Smoking, morever, is a double hazard. The contamination mechanism can operate in reverse: organisms may pass from a soiled object to the hands, to the cigarette, to the lips and mouth. It is absolutely essential that any foodhandler who has been smoking—or doing anything that can contaminate the hands—wash his or her hands thoroughly before returning to work.

Chewing gum is another source of possible contamination, mainly because of the annoying habits of some gum-chewers. Blowing bubbles, stretching the gum with the fingers, and parking gum under counters are among gum-chewing habits that should be forbidden around foodhandling. Aside from the annoyance of having to clean gum off floors and counters, gum-chewing is a potential food-contaminating action.

Proper Working Attire

The clothing of foodservice employees plays an important role in the prevention of food contamination. Because of this fact, it is essential that employees observe strict standards of personal attire. House rules should cover the items of work clothing, hair-coverings, and jewelry.

Work Clothes.   Soiled work clothes that have gone for days without laundering are bad on two counts. They are offensive to patrons, who may rightfully wonder if the food being served is as unsanitary as the clothes of the person serving it. More significantly, dirty clothing is a repository of disease organisms. One contact with soiled clothing is enough to start the contamination cycle: from the clothing, to the hands, to the food. The foodservice manager must insist on clean uniforms and encourage changes as often as they are necessary. Employees must also be trained to refrain from wiping hands on clothing, using clothing as hand protection to move hot food vessels, or from wearing clothing that needs constant adjustment.

No surgeon would wear a surgical gown on the way to the hospital, or street clothes while in the operating room, for fear of contaminating the patient with dirt and germs from the street. For essentially the same reason, work clothes should be donned in the foodservice establishment and not worn while commuting to work. Street clothes should not be worn in food preparation or serving areas.

Hair Restraints.   Hair is a prime breeding ground for bacteria. It is also a most unappetizing item for diners to find in their food. For these reasons, and to comply with many local health codes, employees are required to wear hairnets, bands, or caps to keep hair from contaminating food. Restraints serve a double purpose in that they also discourage employees from running their fingers through their hair, scratching their scalps, or otherwise contaminating their hands by touching their hair. Employees should be discouraged from these habits.

Jewelry.   Some items of personal decoration or jewelry—an ornate ring, bracelet, or watch, for example—are not only soil collectors and difficult to keep clean but can also become caught in machinery or catch on sharp or hot objects.

Prohibited Habits and Actions

Even if a worker has observed the rules of personal cleanliness, actions of that worker may still be dangerous to food safety. Safe food-handling practices will further cut down the risk that employees will contaminate food.

Unfortunately, even if employees are aware of safe foodhandling practices and the rationale behind them and attempt to follow these practices, they may not always stop to think of sanitation when they seek more convenient ways of doing their work. Many shortcuts practiced almost universally among foodhandlers are unsanitary. It is not enough, therefore, to simply include "Don't handle food-contact surfaces" among the house rules. The manager must be aware of employee practices and include in the rules a specific list of the worst habits to be broken.

The following practices are typical of the habits that must be eliminated:

- Using wiping cloths to remove perspiration
- Stacking plates of food in order to carry more at one time
- Washing hands in sinks used to prepare foods
- Spitting on the floor or into sinks
- Coughing or sneezing unguardedly in a food preparation area
- Picking up bread, rolls, butter pats, or ice with the bare hands

- Handling place settings or food after wiping tables or bussing soiled dishes
- Touching the food-contact surface of tableware—the tines of a fork instead of the handle, the rim of a cup instead of the handle—with bare hands
- Tasting food with a finger, or using the same spoon for tasting repeatedly
- Leaving foods uncovered for long periods of time

To bring this "endless" list to a practical end, let us remember one simple and easy rule: *Hands that have touched contamination must never touch food without prior hand washing.*

In summary, the house rules should paint a picture of a model foodhandler—one who

- Is in good health
- Has clean personal habits
- Handles food safely
- Appreciates the need for sanitary practices

Management's Responsibility

Setting up the numerous and complex rules necessary for safe foodhandling is a beginning—not an end. Management must also make it possible for sanitation rules to be observed. In order to do this, management must provide adequate facilities and must assign jobs in such a way as to ensure the practice of sanitation rules.

Adequate Facilities

As in every aspect of a foodservice operation, safe foodhandling requires proper equipment—in this case, adequate washing and dressing-room facilities. Making it convenient and comfortable for workers to follow the sanitation rules will encourage compliance.

Workers need proper facilities from the moment they arrive on the job. First, there should be a dressing room, where employees can change into work clothes and clean up, and lockers for the safekeeping of clothing and personal effects. Since workers are not to wear street clothes at work, there must be a place for them to change into uniforms. Because the wearing of ornate jewelry should be prohibited, a safe place must be provided for the worker to leave personal items during work hours. Facilities should be conveniently located and clean, well-lighted, and uncluttered. If they are not—if they are dingy, cramped, or hard to reach—workers will avoid using them.

A rest or "break" area separate from the foodhandling areas is also desirable and, in fact, is required under the ordinances in some localities. This area should be located in a place where workers can smoke and eat without endangering food, equipment, or utensils.

Employee restrooms, equipped with self-closing doors, ought to be provided, separate from those for customers. If workers need to shower at the beginning or end of the day, adequate shower facilities and supplies must be provided.

Hand-washing stations for employees should be located in the restrooms and in other convenient locations throughout the facility. If the lavatory is too hard to reach, workers will be tempted to wash their hands in a sink in which food or utensils are cleaned—a likely means of cross-contamination. Ideally, the hand-washing station needs to have faucets that are foot-, knee-, or elbow-operated. Self-closing, hand-operated faucets are also acceptable (see Exhibit 7.2).

The hand-washing facility should be supplied with hot water and cold water through a mixing faucet, at a temperature between 110° and 120°F (43.3° and 48.9°C). If the water is uncomfortably hot or cold, workers will avoid necessary hand washing.

Soap dispensing equipment should be provided in sufficient quantity near the washstands. Remotely operated liquid soap dispensers are strongly recommended for use

Exhibit 7.2   A proper hand-washing station

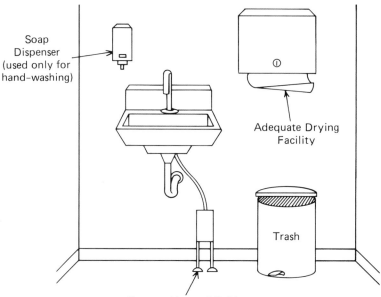

Soap Dispenser (used only for hand-washing)

Adequate Drying Facility

Trash

Remote Hot and Cold Water Foot Pedals

in a food service. Hand-operated soap dispensers and bars of soap can be means of transferring micro-organisms.

For hand drying, management may supply disposable sanitary towels or forced-air blowers. There are too many possibilities for contamination with retractable cloth dispensers. Some authorities consider the blowers to be the most sanitary drying method, but workers are inclined to consider them too slow and may resort to the unsanitary practice of wiping their hands on their clothes and aprons. If paper towels are used, easily cleaned disposal receptacles that do not require touching of the disposal unit must be provided.

Hand-drying facilities should also be available at food-preparation and utensil sinks to be used by workers performing tasks at these sinks. Provision of towels at these sinks should not be taken to mean that hand washing can take place there, however. Proper drying facilities should discourage workers from using aprons or wiping cloths to dry hands.

Job Requirements

Management must be aware of contamination possibilities when assigning job responsibilities. This principle applies especially to carry-out operations but is an important point to remember in any foodservice operation. Training employees in sanitary habits will be pointless if a worker is assigned to cook and wrap food, clear off tables, and then return to the food-preparation area.

Training the Safe Foodhandler

Let's say that the manager has established the policies for safe foodhandling and provided the facilities so that strict observance is physically possible. Now he or she must develop the right attitudes among workers so that they will obey the rules willingly and consistently. Attitude development calls for a continuous program of instruction and motivation. A one-time lecture or crash course will not do the job.

(Chapter 13 of this text will be devoted entirely to training methods and principles in the important task of instructing foodhandlers in sanitation.)

Supervision for Sanitation

No program for safe foodhandling practices can succeed without constant supervision. Supervision is the audit of the training system, ensuring that the rules are being followed. It is the cement that holds the building blocks of the sanitation program together.

Supervising Employees

In the heat of action at peak serving periods, even the most conscientious employee may falter. One person may sweep a lock of hair back with a bare hand; another may disjoint raw poultry and then, without hand washing, slice baked ham. Still another may neglect to trade a heavily soiled uniform for a clean one. To check these errors, a supervisor must always be on the alert to spot unsafe practices that may creep into an employee's work habits. Good supervision reinforced with a continuous training program should help all employees—new and old—follow the rules.

One important facet of foodhandler supervision is to apply the same health standards to regulate workers that are used in screening prospective employees. In a discreet manner, employees should be checked daily for in-fected cuts, burns, boils, respiratory symptoms, and other evidence of infection that can be transmitted through food.

Under the law in many localities, the proprietor who knows or suspects that an employee has a contagious disease, or is a carrier, must notify health authorities immediately. Depending on the disease, the employee may continue to work after medical treatment. (The employee may, for example, be required to wear rubber gloves because of a skin infection, or be assigned to another job that does not involve direct contact with food.) More serious ailments may require treatment that excludes the worker from the establishment for a considerable period of time. In extreme cases, a worker may be declared indefinitely ineligible for foodservice employment.

As in other management positions requiring continuous surveillance of the operation, monitoring a safe food service means developing good supervision routines.

It should become second nature for the manager to run through a mental checklist as he or she makes daily rounds.

1. Are workers wearing clean uniforms?
2. Are they free of body odors?
3. Is the clean-hands policy being strictly observed?
4. Are workers wearing hats, hairnets, or other hair restraints?
5. Are any workers observed fingering a pimple or scratching at the head or face?
6. Are they smoking, eating, or chewing gum in food-preparation or serving areas?
7. Are their fingernails short and clean?
8. Are they spitting in unauthorized places—in sinks, on the floor, in a disposal area?
9. Are they coughing or sneezing in their hands?

10. Are they wearing ornate rings, dangling bracelets, or other easily soiled personal decorations while handling food?

11. Are they using wiping cloths to remove perspiration from their faces?

Ideally, the employee should feel free to report that he or she has an infection. This conscientious action will be more likely to occur, however, if the employee knows that no penalty involving loss of work and pay will occur. As discussed earlier, the worker may be temporarily given another job responsibility. There is no simple answer to this problem, but the manager must strive to maintain a climate in which no member of the staff will be discouraged from coming forward with information about health hazards.

Self-Supervision for Managers and Supervisors

While the manager and the supervisor are watching the employees, the manager and supervisor should also be watching themselves. One of the strongest tools of management is to set a good example. The cook who sees the manager walking through a food preparation area while smoking a cigarette probably thinks, "If the boss can do it, why can't I?"

The leader who does not follow the rules will not lead effectively, and a leader cannot lead in the desired direction unless he or she knows the way. Some managers have never been trained in sanitation or have been trained but do not appreciate its importance.

It is natural for a person to think that he or she could never be the source of a sanitation problem. The supervisor is probably the most experienced person in the operation—and unfortunately, may be the most immune to learning. If managers and supervisors will remember the cardinal rule—that their primary function is to serve safe food to their customers in a safe manner—they will take the time for proper learning and training.

A manager confronted with a reluctant supervisor may try a subtle technique to change that attitude—the supervisor should be asked to make a sanitary survey of another department or operation. Unsafe practices observed by the supervisor in such an inspection will very likely suggest possible defects in his or her own department and will bring home the need for rules, training, and supervision.

SUMMARY

Most food contamination is caused by foodhandlers with skin infections and by bacteria found in the respiratory system or the intestinal tract or in other areas of the body. These mirco-organisms are transmitted from the body to the food by unclean hands, as well as by coughing and sneezing.

In most localities, the foodservice manager is required by law to prevent individuals with communicable diseases from working in contact with food and to report diseased employees to the regulatory agency. Even if no such laws exists, good business practice would require the same restraints.

The manager is responsible for the building of a sanitary barrier to protect customers from contaminated food. This can be accomplished by the manager carefully screening out potentially health-hazardous persons at the hiring stage, establishing for employees clearly understood rules against unsafe personal habits and foodhandling practices, providing for continuous training of employees, encouraging diligent supervision and correction of rule-breaking, and by the manager setting a good personal example.

A CASE IN POINT

Salmonellosis was the illness transmitted to a number of people who attended a "Hawaiian Luau Night" at a social club.

The event had been catered by Chic Catering. A wide variety of meats were served at the party. After the Health Department received the victims' histories, they questioned the caterer and his employees. One assistant was found to have had diarrhea the day of the luau. Upon questioning, the caterer said that the assistant had made a number of trips to the bathroom but had been allowed to go on working with food. Also he said that some of the meats might have been left out at room temperatures for a period of time. Inadequate hand-washing facilities might also have contributed to the problem.

Before leaving the catering facility, the inspector observed the assistant licking his fingers periodically to moisten them while separating pieces of wax paper to wrap sandwiches.

What must the caterer do now?

STUDY QUESTIONS

1. Why is uncovered sneezing so hazardous in a foodservice operation?
2. What steps should a manager take to build a sanitary barrier between the product and the people who prepare, serve, and consume it?
3. To ensure a staff of safe foodhandlers, what three guides should the manager follow in hiring new employees?
4. Why should the manager bother with writing down and posting house rules for personal cleanliness and safe foodhandling?
5. What five activities must be followed in hand washing?
6. What are the correct hand-washing procedures for foodservice workers?
7. Why should a manager explain the reasons behind house sanitation rules?
8. A worker accidentally cuts a finger but wishes to continue work as a salad preparer. What should the manager do?
9. Where in a foodservice operation may employees be allowed to smoke?
10. Why is smoking around food such a hazardous activity?
11. What two purposes does wearing hair restraints serve?
12. What should the house rules state about the tasting of food?
13. What are the four qualities of a model foodhandler listed in this text?
14. Where should employee hand-washing stations be located?
15. What is one method for supervising employees in sanitary food practices?

MORE ON THE SUBJECT

LONGREE, KARLA, and GERTRUDE G. BLAKER. *Sanitary Techniques in Food Service, 2d ed.* New York: Wiley, 1982. 271 pages. This text provides practical guidance for the foodhandler in culinary sanitation. Designed as a teaching aid for vocational training, the book contains many charts and tables depicting safe operating procedures. It also includes new material on foods prepared away from the serving premises, new equipment, changes in the food supply, and changes in micro-biological problems.

ANSWER TO A CASE IN POINT

Many employees, especially hourly workers, will go on working even if they're sick. In the foodservice field, however, this can be more hazardous than in other industries. Foodservice managers must develop a standard policy that workers who are ill will not be given foodhandling duties but will either be reassigned other tasks or sent home.

Managers must also use their powers of observation. Here, the caterer allowed the assistant to go on working even though he had a clear-cut clue that the person was sick. Also, the employee had developed an unsanitary habit that should have been corrected. *Training* could have been the key to preventing this whole incident.

Hand-washing facilities need to have things just right or employees will be discouraged from necessary and regular washing. There must be plenty of liquid or powder soap, hot—but not too hot—and cold running water, and paper towels or blow dryers. Posted directions on how to properly wash hands are helpful.

Part III
The Sanitary and
Safe Food Environment

8
Sanitary Facilities and Equipment

Maintaining standards of sanitation in an improperly designed food service is like trying to carry water in a colander: much time and energy are wasted, and little is accomplished.

A well-designed foodservice facility and sanitation go together. Proper sanitation procedures are made easier by good facilities and equipment design. Otherwise, the relatively simple jobs in cleaning and sanitizing become too difficult. When that happens, the human reactions are to spend less effort in performing them and to settle for less than desirable results. Many breakdowns in sanitation, including pest infestation, are caused by facilities that are simply too hard to keep clean.

A *plan* is at the heart of any foodservice design, and food preparation and storage areas in particular must be planned with sanitation in mind. There are a number of requirements for the sanitary design of a foodservice facility.

The first requirement for sanitary design of a food service is *cleanability*. An item or surface is cleanable if it is exposed for inspection or for cleaning without difficulty and if it is constructed so that soil can be removed effectively by normal cleaning methods. The fewer inaccessible places for soil, pests, and microorganisms to collect, the easier it will be to keep the establishment clean. The easier the establishment is to clean, the closer it will be to achieving an environment free of contamination. Any spot that cannot be readily cleaned may very soon become infested.

Various other factors also enter into sanitary design. For example, the layout of equipment must be such that it is not possible to contaminate food in preparation with refuse from dirty dishes. Toxic or potentially toxic materials may not be used for food-contact surfaces. (A *food-contact surface* is one that is normally in contact with food, or one from which food could drip or drain onto surfaces that normally contact food.) The design of utilities is also important in creating an environment where cleaning and sanitizing become easier to accomplish. Equipment should be installed so that parts that are not food-contact surfaces can not touch or drop into food.

This chapter, then, will focus on the following four subjects of importance in the creation of a sanitary environment for food:

- Construction of walls, floors, and ceilings for easy maintenance
- Arrangement and design of equipment and fixtures to comply with sanitation standards
- Design of utilities to prevent contamination and make cleaning and sanitizing easier
- Proper disposal of garbage to avoid contaminating food and attracting pests

Design for sanitation should begin when a facility is being planned. Many managers, though, inherit an established foodservice facility. They can work to improve the food environment, however, every time they remodel the facility, make repairs, or purchase new equipment. Built-in sanitation should be sought in every structural and mechanical feature.

SANITARY DESIGN AND THE LAW: PLAN REVIEW

In most communities the sanitary design of a foodservice facility is largely governed by law. Public health, building, and zoning departments may all have power to regulate construction of a facility. Many jurisdictions provide for the review and approval of plans prior to new construction or extensive remodeling. Local health authorities often provide checklists of features they consider desirable or necessary for good sanitation. A manager should provide information on sanitation requirements to the architect and/or interior designer and check to see that these are met in the plan.

Then the manager (or the architect) should take the plans for review to the health department and the agency that regulates building safety codes. *A plan review is essential.* Some health departments will provide guides to submitting plans, and the manager should ask for a copy.

Even if local laws do not require it, a manager should have plans reviewed by the local public health agency. In addition to ensuring compliance with sanitation requirements, such reviews can save time and money in the long run, not to mention frustration during cleaning time. This holds true for remodeling or conversion of a facility as well as for new construction. The plan should include the proposed layout, the mechanical plans, and lists of the construction materials of work areas and the types and models of proposed fixed equipment and facilities. Factors that must be considered when preparing a plan are the menu, the service methods and standards, the atmosphere, the hours, and the rate of patron turnover.

Before granting a permit allowing a facility to operate, the local health department will usually conduct a pre-opening inspection to ensure that all design and installation requirements have been met. At the time of the opening, another inspection will be done to check that sanitation procedures are being followed during regular operation. Chapter 14 covers inspections.

INTERIOR CONSTRUCTION DESIGN

Materials for floors, walls, and ceilings should be selected for ease in cleaning and maintenance, as well as for appearance. Heavy drapes may lend a rich feeling to a dining room, but they are dust collectors and are difficult to clean in place. Too often materials are chosen solely on the basis of appearance when first installed.

In judging any covering material, the manager should ask the following questions:

- Can it stand up to the anticipated wear and tear?
- Is it so porous or so absorbent that it will retain soil?
- Does it have a smooth surface, or is it full of crevices that will hold dirt?
- Can it be painted or otherwise finished if desired?
- Will it be serviceable over a long period, or will it require frequent refinishing, touching up, or replacement?

Flooring

The choice of floor covering—and the price range—is almost unlimited. Exhibit 8.1 lists the advantages and disadvantages of several common floor coverings. Floor coverings are usually classified on the basis of their resiliency; that is, on the basis of their ability to withstand shock. Resilient floors include asphalt, linoleum, and vinyl. In the group of nonresilient coverings are concrete, marble, quarry tiles, terrazzo, and others.

A more important consideration for the foodservice manager is the degree of absorbency or porosity; that is, the extent to which a floor covering can be permeated by liquids. When liquids are absorbed, the flooring can be damaged, and the elimination of micro-organisms becomes almost impossible. Nonabsorbent floor-covering materials should be used in all food preparation and storage areas. This requirement obviously rules out the use of carpeting, rugs, or similar materials.

Although absorbency is the most important consideration in choosing floor-covering material, the manager will naturally have some other factors in mind as well. Comfort, quietness underfoot, and ease of maintenance are all desirable qualities. The floor should not be slippery, even when wet. Resistance to grease

Exhibit 8.1   Advantages and disadvantages of common flooring materials

Material	Description	Advantages	Disadvantages
Asphalt	Mixture of asbestos, lime rock, fillers, and pigments, with an asphalt or resin binder	Resilient, inexpensive, resistant to water and acids	Buckles under heavy weight; does not wear well when exposed to grease or soap
Carpeting	Fabric covering	Resilient, absorbs sound, shock; good appearance	Not to be used in food preparation areas. Sometimes problems with maintenance elsewhere
Ceramic tiles	Clay mixed with water and fire	Nonresilient; useful for walls; nonabsorbent	Too slippery for use on floors
Concrete	Mixture of portland cement, sand, and gravel	Nonresilient; inexpensive	Porous; not recommended for use in food preparation areas
Linoleum	Mixture of linseed oil, resins and cork pressed on burlap	Resilient; nonabsorbent	Cannot withstand concentrated weight
Marble	Natural, polished stone	Nonresilient; nonabsorbent; good appearance	Expensive; slippery
Plastic	Synthetics with epoxy resins, polyester, polyurethane, and silicone	Mostly resilient; nonabsorbent	Should not be exposed to solvents or alkalies
Rubber	Rubber, possibly with asbestos fibers. Comes in rolls, sheets, and tiles	Anti-slip; resilient	Affected by oil, solvents, strong soaps and alkalies
Quarry tiles	Natural stone	Nonresilient; nonabsorbent	Slippery when wet, unless an abrasive is added

Material	Description	Advantages	Disadvantages
Terrazzo	Mixture of marble chips and portland cement	Nonresilient; nonabsorbent. If sealed properly, good appearance	Slippery when wet
Commercial-grade vinyl tiles	Compound of resins and filler and stabilized	Resilient; resistant to water, grease, oil	Water seepage between tiles can lift them, making floor dangerous and providing crevices for soil and pests
Wood	Maple, oak	Absorbent; sometimes inexpensive; good appearance	Provides pockets for dust, insects. Unacceptable for use in food preparation areas. Sealed wood may be used in serving areas

stains, cleaning-compound corrosion, wear, and color changes will make the floor long-lasting and economical.

In addition to these general requirements, each area of a food service has its own particular needs in a floor covering; common sense will often indicate what belongs where. In most operations it is the kitchen that imposes the greatest demands on floor coverings. Materials such as carpeting and sealed wood, which may be suitable for dining rooms, will be difficult to clean and will not wear well under the constant spilling and heavy use they get in the kitchen. Non-slip textures should be used in traffic areas. All floor coverings should be nontoxic. Prohibited floor coverings include sawdust, wood shavings, baked clay, and earth.

Kitchen floors may be of marble, terrazzo, natural quarry tile, asphalt tile, or other equally nonabsorbent, easily cleanable materials.

Poured seamless concrete may be used if it has been adequately sealed to minimize porosity. All floors must be kept clean and in good repair. Sealant must be renewed as needed, and lifted or cracked tiles must be replaced immediately to avoid giving soil and pests a place to collect. Areas where water is likely to collect *must* be provided with adequate floor drains.

Except in food preparation, warewashing, and storage areas, carpeting has found favor because it absorbs sound and shock. Carpeting is best limited to serving areas. Carpeting should be closely woven to facilitate cleaning. Although it is available in fibers that are easy to clean and inexpensive to maintain, carpeting does require daily vacuuming and regular shampooing to remove soil.

Exhibit 8.2   Coving is a curved, sealed edge between the floor and wall. (Source: The Food and Drug Administration)

The choice of floor covering is not the only aspect of built-in sanitation affecting floors. The way the floor is constructed is also important. Sharp corners should be avoided. Coving is often required. Coving is a curved sealed edge between the floor and wall (see Exhibit 8.2). Coving at a floor-to-wall joint makes cleaning easier, thereby preventing accumulation of bits of food that attract insects and rodents. It also eliminates hiding places for insects. Concrete, cement, and terrazzo floors should be sealed to make the floors nonabsorbent and durable and to reduce possible health hazards from cement dust.

Walls and Ceilings

Some of the same factors to be considered in judging floor coverings also apply in the selection of wall and ceiling materials. Comfort and safety are of less concern, but cleanability and noise reduction are important. Color is also significant; walls and ceilings in food preparation areas must be light in color in order to distribute light and make soil more visible for cleaning. Location should be considered when selecting wall and ceiling materials. What may work well in one part of the facility may be disastrous in another part because of factors such as splashing and heat.

A number of suitable materials are available for the walls in various parts of a food service. Ceramic tile is a popular wall covering for application in almost every area. The grouting should be smooth, waterproof, and continuous—with no holes to collect soil or to harbor vermin. Stainless steel, with its resistance to moisture and its durability, is often used in food-preparation areas where the humidity is high and wear and tear is considerable.

Painted plaster or cinder-block walls are appropriate for relatively dry areas if they are sealed with soil-resistant and easy-to-wash glossy paints—epoxy, acrylic enamel, and similar materials. Toxic paints, such as those that have a lead base, must *never* be used in a foodservice facility, since flaking and chipping can result in food contamination.

Like floors and walls, ceilings should be covered in smooth, nonabsorbent, easily cleanable materials. Those coverings that improve the distribution of light and absorb sound are the best selections. Smooth sealed plaster, plastic laminated panels, plastic coated tiles, or panels of other materials coated in plastic are all possible choices. Studs, joists, and rafters should not be exposed in food preparation areas. If exposed in other areas for decorative purposes, they should be finished for easy cleaning.

Dining rooms, bars, and lobbies ought to have an appealing appearance to patrons, but *interiors chosen only for good looks may backfire.* Drapes, sconces, pediments, and fixtures that soil easily or are hard to reach can become eyesores, as well as hiding places for dirt and vermin, as they gather dust and cobwebs.

The manager who does not specify cleanability and built-in sanitation when giving instructions to the interior decorator will very shortly regret that omission.

EQUIPMENT

The task of choosing equipment designed for sanitation has been made simpler by a number of equipment standards provided by organizations and manufacturers. The National Sanitation Foundation's Food Service Equipment Standards is one of these standards. When purchasing new equipment, the foodservice manager should specify that equipment must comply with generally accepted standards. Although it is up to the equipment manufacturer to know the standards thoroughly, the foodservice manager should be aware of their general characteristics. The National Sanitation Foundation, for example, makes the following recommendations:

1. Equipment should contain the smallest number of parts necessary to do the job effectively.
2. Equipment should be easy to disassemble and to clean. It should be possible to reach all food-contact parts without having to use tools.
3. All materials should be nontoxic and impart no significant color, odor, or taste to food. They should be nonabsorbent and should not react in any way with food products or cleaning compounds.
4. Internal corners and edges exposed to food should be rounded off. Solder is not an acceptable rounding material. External corners and angles are to be sealed and finished smooth.
5. All surfaces should be smooth and free of pits, crevices, ledges, inside threads and shoulders, bolts, and rivet heads.

6. Coating materials—especially those on food-contact surfaces—should resist cracking and chipping.
7. Waste and waste liquid should be easily removed. Beverage dispensers, for example, should have removable trays for overflows and dripped liquid.
8. Any parts that are difficult to clean should be protected from dirt.
9. Equipment should not promote unsanitary practices on the part of employees. A cantilevered kettle, for example, should be easy to clean without spillage.

Foodservice managers should look for the NSF seal of approval on commercial foodservice equipment or request documentation from the dealer that it meets NSF construction standards.

Finally, in general, *only commercial foodservice equipment should be used in foodservice operations.* Household equipment is not usually built to withstand the heavy use found in food services.

Although all equipment used in a foodservice operation should meet the standards such as those set forth by the NSF, certain items require particular attention. A discussion of some of these items follows.

Dishwashers

Joints and seams inside the tanks of automatic dishwashers must be smooth and sealed to avoid accumulating soil and water in the machine. Piping to and from the dishwasher should be as short as possible to prevent the loss of heat from the water entering the machine and to avoid creating hard-to-clean surfaces. The main structure of the machine must be raised at least six inches off the floor, or higher if necessary, to permit easy cleaning underneath.

Materials used in constructing dishwashing machines should be able to withstand wear, including the action of detergents, and not be easily penetrated by vermin. Materials in the dish zone should be smooth, corrosion-resistant, nonabsorbent, and nontoxic.

Thermometers must be mounted on each water tank of the dishwasher and situated so that they can easily be read by the operator. Proper temperature and speed requirements, as well as pressure and detergent concentration information, should be posted in a conspicuous place on or near the machine. Further information on the characteristics and effective use of mechanical dishwashing machines may be found in chapter 9.

Cutting Boards

A kitchen item as traditional as the chef's hat, the wooden cutting board can easily become a source of contamination. The wood becomes crisscrossed with cuts that are hideaways for micro-organisms. Hard rubber or plastic blocks are preferable and are required in many areas. They do not score or chip easily, thus preventing food contamination. Plus they can be sanitized in the dishwasher or manually by immersion. Where wood is used, such as in baker's tables, it must be of a nonabsorbent variety, such as hard maple.

Any cutting board should be free of seams and cracks, may not contain any toxic substances, and should not impart an odor or taste to the food being cut. Separate cutting boards should be used for raw and cooked foods in order to prevent cross-contamination.

Clean-In-Place Equipment

Some equipment, such as certain automatic ice-making machines and hand-operated beverage dispensers, are designed to be cleaned by having a sanitizing solution passed through them. These machines must be constructed so that the cleaning and sanitizing solution remains within a fixed system of tubes and pipes and cannot leak into the rest of the machine. All food-contact surfaces must be reached by the solution.

Clean-in-place equipment must be self-draining and capable of complete evacuation, to ensure that no cleaning solution is left in the machine to get into food. Some means of inspection, preferably by exposing a part of the machine, must be provided.

Refrigerators and Freezers

It is essential that refrigerators and freezers be easy to clean. Desirable features are described in chapter 5.

ARRANGEMENT AND INSTALLATION OF EQUIPMENT

The placement of equipment within the food-service establishment is usually based on considerations of economy and efficiency. Nevertheless, sanitation must also enter into decisions about layouts. Kitchens that work best establish a flow for quick, easy, and sanitary foodhandling. Equipment must be arranged so that chances for food contamination are not created and so that equipment is easily accessible and cleanable. Any small spaces or crevices created by the improper placement of equipment will be difficult to keep clean and prove attractive to pests. For example, food preparation equipment should never be placed under an open stairway. Waste processing areas and food preparation areas should be kept as far apart as possible. It is not wise to put the soiled-dish table next to the vegetable-preparation sink. Storage areas should be near the receiving area to avoid delays in storing perishable food items. An added bonus of a good layout is increased productivity (see Exhibits 8.3 and 8.4).

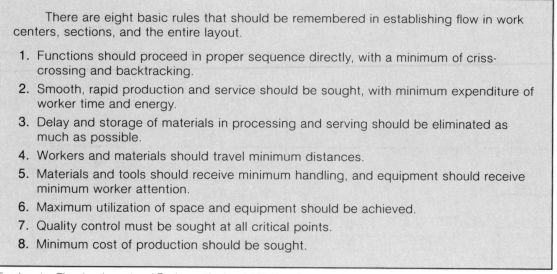

Exhibit 8.3   Considerations in layout design

There are eight basic rules that should be remembered in establishing flow in work centers, sections, and the entire layout.

1. Functions should proceed in proper sequence directly, with a minimum of criss-crossing and backtracking.
2. Smooth, rapid production and service should be sought, with minimum expenditure of worker time and energy.
3. Delay and storage of materials in processing and serving should be eliminated as much as possible.
4. Workers and materials should travel minimum distances.
5. Materials and tools should receive minimum handling, and equipment should receive minimum worker attention.
6. Maximum utilization of space and equipment should be achieved.
7. Quality control must be sought at all critical points.
8. Minimum cost of production should be sought.

Foodservice Planning: Layout and Equipment by Lendal H. Kotschevar and Margaret E. Terrell. Copyright 1961, 1977 by John Wiley & Sons, Inc. Reprinted by permission.

For the most part, arranging equipment for sanitation requires only common sense. Installing equipment, however, is a more demanding enterprise. The primary sanitation goals in installing equipment are to allow for easy cleaning and to eliminate hiding and breeding places for pests. A few general principles for installation are described in the following paragraphs.

Mobile equipment—equipment that can be moved by one person—allows easy cleaning of walls and floors and is being used with increasing frequency in foodservice operations. Equipment that is not mobile should be sealed to the wall or to adjoining equipment or should be kept far enough from the wall or adjoining equipment to permit easy cleaning. The recommended distance from the wall, or between pieces of equipment, depends on the size of the equipment and the amount of surface to be cleaned.

Equipment that is not mobile should be mounted at least six inches off the floor or sealed to a masonry base to avoid uncleanable spaces below it or behind it. If sealed to the floor, a one- to four-inch toe space should be provided.

When equipment is sealed to the floor or wall, it is important that the sealant be nontoxic. Sealant should not be used to cover up wide gaps caused by faulty construction. Such buried mistakes will ultimately be exposed, opening up new cracks to soil and insects (see Exhibit 8.5).

Some pieces of equipment may be supported by a bracket attached to the wall (see cantilever mounting, Exhibit 8.6) in such a way as to allow cleaning underneath. If equipment is designed to be free-standing, however, problems may result from mounting it on the wall. For example, a unit's rounded, splash-back top, which is quite desirable when the unit is accessible for cleaning, will form an uncleanable gully if the unit is mounted on a wall.

Exhibit 8.4   Simplified foodservice floor plan. Arrows indicate normal work-flow patterns

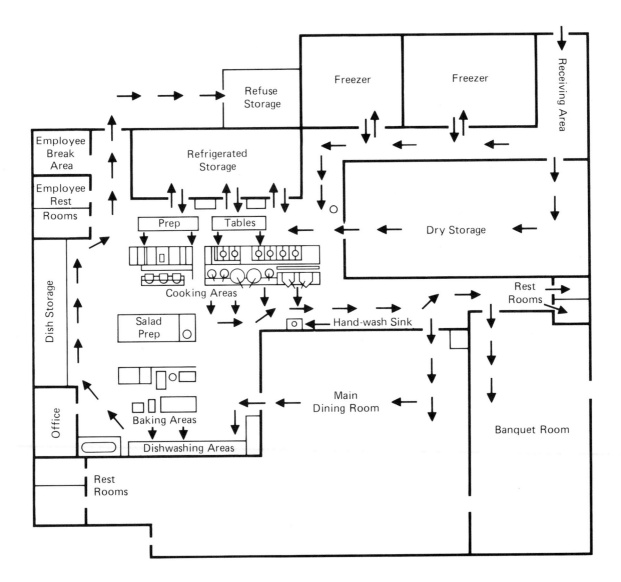

Exhibit 8.5   Acceptable floor mounting of equipment for easy cleaning

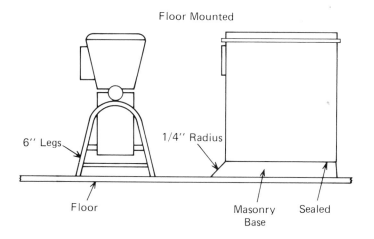

Floor Mounted

6″ Legs

1/4″ Radius

Floor

Masonry Base

Sealed

Exhibit 8.6   Wall mounting allows free access for cleaning under a large kettle.

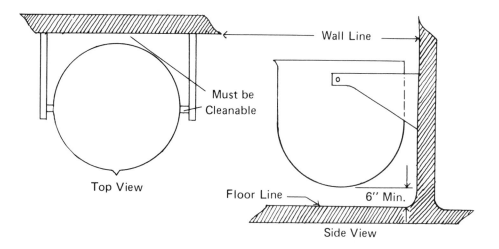

Wall Line

Must be Cleanable

Top View

Floor Line

6″ Min.

Side View

Countertop equipment can also pose cleaning problems. If an item kept on a counter cannot be moved easily by one person, it should be mounted on legs that will provide a minimum four-inch clearance between the base of the equipment and the countertop, or sealed to the countertop with a nontoxic food-grade sealant.

UTILITIES

It seems that nothing enters or leaves a food service without having some impact, however indirect, on sanitation. The provision of air, water, lighting, garbage and sewage disposal—these and other services require a great amount of planning. Two goals must be met in the sanitary design of utilities: first, utilities themselves must not contribute in any way to contamination within the food service; and second, the resources provided by utilities must be in sufficient quantity to meet the cleaning needs of the establishment.

Water Supply

Any in-town foodservice operation usually has no major problem in obtaining a safe water supply. But no matter where the facility is located, variations in water pressure may occur. A drop in water pressure can ruin the efficiency of an automatic spray-type dishwasher so that the tableware will not be cleaned as it should be. The alert manager will keep tabs on the adequacy of the water supply and take extra precautions when the pressure is reduced.

Pollution and contamination of water are not the same things. Pollution is the presence of substances not normally in the water supply that may affect the quality, odor, taste, and in some cases, the use of the water. Contamination, on the other hand, affects the safety of the water and is always dangerous.

A private water supply, such as an individual well, should be regularly inspected to determine that it is safe. Most local health departments will perform this analysis on request. If bottled water is used, it must come from sources that comply with the law. In addition, the water must be dispensed from its original container.

Hot Water

Providing enough hot water of proper temperature seems to be a universal problem for establishments serving the public; this problem is not unique to foodservice operations. Too often, new demands are placed on the hot water supply—through remodeling and expansions—without regard for the heater's capacity. Water heaters should be checked consistently to ensure their effectiveness.

Important factors to consider in evaluating a water heater include its recovery rate (the speed with which the heater produces hot water), the size of the holding tank, and the location of the heater. To maintain the right temperature for heat sanitizing by machine—180°F (82.2°C)—the installation of a booster heater near the dishwashing machine is usually necessary. If the booster is located more than five feet from the dishwasher, water will sit in the pipes and cool while the machine is off. In this instance, a recirculation device must be used to circulate the hot water through the heater to maintain the desired water temperature.

Water Treatment

Foodservice managers should also be aware of water treatment methods in their area. The amount of chemical substances in the water can affect the sanitizing capacity of dishwashers. Calcium can cause scaling on equipment. Of course, water hardness is also a problem for hot water sanitizing. If a foodservice manager knows the amount of the chemical substances added and the degree of water hardness, he or she can take steps to protect equipment and ensure effective sanitizing procedures. If problems exist, the manager may want to consult with a reputable water treatment firm to provide a solution.

Plumbing and Sewage

In almost every community in the United States, plumbing design is regulated by law—and with good reason. In few areas of food service can improper design pose such serious potential dangers. Here we cite only one of many harrowing examples. In 1967, nearly a quarter of the students and faculty at a small private college in Pennsylvania became ill with gastroenteritis contracted from the food and water at the school cafeteria. A broken water main in the kitchen had caused a drop in pressure in the system, and contaminated water had been siphoned into the water supply through cross-connections with the sewage system. Illnesses can result from food contamination or from contamination of the potable water supply. Plumbing hazards have been implicated in outbreaks of typhoid fever, dysentery, hepatitis, and other gastrointestinal illnesses. Thus, plumbing hazards represent a serious threat to sanitation efforts and the health of patrons. The major hazards, which are the results of improperly installed or maintained plumbing equipment, include cross-connections, overhead pipe leakage, and drainage-system stoppage. Knowledge of plumbing systems and their hazards cannot be left to the local plumber. Foodservice managers must take responsibility for studying their own systems and recognizing and preventing problems.

The greatest challenge to water safeness comes from cross-connections. A *cross-connection* is any physical link through which contaminants from drains, sewers, waste pipes, or other unapproved sources can enter a potable water supply. The connection may be direct, as when a drinking fountain is mistakenly connected to a line holding untreated water for fire fighting; or through a valve, as when the water supply feeds into an unapproved well for the purpose of emergency priming. Water supply outlets submerged in an unapproved source, such as a faucet located below the floodline of a sink, are also cross-connections.

The danger from cross-connections rests in the possibility of *backflow*. Backflow is simply the flow of contaminants from unapproved or undrinkable sources into potable water distributing systems. Back-siphonage is one form of backflow that can occur whenever the pressure in the water supply drops below that of the contaminating supply. For example, when lawn sprinkler usage is very high, or when a large fire is being fought, the pressure in the municipal water supply may be greatly reduced, while the pressure in the sewage system remains the same. If cross-connections exist between the two systems, contaminants from the sewage may flow into the lower-pressured potable water supply.

Backflow can also occur when a hose is attached to a faucet, as is frequently done for cleaning purposes. Say, for example, a hose is attached to the faucet of a vegetable sink. The hose is to be used to sprinkle the flowers outside, and part of the nozzle is exposed to the ground. A change in water pressure could contaminate the potable supply to the sink. If the nozzle is left lying in a basin, bucket, or pool of water, a cross-connection is established. If heavy usage elsewhere in the supply system causes the water pressure to be reduced below the atmospheric pressure—that is, the pressure of the air on the water in which the nozzle is lying—contaminated water can then be drawn through the hose and into the potable water supply. A hose should not be attached to a faucet *unless* a backflow prevention device, such as a hose bibb vacuum breaker, is also attached. It is best to use a utility sink, such as one for cleaning mops for such purposes, or have an outside water supply system installed.

Exhibit 8.7   An air gap to prevent backflow

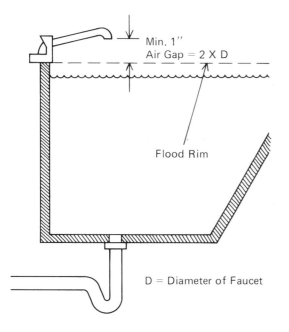

Min. 1″
Air Gap = 2 X D

Flood Rim

D = Diameter of Faucet

Backflow cannot occur without a cross-connection. If cross-connections do exist, they must be protected with backflow preventers. It is not sufficient to rely on a valve between systems—valves can leak or be left open.

The only absolutely reliable backflow preventive device is the air gap. An *air gap* is an unobstructed, vertical distance through the air that separates an outlet of the potable water supply from any potentially contaminated source. More to the point, it usually separates the faucet or source of the potable water from contaminated water or from a system from which contaminated water may enter. Exhibit 8.7 illustrates the air gap that protects the faucet in a sink. The air gap must measure twice the diameter of the outlet, and in no case may the air gap be less than one inch. Thus, if a faucet has an opening with a diameter of one inch, the air gap between it and the flood-line of the sink must be at least two inches. Other types of air gaps may be below the sink and separate waste water sources from the potable water supply (see Exhibit 8.8).

Where an air gap is not feasible—between two piping systems or where a hose is attached to a faucet—vacuum breakers, reduced pressure zone backflow preventers, or other approved devices must be installed to guard against the possibility of contamination. *Properly trapped* open sinks do not require an air gap.

Local plumbing codes vary widely on what kinds of connections are permitted and what kinds of protection are required. If you are in any doubt about the plumbing in your establishment, check with your local health department or other agencies with responsibility for water supply. Upgrade your system to meet the minimum standards.

Even systems free of cross-connections can endanger food. Overhead waste-water drain lines can leak contaminants into food and cannot be permitted. Even lines carrying potable water can be hazardous overhead, since water can condense on the pipes and drip onto food. All piping should be made of sturdy, leak-proof materials and should be serviced immediately if leaks do occur. Overhead lines are sometimes acceptable when they are part of a fire-protection system required by law, but they should still not pass directly over areas where food is likely to sit out. Putting overhead lines above false ceilings only hides the problem. Water can always leak through the ceiling.

Sufficient drains must be provided to handle the waste water produced by the operation. Any area subject to heavy water exposure, such as a kitchen cleaned by hosing down, should have its own floor drain. There should be no direct connection between the sewage system and any drains originating from sys-

Exhibit 8.8 Sinks with air gap underneath (Source: Michigan Department of Public Health)

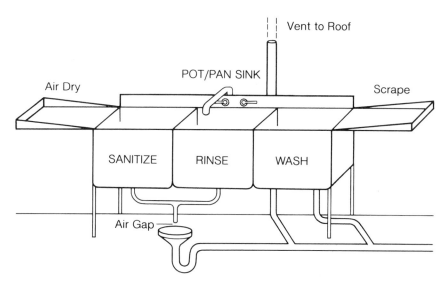

tems in which food, food equipment, or dishware is placed. Waste coming from equipment and the potable supply should be channeled into an open, accessible waste sink, floor drain, or other fixture that is properly trapped and well vented. The drainage system should be designed to keep floors from being flooded—another sanitation hazard. All food and food-contact equipment and utensils must be kept off the floor to prevent contamination by water backing up through the floor drains.

Sewage is the most dangerous reservoir of pathogens that can be found in a food service. It is absolutely essential that there be no possibility of contamination of food from such a source.

The piping of any nonpotable water system should be clearly identified so that it is readily distinguishable from piping carrying potable water.

Ventilation

Ventilation of the food preparation area has ten functions.

1. To reduce the possibility of fires resulting from accumulated grease
2. To promote the comfort of employees and patrons by reducing heat
3. To eliminate condensation, which may drip from walls and ceilings onto food
4. To reduce the accumulation of dirt in the food-preparation area
5. To prevent the concentration of toxic gases
6. To reduce odors, gases, and fumes
7. To reduce humidity and steam
8. To reduce mold growth
9. To keep insects out
10. To prevent food contamination by removing potential contaminants and keeping them from dripping onto food

Exhibit 8.9   Rate of ventilation for
cooking range (Source: Ohio Department
of Public Health)

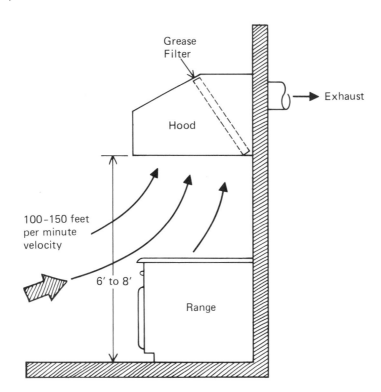

In foodservice facilities, ventilation usually involves the removal of exhaust from equipment. Relying on open windows and doors to ventilate is not only unsanitary; it is inadequate. Mechanical ventilation equipment must be used in areas for cooking, frying, grilling, and dishwashing. Exhaust hoods are frequently used over cooking equipment, steam tables, dishwashers, pot washers, and coffee urns. Hood filters or grease extractors must be tight-fitting, removable, and cleanable.

Ventilation is measured by the rate at which air changes are made in a given time period. For example, a greater ventilation velocity is required over a cooking range than over a utensil sink (see Exhibit 8.9).

Since so much air is removed through exhaust hoods, provisions must be made to take in clean air to replace it. This replacement air is called *makeup air*. Air must be replaced, without creating drafts, either through the natural flow of air through a grating or by mechanical air-changing devices (see Exhibit 8.10). All outside air intakes must be screened to prevent the entrance of insects.

In many areas of the United States, clean-air ordinances restrict the nature of exhausts vented to the outside from retail and other establishments. Any ventilation equipment leading to the outside should be designed to keep insects out. Exhaust air from cooking

Exhibit 8.10   Fresh air supply installation (*The Management of Maintenance and Engineering Systems in Hospitality*

Industries by Frank D. Borsenik. Copyright © 1979 by John Wiley & Sons, Inc. Reprinted by permission.)

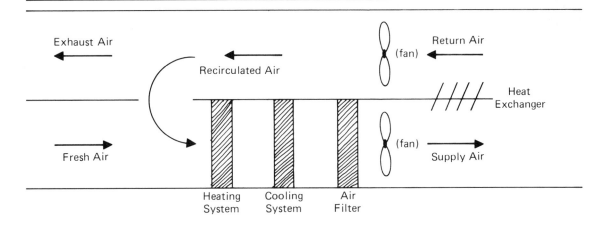

areas, which is thick with food odors, smoke, and grease, may have to be purified. It is the manager's responsibility to see that the installation is in compliance with applicable regulations.

Lighting

Good lighting in a foodservice facility generally results in improved employee work habits, easier cleaning, and a safer work environment. Building and health codes usually set minimum acceptable levels of lighting, usually based on footcandles. A *footcandle* is a unit of illumination one foot from a uniform source of light. One such code has the following minimum requirements: 20 footcandles at a point 30 inches above the floor in food-preparation areas and areas where utensils and dishes are being washed; 10 footcandles at a point 30 inches above the floor in walk-in refrigerators and dry storage areas whenever in use, and in all other areas during cleaning.

Rheostats may be useful in dining areas where a low intensity of light is desired during serving hours. Spotlights over work stations should be positioned so that the employee does not cast a shadow on the work surface.

The location of lighting fixtures is also important in minimizing contamination that may result from shattered glass bulbs or fluorescent tubes. Good location also prevents shadow formations which can hide dirt.

Protective globes or sleeves should be provided for all fixtures located over or in food preparation, storage, service, or display facilities, and in places where utensils and equipment are cleaned and stored. Shatterproof bulbs are available.

Electricity

Electricity does not pose any threat of contamination to the foodservice establishment. However, electrical supplies should be sufficient for the needs of the establishment, including cleaning needs. If carpeting is chosen for the dining room, then sufficient outlets of the proper kind are needed for vacuum cleaners or shampooers.

Electrical wiring must not be allowed to become frayed or to get wet. Electric facilities should be installed so that exposed conduits do not have to be run over exterior wall surfaces at a later time. These exposed conduits pose additional cleaning problems.

Toilet and Lavatory Accommodations

Local building and health codes usually specify how many lavatories, water closets, and urinals are required by a food service to meet the needs of both diners and employees.

It is best if separate toilet and lavatory facilities are provided for employees and diners. In any event, customers must never have to pass through the food-preparation area to reach the restrooms.

Restroom facilities must be convenient, sanitary, and adequately stocked. At least one warm-air dryer should be installed in each guest restroom. Warm-air dryers are the most sanitary means of drying the hands, but some diners may consider them an inconvenience. The inclusion of at least one blow dryer, however, may save the establishment from a health violation should the towels run out.

Requirements specifically for employee restrooms and hand-washing stations are more stringent and are covered in detail in chapter 7.

Garbage and Trash Disposal

Garbage is a dangerous commodity in a food-service operation because it attracts pests and because it can contaminate food items, equipment, and utensils. A few general rules on handling garbage deserve mention here.

1. Garbage containers must be leakproof, water-tight, easily cleanable, pest-proof, and durable. These containers should be made of metal or an approved plastic. Plastic bags and wet-strength paper bags may be used to line these containers. Containers kept outdoors or in food-preparation areas must have tight-fitting lids. These containers should be kept covered when not in use. There should be a sufficient number of containers for the refuse normally created.

2. Garbage must not be allowed to accumulate anywhere but in regular garbage containers.

3. Garbage should be removed from food-preparation areas as soon as possible and should be disposed of often enough to prevent the formation of odor and the attraction of pests.

4. Garbage storage areas, inside or outside, should be large enough for the amount of garbage that will accumulate. Inside garbage storage areas should be easily cleanable and pest-proof. If the operation produces a lot of garbage, or if long holding times are anticipated, it may be wise to refrigerate the indoor storage area.

5. Garbage and refuse containers, including dumpsters and compactor systems located outside, should be easily cleanable and stored on or above a smooth surface of nonabsorbent material like concrete.

6. Soiled garbage containers from inside and outside areas should be cleaned frequently to prevent insect and rodent problems. The containers should be cleaned thoroughly on the inside and the outside.

7. An area equipped with hot and cold water and a floor drain must be provided for washing garbage cans. This area must be located so that food in preparation or storage will not be contaminated when the cans are washed.

The volume of trash found in a food service can be reduced through the use of pulpers or mechanical compactors. Pulpers grind refuse into small parts that are flushed with water. The water is then removed so that the processed solid wastes can be trucked away. Mechanical compacting of dry bulky wastes, such as cans and cartons, is particularly valuable in establishments that are cramped for space. This process reduces garbage volume to as little as one-fifth of its original bulk. Use of a compactor requires access to a drain, water for cleaning, and usually a power source.

Incineration of burnable trash and garbage is permitted in some areas, provided that the incinerator is constructed so as to meet all federal and local clean-air standards. Garbage, because of its high moisture content, does not burn very well. If a food service has a large amount of burnable trash that justifies the use of an incinerator, the manager will usually need to obtain a permit before using an old incinerator or installing a new one. Incinerators should never be used as temporary collection containers for waste.

The manager should give sanitation high priority whenever planning a new food service or remodeling or expanding an old one. In most communities, plans for new construction or extensive remodeling are subject to review and approval by local regulatory agencies.

The manager can seek built-in sanitation in three aspects of the facility: construction of floors, walls, and ceilings; choice and placement of equipment; and design of utilities.

Avoid the inclination to select floor, wall, and ceiling coverings solely on the basis of good appearance. In the long run it will pay off to consider their cleanability and durability.

Much the same can be said of equipment to be used anywhere in a foodservice operation. Crevices or surfaces that catch dirt can harbor micro-organisms as well. Equipment should be placed so that all areas around and under it are accessible to cleaning apparatus.

A food service with built-in sanitation will also have utilities designed for easy cleaning and freedom from the danger of contamination. Included in this category are water supply, plumbing and sewage installations, ventilation and lighting systems, toilet facilities, and garbage-disposal systems.

SUMMARY

The food service that is difficult to clean will in all probability not be cleaned well. Sanitation efforts will be greatly facilitated if the establishment is designed and equipped with easy cleaning, or built-in sanitation, in mind.

A CASE IN POINT

In mid-August of 1970, two patients at an Iowa hospital were diagnosed as suffering from a form of salmonellosis—the disease caused by ingestion of *Salmonella* organisms. Although investigators did not realize it at the time, both patients had eaten chicken at the same restaurant. One of them, in fact, was a busboy there.

During September of the same year, nearly 250 cases of salmonellosis were reported in the area. Victims suffered from diarrhea, fever, nausea, and, on occasion, vomiting. All cases were attributed to food consumed at the restaurant in question. Interestingly enough, only those guests who had eaten sliced roast beef, ham, or prime rib at the restaurant became ill during September. Moreover, a high percentage of the employees working in the banquet rooms of the restaurant became ill, but the busboy mentioned earlier was the only employee from the buffet area who suffered from salmonellosis. What was most puzzling, though, was that the level of sanitation in the restaurant was generally quite high. Eventually it was found that *Salmonella* organisms from contaminated meat were sequestered in a hard-to-clean meat slicer serving the banquet area.

Investigators concluded that the *Salmonella* organisms had probably been brought to the restaurant on the chicken that made the first two victims ill. Workers throughout the restaurant then became the carriers of the *Salmonella* organisms. Cross-contamination probably resulted from the meat slicer being used for different food products and not being thoroughly cleaned between uses. As a result of the general high level of sanitation in the restaurant, no outbreaks among patrons occurred until later in the fall.

What is the lesson to be learned from this case?
Why do you think people became ill from eating the sliced roast beef, ham, or prime rib?

STUDY QUESTIONS

1. What is meant by cleanability? What is its importance in a foodservice establishment?
2. What is the most important sanitation requirement to consider in choosing a floor-covering material? Name several flooring materials that meet this requirement.
3. List at least three of the general characteristics recommended by the National Sanitation Foundation in their standards for foodservice equipment.
4. What is a food-contact surface?
5. How far off the floor should the main structure of a dishwasher or other item of equipment be? Why?
6. What factors should be remembered in arranging and installing immobile equipment?
7. Define the following terms: cross-connection; backflow.
8. How can backflow be prevented?
9. List at least three functions of ventilation in a food service.
10. What danger can arise from overhead water or waste lines?
11. What requirements must be met by a sanitary garbage container?

MORE ON THE SUBJECT

AMERICAN INSTITUTE OF MAINTENANCE. *Floor Care Materials.* Glendale, Ca., 1973, 71 pages. Also *Floor Care Guide.* 1973, 79 pages. These publications provide guides to floor cleaning and floor materials.

KOTSCHEVAR, LENDAL H., and MARGARET E. TERRELL. *Foodservice Planning: Layout and Equipment.* Rev. ed. New York: Wiley, 1977. 607 pages. The book offers a complete guide to planning the layout of a food service and provides practical tips for designers and managers.

NATIONAL SANITATION FOUNDATION. *Foodservice Equipment Standards.* Ann Arbor, Michigan, 1978, 288 pages. All NSF standards concerning foodservice equipment are gathered together in this single volume. This book is the authoritative guide for managers and designers.

OHIO DEPARTMENT OF HEALTH. *A Guide to Food Service Operation Planning.* Revised 1977. Ohio Department of Health Publication Number 2115.32. 20 pages. This brief, readable guide contains numerous helpful illustrations and photographs.

U.S. ENVIRONMENTAL PROTECTION AGENCY. Office Of Water Programs. Water Supply Division. *Cross-Connection Control Manual.* Washington, D.C., 1973, 57 pages. This education pamphlet explains the physical principles behind backflow and describes various means of preventing its occurrence. It includes a number of chilling but informative examples of the dangers of cross-connections.

ANSWER TO A CASE IN POINT

Foodservice equipment must be purchased with cleanability considered. If it is not, its very use invites poor sanitation. Meat slicers may be difficult to keep clean. For one thing, removing the blades can be dangerous if done incorrectly. It is a job that many workers prefer to leave undone. Yet a failure to clean slicers properly can result in cross-contamination of foods. Although *Salmonella* organisms are destroyed by high heat, foods like sliced roast beef, sliced ham, and prime rib are often served without their being reheated to high temperatures. Foodservice equipment purchased without cleanability in mind can become efficient vehicles of cross-contamination. The manager must seek ease of cleaning in all equipment for the sake of sanitation and employee safety. The manager must also see to it that rules of sanitation are enforced, whether those rules are easy to carry out or not.

This case reminds us of another important fact: often carriers of disease organisms do not reveal symptoms of the disease. Keeping people who are obviously ill away from the job does not eliminate the need for good personal hygiene and sanitation habits on the part of all workers.

9
Cleaning and Sanitizing

At this point in our study of sanitation, we are really doing quite well. We have learned how to purchase safe food, how to store it out of the danger zone, cook it thoroughly, garnish it attractively, and serve it to appreciative customers in a safe, sanitary, well-designed establishment. Unfortunately, no matter how delicious the food, the customers will not really clean their plates. The tableware—as well as the pots, pans, utensils, and equipment used to turn out culinary marvels—has been contaminated.

Fortunately, a whole arsenal of cleaning and sanitizing procedures and products is at our disposal to ward off this contamination. All we need to do is find out what these procedures and products are and how to apply them properly. The following topics are discussed:

- Cleaning as the result of the application of a cleaning agent under sufficient pressure for an adequate period of time
- Sanitizing through the use of heat or the application of chemical compounds
- Mechanical and manual methods for cleaning and sanitizing
- Storage of clean and sanitary equipment and utensils

CLEAN *AND* SANITARY

A clean *and* sanitary establishment is the result of a planned program, properly supervised and followed on schedule. However, when the going gets rough and workers are rushed trying to meet the needs of customers, correct practices are often neglected. Only a manager who is knowledgeable and alert can prevent these breakdowns in good sanitation discipline. He or she must know how a cleaning/sanitizing job should be done, instruct workers accordingly, and then see to it that instructions are carried out.

The concepts of "clean" and "sanitary" have already been explained. The distinction is worth repeating because of its importance to cleaning and sanitizing operations. *Cleaning* is the removal of matter from a surface where it does not belong. *Sanitizing* is the reduction to safe levels of the number of disease-causing bacteria. The materials and procedures used in these two processes are *not* identical.

Cleaning and sanitizing form the basis of good housekeeping and together result in this fundamental foodservice sanitation rule: *All food-contact surfaces must be cleaned and sanitized after every use.* This rule applies not only to tableware and pots and pans, but also to stationary equipment used in the preparation of food and even to equipment used in cleaning other food-contact surfaces. All surfaces coming into contact with food (whether plates, pots, or potato peelers) must be cleaned and sanitized after each use, after any interruption of service during which they may have become contaminated, or at regularly scheduled intervals if they are in constant use.

CLEANING PRINCIPLES

Effective cleaning is a lot more complicated than the simple combination of soap, water, and elbow grease. As one writer put it, "Cleaning is a practical application of chemistry."

Cleaning takes place when a cleaning agent contacts a soiled surface under sufficient pressure and for a long enough time to penetrate the soil and remove it. Many cleaning agents are designed to be dissolved in water, while others such as powders used for the dry cleaning of some floors are meant to be used "as is."

Exhibit 9.1   Measures of water hardness

	Soft	Moderately Hard	Hard	Very Hard
Grains per gallon	0.0–3.5	3.6–7.0	7.1–10.5	10.6–
Parts per million or milligrams per liter	0.0–60	61–120	121–180	More than 180

Source: U.S. Geological Survey

Factors in the Cleaning Process

Many variables affect the outcome of the cleaning process. These variables should be taken into account before the process is started.

1. *Type and condition of soil.* Soils and stains can be classified as protein-based (blood, egg); grease- or oil-type (margarine, animal fat); and acid or alkaline (tea, dust, perspiration). In addition, the condition of the soil—fresh, ground-in, soft, dried, or baked on— affects the ease of removal.

2. *Type of water.* If water is used as part of the cleaning process, it must of course be potable. Dirty water limits the effectiveness of the cleaning agent.

   Water hardness—the amount of mineral impurities in the water—also affects cleaning properties. Water containing calcium, magnesium, and iron is "hard" water. Water hardness is measured in parts per million or grams (or grains) per gallon (see Exhibit 9.1). Cleaning in hard water is more difficult. The mineral deposits may interact with the detergent causing a sticky substance that leaves a film on dishes. Also, hard water causes "scale," or lime deposits, to form on equipment. These deposits can render some detergents ineffective. Some detergents are formulated for use in hard-water areas, but other detergents may be made ineffective by hard water.

3. *Temperature of water.* In general, the higher the temperature of the water in which the cleaning agent is dissolved, the faster the chemical reaction and the more effective the cleaning action. The exceptions to this rule, of course, are chemical cleaning agents specifically designed to be used in cold water.

   For manual cleaning, water should be as hot as the person working with it can stand. In manual, hot-water cleaning the minimum temperature should be about 75°F (23.9°C) or a maximum of 110°F (43.3°C). Machine dishwashing requirements will vary. Generally in a machine using hot water, the water supply for pre-wash should be at 85°F (29.4°C) to 110°F (43.3°C), and the wash cycle temperatures between 140° and 160°F (60° and 71.1°C). Chemical sanitizing dishwashers usually use water between 120° and 140°F (48.9° and 60°C) during the wash cycle.

4. *Surface being cleaned.* The surface may be hard or soft, easily damaged or corrosion-resistant. Different surfaces demand different cleaning agents. Cleaning should be considered when the equipment is purchased.

5. *Type of cleaning agent.* Soap, for example, may leave a greasy film under certain conditions; abrasives may scratch some surfaces. Some cleaners are only used for special purposes. For example, a mildly alkaline cleaner may be used for washing painted walls, while a highly alkaline cleaner may be used for hot-water dishwashing machines. Acid cleaners may be used to remove lime buildup from dishwashers.

6. *Pressure to be applied.* In many cleaning operations, pressure (scouring action) consists primarily of "elbow grease" or the friction from a brush or other cleaning implement. The purpose of pressure is simply to remove the loosened soil from the surface of the object. Obviously, the amount of pressure will affect the success of the outcome. Other sources of pressure include the spray action in mechanical dishwashers and the turbulence created when water is forced through equipment with clean-in-place systems.

7. *Duration of treatment.* All other factors being equal, cleaning effectiveness increases with the time of exposure to the cleaning agent.

Cleaning Agents

The role of a cleaning agent is to loosen soil from the surface of the object being cleaned and keep it "suspended" so that it is not redeposited on the item. Broadly defined, a cleaning agent is anything—steam, water, soap, or sand—that removes soil. Ordinarily, however, the word *refers* to chemical compounds specifically formulated for special cleaning purposes—for use on floors or in dishwashing machines, for removing mineral deposits, and so on.

A particular cleaning agent should be selected for its special cleaning properties. A compound that is powerful in one situation may prove totally ineffective in another. In addition to being effective and compatible with its intended use, a cleaning agent should fit the needs of the facility. It must be stable while being used, noncorrosive, nontoxic or safe when applied as directed, and economical. Since some cleaning agents are more effective then others, the quantities required to do a job should be considered in making cost comparisons.

It's wise to consult suppliers in determining which chemical compounds are suitable for specific needs. The advice of a foodservice operator down the street may not be dependable. Cleaning agents that work well in one place may not be suitable in another.

Cleaning agents may be divided into three categories: detergents, abrasive cleaners, and acid cleaners.

Detergents

Soap is the oldest manufactured detergent and is still one of the most effective in removing soil. Unfortunately, soap reacts with the mineral salts in hard water to form insoluble precipitates, or what is familiar to most people as "bathtub ring." This fact, plus soap's poor rinsability, limits its use to hand washing in the foodservice industry.

For most purposes, including the cleaning of food-contact surfaces, soap has been replaced by synthetic detergents. Synthetic detergents have been designed to meet almost any cleaning requirement. They can work in hard water without difficulty, are easily rinsable, and can be high- or low-sudsing. In addition, they are chemically compatible with many other compounds, with the result that a single product can be formulated to answer several types of cleaning needs.

All detergents contain surface-active agents or surfactants. *Surfactants* reduce surface tension at the points where the detergent meets the soiled surface, allowing the detergents to penetrate quickly and get on with the job of loosening and dispersing the soil.

Most synthetic detergents used in foodservice operations are built up by the addition of alkaline salts. General-purpose detergents are mildly alkaline and are effective for removal of soil from floors, walls, ceilings, and most equipment and utensils. Heavy-duty detergents are highly alkaline and are reserved for use in removing wax and baked-on grease. Detergents used in dishwashing machines are also highly alkaline.

Most packaged detergents are effective if used as directed. They can be worse than worthless, however, if used under the wrong conditions or for the wrong purposes. Handwashing soap will not delime a dishmachine no matter how much of it is applied.

All label instructions should be read for information regarding appropriate uses, concentrations, temperature requirements, and possible hazards; and if this information is not clear, the supplier should be contacted.

CAUTION: Under no circumstances should a foodservice manager or employee attempt to formulate his or her own detergents. Unless the workers know exactly what they are doing—unless they have the knowledge of a trained chemist—the result could be very dangerous to employees and patrons and damaging to the facility. At best, the compound produced will probably not achieve the desired result. By the same token one type of detergent should never be substituted for another. Using a machine dishwashing detergent for manual washing is dangerous.

Acid Cleaners

The detergents described previously are alkaline in nature. However, there are certain types of soil that are not affected by alkaline cleaners. The lime encrustations in dishwashing machines, the rust stains that develop in washrooms, and the tarnish that darkens copper and brass are examples. Acid cleaners—in formulas that sometimes also contain detergents—are used for these cleaning purposes.

The kind and strength of the acid varies with the purpose of the cleaner. Whatever their strength, acid cleaners must be selected and applied carefully lest they damage the surface being cleaned or the skin of the user.

Abrasive Cleaners

Sometimes soil is attached so firmly to a surface that alkaline or acid cleaners will not work. In these cases a cleaner containing a scouring agent—usually finely ground feldspar or silica—is used to attack the soil. Worn, pitted porcelain, rusty metals, or badly soiled floors benefit from the use of abrasive cleaners.

Abrasives should be used with caution in a foodservice facility. Since they may mar smooth surfaces, especially plexiglass or plastic, abrasives should be applied with care to food-contact surfaces.

SANITIZING PRINCIPLES

After a surface has been thoroughly cleaned, it may be sanitized. In the case of a food-contact surface, it *must* be sanitized. The term "sanitized," you will recall, means that the bacterial contamination of an object or surface has been reduced to a safe level. It is a step above "clean"—which is merely the absence of soil—but a step below "sterile"—which is the absence of all living organisms.

A conscientious manager may wonder, "Why don't we just sterilize everything and be on the safe side?" The answer is that sterilization is quite expensive, and unless all persons involved have highly communicable diseases, it is not necessary.

At the other extreme, the pot washer may mutter, "Why do I have to sanitize this pot? We're just going to cook in it, and the heat from the cooking process will kill the bacteria." There is no guarantee that the heat involved in cooking will heat all parts of the item to a high enough temperature for a long enough time to effectively sanitize it. Also there is no assurance that the pot will be used for cooking at all. It may be used for mixing when no heat treatment is involved.

Sanitization can be accomplished in two ways: either the object may be heated to a high enough temperature to kill micro-organisms; or it can be treated with a chemical sanitizing compound. In either case the object must be thoroughly clean and completely rinsed in order for the sanitizing process to work. Caked-on soils not removed by cleaning, for example, may shield bacteria from a sanitizing solution. Sanitization, in short, is no substitute for good cleaning.

Heat Sanitization

Exposing a clean object to sufficiently high heat for a sufficient length of time will sanitize it. Generally, the higher the heat, the shorter the time required to kill harmful organisms. The purpose of heat sanitizing is to bring the food-contact surface to a temperature that will kill most harmful micro-organisms, usually 162° to 165°F (72.2° to 73.9°C) or over. Heat sanitization can be used in either mechanical or manual warewashing operations.

One method of heat sanitizing is by immersing an object in water maintained at a temperature of 170°F (76.7°C) for *no less* than 30 seconds. Water at this temperature can also be run through equipment designed for cleaning in place, provided that the water can be kept hot enough and that a thermometer is mounted at the outlet of the system. Manual immersion may be accomplished by use of racks to lower the items into the water. For clean-in-place applications, the hot water should run through the machine for as long a time as the manufacturer's operating manual indicates.

The most common method of hot-water sanitizing is to use very hot water in the rinse cycle of a high-temperature dishwashing machine. Here the rinse must be sprayed on the dishes at a certain volume and pressure for a prescribed period of time. The water temperature should be at least 180°F (82.2°C), but should not be more than 200°F (93.3°C). At higher temperatures, the water will vaporize before sanitizing the dishes.

Still another means of heat sanitization is through the use of live, additive-free steam. This method may be used on equipment that is too large to be immersed, provided that the equipment is capable of confining the steam. Steam used on assembled equipment should be at a temperature of at least 200°F (93.3°C). It is important to note, however, that the temperature at the surface of the object being sanitized is what counts, not the temperature of the steam in the line. Water or steam may be quite hot when it leaves its source, but it will cool very quickly in contact with a cool object.

Chemical Sanitization

Sanitization can be achieved through the use of chemical compounds capable of destroying disease-causing bacteria. Chemical sanitizers have found wide acceptance in the foodservice industry. They are rigorously regulated by the U.S. Environmental Protection Agency, which registers them as pesticides. Consequently, any product that uses the word "sanitize" on its label and bears an EPA registration number will, if used as directed, reduce bacteria to levels acceptable to most local regulatory agencies.

EPA labeling requirements are quite strict, so the user can count on the information on the label of the sanitizer to be accurate and complete. This information will include what concentrations to use, data on minimum effectiveness, and warnings of possible health hazards.

Chemical sanitizing is done in two ways: either by immersing an object in the correct concentration of sanitizer for one minute; or by rinsing, swabbing, or spraying *double the usual* recommended concentration of sanitizer on the surface to be sanitized. There are exceptions: quaternary ammonium (quats) sanitizers may not be sprayed at more than recommended amounts on food-contact surfaces.

The strength of the sanitizing solution must be tested frequently, since the sanitizing agent is depleted in the process of killing bacteria. The solution must be changed when it is no longer effective. Test kits are usually provided free of charge by the sanitizer manufacturer for this purpose.

Some sanitizing agents are toxic to humans as well as to bacteria; they therefore are acceptable for use only on nonfood-contact surfaces. Others may not be toxic, but they impart undesirable flavors and odors and are therefore unfit for foodservice use. Managers should check to see that sanitizers in this category have not been selected.

Kinds of Sanitizers

Three of the most common chemicals used in sanitizing are chlorine, iodine, and quaternary ammonium (quats). The properties of these agents differ somewhat.

Chlorine and iodine compounds have some properties in common. They will kill most bacteria if used correctly and are not greatly affected by water hardness. They will lose effectiveness in water that is too alkaline. Because of this last factor, it is necessary to apply a thorough rinse to items that have been cleaned with general-purpose or heavy-duty detergents, which are usually alkaline, before applying the sanitizers. These compounds may be affected by adverse temperatures. Both compounds are relatively non-irritating to skin.

There are also some differences between chlorine and iodine compounds. Iodine compounds (iodophors) have a built-in indicator of concentration—the stronger the solution, the deeper its amber color. Iodine compounds may be selective in their ability to kill certain micro-organisms. Chlorine compounds are more likely than iodophors to attack metal. Some chlorine compounds may leave a mild odor on dishes if the items are not completely clean.

Quats are relatively noncorrosive and are effective in both acid and alkaline solutions. They are generally non-irritating to skin. Some quats may not be compatible with certain soaps or detergents. The bacteria-killing power of a particular quaternary ammonium compound may be limited, but a blend of quat compounds can dispatch a great variety of micro-organisms. A high degree of water hardness (over 500 parts per million) will make some quats less effective. Quats may not be sprayed at double the recommended amounts. The FDA specifies a concentration of 200 ppm. Therefore, quats should probably not be used for spray- or swab-sanitizing of food-contact surfaces. Since quaternary ammonium compounds are manufactured according to many different formulas, it is necessary to read the label to make sure that the particular formula in question suits the sanitizing needs of the operation. Many quats are not FDA approved for foodservice operations, and many state and local health departments do not accept quats as sanitizers.

A number of factors affect the action of chemical sanitizers and should be considered by management before use.

1. *Contact.* In order for the sanitizer to kill a sufficient number of micro-organisms, the sanitizer must make contact with the item for an amount of time specified by the manufacturer. Package instructions should not be short-circuited no matter what the method of application used.
2. *Selectivity.* Chemical sanitizers may be selective in their capacity to kill certain micro-organisms. Both iodine and quaternary compounds are somewhat selective.

3. *Concentration.* Proper concentration of sanitizers is a critical factor. Concentrations below the required minimum will result in a failure to sanitize equipment and utensils. Concentrations higher than necessary can cause taste and odor problems, are a waste of money, a health department violation, and can even poison someone. Test kits are available for most sanitizers. It is essential to follow the manufacturer's instructions for each type of sanitizer and check the strength often.

4. *Temperature.* The temperature of the solution is very crucial. The water must be warm enough to increase the activity of the solution but not be too warm. A minimum temperature of 75°F (23.9°C) is required. Generally, sanitizers work best at temperatures between 75° and 120°F (23.9° and 48.9°C). At higher temperatures chlorine compounds may corrode some metal items and chlorine and iodine compounds may leave the solution.

5. *Solution pH.* The pH level of some detergents can affect some sanitizers. The manager must check to see that the detergent residue is thoroughly rinsed off prior to sanitizing.

Exhibit 9.2 summarizes the properties of chlorine, iodine, and quaternary ammonium sanitizers. As the exhibit indicates, concentrations necessary to kill bacteria are higher for clean-in-place and power-spray applications than for the immersion method.

Some sanitizers are blended with detergents to make *detergent-sanitizers.* These products will sanitize effectively, but sanitization must still be a separate step from cleaning. In other words, the same product must be used twice—once to clean and once to sanitize. In general, detergent-sanitizers are more expensive than regular detergents and are more limited in their applications than detergents. Some are not meant to be used on food-contact surfaces.

MACHINE CLEANING AND SANITIZING

Dishwashing machines, properly operated and maintained, can be reliable in removing soil and bacteria from tableware and kitchen implements. Because of this factor and the needs of high-volume operations, the foodservice industry has increasingly moved to the use of dishwashing machines, both hot-water and chemical-sanitizing types.

Purchase of dishwashing equipment can represent a sizeable investment, so individual requirements should be carefully considered before a decision is made. A successful machine cleaning and sanitizing program requires

- Sufficient water supplies for the entire washing operation, including hot-water sanitizing
- An efficient layout in the dishwashing area to utilize personnel and machine to best advantage and to prevent recontamination of clean dishes by soiled ones (see Exhibit 9.3)
- Workers who know how to operate and maintain the equipment, and who are knowledgeable about the correct use of required detergents and other chemicals
- A protected dish-handling and storage area to maintain sanitary dishware
- Regular inspection of the finished product—the washed and sanitized items—to ensure that the machine is performing up to par
- Regular inspection of the whole operation by management to make certain that correct procedures are being followed

Exhibit 9.2   Chemical sanitizing agents

	Chlorine	Iodine	Quaternary Ammonia
Minimum Concentration			
—*For Immersion*	50 parts per million (ppm)	12.5 ppm	200 ppm
—*For Power Spray or Cleaning in Place*	100 ppm	25 ppm	
Temperature of Solution	75°F/23.9°C+	75°–120°F/ 23.9°–48.9°C Iodine will leave solution at 120°F/ 48.9°C	75°F/23.9°C+
Time for Sanitizing			
—*For Immersion*	1 minute	1 minute	1 minute; however, some products require longer contact time; read label.
—*For Power Spray or Cleaning in Place*	Follow manufacturer's instructions.	Follow manufacturer's instructions.	Follow manufacturer's instructions.

Types of Dishwashing Machines

Dishwashing machines vary widely in size, style, and capabilities; however, they fall into two basic types. There are high-temperature machines that use hot water as the sanitizing agent in the final rinse and chemical-sanitizing machines that use a chemical agent for sanitizing.

Mechanical dishwashing machines come in all sizes and configurations and in a variety of time and temperature combinations to achieve the same results. Selecting the size and type of machine depends upon the nature and volume of the utensils to be cleaned and upon dishwashing schedules. Since such a machine is a big investment, the operator/manager needs to consult with manufacturers' representatives to learn which machine matches his or her needs.

High-Temperature Machines

Effective hot water sanitizing by a machine depends on several factors. First, the volume of water passed over the item must be of sufficient velocity to remove soil. Second, the amount of time the item is exposed to the high

	Chlorine	Iodine	Quaternary Ammonia
pH (Detergent Residue Raises pH of Solution)	Must be below pH 10.	Must be below pH 5.5.	Most effective around pH 7 but varies with compound.
Corrosiveness	Corrosive to some substances.	Noncorrosive.	Noncorrosive.
Response to Organic Contaminants in Water	Quickly inactivated.	Made less effective.	Not easily affected.
Response to Hard Water	Not affected.	Not affected.	Some compounds inactivated but varies with formulation; read label. Hardness over 500 ppm is undesirable for some quats.
Indication of Strength of Solution	Test kit required.	Amber color indicates effective solution, but test kits must also be used.	Test kit required. Follow label instructions closely.

temperature is important. Finally, the temperature of the water for the final rinse must be at least 180°F (82.2°C). Since most general-purpose water heaters do not bring water to such high temperatures, a *booster heater* is usually required to bring water to 180°F (82.2°C). If obtaining a *constant* supply of hot water is a problem, the operator should consider buying a chemical-sanitizing machine. High-temperature machines include the following models:

1. *A single-tank, stationary-rack type with doors.* This machine will hold a rack of dishes that may either be moved during washing on a conveyor or remain stationary. Dishes are washed by detergent and water from below and sometimes from above. The wash cycle is followed by a hot water spray.

2. *The conveyor machine.* The conveyor moves the dishes through the various cycles including washing, rinsing, and sanitizing.

3. *A carousel or merry-go-round type.* A conveyor, multi-tank machine, moves a rack of dishes on a conveyor or dishes

Exhibit 9.3 Efficient working space for mechanical dishwashing function (*Programmed Cleaning Guide*. Copyright © 1984 by The Soap and Detergent Association. Reprinted by permission.)

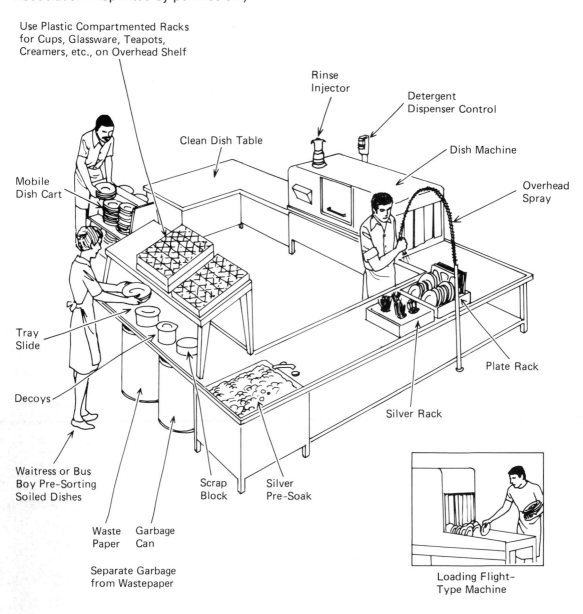

Use Plastic Compartmented Racks for Cups, Glassware, Teapots, Creamers, etc., on Overhead Shelf

Rinse Injector

Detergent Dispenser Control

Clean Dish Table

Dish Machine

Mobile Dish Cart

Overhead Spray

Tray Slide

Plate Rack

Decoys

Silver Rack

Waitress or Bus Boy Pre-Sorting Soiled Dishes

Scrap Block

Silver Pre-Soak

Waste Paper

Garbage Can

Separate Garbage from Wastepaper

Loading Flight-Type Machine

on built-in racks. Dishes must be removed after the final rinse, or they will continue to go through the machine.

4. *A flight-type.* This machine has several tanks with conveyors that hold dishes in place with pegs or bars, making racking unnecessary.

Temperatures during the wash cycle may vary from machine to machine, but typically they should be between 140° and 160°F (60° and 71.1°C), temperatures necessary to dissolve grease and loosen soil. For high-temperature machines with a pre-wash cycle, the temperature during that cycle should be between 80° and 110°F (26.7° and 43.3°C). These are the minimum temperatures needed to remove gross soil and particles of food.

Chemical-Sanitizing Machines

Low-temperature machines are used for chemical sanitizing. Effective chemical sanitizing requires that the water temperature be sufficient to activate the sanitizing chemical but not so hot as to cause it to leave the solution.

The water temperatures for chemical sanitizing are typically between 120° and 140°F (48.9° and 60°C). It is important that the proper concentration of the sanitizing chemical be used. The solution should be automatically dispensed into the final rinse water. There are two kinds of chemical sanitizing dishwashing machines.

1. *The batch-type machine.* This machine combines the wash cycle and rinse cycle in a single tank. Each cycle is timed, and the machine automatically dispenses both the detergent and the sanitizing chemical.

2. *The door-type recirculating machine.* This machine is similar to the batch-type machine. The major difference is that the door-type machine is not completely drained of water between cycles, so that the wash water is diluted with fresh water and reused from cycle to cycle.

Whatever the type of dishwashing machine, the following requirements should ordinarily be met:

- Thermometers should be provided indicating the temperature of the water in each tank of the machine and showing the temperature of the final rinse water as it enters the manifold.

- Dish tables of adequate size should be provided to handle both soiled or cleaned equipment, tableware, and utensils.

- Unless the machine has a pre-wash cycle, items to be cleaned must be scraped or soaked to remove food debris before being washed in the machine.

- In compartmented machines (except for the door-type), the rinse water tanks should be protected by some device that prevents the flow of wash water into the rinse water.

- In conveyor-type machines, conveyor speed should be accurately timed to make sure the items receive proper exposure.

- Spray-type dishwashing machines should come equipped with some device that allows the operator to check on the pressure of the wash and final rinse water.

- All dishwashing machines should be cleaned at least once a day or more frequently when the circumstances warrant.

Problems and Cures

Although dishwashing machines can be the most reliable way to clean and sanitize tableware and utensils, they can also be the source of innumerable problems if installed or operated incorrectly. Exhibit 9.4 summarizes some of these problems, with possible causes and cures.

Exhibit 9.4 Dishwashing problems and cures

Symptom	Possible Cause	Suggested Cure
Soiled Dishes	Insufficient detergent.	Use enough detergent in wash water to ensure complete soil removal and suspension.
	Wash water temperature too low.	Keep water temperature within recommended ranges to dissolve food residues and to facilitate heat accumulation (for sanitation).
	Inadequate wash and rinse times.	Allow sufficient time for wash and rinse operations to be effective. (Time should be automatically controlled by timer or by conveyor speed.)
	Improperly cleaned equipment.	Unclog rinse and wash nozzles to maintain proper pressure-spray pattern and flow conditions. Overflow must be open. Keep wash water as clean as possible by pre-scraping dishes, etc. *Change water in tanks at proper intervals.*
	Improper racking	Check to make sure racking or placement is done according to size and type. Silverware should always be pre-soaked and placed in silver holders without sorting. Avoid masking or shielding.
Films	Water hardness.	Use an external softening process. Use proper detergent to provide internal conditioning. Check temperature of wash and rinse water. Water maintained above recommended temperature ranges may precipitate film.
	Detergent carryover.	Maintain adequate pressure and volume of rinse water, or worn wash jets or improper angle of wash spray might cause wash solution to splash over into final rinse spray.
	Improperly cleaned or rinsed equipment.	Prevent scale buildup in equipment by adopting frequent and adequate cleaning practices. Maintain adequate pressure and volume of water.

Reprinted by permission of the National Sanitation Foundation from "Recommended Field Evaluation Procedures for Spray-Type Dishwashing Machines."

Symptom	Possible Cause	Suggested Cure
Greasy Films	Low pH. Insufficient detergent. Low water temperature. Improperly cleaned equipment.	Maintain adequate alkalinity to saponify greases; check detergent, water temperature. Unclog all wash and rinse nozzles to provide proper spray action. Clogged rinse nozzles may also interfere with wash tank overflow. Change water in tanks at proper intervals.
Streaking	Alkalinity in the water. Highly dissolved solids in water.	Use an external treatment method to reduce alkalinity. Within reason (up to 300–400 ppm), selection of proper rinse additive will eliminate streaking. Above this range external treatment is required to reduce solids.
	Improperly cleaned or rinsed equipment.	Maintain adequate pressure and volume of rinse water. Alkaline cleaners used for washing must be thoroughly rinsed from dishes.
Spotting	Rinse water hardness.	Provide external or internal softening. Use additional rinse additive.
	Rinse water temperature too high or too low.	Check rinse water temperature. Dishes may be flash drying, or water may be drying on dishes rather than draining off.
	Inadequate time between rinsing and storage.	Allow sufficient time for air drying.
Foaming	Detergent. Dissolved or suspended solids in water.	Change to a low sudsing product. Use an appropriate treatment method to reduce the solid content of the water.
	Food soil.	Adequately remove gross soil before washing. The decomposition of carbohydrates, proteins or fats may cause foaming during the wash cycle. Change water in tanks at proper intervals.
Coffee, tea, metal staining	Improper detergent.	Food dye or metal stains, particularly where plastic dishware is used, normally requires a chlorinated machine washing detergent for proper destaining.
	Improperly cleaned equipment.	Keep all wash sprays and rinse nozzles open. Keep equipment free from deposits of films or materials which could cause foam build-up in future wash cycles.

Exhibit 9.5   A three-compartment sink for manual sanitizing

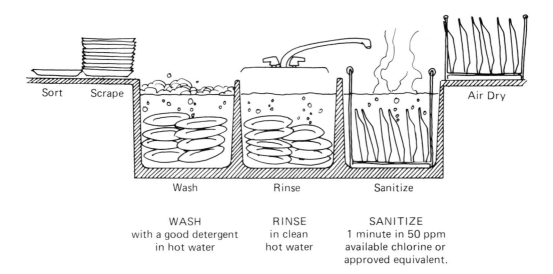

WASH	RINSE	SANITIZE
with a good detergent in hot water	in clean hot water	1 minute in 50 ppm available chlorine or approved equivalent.

MANUAL CLEANING AND SANITIZING

Regular cleaning and sanitizing of equipment, utensils, and work or serving surfaces reduces the possibility of food contamination and the transmission of disease organisms to customers and employees. Thorough cleaning not only removes obvious soil, but also prevents the accumulation of food particles, which may support the growth of illness-causing and spoilage organisms. Although cleaning removes the visible soil, sanitizing reduces the unseen micro-organisms that may be present on tableware such as cups, glasses, bowls, plates, and flatware.

Work Area

The first requirement for cleaning and sanitizing most portable food-contact items is a washing area away from the food preparation area. This work station should be equipped with at least three sinks or sink compartments, separate drainboards for clean and for soiled items, and an area for scraping and rinsing food soil into a garbage container for disposal (see Exhibit 9.5).

If hot water will be used to sanitize, the third sink or compartment of the sink must be equipped with a heating unit to maintain water at the desired 170°F (76.7°C). A thermometer must also be mounted in the sink or sink compartment to indicate accurately the temperature. A clock with a second hand should be easily visible so that washers do not have to estimate the time of immersion. Long-handled tongs, hooks, and baskets or racks will also be needed to dip clean items into the sanitizing bath of hot water or chemical sanitizer so that they need not be handled.

Requirements for cleaning and sanitizing equipment vary from locality to locality, so you should check regulations as they apply in your area. In some areas, two-sink units are permitted for manual cleaning and sanitizing of pots and pans.

Cleaning and Sanitizing by Immersion

Whatever the item, manual immersion cleaning and sanitizing involve the same six steps.

1. Clean the sinks and the work surfaces before each use.
2. Presoak and scrape items to be cleaned to remove gross food soil that may deactivate the detergent. This step should be done on a scraping table or other area where garbage can be disposed of without contaminating clean equipment and utensils. Items to be cleaned should be sorted; silverware should be pre-soaked in a solution designed for that purpose.
3. Wash in the first sink in a clean detergent solution at about 120°F (48.9°C), using a brush or dishmop to loosen and remove any remaining soil.
4. Rinse in the second sink in clear, potable water at about 120° to 140°F (48.9° to 60°C) to remove all traces of food soil and detergent that may interfere with the operation of the sanitizing agent.
5. Sanitize in the third sink by immersing items in hot water at 170°F (76.7°C) for 30 seconds or in a chemical sanitizer solution for one minute. If a chemical sanitizer is used, a good practice is to mix the sanitizing solution initially to twice the recommended strength for immersion. Thus, water carried over from the rinse sink will not dilute the sanitizing solution below the minimum concentration for effectiveness. Be sure that all surfaces contact the sanitizing chemical or water for the prescribed length of time—in particular, beware of air bubbles inside inverted containers that might shield the interior from the sanitizer.
6. Air dry. Do not wipe dry. Wiping can recontaminate all your newly sanitized utensils and equipment.

Sanitizing wooden cutting boards presents a special problem. Even those that meet public-health standards are difficult to sanitize and should certainly be discarded or refinished when they become badly scored by knife blades. If wooden boards must be used, they should be scrubbed with a nontoxic detergent solution and stiff-bristled nylon brush, rinsed and treated with a sanitizing solution after every use. Wooden cutting boards should never be submerged in a sanitizing solution.

Cleaning and Sanitizing Stationary Equipment

Stationary food preparation equipment should come with manufacturer's instructions for disassembly and cleaning and should be followed. If they are not available, these general instructions may be applied.

1. For general equipment cleaning, unplug the unit if it is electrically powered.
2. Remove whatever parts you can, and wash and sanitize them as described in the previous section.
3. Wash remaining food-contact surfaces and rinse with a solution of chemical sanitizer mixed to twice the strength required for immersion sanitizing.
4. Wipe down the nonfood-contact surfaces and allow all parts to air dry before reassembling.

Cloths used for wiping down stationary equipment and other surfaces should be wrung out frequently in a sanitizing solution, stored in the solution when not in use, and laundered daily or more often if necessary. Cloths used for food-contact surfaces should be kept separate from other wiping cloths.

Some stationary items are designed to have detergent and sanitizing solutions pumped through them. For items that are equipped for cleaning in place, the manufacturer's instructions should be consulted. Equipment can also be cleaned and sanitized through the use of power-spray equipment. To be sanitized in this way, the object must be sprayed for two to three minutes with a double-strength solution of the sanitizer.

STORAGE

When all tableware, utensils, and equipment are clean and sanitary, they must be kept that way. The objects must be transported to clean and protected storage areas. Wheeled dish tables or carts, if they are easily maneuverable, provide the best means of transportation in many instances. These dish carts must, of course, be clean and sanitized.

The storage area must be more than six inches off the floor and be protected from splash, dust, and contact with food. All items must be accessible without the necessity of touching surfaces, which will then contact food or the customer's mouth. For example, glasses and cups should be stored inverted.

The food-contact surfaces of fixed equipment must also be covered or otherwise protected when not in use.

SUMMARY

All the work that goes into preparing and presenting wholesome and sanitary food can be undone by the failure to keep utensils and equipment clean and sanitary. All food-contact surfaces must be cleaned and sanitized after every use or interruption of use.

Cleaning is the application of a detergent solution at the proper temperature and under pressure for a long enough time to remove soil from the surface of an object. Detergents are formulated to meet every cleaning need.

Clean items may be sanitized in one of two ways: either by heating them to 170°F (76.7°C) for a long enough time to kill the bacteria, or by immersing them in a strong enough solution of a chemical sanitizer.

Dishwashing machines can be the most reliable tools for cleaning utensils and equipment if the machines are installed and used properly.

Manual cleaning and sanitizing can be as effective as machine cleaning *if it is done carefully.* The six steps in manual cleaning are pre-cleaning the wash compartment or work surface, pre-soaking or pre-flushing the items to be cleaned, washing, rinsing, sanitizing, and air drying.

A protected storage area is necessary to keep clean and sanitary utensils and equipment from becoming contaminated before use.

A CASE IN POINT

The student workers in a university cafeteria scraped every dish and utensil and placed them in the racks where they were then automatically fed into a conveyor-type dishwasher. When the washing and rinse cycles were complete, the racks were placed on a table where the dishes and utensils were dried manually, as there was no room or time to air-dry them. They were used immediately for dinner.

Twenty-five students became very ill with hepatitis soon after. One of the students who worked in the dishroom tested positive for the hepatitis virus.

How do you think this outbreak may have occurred?

STUDY QUESTIONS

1. What is the fundamental foodservice rule about cleaning and sanitizing food-contact surfaces?
2. What are the variables that should be taken into account in the cleaning process?
3. In selecting a cleaning agent, what requirements should a foodservice manager consider?
4. What is a synthetic detergent?
5. Why does soap have a limited usefulness in a foodservice facility?
6. Which is more alkaline—heavy-duty or general-purpose detergents?
7. Why should foodservice managers refrain from formulating their own detergents?
8. For what cleaning purposes should acid cleaners be used?
9. When should abrasive cleaners be applied?
10. Do the terms "sterile" and "sanitary" have the same meaning? If not, what is the difference?
11. What two general methods may be used in sanitizing?
12. What are the heat requirements for sanitizing with water using manual methods?
13. What two methods may be used for chemical sanitizing?
14. Describe the differences and similarities among chlorine, iodine, and quaternary ammonia sanitizers.
15. What is a detergent sanitizer? How may it be used?
16. Describe the six steps in manual cleaning and sanitizing.
17. Why are a thermometer and a clock necessary in the manual dishwashing area?
18. What are some of the factors for a successful mechanical dishwashing operation?
19. What are some of the factors that should be considered in selecting a mechanical dishwashing machine and in setting up its successful operation?
20. How often should dishwashing machines be cleaned?
21. How should clean and sanitary tableware, utensils, and equipment be stored?

MORE ON THE SUBJECT

LONGREE, KARLA, and GERTRUDE G. BLAKER. *Sanitary Techniques in Food Service,* 2d ed. New York: Wiley, 1982. 271 pages. Part III, Section B gives examples of specific procedures for cleaning and sanitizing numerous kinds of kitchen equipment.

NATIONAL SANITATION FOUNDATION. *Food Service Standards.* Ann Arbor, Michigan, 1976. 309 pages. Standard Number 3 covers dishwashing machines. Standard Number 29 includes some information on the requirements for detergent and chemical feeders.

OHIO DEPARTMENT OF HEALTH. *Dishwashing.* Publication Number 2122.32. This pamphlet covers all facets of manual and mechanical dish, silver, and glass washing, with clear diagrams, drawings, and photographs. It is based on Ohio Public Health Ordinances, so specifics should be checked out with the local regulatory agency.

THE SOAP AND DETERGENT ASSOCIATION. *Programmed Cleaning Guide for the Environmental Sanitarian.* New York, 1984. This guide provides a look at overall cleaning and sanitizing procedures including floor care, warewashing, food sanitation, and laundering.

THE SOAP AND DETERGENT ASSOCIATION. *Understanding Automatic Dishwashing.* 10 pages. This publication offers a brief survey of detergent ingredients and water action requirements for automatic dishwashers.

U.S. DEPARTMENT OF HEALTH AND HUMAN SERVICES, Food and Drug Administration. *Food Service Sanitation Manual.* Washington, D.C., 1976. Chapter 5 of the Model Food Service Sanitation Ordinance deals with cleaning, sanitizing, and storage of equipment and utensils.

ANSWER TO A CASE IN POINT

Sanitary dishes can be re-contaminated by handling. In this case the worker contaminated a number of utensils and dishes with hepatitis virus, which then survived long enough to make contact with the food and from the food with the human hosts.

Dishes and utensils should always be air-dried and should not be handled, if possible, until ready for use. Unsanitary towels and hands only undo the work of cleaning and sanitizing.

10
Organizing a Cleaning Program

Foodservice facilities require constant cleanup. Every time a meal is served, the cleaning and sanitizing that has gone before is at least partly undone. Each customer, directly or indirectly, leaves behind a trail of dishes and disorder that must be quickly cleared away. The cleaning work is, quite literally, never done.

Effective and efficient cleaning does not come about by accident. It results from the manager's deliberate efforts to understand the precise cleaning needs of the foodservice establishment, to provide the necessary equipment and cleaning agents to fill these needs, and to make full use of available workers and materials. In this book we give the name *cleaning program* to the system that the manager devises in order to organize all the cleaning tasks in the establishment.

The advantages of a good cleaning program are innumerable. Among other things, having a cleaning program

- Forces the manager to plan ahead and make the best use of resources
- Helps to distribute the work load fairly, giving employees less reason to think they are being forced to do more than their share
- Reduces duplication of efforts on the part of employees
- Pinpoints responsibility for specific tasks, thereby making it more likely that work will be done conscientiously
- Encourages forethought in providing substitutes for vacationing workers and in contracting for cleaning by outside specialists
- Establishes a logical basis for such supervisory tasks as inspections
- Saves employee time that might be spent in deciding what to do next, or in organizing a job

- Provides a useful tool for familiarizing new employees with cleaning routines and with the management's approach to sanitation
- Most importantly, ensures that necessary sanitation tasks are not overlooked

Chapter 9 presented the principles involved in cleaning and sanitizing. This chapter will discuss ways of guaranteeing that those principles are applied when, where, and as they should be, through the use of an organized and planned cleaning program. The basic steps to be followed in the design and implementation of a cleaning program are the following:

- Surveying cleaning needs
- Accumulating cleaning materials
- Devising a cleaning schedule
- Introducing the program to those who must carry it out
- Supervising implementation of the schedule
- Monitoring and evaluation of the program, materials, and procedures

SURVEYING CLEANING NEEDS

If you are a manager, one way to begin designing your cleaning program is to walk through every room of your establishment, clipboard in hand, and write down each area, surface, and piece of equipment that ever needs to be cleaned, from the garbage dock to the potted plants in the foyer. Try to examine your place from a fresh viewpoint, looking for spots that might be neglected simply because you are so familiar with your layout that you do not notice them.

Whatever else you do in making your survey, do *not* ignore the restrooms. Many otherwise sanitary restaurants have alienated customer and sanitarian alike with their neglected toilet facilities. Most customers will base their opinions of a restaurant's cleanliness on the condition of its restrooms. And, of course, an unsanitary washroom is a friendly environment for dangerous micro-organisms.

When surveying the restrooms, carefully note all floors, walls, counters, sinks, mirrors, dispensers, toilets, urinals, partitions, and waste receptacles. All these must be kept scrupulously clean. Include frequent refilling of toilet paper, soap, and sanitary supplies on the list of cleaning jobs. Do not underestimate your cleaning needs in this area: the restroom hasn't been invented that can be too clean.

When you have compiled a list of cleaning jobs to be done throughout the entire establishment, estimate the amount of time necessary for each task. Decide whether each job can be done most efficiently by one, two, or more people. Note all the equipment and materials that are required to do each job.

Keep in mind that many items require several different kinds of cleaning. Steam tables, for example, need periodic deliming in addition to cleaning and sanitizing. Floors may require daily dust removal, weekly scrubbing, and periodic resealing. Don't forget to assign responsibility for seasonal cleaning tasks either to employees or to outside cleaning specialists. Don't forget, either, about the cleaning requirements of outside areas such as refuse storage, parking lots, and so on.

While you are taking a good hard look at your cleaning needs, you should examine critically the ways in which the cleaning is currently being done. Are there any procedures that could be improved with a little concentrated thinking? People are apt to perform their regular tasks according to habitual methods, even when possible improvements are obvious.

ACCUMULATING AND SELECTING CLEANING MATERIALS

Providing adequate and appropriate sanitation tools is the next step in guaranteeing efficient cleaning. Prepare a checklist that covers each area of the operation and every major piece of equipment. Metal scrapers, heavy rubber gloves, clean cloths, brooms (vertical and push-type), wet mops, dust mops, double buckets with mop presses, and dust pans should all be on your shopping list. Be sure that adequate supplies of detergents and sanitizing agents are also at hand (see Exhibit 10.1).

Brushes of natural fibers, nylon, or plastic are common cleaning tools. They are used in manual as well as mechanical operations. The type of brush selected is a matter of individual preference, but it should be noted that some wood-backed fiber brushes are themselves hard to keep clean. Nylon and plastic brushes with composition backing, in contrast, are easily cleaned and ideal for many hand- or mechanical-cleaning operations. They have strong, flexible uniform bristles that wear well, are nonabrasive, and do not absorb too much water. They also must be resistant to chemicals.

Avoid wire brushes, steel wool, coarse abrasives, and anything else that will mar the surface being cleaned. A scratched surface provides soil with a new harborage that may be difficult to clean with ordinary detergents.

When you have selected supplies, see that they are kept in a well-lighted storage area where they are easily identifiable and accessible and where they cannot contaminate food.

Exhibit 10.1   Cleaning tools

General Supplies

Paddle scrapers
Window squeegees
Floor squeegees
Putty knives
Hoses
Dustpans
Mops (light and heavy duty)
Mop bucket and wringer
Buckets (various sizes)
Brooms (light and heavy duty)

Brushes

Glass washer
Tableware
Bottle
Tube
Scrub
Plumbing
Toilet
General cleaning

Cloths

Washcloths
Counter cloths
Dustcloths
Special cheesecloths

Sponges

Varying grades and sizes
For non-stick surfaces

Heavy Equipment

Vacuum cleaner
Carpet sweeper
Wax applicator
Floor scrubber/polisher

Worker Supplies

Plastic disposable gloves
Steel reinforced gloves
Goggles
Aprons

If a worker is unable to find the tool or product specified for a job, whatever is handy will frequently be used. Results of such carelessness can range from inefficiency to disaster.

Be sure, too, that equipment you keep on hand matches the needs you have identified in your survey of cleaning jobs. Needless to say, if you have scheduled two people to mop the floor, you should provide two mops. If you want the dining room vacuumed, check to see that there are enough cords and electrical outlets to reach all parts of the room.

It is also a good idea to investigate new materials and equipment that might be suitable for the establishment. A wet/dry vacuum with attachments could well be the most versatile and economical worker on your payroll. You may also wish to investigate the wide variety of power cleaning tools and look into advances in chemical cleaning agents.

The physical facility must be considered in any cleaning program. Floor drains should be in every area that must be mopped regularly. It is best to set aside a specific area for storing

Exhibit 10.2   Cleaning supplies storage area

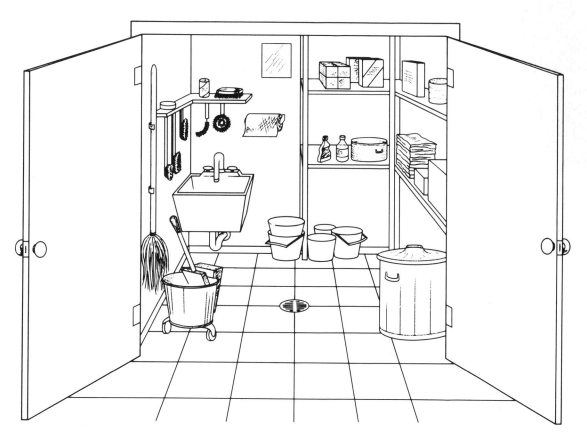

cleaning supplies. It should be located away from food preparation and storage areas to prevent contamination of foods by such supplies. This area should include storage space for cleaning supplies, including hooks for hanging mops, brooms, and brushes and shelves for chemical cleaners and detergents. There should be a proper sink to fill mop buckets, rinse and clean mops, and for cleaning brushes and sponges. Hand-washing, food-preparation, and equipment-cleaning sinks must never be used for cleaning mops or brushes. A floor drain is necessary to rid the area of waste water or spillage (see Exhibit 10.2).

Remember, though, that if you select novel materials and tools, you will have to train workers in their use and maintenance and provide competent supervision. All too often, costly machines are not used to full effect because of poor maintenance, misapplication, or misunderstanding on the part of employees.

Cleaning equipment must itself be kept clean. Mops and washcloths should be laundered regularly—but separately. Brushes must also be washed to get rid of dirt. Greasy rags and blackened mops do not belong in a food-service facility.

DEVISING THE MASTER CLEANING SCHEDULE

The two steps described thus far will yield a good deal of information about jobs to be done, as well as the materials, employees, and time needed to do them. The next step is to tabulate all this information in the form of a master cleaning schedule.

The *master cleaning schedule* is a summary of all the cleaning operations in the establishment. As such, it should include a comprehensive list of *what* is to be cleaned. For each item on this list there should be an entry indicating *who* is to clean the item, *when* it is to be cleaned, and *how* the job is to be done. Exhibit 10.3 presents a partial sample cleaning schedule. A full cleaning schedule can follow the same general outline.

What Is to Be Cleaned

The section of the schedule describing what is to be cleaned should constitute a detailed and comprehensive list. It is not enough to say, "The restroom," without specifying floors, walls, mirrors, partitions, fixtures, and so on.

The list should be arranged on some logical basis so that nothing will be overlooked. For example, all the cleaning jobs in one room may be placed together on the list. Alternatively, the schedule may list jobs in the order in which they are to be performed, or according to the person responsible for them. Many schedules are arranged in alphabetical order. Although an alphabetical arrangement is useful if an employee or manager wishes to learn when a particular item is to be cleaned, it does not give the manager a coordinated picture of the entire cleaning program.

Who Is to Clean It

Someone should be responsible for every item on the list of jobs. As the manager composes the schedule, it will become apparent when one person has been assigned too many duties, or has been asked to be in two places at the same time. One of the advantages of making up a schedule is that precisely such conflicts can be detected before they result in serious problems.

Cleaning tasks can be assigned to the workers on several bases. In general, workers should be held responsible for continuous cleaning of their own work areas, a "clean-as-you-go" policy. Such a method of work assignment encourages employees to limit their own untidiness and to clean well the area they themselves must use.

Distribution of larger jobs will depend in part on the size of the facility's staff. If all the cleaning must be done by one utility worker and the dining room and kitchen crews, then it becomes necessary to work large jobs into the staff's slack periods.

Rotating cleaning assignments helps to prevent people from becoming bored. This method will also distribute the more unpleasant tasks fairly among workers.

When It Is to Be Cleaned

Major cleanup tasks are to be carried out at a time when contamination of foods is least likely to occur and interference with service is minimized. The kitchen should not be mopped during the preparation of food. Vacuuming the dining room floor should be reserved for a time when customers are not present. The dust and splash raised by mopping and vacuuming can contaminate food, and electrical cords and wet floors pose obvious safety hazards. At the same time, it is desirable to clean as soon as possible after soiling, to prevent dirt from drying and hardening and to avoid the multiplication of bacteria to enormous numbers. A balance must be found among the sometimes competing demands of service and sanitation.

Food-contact surfaces, of course, must be cleaned and sanitized after every use, after interruption of service, and, if they are in continuous use, at regularly scheduled intervals throughout the day. The food-contact surfaces of grills, griddles, cooking devices, and microwave oven cavities and door seals should be cleaned once a day.

Exhibit 10.3   Sample cleaning schedule (partial) for food preparation area

Item	When	What	Use	Who
Floors	As soon as possible	Wipe up spills	Cloth, mop and bucket, broom and dustpan	
	Once per shift, between rushes	Damp mop	Mop, bucket	
	Weekly, Thurs. evening	Scrub	Brushes, bucket, detergent (brand)	
	January, June	Strip, reseal	See procedure	
Walls and ceilings	As soon as possible	Wipe up splashes	Clean cloth, detergent (brand)	
	February, August	Wash walls		Contracted Specialists
Work tables	Between uses and at end of day	Clean and sanitize tops	See cleaning procedure for each table	
	Weekly, Sat. P.M.	Empty, clean and sanitize drawers, clean frame, shelf	See cleaning procedure for each table	
Hoods and filters	When necessary	Empty grease traps	Container for grease	
	Daily, closing	Clean inside and out	See cleaning procedure	
	Weekly, Wed. evening	Clean filters	Dishwashing machine	
Broiler	When necessary	Empty drip pan Wipe down	Container for grease Clean cloth	
	After each use	Clean grid tray, inside, outside, top	See cleaning procedure for each broiler	

Exhibit 10.4   Sample cleaning procedure: How to clean a food slicer

When	How	Use
After each use	1. Turn off machine.	
	2. Remove electric cord from socket.	
	3. Set blade control to zero.	
	4. Remove meat carriage. (a) Turn knob at bottom of carriage.	
	5. Remove the back blade guard. (a) Loosen knob on the guard.	
	6. Remove the top blade guard. (a) Loosen knob at center of blade.	
	7. Take parts to pot-and-pan sink, scrub.	Hot machine detergent solution, gong brush.
	8. Rinse.	Clean hot water, 170°F (76.7°C) for 1 minute. Use double S hook to remove parts from hot water.
	9. Allow parts to air dry on clean surface.	

Sanitary Techniques in Food Service by Karla Longree and Gertrude G. Blaker. Copyright 1971, 1982 by John Wiley & Sons, Inc. Reprinted by permission.

Other surfaces should be cleaned often enough to keep them free of dust, dirt, food particles, and debris. The frequency with which they are cleaned will depend upon the type of food served, the kinds of surfaces to be cleaned, and such factors as the quality of ventilation in the kitchen.

Restrooms must be cleaned at least once a day, or more frequently if necessary to keep them pleasant and sanitary. Toilet bowls and urinals must also be sanitized once or more a day.

Enough *time* must be set aside for cleaning. It is wise to schedule cleaning in a normal work shift. Employees who work an eight-hour day are going to be reluctant to stay after hours to clean. If late night banquets and irregular closing times are the rule, the cleaning schedule should be adjusted accordingly.

Other goals to consider in scheduling cleaning operations include even-spacing of periodic cleaning and arranging of jobs in the proper order. For example, it is not wise to schedule all weekly jobs on the same day of the week, nor does it make much sense to do semiannual floor resealing in September and again in November. Utensil drawers and clean-dish shelves are best cleaned before and not after the newly sanitized utensils and dishes are brought in from the dishwashing room.

When	How	Use
	10. Wash blade and machine shell. CAUTION: PROCEED WITH CARE WHILE BLADE IS EXPOSED.	Use damp bunched cloth* (fold cloth to several thicknesses) dipped in hot machine detergent solution.
	11. Rinse.	Clean hot water, clean bunched cloth.
	12. Sanitize blade, allow to air dry.	Clean water, chemical sanitizer, clean bunched cloth.
	13. Replace front blade guard immediately after cleaning shell. (a) Tighten knob.	
	14. Replace back blade guard. (a) Tighten knob.	
	15. Replace meat carriage. (a) Tighten knob.	
	16. Leave blade control at zero.	
	17. Replace electric cord into socket.	

*A cloth folded to several thicknesses

How It Is to Be Cleaned

It is very important to provide, in writing, clear and detailed procedures for cleaning all areas and items of equipment, in order to keep workers from improvising their own techniques. For practical reasons, however, the manager will probably not want to include such detailed treatment in the actual schedule, even though the information is an integral part of the cleaning program. Cleaning instructions can be posted near the item they describe, so that workers do not have to run back and forth to the cleaning schedule for directions.

The cleaning procedures should be written in a simple manner. They should lead the worker—novice or veteran—step-by-step through the cleaning process. Tools and cleaning agents to be used should be specified by name, never by such expressions as "that runny pink stuff." Any unusual hazards involved in the job or special precautions that must be taken, should be clearly stated. Manufacturers' instructions for cleaning pieces of equipment can be of assistance to the manager in the preparation of cleaning procedures. When instructions are not available from the equipment manufacturer, the manager should consider modifying the sample cleaning procedures provided by manufacturers of cleaning agents. Exhibit 10.4 presents a sample procedure form for cleaning a food slicer.

Exhibit 10.5   Individual cleaning schedules

Schedule for _____(Name)_____ .				
Week of _____ .				
Monday	**Tuesday**	**Wednesday**	**Thursday**	**Friday**
Waitress station #1	*Waitress station #2*	*Waitress station #3*	*Waitress station #1*	*Waitress station #2*
Juice machine	Ice cream freezer	Coffee machine	Juice machine	Ice cream freezer
Refill paper supply	Cocoa machine	Catsup, mustard containers	Refill paper supply	Cocoa machine
Dust and wipe shelves under counter	Dust dining room window sill, booth partitions	Sugar, salt, pepper containers	Dust and wipe shelves under counter	Dust dining room window sill, booth partitions

INTRODUCING THE PROGRAM

Preparing a cleaning program and writing schedules and procedures is quite an effort. Unfortunately, the effort is a wasted one if nobody but the manager works to carry the program out. The manager must devote time and energy to acquainting the employees with the schedule and to enlisting their support for the program.

It is more than likely that the master schedule will be too detailed and bulky to mean much to employees. The manager will probably want to break it down into several smaller schedules. These may include schedules for each room or area, individual schedules of each employee's duties, and daily schedules of immediate tasks. These smaller schedules may refer to employees by name, thus heightening their sense of responsibility. The master schedule will probably use employee titles, to take account of high turnover. Exhibit 10.5 depicts a schedule of one employee's duties. Note that a waitress is assigned to several different stations during one week.

The manager should organize a meeting to present the cleaning program to employees. During the meeting he or she can demonstrate any new procedures or cleaning tools being introduced. These should also include the safety procedures required during cleaning. In addition, the meeting will offer an opportunity to explain the reasons behind the program, and to discuss the importance of following the procedures exactly as they are spelled out. If people understand *why* they are being asked to do something a certain way, they will be less likely to deviate from specified procedures. They will also feel that the manager has more confidence in their intelligence than if they are simply told, "Do it this way."

SUPERVISING IMPLEMENTATION

Once the cleaning program is in operation, the manager must still evaluate its effectiveness. Even the most conscientious employees may ignore proper procedures in the rush of business or out of sheer forgetfulness. It is the manager's job to see to it—through continual supervision and self-inspection—that such departures from the rules do not occur.

One of the most important factors in keeping people aware of the cleaning schedule is the manager's continued interest. The cleaning program should not be allowed to degenerate into last week's "idea of the week." The manager should let people know that the schedule is expected to continue to function on a permanent basis. Of course, the schedule as originally written cannot be chiseled in stone. Changes in the menu and the personnel, and the hundred other variables that beset a food service, will necessitate changes in the schedule. But if the manager takes the time to explain these departures, and keeps the posted schedules up to date, people will be reassured that the schedule is still operative.

The schedule should be used to introduce new employees to the cleaning program. It may also be used for making up self-inspection sheets for individual workers and a master inspection sheet for the manager. By making use of these tools the manager can ensure that the food service is as clean and sanitary as it should be.

MONITORING THE PROGRAM

A cleaning program that is flexible enough allows for changes in personnel and equipment. A manager should regularly review the cleaning program and consider the following questions:

1. Is the program correct for the facility, or should it be revised?
2. Do I have the proper tools for the staff to do each task correctly and quickly?
3. Is the staff given enough *time* to clean during operation and after closing?
4. Do I have enough personnel for cleaning?
5. Is the program being implemented properly, or are shortcuts being taken?
6. Are cleaning workers properly trained?

SUMMARY

Clean and sanitary conditions in a foodservice operation do not spring into being on their own, or as the result of random efforts on the part of management and staff. Such conditions are the product of an organized and planned *cleaning program*.

The first step in designing such a program is for the manager to survey the establishment, noting all its cleaning requirements. Cleaning procedures, materials, and equipment must all be scrutinized in order to reveal possible areas for improvement.

Next, the necessary cleaning materials should be collected in appropriate quantities. These cleaning agents and tools must be kept in safe, well-lighted, and convenient storage areas.

To ensure that every job is done when and as it should be, a major cleaning schedule as well as cleaning procedures should be created and posted prominently. The schedule and procedures should state clearly and in detail what is to be cleaned, who is to clean it, and when and how the cleaning is to be done.

A special effort should be made to introduce the schedule to the employees who will have to carry it out. Taking the time to enlist their support for the cleaning program will pay off with greater cooperation on their part.

After the cleaning program has been implemented, the manager must constantly monitor its functioning. Monitoring will help prevent deviation from the correct cleaning procedures and demonstrate the manager's continued interest in the program.

A CASE IN POINT

It was only 9:05 in the morning, but already Tim, the manager, could tell it was going to be a bad day. The executives from American Widget looked annoyed as they munched unenthusiastically on complimentary doughnuts and waited for Tim and the busboy to finish cleaning the private room that American Widget had hired for 9:00 A.M. Tim had opened the banquet room just before 9 o'clock to find, to his dismay, that the remains of the Pine Valley Martial Arts Club Annual Banquet were still strewn about the room.

Later, Tim sat down with his cleaning schedule and tried to determine what had gone wrong. The banquet was supposed to have ended at 11:30 the previous night. The assistant dishwasher was scheduled to clean the room at midnight when he got out of the dishroom and before he went home at 12:30 A.M. But a note from Norman, the night manager, told Tim that the banquet had been a wild one and that the last guest had not staggered out until long after the 1:00 A.M. closing time. The dishwasher had punched out at 12:30 A.M. as he always did. Tim sighed.

What do you think went wrong?
How can Tim prevent this from happening again?

STUDY QUESTIONS

1. List five advantages of developing an organized cleaning program.
2. What are the basic steps to be followed in designing and implementing a cleaning program?
3. Give an example of a piece of foodservice equipment that may require more than one kind of cleaning. Give examples not listed in the book.
4. What disadvantage is associated with some wood-backed brushes?
5. What special responsibility must a manager fulfill if he or she purchases a piece of cleaning equipment with which the employees are not familiar?
6. What are the four categories of information that should be present on a cleaning schedule?
7. Give three ways of listing cleaning jobs on a cleaning schedule.
8. Why should workers be made responsible for cleaning their own work stations?
9. What is the difference between a cleaning schedule and a cleaning procedure?
10. What is the chief advantage to developing written cleaning procedures?
11. What steps must be taken after the cleaning program is implemented?

MORE ON THE SUBJECT

AMERICAN INSTITUTE OF MAINTENANCE. (1) *Floor Care Guide.* Glendale, California, 1973. 79 pages. (2) *Selection and Care of Cleaning Equipment Including Mechanical Maintenance.* Glendale, California, 1973. 80 pages. (3) *Selecting Proper Floor Care Materials Including Questions and Answers.* Glendale, California, 1973. 71 pages. These three pamphlets offer a wealth of specific information on the topics covered. In addition, *Selecting Proper Floor Care Materials* also includes a discussion of the properties of various cleaners and floor finishes.

FELDMAN, EDWIN B. *Housekeeping Handbook for Institutions, Business, and Industry.* New York: Frederick Fell, Inc., 1974. 423 pages. Though primarily concerned with the cleaning of industrial and high-rise structures, this book still offers much useful and practical information on cleaning methods and on training of workers.

LONGREE, KARLA, and GERTRUDE G. BLAKER. *Sanitary Techniques in Food Service.* 2d ed. New York: Wiley, 1982. 271 pages. Sections A and B of Part III present outlines of procedures for cleaning facilities, equipment, and utensils.

ANSWER TO A CASE IN POINT

Schedules don't clean dining rooms—people do. Tim had made his schedule too rigid, for there was really no way of knowing when the banquet would actually end. Perhaps it would have been unreasonable to expect the dishwasher to wait around, no matter how long the banquet lasted, to clean the room; but if Tim had succeeded in enlisting the dishwasher's support for the whole idea of a cleaning program, the dishwasher might have been motivated to tell Norman that the room could not be cleaned. Norman, too, should have been concerned enough to inspect the room. Tim got compliance with the letter, not the spirit, of his cleaning instructions. In the unpredictable business of running a foodservice operation, allowances must be made for special situations. Tim should prepare a cleaning schedule for late banquets and let workers know that cleaning is part of their jobs, no matter what time it is.

11
Pest Control

From time immemorial, humanity has been shooing, swatting, and swearing at flies. The rodent menace can be traced back to the earliest human records. The cockroach has existed through the centuries. Some species have even developed resistance to human attempts to vanquish them. With today's advanced knowledge, however, there is no reason to tolerate these or other pests in a foodservice operation.

Foodservice managers can guard the premises against insects, rodents, and other vermin if they know the habits and points of vulnerability of these pests. This chapter will discuss the most common pests and describe methods for detecting their presence, as well as measures available for controlling them.

Most pests carry disease-causing organisms. Insects and rodents cause considerable spoilage and waste, to say nothing of loss of patronage. A rat, for example, eats a tremendous amount of food for its size, and with its hair and droppings contaminates much more food than it actually eats.

Pests can be effectively controlled by following three common-sense rules:

- Keep pests out of the foodservice facility by pest-proofing the building.
- Deprive pests of food and shelter by following good housekeeping practices.
- Work with a licensed pest control operator to rid the operation of pests that do enter.

COCKROACHES

Cockroaches are among the most frequent and most bothersome insect pests ever to enter foodservice operations. Efforts to control them are complicated by their resistance to chemicals and population dynamics. In her short lifetime—of only about 60 days to two years, depending on the species—the female cockroach may produce offspring in the *millions*.

In past centuries, particularly the nineteenth, cockroaches were so numerous and attempts to eliminate them were so futile that people began to consider them an unavoidable evil. This toleration was encouraged by the belief that cockroaches had little to do with the transmission of disease to humans.

Today we know better. Although cockroaches have not been identified as the *main* cause of any particular epidemic, they are known to be *carriers* of disease organisms such as *Salmonella* bacteria and the viruses that cause poliomyelitis. Even if cockroaches had no relationship to human illnesses, their disgusting appearance and vile odor would put elimination of them high on the list of priorities for a foodservice manager.

Kinds of Cockroaches

At least three different kinds of cockroaches plague commercial establishments in the United States. Identification of the particular kind of cockroach infesting an establishment is often helpful in working with a pest control operator (PCO) to determine the control techniques to be used.

German Cockroach

About ½ inch (13 mm) long and pale brown in color, the German cockroach has two dark stripes on its body. The German cockroach often enters the facility in cases or cartons of supplies. It is particularly fond of foods like potatoes, onions, and bottled drinks. It prefers warm crevices near stoves or other sources of heat, including the motors of refrigerators and soft-drink machines, drinks more water than cockroaches of other species, and reproduces extremely quickly. The German cockroach may be found at any level in a room—from floor to ceiling—and is especially common in restaurants. The German cockroach has proved hardy and is resistant to some sprays. It may

Exhibit 11.1   Characteristic appearances of three types of cockroaches likely to infest foodservice operations (*B* and *C*, *Handbook of Pest Control, Sixth Edition,* by Arnold Mallis. Copyright © 1982 by Franzak & Foster Company, Cleveland, Ohio. Reprinted by permission.)

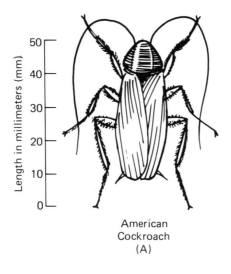

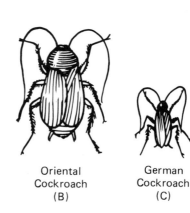

American Cockroach (A)

Oriental Cockroach (B)

German Cockroach (C)

live for three to six months. It reproduces rapidly, and the female carries her eggs around until they are ready to hatch. This species is usually only active at night. Its presence during the day indicates a heavy infestation.

Oriental Cockroach

The Oriental cockroach grows to a length of about 1 inch (25 mm) and has a shiny, dark-brown color. This cockroach is generally found at floor level in buildings and around water pipes. It has a distinct odor. The life cycle of the Oriental cockroach is about two years, and the female may produce up to 18 egg capsules.

American Cockroach

Reddish-brown in color, the American cockroach is about 1½ inches (38 mm) long. It tends to inhabit more or less open, wet places, such as drainage areas and sewers. The American

cockroach may live from one to two years. The female may produce up to 50 egg capsules, containing 16 nymphs.

Exhibit 11.1 shows examples of the adult forms of the German, Oriental, and American cockroaches.

Detecting the Presence of Cockroaches

Cockroaches may be found virtually anywhere in a foodservice establishment. They tend to hide and to lay eggs in dark, warm, moist, hard-to-clean places; narrow spaces in and between equipment and shelves and under shelf liners are favorite harborages, as are spaces under pipes, between pipes and walls, or where pipes pass unsealed through walls or floors. Although cockroaches prefer the dark, they will come out into the light if they get hungry enough.

Exhibit 11.2   A comparison of the droppings of the Norway rat, the roof rat, the house mouse, and the American cockroach. Proper identification of droppings will simplify control measures.

Norway Rat
Average length 3/4 inch (19 mm)

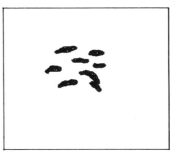

House Mouse
Average length 1/4 inch (6 mm)

Roof Rat
Average length 1/2 inch (13 mm)

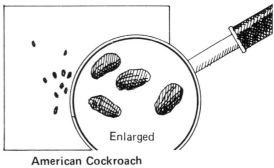

Enlarged

American Cockroach
Average length 1/25 inch (1 mm)

The simplest way to check for cockroach infestation is to enter a darkened storeroom or food preparation area and see whether the bugs scurry away as soon as the lights are turned on. A strong, oily odor can also signal the presence of cockroaches in a room. This odor arises from a substance given off by certain glands in the insect. Finally, cockroaches leave their feces practically everywhere they go. Cockroach droppings are small, black or dark brown, and almost spherical in shape (see Exhibit 11.2).

Preventing Cockroach Infestation

Ridding an establishment of cockroaches is not easy, but it can be done. Taking the following steps will deprive cockroaches—and virtually all insects—of their four basic requirements of food, water, shelter, and access to the establishment.

1. *Eliminate food and water sources through frequent and careful cleaning.* Careful cleaning reduces the food supply for insects, destroys many insect eggs, and may reveal new infestations before

they become serious. Clean hard-to-reach corners and crevices and under and behind equipment. Clean up grease around ranges and ventilation areas. Garbage must be removed promptly, and food should never be left uncovered.

Wipe up spills immediately. Do not allow puddles from cleaning or other activities to remain on the floor. Do not store wet mops or brushes in the food preparation area.

Pick up crumbs and other scraps of food as quickly as possible. Remember that roaches can and will eat practically anything. A mere crust of bread can support an entire roach population. Since most insects, including cockroaches, become inactive at temperatures below 40°F (4.4°C), refrigerating such items as cocoa, powdered milk, and nuts can reduce cockroach infestation. If dry products must be stored for any length of time, rotate them and clean storage areas regularly. This disturbs roaches and makes it hard for them to breed. Never store food products right up against the wall or on the floor. A six-inch space should always be left between stored products and walls and floors.

2. *Deprive cockroaches of shelter and hiding places.* Structural defects, particularly in older buildings, allow cockroaches to enter and provide them with plenty of hiding places. Fill *all* cracks in floors and walls with a suitable material such as silicone caulking or putty. Be sure to close off spaces where large pieces of equipment are improperly fitted to their bases or to the floor; these spaces are favorite homes for cockroaches. Unsanitary conditions in lavatories and toilet areas will also attract cockroaches and should be corrected.

Storing food and supplies away from the walls and floors eliminates hiding places for cockroaches. Do not let crates, boards, empty boxes, bags, or other rubbish pile up in areas not designed for storing those items. Provide good ventilation in storerooms and food preparation areas. Cockroaches and other insects thrive in moist, poorly ventilated rooms.

Don't overlook employee lockers or break areas. Be sure employees don't leave exposed food around. They should clean their lockers regularly. Soiled uniforms and other laundry items like dirty linens or towels should not be left in lockers.

3. *Deprive roaches of easy access to the operation.* Roaches are notorious hitchhikers. They or their eggs may be brought into the establishment in boxes, bags, and cartons of produce, meat, or other supplies. Examine incoming cartons carefully, and destroy any cockroaches that may be hiding in them. Examine paper goods such as bags and napkins. Refuse any shipment of foodstuffs in which cockroaches are found, even if there is only one. Remove cartons and boxes from the premises as soon as supplies have been unpacked.

FLIES

The common housefly is an even greater menace to human health than is the cockroach. A single fly is a veritable repository for a large variety of bacteria and can carry disease-causing viruses as well. Flies can transmit a variety of human diseases, including typhoid, dysentery, infantile diarrhea, and streptococcal and staphylococcal foodborne illnesses.

Flies are transmitters of disease primarily because they feed on human and animal wastes. The dangerous bacteria present in these wastes sticks to the mouth, footpads, and hairs of flies and may then be deposited in food intended for human consumption. Fly feces, which contain disease-bearing organisms, can also contaminate human food. Flies defecate every four to five minutes. Moreover, since flies have no teeth and must take their nourishment in liquid form, they spit on solid food and let the food dissolve before consuming it. Fly spittle, or vomitus, is swarming with bacteria and contaminates food, surfaces, and utensils. A single fly can contaminate food with enough bacteria to cause illness.

As if all this weren't enough, flies are annoying and some outside flies can bite. The presence of flies in an establishment should not be tolerated.

Some Facts About Flies

The following list of habits and characteristics of houseflies should be helpful in combating these pests:

1. Flies can enter a building that has openings not much larger than the head of a pin.
2. Although they rarely travel very far from where they are hatched, flies may be lured to the sources of attractive odors. Flies may also be carried long distances by air currents.
3. One female fly can produce thousands of offspring in a single breeding season.
4. Flies have favorite resting places. They are especially fond of places protected from the wind, and of edges such as clotheslines, garbage can rims, and electric wires.
5. Moist, warm, decaying material protected from sunlight is required for fly eggs to hatch and fly larvae, or maggots, to grow. Flies also favor animal and

human waste areas for depositing their eggs (see Exhibit 11.3). An uncovered garbage can is an ideal breeding place.

Keeping Flies Away

In order to keep flies away from food, it is necessary to prevent their entry into the foodservice facility in the first place. Here are some techniques for keeping flies out of the establishment.

1. Follow proper cleaning procedures and promptly remove wastes from food preparation and service areas.
2. Use screens on all outside doors, windows, and other openings and keep all screens in good repair. The U.S. Public Health Service recommends screens of not less than 16 mesh per inch.
3. When receiving supplies, leave doors and screens open for the shortest time possible. All doors should be self-closing. The use of air doors or "fly fans" may be helpful in many installations. The air doors form a shield of air that flies avoid. These air door units must be of adequate width and provide sufficient air velocity to cover the entire door area. Positive air ventilation that forces air out of storage areas or out of the building is also helpful (see Exhibit 11.4). Such devices *by themselves* do not usually control flies. Good sanitation is still important.
4. Do away with breeding places by making sure that garbage is picked up at least once every four days. Garbage containers must be placed as far from the building as possible to avoid attracting flies. You can determine whether a garbage can or pile is a breeding place for flies by checking for maggots, which are white, moist-looking, and about a ½-inch (1.2 cm) long. In

Exhibit 11.3 Transmittal of disease-causing organisms by flies (Source: U.S. Department of Health and Human Services, Centers for Disease Control, Atlanta, Ga.)

addition, make sure area residents are not using your property for a dog toilet. If you have a lot of flies, something either on the inside or outside is attracting them and encouraging them to breed.

Whether or not it is currently a breeding place, the garbage-disposal area should always be neat and clean. Outdoor garbage storage should be as far as possible from entrance doors. Refrigerating garbage that must be stored indoors will assist greatly in keeping flies away.

Enough containers should be provided to hold all of the garbage and refuse that accumulates between pickups. Garbage should be wrapped in paper or placed in plastic bags to

Exhibit 11.4 An air door must be of adequate width and provide sufficient air velocity to cover the entire door area (Photograph courtesy of Mars Sales Company, Inc., El Segundo, Calif.)

reduce access for flies and to keep wet garbage from leaking into the containers. Garbage container lids should fit tightly, and boxes and bags should never be used in place of galvanized metal or heavy-duty plastic containers. Even if flies hatch elsewhere, accessible waste in or outside garbage containers will attract them.

OPERATOR METHODS OF KILLING COCKROACHES AND FLIES

It is an unfortunate fact of life that insects may be present in a dining facility no matter how good the sanitation and housekeeping practices are. Infestation can result from poor sanitation on the part of other tenants in the same or adjoining building or from infrequent refuse collection. But proper safeguards, aggressively applied, will reduce the severity of an infestation and make control measures more effective.

Many non-chemical methods for eliminating cockroaches and flies have been invented. Although the average foodservice operator may want to rely on chemical control of insects, it is best to consider *both* safety and effectiveness when checking out control methods. The manager may want to consider a variety of methods depending on safety and the size of the problem. In general, the chemical approach is best done by a licensed pest control operator.

Electrocutor Traps

Electrocutor insect traps, also called fly grids or "zappers," are coming into popular use in foodservice establishments, especially those with outside serving areas. These light traps "zap" or electrocute flying insects that come into contact with them.

Vapor lights are best used outside. If placed outside away from doors or entry areas, these devices can keep flies from entering the establishment. Vapor lights should be placed away from entrances, however, to avoid *attracting* flying insects to these areas. Other zappers are for inside. Inside zappers are best used in garbage areas or in dry storage areas.

Zappers should be kept away from inside serving areas, if possible. They are unsightly to patrons, who may not want to watch flies being electrocuted while they're dining. They should *never* be installed in any location where the dead insects may drop onto food. Zappers to kill flies are best kept close to the floor. Correct location is critical.

Zappers are useful for determining what type of insect problem exists. Some managers may be surprised at what they catch. Zappers should carry the Underwriters Laboratories seal. It is important that the trays to catch the corpses are regularly emptied and cleaned. Bulbs for zappers must be replaced regularly.

Glue Traps

Glue traps are cardboard containers opened at both ends, which allow cockroaches to enter and be trapped by the glue on the container floor. They may be used to find out the size of the cockroach problem. If the problem appears quite small or isolated, glue traps may be all that is necessary.

Repellents

Repellents are sprays, powders, or liquids that work to keep bugs away from a specific area and not necessarily to kill them. Repellents can sometimes be applied in hollows inside and around the outsides of walls or other areas that are difficult to reach. Like all methods of chemical control, they must be used with caution.

Sprays

Insecticide sprays are used frequently in the control of cockroaches and flies. These sprays are designated as residual, contact, or space sprays, depending on the way they work and the method of application.

A *residual spray* is applied directly to surfaces and leaves a deposit that kills insects contacting it. Residual sprays are applied near the hiding places of roaches and on the favorite resting and breeding places of flies. To be effective, the spray must form a thin, uniform layer on the treated surface.

A *contact spray* must touch the insect to kill it. The spray is usually applied to a group of insects, such as a cluster of cockroaches in a corner or crack.

A *space spray* discharges a mist into the air for killing insects. Because the application of space sprays can easily contaminate food, uses of this form of pesticide in foodservice facilities are limited.

Application of insecticides by *automatic dispensing devices* is permitted in foodservice operations only if (1) the ingredients or combinations of ingredients approved by the EPA are used; (2) if dispensers are installed according to manufacturer's instructions; and (3) if they are located so that there is no drippage or condensation onto exposed food or food-contact surfaces. All foods and food-contact utensils must be removed from an area being sprayed to avoid contamination. Any immovable equipment such as counters and ovens should be covered *and* cleaned off after spraying.

OTHER INSECT PESTS

In addition to flies and cockroaches, the insects that plague foodservice operations include beetles, moths, and ants. Insects such as flour moths and beetles are generally found in dry storage areas. The insects themselves, their webbing, clumped-together food particles, holes in food, and holes in packaging will be visible. Good ventilation, use of cool storage areas, regular cleaning and rotation of stock will help to control these pests.

Ants sometimes make their nests in the walls and floors of establishments, especially in the vicinity of stoves or hot water pipes. They often enter from the outside. Arches around windows and doors should be checked for cracks. Crevices around stoves, refrigerators, and sinks should be sealed, or if that is not possible, kept clean and free of food particles. Ants are partial to sticky sweets and to grease. Don't allow food residue to collect and attract ants. Spills should be cleaned up thoroughly and immediately. If serious ant infestation is suspected, sponges dipped in syrup as baits will locate where the ants are coming from.

Remember that beetles, moths, and ants can thrive on very small amounts of food. Good housekeeping and proper storage of food are the best safeguards against these pests.

RATS AND MICE

Rats and mice are among humanity's most cunning and capable enemies. They have highly developed senses of touch, smell, and hearing and can identify new or unfamiliar objects in their environment. Rats can wriggle through openings the size of a quarter. A mouse needs a hole only as large as a nickel to gain access to a building. Rats have a reach of up to 18 inches. They can climb vertical brick walls and jump up to three feet vertically and four feet horizontally. Both rats and mice are strong swimmers and are capable of swimming up through floor drains and toilet bowl traps. Rats and mice also have an excellent sense of balance: a falling rodent always lands on its feet. Some rats can maintain their balance even when walking on suspended wires.

Rats are prolific breeders. A single pair of rats can produce 50 offspring in one year. Rats and mice only live about one year, but they do enough damage to their environment to make up for their short life span. Rodents are dangerous and destructive. It has been estimated that rats cause anywhere from $1–10 billion a year in economic loss to this country through consumption and contamination of food and structural damage to property, including damage from fires caused by rats gnawing electrical wiring.

More important to the foodservice manager than such economic problems is the serious health hazard posed by rodent contamination of food and utensils. Rodents can be directly or indirectly involved in the transmission of such diseases as salmonellosis, leptospirosis, and murine typhus. One rat pill, or fecal dropping, can contain several million bacteria. Even if the pill does not get into food directly, it will become dry and fall apart or be crushed. Rats and mice have simple digestive systems, with very little bladder control. Therefore, they will urinate and defecate *as they move* around the facility. The particles then may be blown or carried into food. Don't assume that if you see only one or two droppings that you have a *minor* problem.

Kinds of Rodents

The most common kind of rat in the United States is the *Norway rat,* sometimes known as the sewer rat, brown rat, barn rat, or wharf rat. Norway rats are heavy, usually brown in color, and 7 to 10 inches (18 to 25 cm) long, excluding the tail. The Norway rat is found in every state of the United States. The roof rat, on the other hand, is generally found in this country only in the South, the states of the Pacific Coast, and Hawaii. The roof rat is more slender and graceful than the Norway rat, and

only 6½ to 8 inches (16.5 to 20 cm) long, excluding the tail. The house mouse, found everywhere in this country, has a body length of 2½ to 3½ inches (6 to 9 cm) and large, prominent ears. Exhibit 11.5 presents the identifying characteristics of these three types of rodents.

Signs of Rodent Infestation

Because rats and mice tend to hide during the day, they may be present in your establishment even if you do not see them. The following signs can help you determine whether you have an infestation and, if so, how extensive and recent it is.

Droppings

The presence of droppings, or feces, is one of the telltale signs of rodent infestation. Rat droppings are from ½ to ¾ inch (13 to 19 mm) in length and up to a ¼ inch (6 mm) in diameter. House mouse feces are much smaller, usually only an ⅛ inch (3 mm) in length. If the droppings are black and shiny and of a pasty consistency, a rodent has recently been in the vicinity. Older feces are brownish in color and fall apart when touched with a stick. Exhibit 11.2 shows the relative size of rodent and cockroach droppings.

Grease Marks (Rub Marks) and Runways

Since rats and mice almost always follow the same path or runway between their nests and sources of food, the grease and dirt from their bodies form visible streaks on floors and other surfaces. Rodents prefer to keep in contact with vertical surfaces when they travel, so look for runways along walls, steps, and roof rafters, in the corners of cupboards, and along inner sides of pipes. Exhibit 11.6 shows a typical rodent runway.

Exhibit 11.5   Field identification of
domestic rodents

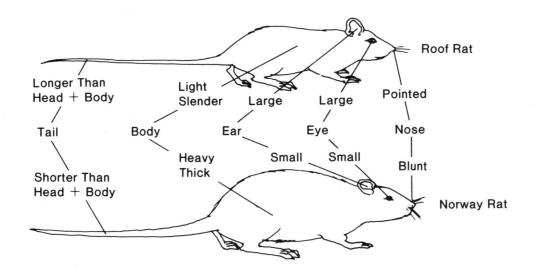

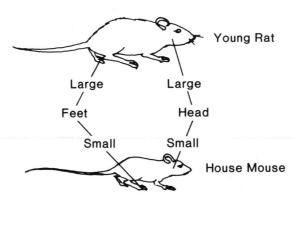

Scale in Inches

0   1   2   3

Exhibit 11.6 "Swing marks" on the overhead beam indicate the runway of a roof rat

Exhibit 11.7 Rat burrows (Source: The Food and Drug Administration)

Gnawings

Rats gnaw to reach sources of food and drink and to keep their teeth short. Their incisor teeth are so strong that rats have been known to gnaw through lead pipes and unhardened concrete, as well as sacks, wood, and paperboard. If gnawings are recent, teeth marks should be visible.

Tracks

Rat and mouse tracks can be seen most clearly on dusty surfaces by light shining from an acute angle. Talc spread in areas of suspected rodent activity will make new tracks visible.

Burrows

Rats also dig underground to enter buildings. Regular checks around the outside of a building may reveal rat-sized holes. Before closing them up, however, it is necessary to eliminate the rats inside (see Exhibit 11.7).

Preventing Rodent Infestation

Proper sanitation is the best weapon in the fight against rodents. Without food, shelter, or water, a population of rats or mice cannot survive in a foodservice establishment. Even the most effective poisoning and trapping campaign will bring about only a temporary reduction in a rodent population unless the following preventive measures are adopted.

Keep Them Out

The first step in rat-proofing an establishment is to find and eliminate all the possible ways for rodents to enter. Ill-fitting doors and weak masonry around external pipes provide easy access for rodents. Doors can be flashed with metal, and holes near pipes can be covered with sheet metal or filled with concrete (see Exhibit 11.8). Vents and basement windows should be protected by mesh screens. Basement and other floor drains should be covered

Exhibit 11.8   Stoppage of openings around pipes (Source: U.S. Department of Health and Human Services, Centers for Disease Control, Atlanta, Ga.)

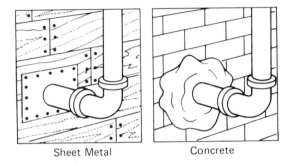

Sheet Metal   Concrete

by a perforated metal cap with a removable hinge (see Exhibit 11.9). (Accustomed to life in sewers, rats have no difficulty swimming into houses and commercial institutions.)

Improperly closed door thresholds are also an invitation to rodents. When wheeled carts are in use in a facility, door thresholds are often removed to facilitate movement of the carts through the doorways. This operation results in a gap being left between the closed door and the floor, through which pests can enter. If a building is tightly sealed, however, rodents will have a difficult time entering. The foodservice manager can then deal exclusively with the vermin population that might develop *inside* the facility.

Exhibit 11.9   Floor drain covered by a perforated metal cap with a removable hinge (Source: U.S. Department of Health and Human Services, Centers for Disease Control, Atlanta, Ga.)

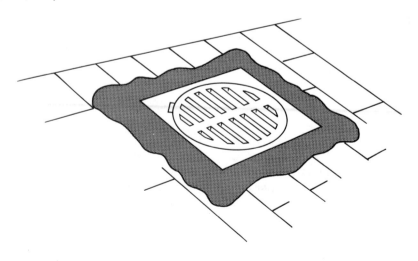

Decaying masonry in building foundations allows rats to burrow into buildings. An L-shaped concrete wall—4 inches thick, extending 24 inches down and 12 inches out—blocks such entrances (see Exhibit 11.10). Transoms, letter drops, and fan openings also provide access for rats and should be treated accordingly.

Destroy Their Hiding Places

Rats build nests in crowded storage rooms, in areas where garbage is placed, and along walls under boards, crates, or other such refuse. The foodservice operator can and must eliminate rodent hiding places on or near the premises.

Exhibit 11.10   L-shaped wall to keep out rats (Source: U.S. Department of Health and Human Services, Centers for Disease Control, Atlanta, Ga.)

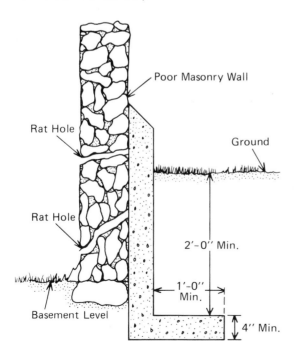

Garbage cans should be of heavy-duty plastic or galvanized metal and should have tight-fitting lids. Containers should be placed on racks at least 18 inches above the ground or on concrete blocks. Garbage cans or dumpsters should be placed as far from the building as possible, and lids kept tightly closed. Such arrangements eliminate possible hiding places for rodents beneath the containers.

All foodstuffs in storerooms should be placed on racks at least six inches above the floor and should be kept away from the walls. Painting a white strip around the edge of the floor of a storeroom will not only encourage workers to stack material away from the walls but will also make identification of rodent signs (tracks, rubbings, droppings, hairs) much easier. Boards, crates, and so forth, should be stored on racks away from walls.

Starve Them

Food sources for rodents can be reduced by careful storage and proper cleaning. Clean up spills immediately, sweep floors regularly, and remove garbage from the premises as soon as possible. Once commercial food containers have been opened, the supplies from them should be stored in properly constructed, covered containers.

Operator Methods of Controlling Rodents

On any list of nightmares that ruin the sleep of a foodservice manager, this one must rank high. The establishment is crowded with diners. Suddenly, their conversation stops and their forks poise midway above their plates. A rat has been spotted scurrying through the room.

When rats come to dinner, or when you discover the presence of rats or mice through the telltale signs described earlier, it is obvious that some cardinal rule of pest prevention has been violated. As with other pests, the best way to control rats and mice is to make the environment unsuitable for them. If available food and shelter are reduced, the rodent population will be reduced proportionately. But what can be done if preventive measures don't solve the problem? The following paragraphs list techniques for killing rodent pests.

Trapping

The use of traps is a slow, but generally safe, method of killing rats and mice. Traps should be placed at right angles to rodent runways, with the baited or trigger end toward the wall. Traps can be baited with any one of a number of different kinds of food: fresh ground meat, pet food, and peanut butter all make satisfactory baits. Traps should be checked every day, and baits should be kept fresh. Since rodents are accustomed to human smells, odors from trapped rats or from human hands will not keep rats away from traps.

Glue Boards

A quantity of rat-size or mice-size glue traps, strategically placed, can be effective in controlling rats and mice. They do not contain poison and are safe for use in foodservice areas. Like traps, glue boards should be placed in areas where rats and mice run through. If possible, they should be tacked down so that the trapped rats don't attempt to drag them back to their nests. They should be removed as soon as a rat appears dead and it is safe to do so.

Poisoning

Since they are dangerous to humans as well as to rodents, poison baits should be used with extreme caution, only as a last resort, and only on the advice of a licensed pest control operator. Nevertheless, poisoning can be a very effective method of rat control.

The most commonly used rodenticide poisons are the anticoagulants such as warfarin, fumarin, Pival, PMP, Brodifacoum, and Bromodiolone. These are multiple-dose poisons—the rodent must eat some of them on several occasions. This multiple-dose feature provides a safety factor for a child who may accidentally eat a portion of the poisoned bait.

Although the multiple-dose anticoagulants are safer than other poisons, they require careful application and maintenance. Baits must be prepared according to package directions and placed along rodent runways or near breeding sites. Children will be protected from baits placed beneath shelters or in bait boxes, under boards, or in pipes or cans. Fresh baits must be put out every day for at least two weeks if the anticoagulant poison is to be effective in reducing rodent infestation. They must never be placed where they may be confused with food items or may be dropped onto food.

The anticoagulant rodenticides are available in many forms: as ready-to-use baits that can be placed on plastic or cardboard trays in rodent runways; in pellet form, mixed with grain, for use in rodent burrows and dead spaces between walls; in small plastic packages to be tossed into rodent hiding places; in bait blocks; in concentrated form; and as salts that are to be mixed with water.

Whatever the form of bait used, the manager should be sure to use an adequate amount of bait. In addition, the location of all bait containers should be recorded so that an inspection can be made quickly and any bait that has been consumed can be replaced. If a bait remains undisturbed after several inspections, it should be moved to another location.

If several types of baits are distributed at the same time, a different-colored paper wrapper for each type will help quickly determine which type the rats prefer.

Baits should be generous. Rodents travel limited distances from their burrows or hiding places—usually a maximum of 150 feet for rats, and 30 feet for mice. If baits are too few in number, or poorly placed, rodents may not find them. It is wise to bait liberally where signs of rodent activity are numerous and recent. The baits should be inspected regularly and fresh ones provided when needed.

It should be noted that some of the most commonly used single-dose poisons are effective against Norway rats only. *Caution.* Never touch a dead or dying rat with your hands. If it is still alive, it may fight back and bite. If the rat is dead, the fleas will abandon the body as soon as the body temperature begins to drop.

BIRDS

Birds such as sparrows, starlings, and pigeons may also present problems for a food-service facility. These birds leave unsightly droppings that sometimes carry fungi capable of infecting human beings. The droppings themselves can damage buildings. The birds themselves may be carriers of mites and of organisms that cause encephalitis, psittacosis, and other diseases.

The most effective procedure in dealing with pest birds is to employ a pest-control operator who specializes in bird control. The operator has the knowledge and equipment required for safe use of chemicals in combating birds, and knows which birds are protected by law.

Any bird population can be effectively controlled, although doing so is not always a simple matter. Good sanitation practices will keep birds from being attracted by food on the property. Screening should of course be installed on windows, ventilator openings, and doorways.

If these measures fail, more direct techniques are available, within varying legal limits. Migratory birds are protected by federal law. Many state and local laws specify not only what birds may be controlled, but also what methods of control may be used. The legality of any control methods should, therefore, be checked in advance with local conservation officials and representatives of the U.S. Fish and Wildlife Service.

Live-trapping is usually an acceptable method of bird control. Pastes that repel birds and wires that administer a mild electric shock are also effective in preventing birds from roosting. They are generally safe and can permanently discourage birds from using the facility for nesting. The latter method is fairly expensive and requires frequent inspection and maintenance. Netting may also be used around outside displays such as signs or statues to keep birds from roosting on these. Noisemaking devices and flashing lights have little effect on birds because the birds soon become accustomed to these irritants. Removing nests, spraying the birds themselves with water, and similar forms of harassment may be successful if carried out repeatedly.

PESTICIDES

For some operators, an immediate reaction upon seeing, say a few cockroaches, is to run to the hardware store for a can of insecticide and bombard the facility with it. This is a faulty approach for a number of reasons:

1. *Chemical pesticides are no substitute for good sanitation.* In the long run, proper sanitary measures are more effective and more economical than any poison. No matter how effective the pesticide program may be, rodents and insects will return when unsanitary conditions prevail.

2. *The safest assumption to make about pesticides is that any time they are used or stored in the establishment, a hazard exists to the food supply, customers, and employees.* Pesticides may be toxic to humans, and some may also cause fire or explosion. Since the manager is ultimately responsible for the safety of the entire operation, he or she must always see to it that hazards are minimized.

3. *Pesticide use is not a simple procedure.* Determining the most appropriate pesticide for a particular pest, where it is to be applied, and the most effective method of application often requires information and training not readily available to the foodservice manager. In some areas pests have developed populations that are resistant to common pesticides. This does not mean that a given rat or cockroach becomes immune to a specific poison in the same way that human beings become immune to a disease. Rather, within a population of pests those that are naturally immune to a poison survive its use and breed resistant strains of the pest.

    A solution to the growing problem of immunity has not yet been found, though research is moving ahead. Because this is a complicated problem varying from pest to pest and with each section of the country, it is best to work with a professional pest control operator who knows the proper methods to rid an operation of pests.

4. *Pesticide use is regulated by the federal government.* Chemical pesticides have come under increasingly tight legal restrictions in recent years. Numerous new state and local regulations govern the use of pesticides. In addition, the Federal Environmental Pesticide Control Act of 1972 seeks to ensure protection of human beings and the environment from improper use of pesticides. The act prohibits the use of pesticides in any manner inconsistent with the instructions on the label of the pesticide container and requires that all pesticides be classified as being for "general use" or for "restricted use." General-use pesticides are those that will not ordinarily cause unreasonably adverse effects either on the user or on the environment when used in accordance with the instructions on the container labels or according to widespread practice. Restricted-use pesticides are those that may cause adverse effects either on the user or on the environment. These pesticides may only be applied by, or under the supervision of, competent persons certified by the individual states in cooperation with the Federal Environmental Protection Agency.

    If you have any doubts about the legality of a pesticide that you or your pest control operator wish to use, consult your state regulatory agency or other appropriate authority.

Pesticide Use

Although pesticide use can be effective against a variety of pests, it should always be a last resort. Even then, pesticides are best used by a pest control operator. For safety and effectiveness, this is the best solution to a consistent pest problem. Pest control methods such as misting, dusting, and gassing should *always* be left to a licensed pest control operator. However they are used or whoever uses them, precautions should always be observed.

Precautions in Use of Pesticides

1. Be sure pesticide containers are properly identified and labeled.

2. Read and follow package directions carefully. Use any pesticide only for the purposes for which it is designed. An insecticide effective against one type of insect may be totally ineffective against another.

3. Use the weakest poison that will do the job, and use it in the proper concentration. *When it comes to poison, it's dangerous to reason that if one dose is good, a double dose will be better.* Effective results occur because of *thorough treatment,* not a double dose of poison.

4. Distinguish between oil-based and water-based sprays. Oil-based sprays are used where water might cause an electrical short circuit, stain wallpaper, shrink fabric, or cause mildew. Water-based sprays are used around hot ovens or pilot lights where fire is a possibility, or any place where oil might cause damage to rubber or asphalt, or where the odor of oil is objectionable.

5. Avoid *any* possibility of contaminating food utensils with pesticides. Always consider the rule of nature that "if an accident can happen, it will."

6. If pesticides are used or stored, post emergency measures for treating accidental poisoning.

Precautions in Storage and Disposal of Pesticides

If pesticides are being used, the foodservice manager should consult with a pest control operator about where to store them and how to dispose of them. The manager should routinely inspect pesticide supplies and discard those no longer in use. The following list itemizes precautions to be taken in storing pesticides:

1. Never permit a pesticide to be transferred from its labeled package to any other kind of storage container. One of the most common causes of pesticide poisoning is the bad habit of storing pesticides in empty food containers.

2. Store pesticides in a *locked* cabinet well removed from foodhandling and storage areas. Pesticides should be stored separate from other poisonous or toxic materials such as detergents, caustics, and other chemicals.

3. Aerosol "bombs" or other pressurized spray cans should never be stored in an area where they may become overheated. If they reach too high a temperature, they could explode violently. Pressurized pesticide containers should be stored in a cool place and should not be exposed to temperatures higher than 120°F (48.9°C).

Pesticides constitute a hazard until they are disposed of properly. Here are some precautions for disposing of pesticides.

1. Dispose of bags, cartons, bottles, or cans as soon as they become empty. Containers for pesticides are a potential hazard even when they appear empty, since particles of toxic material may still be present.

2. Rinse bottles and nonaerosol or unpressurized cans three times in a disposal drain—never in a sink used for food, dishware, or utensils—and then destroy them. Paper and cardboard may be incinerated.

3. Break bottles and crush unpressurized cans, wrap the remains in paper, and place them in rubbish containers.

4. Because of the probability of explosion, do not burn empty aerosol cans. Pressurized spray cans should not be crushed in a compactor or punctured.

WORKING WITH A PEST CONTROL OPERATOR

Foodservice managers will work with a variety of professionals during their careers. Lawyers, accountants, menu designers, and others all provide services to foodservice operators. As foodservice management requires skill and expertise, technical jobs such as pest control are also best performed by experts. A licensed pest control operator (PCO) has the technical background to work with a foodservice manager to solve a pest problem. As a team, the manager and the PCO can rid the operation of pests and keep them from returning. If a pest problem persists despite a variety of non-chemical methods, employing the services of a PCO is a sound alternative to pesticide use. The following factors should be considered:

1. A skilled pest control operator can recommend an *integrated pest management program*. The program may include all or a variety of control methods—such as correcting sanitary procedures, chemical treatment, non-chemical solutions, and sealing of cracks and crevices to keep pests away. Pest problems are rarely solved by simplistic measures, such as spraying or poisons. A PCO who evaluates an operation's sanitation procedures and points out gaps is aware of this. If the pest problem is the result of bad sanitation, poor building conditions, or pesticide resistance, spraying chemicals at pests is not going to remove them for good.

2. Staying on the safe side of the pesticide issue and relying on the expertise of a pest control operator is a logical approach. Pesticide use is a tricky business. Most states require pest control operators to know which pesticides can be used in a foodservice facility, and those that may be used under certain restrictions.

3. Pest control technology is changing and pest control operators are expected to keep up with new developments. Hiring a licensed pest control operator can help ensure that the foodservice manager receives up-to-date control services for the type of pest infesting the establishment.

4. A pest control operator can work during slow business periods or before the operation opens. This flexibility frees managers and other workers to concentrate on other tasks. Of course, it is necessary for the manager to know where the PCO is and what he or she is doing. Still the major, technical job of pest control is best delegated.

How to Select a Pest Control Operator

The selection of a pest control operator merits the same care that would be used in hiring a lawyer, a decorator, or an accountant. A little research is wise.

1. Talk to friends in the foodservice business. Find out who they've used and what kind of job they felt a particular PCO did. Ask about return visits. Did the PCO offer sanitation advice or just spray corners and baseboards? (Remember you're looking for an integrated approach.) Friends may also be able to

tell you about prices and other facts. Any reputable PCO should be able to provide names of former clients as references.

2. Make sure that the PCO is licensed or certified by your state. Certification is required by federal law especially for supervising personnel. Certification usually indicates that the PCO has demonstrated minimal competence by passing an exam on pesticide use and other control procedures.

3. Ask about membership in professional organizations. Membership in a state or local pest control association or the National Pest Control Association is a positive sign. This professional membership is assurance that the PCO is receiving the most up-to-date information on control methods.

4. Be sure that any pest control operator you employ has insurance on his or her work in order to protect your establishment, employees, and customers.

A word of caution. Don't use price as the only deciding factor in choosing a PCO. Expertise is what you're looking for. The lowest bid may prove more costly in the long run.

Working with a PCO: The Teamwork Approach

Okay, you've found your PCO. What happens next? Can you return to the back of the house and leave the PCO to search out nooks and crannies for pests? Not exactly.

There are several steps to achieving a pest-free environment that require cooperation between the PCO and the foodservice manager. These are the contract, the inspection, the treatment procedures, and the follow-up.

Contracting with a PCO

A contract is an essential element in the business relationship between the foodservice manager and PCO. A PCO may have a standard contract. Read it carefully. If possible, have a longer look at it. It should include a warranty of what is to be done, the period of service, legal liability, emergency service, and foodservice obligations.

The Inspection

Most PCOs will want to inspect an operation to find out the extent of the pest problem as well as the sanitary conditions and structural defects that may be contributing to the problem. You should have building plans and a layout available. Of course, employees should be told about the inspection. They should be ready to answer any questions the PCO may have regarding sanitary procedures. The PCO must have complete access to the facility. However, you should point out the areas where the problem is greatest.

After the inspection, the PCO should outline a treatment program for the unit. His or her program should include the materials that will be used, the dates and times of the treatment, and any steps the foodservice manager should take to help eliminate pests. At this point the PCO should point out problem areas in sanitation and structural defects that invite pests.

The Treatment Procedures

It is essential that foodservice managers know which, if any, chemical pesticides are going to be used throughout the operation. As part of the inspection process, local health departments often require written records of hazardous chemicals, when they were used, and where.

If the PCO must store pesticides in the facility left over from treatments, see that they are kept away from food storage or food preparation areas. Also, find out what steps are required during treatment. Do you need to move dishes, cover equipment, or open windows? Ask about non-chemical methods of pest control, especially in areas where these substances may be hazardous.

Mutual cooperation will speed the pest elimination process. Some PCOs will reserve the right to terminate the contract if clients refuse to cooperate by ignoring advice on sanitation or canceling treatments. On the other hand, the foodservice manager must make it clear that the nature of the business requires special care be taken in the treatment plan.

The Follow-Up

Pest control services should include follow-up. The PCO should return after the final treatment to check for pests. A manager should check the facility as well and contact the PCO if pests reappear.

Many large operations, including cafeterias and restaurants, have periodic inspections by pest control companies. For operators with persistent or seasonal problems, building problems, or less-than-clean neighbors, this may be a good idea. Otherwise, annual inspections are usually sufficient.

SUMMARY

Insects and rodents have plagued human beings and destroyed their food supplies throughout history. These pests continue to be a menace in the foodservice operation because they are carriers of foodborne illness and because they reduce profits by spoiling foodstuffs.

To guard the establishment against pests, a foodservice manager should concentrate on the following two areas:

1. Physically prevent pests from entering by closing off any openings in the building and by inspecting incoming supplies.
2. Eliminate sources of food and water, as well as breeding and hiding places, through proper housekeeping measures.

If insect or rodent pests become established, it may be necessary to resort to control measures. Control measures, however, should be considered as a supplement to, not as a substitute for, good sanitation. Although an insect or rodent infestation may be eliminated by use of pesticides, pests will almost certainly return unless the establishment is kept clean and food and water supplies are protected.

Because most pesticides are toxic to humans, these poisons should be selected and applied with great care. Precautions must be observed in the use, storage, and disposal of pesticides. Although the foodservice manager may choose to apply pesticides on occasion, a pest control operator should always be employed for the more complex or hazardous extermination tasks.

Employing a pest control operator is often the best approach to ridding a food service of pests. The PCO should be licensed, insured, and a member of a pest control association. Although the technical work of pest control should be left to the PCO, the manager should know what he or she is using and where. The manager should also cooperate when it comes to correcting faulty sanitary procedures pointed out by the PCO.

A CASE IN POINT

The restaurant located in the middle of town is on the first floor of a landmark building, which has stood since World War I. The restaurant is in a shopping area that includes several other restaurants. The interior of the restaurant is completely remodeled with marble floors and new ceilings. Most of the materials are easy to clean and modern. All of the foodservice equipment is modern and designed for cleanability. The cleaning procedures in food preparation areas are regular and strict. Spills and grease are cleaned up immediately. Dirt is hardly given time to settle anywhere in the kitchen. Stock procedures include frequent stock rotation and metal racks that keep food off the floor and away from the walls.

One week the health inspector comes in. He finds cockroaches behind the sinks, in the vegetable storage area, in the bathrooms, and near the waste areas.

How do you think this infestation happened?
What is your recommendation to the foodservice manager?

STUDY QUESTIONS

1. Name three basic steps for controlling pests in a foodservice operation.
2. What three types of cockroaches are most likely to infest a foodservice facility?
3. Describe typical breeding places for cockroaches.
4. List at least four housekeeping practices that will prevent roach infestation.
5. Name two favorite resting places of flies.
6. Where would you check for maggots?
7. What is the difference between a contact spray and a residual spray?
8. What three types of rodents are most likely to infest a foodservice facility?
9. List three signs that a foodservice facility is infested with rodents.
10. Name at least four ways in which a rodent can gain entrance to a building.
11. List two methods of eliminating rodents from a foodservice facility.
12. What are some of the problems with using pesticides in a foodservice facility?
13. Describe the proper means of storing pesticides.
14. What are the reasons for using the services of a pest control operator?
15. List the steps for selecting a pest control operator.

MORE ON THE SUBJECT

NATIONAL PEST CONTROL ASSOCIATION. *How to Select and Use Pest Control Services.* Available from the National Pest Control Association, Dunn Loring, Virginia, this publication provides information on locating and working with pest control operators.

OHIO DEPARTMENT OF HEALTH. *Insect Control.* Available from the Ohio Department of Health, Columbus, Ohio, this publication provides basic information on the life cycles of flies and cockroaches and methods for controlling these pests.

SCOTT, H. G., and M. R. BOROM. *Rodent-Borne Disease Control through Rodent Stoppage.* U.S. Department of Health and Human Services, Public Health Service, Centers for Disease Control, Atlanta, Georgia. An excellent manual on specific techniques of ratproofing, this publication contains numerous drawings and much information on materials and design.

ANSWER TO A CASE IN POINT

Older buildings often have more nooks and crannies than newer buildings. Decaying building materials and less than sanitary neighbors can make pest control in such buildings difficult. Still, there are probably crevices that could be sealed around the sinks and in the storage areas. It is also important to step up cleaning of the restrooms. Patrons may be unwittingly contributing to the pest problem there. Garbage may have to be taken out of the facility several times during the day.

Rather than resorting to do-it-yourself pesticides, the foodservice manager should call in an expert pest control operator. The PCO should be able to work with the manager to develop a pest control program that includes sanitation advice, pesticides, and non-chemical control methods.

12
Accident Prevention and
Action for Emergencies

The prevention of accidents and the ability to act wisely in an emergency are as much a part of the business of operating a foodservice establishment as the prevention of foodborne illness. Protecting customers from the danger of foodborne illness is of little use if the restaurant is allowed to burn down around them while they eat. Or, to choose a less extreme case, attention to both customer service and sanitation suffers whenever a time-consuming and possibly injurious accident occurs in the establishment. Many accidents also result in the direct contamination of food. In short, accident prevention and sanitation are closely related, *and both contribute to the creation of a safe food service.*

It is easy to think of reasons for eliminating accidents from the foodservice establishment. Some of the major motivations are listed.

1. *Accidents are painful.* Many accidents involve personal injury and also create tension and anxiety among other workers and customers.

2. *Accidents are expensive.* An establishment must carry insurance to cover medical expenses and workman's compensation for employees injured on the job. Frequent accidents will cause these insurance rates to skyrocket.

   Accidents also result in indirect, uninsured costs, including lost and damaged materials, reduced efficiency due to short-handedness or distraction, lost work time of injured workers, cleanup costs after an accident, and the costs of investigating the accident, filling out accident report forms, and the fees of visiting physicians. New employees may have to be trained to replace injured workers, or other methods may have to be found to handle the workload of accident victims. All of these factors cost the foodservice operation money.

3. *Accidents lower morale.* Frequent accidents indicate that the management is not interested enough in the employees' or the customers' welfare to provide safe surroundings.

4. *Accidents damage reputations.* No one wants to eat in a firetrap.

5. *Accidents can result in fines or imprisonment.* Employers are required by law to provide employees with a safe place to work. Employee complaints about safety can initiate government inspections under the *Occupational Safety and Health Act of 1970.* Unsafe conditions found during these inspections can leave the operator of the food service open to legal penalties.

Most people feel that "accidents will happen"; that accidents occur because of chance, bad luck, or because some people are "accident prone." But the truth is that *most accidents can be prevented.* Accident prevention is not easy, but it is by no means impossible.

A well-designed accident-prevention program consists of steps to eliminate physical hazards, to train workers in good safety habits, and to provide constant supervision to see that unsafe conditions and practices do not arise. An accident-prevention program can significantly reduce accidents and injuries in the foodservice establishment.

This chapter will discuss the methods for setting up an accident-prevention program through finding the answers to the following questions:

- What are accidents?
- How are accidents caused?
- What kinds of accidents occur in a foodservice establishment?
- How can accidents be prevented?
- How should emergencies be handled?

No accident-prevention program is fool-proof. Accidents and injuries often occur suddenly. Because of this, emergency procedures for managers and employees are included. *Action* is the key to dealing with an emergency properly. A failure to act could worsen an injury and result in liability for the operator.

ACCIDENTS DEFINED

An *accident* may be defined as an unintended happening resulting in injury, loss, or damage. The event may or may not result from negligence. By this definition, if a dish slips from the hands of a dishwasher into the sink without breaking, it is not an accident. If the dish does break, resulting in the loss of both the dish itself and the time required to clean up the fragments, an accident has occurred. If the dishwasher's hand is cut in the process of cleaning up the broken dish, then personal injury has resulted from the accident. An accident-prevention program seeks to eliminate all accidents, not just those resulting in personal injury.

THE CAUSES OF ACCIDENTS

Accidents in foodservice operations occur more frequently than they should. A combination of poor training and environmental hazards contribute to this frequency. Such threats to safety can be eliminated, or at least minimized.

Accidents are the products of a number of factors. They may begin with unsafe physical conditions, such as loose boards on a stairway or a crowded kitchen, but unsafe conditions alone rarely generate accidents. It is possible to work for years under the most dangerous conditions—as a tightrope walker, for example, or as a demolition expert—and never have an accident. On the other hand, it is en-tirely possible to have a series of accidents in an environment as safe as human ingenuity can possibly make it. The determining factor in most accidents is *human error.*

The Human Hazard

People cause the majority of accidents. People create unsafe conditions. They ignore frayed wire on equipment, stack boxes too high, leave spills on the floor, fail to clean greasy vent filters, and block passages with equipment.

People ignore obvious hazards. They pick up broken glass with their bare hands, refuse to use safety devices on grinders and slicers, lift loads too heavy for them, and stride fearlessly across slick wet floors without a second thought.

People can even manage to have spectacular accidents where there are no hazards at all. Through inattention and carelessness they bump into other people, drop heavy items on their own feet, and close doors and drawers on their fingers.

However, there is hope. People can learn practices that will reduce the possibility of accidents. They can be made to understand that they have an obligation to their employer and themselves to learn how to *prevent* accidents. They can learn to recognize and correct or avoid hazardous conditions.

While the element of human negligence is the most important cause of accidents, it rarely operates without the assistance of preexisting hazards in the environment. Eliminating these unsafe conditions is another important step toward preventing accidents.

The Environmental Hazard

Environmental hazards include both conditions that are unsafe in themselves, such as unguarded meat slicer blades, and conditions that encourage unsafe habits on the part of the workers, such as ladders that are too short to reach upper shelves in the storeroom.

Some environmental hazards cannot be eliminated without full-scale renovation. Steep, narrow stairways or dining rooms located a step or two up or down from the kitchen are hazards of this type. Unsafe architectural features must be recognized and compensated for until economic considerations allow remodeling; they should certainly never be built into new structures or be allowed to survive renovation.

Other less permanent environmental hazards should be remedied as soon as possible after they are recognized. Clogged floor drains that result in floors remaining wet and slippery for long periods of time, furniture or equipment arranged so as to create narrow aisles or inefficient traffic patterns, doors that open into passageways—these conditions can all be corrected with a minimum of expense for a great gain in safety.

Another type of environmental hazard is that which results from negligence. Knives left lying around when not in use and pots and pans placed on stoves so that their handles protrude into aisles are two examples of this type of hazard.

An examination of the kinds of accidents and injuries that occur in foodservice operations will reveal that this type of unnecessary hazard, coupled with other unsafe practices on the part of employees, account for most mishaps.

FOODSERVICE ACCIDENTS AND PREVENTION

A food service can be a dangerous place to work. The nature of the business requires that many items of equipment be sharp or hot. Floors are often wet or greasy. Workers rush from place to place with their arms full and their minds elsewhere. The most common kinds of foodservice injuries and accidents are directly related to the presence of these conditions.

Cuts and Lacerations

Cuts and lacerations are injuries involving breaking of the skin. They result from accidents involving knives, food slicers, choppers, and mixers, poorly designed equipment with sharp edges, and broken glass or other items. These objects may be inherently unsafe because of faulty design and lack of safety features, or they may be handled unsafely by rushed, careless, or untrained employees.

Cuts often result when workers attempt to catch knives they have dropped, instead of stepping out of the way while the knives drop to the floor. Knives left in sinks full of soapy water to be washed later are also frequently the cause of cuts, when unsuspecting dishwashers reach into the sink and grab whatever utensils are there.

Preventing Cuts and Lacerations

Dull blades are implicated in more cutting accidents than are sharp blades. Dull blades are difficult to work with. More pressure must be applied to cut with them; the chance of a dull knife slipping or being dropped is thus also increased. Knives should be sharpened frequently and at regular intervals.

Knives should be stored separately from other utensils and sorted by size. Knives should only be used for the special purpose for which they are intended. Knives should never be left in sinks or on counters where they may be forgotten. Steel gloves are available for workers to wear when cleaning knives and slicer blades. They do not take the place of caution, however.

Power-driven slicers, grinders, and choppers are frequently the causes of severe cuts and lacerations, some even resulting in loss of fingers. Such accidents are preventable. Buying the safest equipment and maintaining it is one safety step. Jewelry, loose sleeves, or ties should never be worn when operating slicers. These items can be drawn into the equipment, resulting in hand cuts or worse. Always disconnect the machine immediately if something does become caught.

Guard devices that prevent machine operators from touching moving blades should be installed wherever possible. Nonsplintering tampers, pushers or plungers, or blocks should be provided for pushing food into grinders and slicers. Sharp edges can also be covered with nontoxic paint to make them more visible. A very effective safety device for dangerous equipment is a *spring switch,* or dead-man control, which allows the machine to operate only while the switch is depressed—if the operator releases the switch, the machine stops. Guards should be provided for all equipment with moving or electrically charged surfaces that could injure workers, including not only cutting and chopping appliances, but also fans, conveyors, and mixers.

Meat slicers and other grinding, chopping, or cutting equipment have to be kept sharp—it is not feasible to change to round-edged blades so that workers won't cut themselves.

Glasses should not be stacked inside one another. Dishes and glasses that are washed manually should be washed separately. Glasses should never be used to scoop ice. If glass breaks in dishwater, the sink should be drained and the pieces carefully removed. Separate garbage containers should be kept for broken glass.

Nails, staples, and protruding sharp edges present further hazards to employees unpacking boxes and crates. If possible, these should be removed or pounded down.

Burns

Burns are a second common foodservice injury. Burns and scalds of varying degrees of severity can result from contact with the hot surfaces of grills, ovens, stove burners, steam tables, fryers, and any other heating equipment that might be in use. Spattered,

splashed, and spilled hot food and drink can also burn skin, as can steam or hot water.

Deep fryers are a source of many very severe burns. The usual temperature of the hot fat in a fryer is at least 300°F (over 149°C), and this fat can splash on a careless worker, particularly if wet, cold food is placed in the fryer.

Poor traffic patterns through the kitchen, allowing insufficient space for avoiding hot equipment, also contribute to the incidence of burns.

Hot equipment that is not designed for easy accessibility, pots and pans with loose handles, and loose connections on steam equipment are examples of other conditions that can lead to burns.

Preventing Burns

Burns from hot equipment and hot liquids can be prevented. Most, if not all, of these types of injuries are due to carelessness.

Traffic in hot-food preparation areas should be kept to a minimum. Pan handles should always be pointed away from traffic, but reachable to workers without knocking over other pans. Stoves should not be crowded with hot pans of food between preparation and serving. Pot holders and gloves should be used for handling hot pans and cookware. Layout and planning promotes safety in this area. Hot pots and pans should be moved minimal distances, if at all.

Steam is another burn hazard. An employee should stand with his or her face away from the pot when removing the lid of a steam kettle. The lid should be removed gradually.

Of course, patrons can also be burned as a result of employee carelessness. Employees need to follow a clear traffic pattern among themselves to avoid collisions when carrying hot liquids. Cups or dishes containing hot foods should never be filled to overflowing. Patrons should be warned if foods and plates are very hot. (Flaming food hazards will be discussed later.)

Hot grease can cause severe burns, and caution must always be used. Food items should not be dropped into hot oil but placed in with tongs or in frying baskets. Protective gloves should be worn. Oil and water *do not mix*. Just-washed food items should dry before they are placed in oil. New oil should not be added to hot oil. The hot oil should be allowed to cool first. Frying baskets must not be overloaded.

Falls

Anything that is not already on the floor can fall. People, pots, boxes, bottles, knives, and napkins can all fall to the floor, causing damage, injury, or inconvenience.

Inanimate objects fall because they have been stacked too high, left on vibrating surfaces, perched precariously on shelves, or dropped by people. They can also cause injury by falling on unwary people who dislodge them as they pass by. If fallen objects land in passageways, they can, in turn, cause people to trip.

Most falls, however, involve more direct causes. Workers frequently lose their footing on floors that are either made of slippery material to begin with or have been made slippery by the presence of food, grease, or water. The danger from slippery floors is compounded by the fact that workers frequently hurry through their tasks in response to the rush of business at mealtimes and by the fact that workers often carry loads of varying sizes as they move to and fro. These loads can obstruct their vision and limit their maneuverability.

When workers fall from heights, injuries are more severe. The most unlikely and unsafe objects are constantly being used to aid foodservice workers in reaching high shelves—boxes, chairs, other shelves, and other workers. Even when safe stools and ladders are employed, it is often without any thought for their safe use.

The bruises, strains, sprained muscles and joints, fractures, and more serious injuries resulting from falls account for a large proportion of foodservice injuries.

Preventing Falls

Falls are usually the result of carelessness and are preventable. Environmental hazards also play a part. Floors should be designed for safety as well as appearance. Carpeting should be tacked down well. Drains will aid in keeping floors dry. Spills must be cleaned immediately. Employees should wear shoes that have hard rubber soles to prevent slipping and that have closed heels and toes to prevent cuts or crushing injuries.

Traffic congestion is a major cause of falls and collisions. Service employees should not have to cross paths with preparation employees and vice-versa. A work-flow system that minimizes traffic should be developed.

Climbing to reach supplies is another cause of falls in foodservice operations. Ladders exist to facilitate climbing but must be used correctly. The top rung of a ladder should not be used as a step or for balance. Boxes, crates, chairs, and the shelves themselves are not made for climbing.

Heavy supplies should be placed on lower shelves and lighter ones on top shelves. Overreaching for supplies should be avoided. If a box looks too heavy for one person, workers should be instructed to ask another employee to help them.

Customers of foodservice operations can be victims of ''slip and fall'' accidents, which can result in liability. Managers and employees need to be on the lookout for hazards such as spills and objects in pathways.

Exhibit 12.1   Los Angeles Fire Department rules for serving flaming foods

Los Angeles operators must have special fire department permits to serve flaming foods or drinks. In addition to the required permit, the following safety measures must be followed:

1. Fuels to heat food may be of jellied or semi-solid type. Liquid fuel in excess of one ounce per table will not be permitted.
2. The preparation of flaming foods and drinks is restricted to the table being served. They shall not be transported or carried through rooms or areas while burning.
3. The person who prepares the flaming food or drink shall have a wet towel immediately available for use in smothering the fire in event of emergency.
4. The serving of flaming drinks or desserts shall be done in a safe manner without flamboyancy or the type of showmanship which would create high flames. The pouring, ladling, or spooning of burning liquids is restricted to a maximum height of eight inches.
5. Crepes suzette shall not be served to more than six persons with one "set up." The pan used shall not be more than one inch in depth. The total amount of flammable beverage used in one "set up" shall not exceed one ounce.

Source: Los Angeles Fire Department

Other Common Accidents and Injuries

The nature of the foodservice operation contributes to the frequency of several other types of accidents in addition to those just mentioned. The large amount of movement required of employees increases the chance that they will bump into equipment, furniture, and each other, causing damage to the facility and injury to themselves. Swinging doors cause injury if not used properly. Windows on these types of doors can help workers avoid collisions. One door should be marked "out" and the other "in". Heavy and awkward items must frequently be lifted, providing opportunities for back strain and other injuries resulting from incorrect lifting techniques. Incorrect lifting can cause serious back injury. Lifting should be done from a knee-bending position, not by leaning forward and picking up the item, that will allow the leg muscles and not the back to lift the weight. Hand trucks should be available if boxes must be moved frequently.

Another type of hazard involves the use of tableside, food-preparation or service displays such as lighting flaming dishes or chopping foods. If this is done with caution, it can be good entertainment for customers. However, careful training and use of safe techniques are necessary to avoid injuries and prevent liability. Flying knives and corks are not fun when they hit someone. Corks should not be allowed to pop. Flaming dishes can be a source of tragedy without scrupulous attention to safety (see Exhibit 12.1 from the Los Angeles Fire Department Rules for Serving Flaming Foods).

Exhibit 12.2   Number of fires by retail classification

Classification	Annual Number of Fires	Loss per Fire
Drug stores	3,300	$ 3,909
Grocery stores	7,800	5,244
Food product plants	4,900	11,959
Laundries	3,100	2,290
Service stations	6,000	2,367
Restaurants	26,800	2,437

Reprinted by permission from "Fire Safety: Can We Do More?" *Restaurant Business,*
Volume 80, Number 6, May 1, 1981.

Foodservice operations use large numbers of electric appliances, which can be hazardous when in poor condition or handled unsafely. Improperly grounded equipment and equipment placed in damp or wet areas can seriously shock unwary operators. An even greater hazard related to electrical equipment, however, is the ever-present danger of fire.

Fires

The National Fire Protection Association estimates that 26,800 fires are reported in restaurants and taverns each year—an average of 73 fires each day (see Exhibit 12.2). More fires occur in foodservice establishments than in any other kind of business operation. Fires cause approximately $65 million of damage to food services annually, in addition to the death or injury of thousands of people. Obviously, the foodservice industry has a fire-prevention problem.

A large percentage of foodservice fires are caused by arson. Some of these are traceable to owners, who in troubled times may want to collect insurance by "torching" the operation.

Arson is also the result of vandalism or attempts to cover up robberies. Foodservice operations have also been targets for arson by disgruntled employees or customers (see Exhibit 12.3).

Over one-third of all accidental fires in food services are caused by faulty wiring and equipment or by improperly operated or positioned electric appliances. Old, frayed wiring, overloaded circuits, and use of the wrong fuses (or worse yet, pennies in the fuse box!) can all lead to fire. Crowding machinery together without providing enough air-circulation space will cause motors to overheat and burn.

Another major cause of fire is grease. Fat in fryers, in ventilation systems, and on walls, equipment, and other surfaces is highly flammable. It not only can contribute to the start of fires, but can also increase the severity of fires begun in other ways. Deep-fat fryers in particular are the source of many severe fires. Fat becomes increasingly volatile and begins to smoke as it is heated, until finally it bursts into flame at its *flash point,* usually between 425° and 500°F (218° and 260°C). Flash points vary with different kinds of oil or fat and should be stated on the label of the container.

Exhibit 12.3   Causes of restaurant fires

Incendiary (Arson)		**32.3%**
Igniting flammable liquids	21.3	
Igniting papers or trash	4.7	
Igniting other or unknown materials	6.3	
Electrical Causes		**22.7**
Faulty wiring	13.4	
Electrical appliances (except cooking and heating)	9.3	
Cooking		**15.8**
Igniting grease or fat not in fryers or ducts	6.3	
Involving deep fat fryers	5.5	
Involving gas	2.4	
Involving other facts	1.6	
Smoking		**14.2**
Igniting paper or trash	11.0	
Igniting furnishings	3.2	
Exhaust Ducts		**7.1**
Ignition of grease in duct	6.3	
Other factors	0.8	
Heating Equipment		**6.3**
Other Causes		**1.6**
TOTAL		**100.0%**

Reprinted by permission from "Fire Safety: Can We Do More?" *Restaurant Business,*
Volume 80, Number 6, May 1, 1981.

Another general source of restaurant fires is the cigarette. Burning cigarettes tossed carelessly into the trash, or discarded near storage areas containing flammable materials, account for hundreds of fires each year. These fires can smolder unnoticed for hours, and then become roaring blazes after closing when no one is there to check them.

Preventing Fires

Despite the statistics, most foodservice fires are preventable. Managers should regularly check their operations, including employee procedures for hazards that could result in fires.

Fires caused by *arson* are usually only preventable by good security. Security includes good locks, regular checks of all areas of the facility, and alarms. A written memo of any threats by former employees or customers should be kept and stored with other personnel records in a metal box.

Fires caused by the *electrical system* and *faulty wiring* can be prevented by regular checks. Managers should look for frayed wiring, overloaded circuits, ventilation around motors, and improper grounding. If any discrepancies are found, they should be corrected immediately.

Grease fires are also preventable. Kitchen range hoods and air ducts must be regularly cleaned to halt grease buildup. Other methods of preventing grease fires are mentioned under the section ''Burns.''

Fires caused by *smoking* are more preventable than the statistics (see Exhibit 12.3) would suggest. The problem is that with both employees and customers smoking, it is essential to police smoking areas to guard against fires. Smoking for employees should not be allowed in dry storage areas. Of course, employees shouldn't smoke in food preparation areas for sanitation reasons, but also because grease, alcohol, and other flammable materials may be present. Smoking should also be forbidden in restrooms, with signs to that effect posted. However, as a caution it is wise to place metal receptacles in restrooms.

The severity of fires is increased by the lack of proper fire protection equipment such as extinguishers, blankets, sprinkler systems, and smoke alarms. Poor housekeeping leaves more combustible material available to feed a fire. Overcrowding of service areas and blocked or poorly marked exits can cause an unfortunate occurrence to escalate into a full-scale tragedy.

THE SAFETY SURVEY

The hazards, accidents, and injuries discussed earlier are common to all types of foodservice operations. In addition, each establishment will have its own unique dangers arising from the layout, the type of food served, the type of labor employed, and other variables. Before attempting to put together a comprehensive accident-prevention program, the foodservice manager should conduct a complete safety survey.

An understanding of the methods of accident prevention needed in a foodservice establishment can be gained by investigating the types of accidents that have occurred in the past at the establishment. This information can be found by checking accident reports and files, if these exist. If these are not available, interviewing employees, especially those who have worked in the operation for a long time, can be helpful. Employees can point out areas where near misses often take place, as well as indicating sources of actual accidents.

The manager should also conduct a clipboard tour of the establishment, in order to compile a complete list of safety hazards. The manager should also keep an eye open for unsafe employee practices as the tour progresses. Every aspect of the operation, including the design of the facility, the housekeeping standards maintained, the positioning and functioning of equipment, the methods of work, and even the overall atmosphere and spirit of the operation should be carefully scrutinized, because each can contribute to the frequency—and the prevention—of accidents.

The Accident Prevention Program

An analysis of the hazards discovered in the course of the safety survey will probably reveal that they fall into two categories: (1) unsafe conditions that can be corrected or reduced through changes in the physical environment, and (2) unsafe conditions and practices that require training and supervision of workers for correction. Some specific precautions have been included in the sections on various hazards. The following changes are more general.

Built-In Safety

Changes in the physical environment that increase the safety of the facility include the correction of dangerous conditions, the installation of guards and warning signs around conditions that cannot be changed, and the provision of safety features.

Eliminating dangerous conditions can be as simple as rearranging the tables in the dining room to allow wider aisles for traffic or installing a railing on a stairway. Putting down abrasive strips or non-skid mats on slippery floors in areas of heavy traffic is another example of this type of correction. Other changes may involve more work and expenditures of money and time. It may be necessary to rewire parts of the facility to relieve overloaded circuits and eliminate the use of flexible cords (such as extension cords) as a substitute for fixed wiring. Floors may need to be repaired or even replaced; for example, if water has caused linoleum to warp and lift in spots, creating unsafe footing, the whole floor may have to be torn up and replaced.

It is unreasonable to expect that all unsafe conditions can be corrected. When correction is impossible, warnings and guards should be furnished. Areas with low overhead clearance or with unexpected changes in floor level should have warning signs posted, and the step or low overhang should be painted a bright color. Low overhead pipes or corners where people could bump their heads should be padded.

Special safety equipment, especially fire-protection equipment, should be provided wherever necessary. The danger of fire is so great in a foodservice establishment that it is foolish to economize in this area. The National Fire Protection Association estimates that fire loss in buildings unprotected by sprinkler systems, for example, is four times as great as in protected buildings.

Fire extinguishers and smoke alarms should be provided in all areas where fires are likely to occur. Extinguishers should be accessible, in plain sight, but not too close to fire hazards, since this location might make it dangerous to approach the extinguisher in the event of a fire. Fire extinguishers for different classes of fires are not the same, and the manager should know the difference and purchase the proper kinds of extinguishers (see Exhibit 12.4) and place them in the areas where those types of fire are likely to occur. (Some extinguishers can be purchased that cover all three types.) It should be remembered that fire extinguishers are for very small fires and cannot be relied upon to put out blazes of any great size. The fire department should be called *before* the fire extinguisher proves to be inadequate—waiting may result in vastly increased damage and loss.

Other fire-protection equipment includes detection systems that alert the occupants of a building, and the fire department as well, to the presence of fire and several kinds of heat-activated sprinkler systems.

Safety Training

Even if all environmental hazards are eliminated, the human hazard will remain. The greatest challenge in the prevention of accidents is simply convincing people that accidents are preventable and that they themselves have a responsibility to prevent accidents.

In order to accomplish this feat, a safety training program should be designed. This training may be combined with instruction on sanitation; in fact, many sanitation techniques will also be good safety habits. New employees should learn safe methods of work when they go through their job orientation. Early safety training has two advantages: it helps to prevent accidents that arise from unfamiliarity with the facility and job procedures; and it ensures that new workers will not form unsafe habits. In addition, studies have shown that the safest way to do a job is often the most efficient way.

Exhibit 12.4 Proper use of fire extinguishers (Source: The National Institute for Occupational Safety and Health)

KIND OF FIRE

DECIDE THE CLASS OF FIRE YOU ARE FIGHTING. . . →

. . .THEN CHECK THE COLUMNS TO THE RIGHT OF THAT CLASS →

CLASS A FIRES

USE THESE EXTINGUISHERS →

ORDINARY COMBUSTIBLES
- WOOD
- PAPER
- CLOTH
ETC.

CLASS B FIRES

USE THESE EXTINGUISHERS →

FLAMMABLE LIQUIDS, GREASE
- GASOLINE
- PAINTS
- OILS, ETC.

CLASS C FIRES

USE THESE EXTINGUISHERS →

ELECTRICAL EQUIPMENT
- MOTORS
- SWITCHES
ETC.

APPROVED TYPE OF EXTINGUISHER

MATCH UP PROPER EXTINGUISHER WITH CLASS OF FIRE SHOWN AT LEFT

FOAM Solution of Aluminum Sulphate and Bicarbonate of Soda	CARBON DIOXIDE Carbon Dioxide Gas Under Pressure	SODA ACID Bicarbonate of Soda Solution and Sulphuric Acid	PUMP TANK Plain Water	GAS CARTRIDGE Water Expelled by Carbon Dioxide Gas	MULTI-PURPOSE DRY CHEMICAL	ORDINARY DRY CHEMICAL
A B	X	A	A	A	A B C	X
A B	B C	X	X	X	A B C	B C
X	B C	X	X	X	A B C	B C

HOW TO OPERATE

FOAM: Don't Play Stream into the Burning Liquid. Allow Foam to Fall Lightly on Fire.

CARBON DIOXIDE: Direct Discharge as Close to Fire as Possible. First at Edge of Flames and Gradually Forward and Upward

SODA-ACID, GAS CARTRIDGE: Direct Stream at Base of Flame

PUMP TANK: Place Foot on Footrest and Direct Stream at Base of Flames

DRY CHEMICAL: Direct at the Base of the Flames. In the Case of Class A Fires, Follow Up by Directing the Dry Chemicals at Remaining Material That is Burning

IMPORTANT! USING THE WRONG TYPE EXTINGUISHER FOR THE CLASS OF FIRE MAYBE DANGEROUS!

Chapter 13, "Employee Sanitation Training," talks about training in some detail. The techniques of sanitation training can easily be extended to safety training. As in the case of sanitation training, safety training can be facilitated through the use of audiovisual learning aids. The National Safety Council, the American Red Cross, and state and local health and fire departments are sources of posters, filmstrips, and other material that can be used in the training process itself or as memory refreshers afterward. Some of these organizations may also provide training to employees.

Safety Supervision

The best memory refresher, of course, is a word from the supervisor. It is the responsibility of management to see that safe practices are carried out in an environment that has been made safe and is being kept that way.

One important element in an accident-prevention program is employee interest in safety. Reminding workers of safety considerations is part of this process, but more can be done. If workers are unhappy in their jobs, if they are frustrated in their efforts to do good work, or if they are physically uncomfortable because of crowding or excessive heat or cold, their attention to safety will be diminished and accidents will become more frequent. The supervisor should be on the lookout for these factors, as well as for more direct influences on safety.

Safety supervision is made simpler by the use of an accident-prevention checklist, similar to the sanitation checklist suggested in chapter 15. A sample list is included here as Exhibit 12.5; modifications should be made to fit individual establishments.

Occupational Safety and Health

Since 1970 employers have been required by the Occupational Safety and Health Act to provide employees with safe working conditions. This law, administered by the Occupational Safety and Health Administration (OSHA), sets standards for a hazard-free working environment, safe equipment, and job procedures designed with safety in mind. Employers with 11 or more workers must also keep records of on-the-job employees' injuries and illnesses. All employers must report an accident that results in death.

Employers may also be inspected by OSHA officers. During these unannounced visits, the employer may accompany the inspector and point out safety steps taken in the operation. The penalties for violations vary but may include stiff fines for serious violations. A thorough accident-prevention program that includes employee training is a positive approach to dealing with OSHA regulations.

TAKING ACTION IN AN EMERGENCY

In spite of all of the manager's and employees' efforts, some accidents will probably occur, and employees or customers may be injured or become ill. It is important to *act* in an emergency. At minimum, acting may mean calling for help if necessary; in emergencies when help is slow in coming, it may include providing first aid. As the foodservice manager, people will expect *you* to be the one to initiate action and take charge, even if you do not administer first aid yourself.

Exhibit 12.5   Accident prevention checklist

Employee Practices

Are all employees aware of hazards existing in their work areas?

Are employees properly instructed on placement of hands to avoid injury when handling potentially hazardous devices such as slicers?

Do employees make use of all guards, hot pads, railings, and other protective devices available to them?

Do employees wear proper shoes which are nonskid and will protect feet from injury?

Do employees wear clothing that cannot get caught in mixers, cutters, grinders, fans, or other equipment?

Is at least one employee on each shift trained in emergency first aid techniques?

Fire Prevention Equipment

Are fire extinguishers conveniently located where fires are most likely to occur?

Are extinguishers adequate in size and of the proper type to control a fire?

Have employees been instructed in the effective use of extinguishers?

Are extinguishers in plain sight?

Are extinguishers kept fully charged and inspected weekly for damage?

Are spinklers or automatic alarms installed if required?

Does all fire prevention equipment comply with local fire prevention agency requirements?

Floors

Are all floors in safe condition—free from broken tile and defective floorboards, worn areas, and items that may cause people to trip or fall?

Are spills and debris removed from the floor immediately?

Where floors are frequently wet, are heavy traffic areas provided with nonskid mats?

Are floors mopped adequately and provided with a protective or nonskid finish to prevent slipping?

Are adequate floor drains provided and properly covered with gratings?

Are all carpets securely tacked or otherwise fastened in place to prevent people from tripping over raised edges?

Serving Area and Dining Room

Are serving counters and tables free of broken parts, wooden or metal slivers, and sharp edges or corners?

Is all tableware regularly inspected for chips, cracks, or flaws? Are defective pieces discarded in a safe manner?

Is the traffic flow coordinated to prevent collisions while people are carrying trays or obtaining food?

Are pictures and wall decorations securely fastened to walls?

Are ceiling fixtures firmly attached and in good repair?

Doors and Exits

Are sidewalks and entrance and exit steps kept clean and in good repair?

Will all exits open from the inside without keys to allow escape from the building?

Can an exit be reached from every point in the building without having to pass through an area of high potential hazard?

Are routes to exits, and the exits themselves, clearly marked?

Are passages to exits kept free of equipment and materials?

Are all exits outward opening?

Are doors hung so they do not open into passageways where they could cause accidents?

Stairs, Ramps, and Ladders

Are stairs and slopes clearly marked and illuminated?

Do stairs have abrasive surfaces to prevent slipping and falling?

Are handrails on open sides of stairways provided?

Are center handrails provided for wide stairs?

Are stairways kept unobstructed?

Is there a 7 foot clearance over each step?

Are the slopes of ramps set to provide maximum safety—not too steep?

Are ladders maintained in good condition and inspected frequently?

Do ladders have nonslip bases?

Ventilation

Is the ventilation adequate in receiving, storage, and dishwashing areas and in walk-in coolers and freezers?

Are vent filters and fresh-air intakes provided in food-preparation, serving, and dining areas?

Are all fans and their moving parts shielded or guarded?

Is gas equipment properly vented?

Electrical Equipment

Is electrical equipment properly grounded, wired, and fused?

Is electrical equipment of approved type and installed properly?

Does it meet the National Electrical Code specifications or local ordinances and bear the seal of the Underwriter's Laboratories?

Are regular inspections of equipment and wiring made by an electrician?

Are electrical switches readily accessible in emergencies?

Are switches located so that employees do not have to lean on or against metal when reaching for them?

Are cords maintained without splices, cracks, or worn areas?

Is wiring kept off surfaces subject to vibration and floors, and out from under equipment?

Is electrical equipment protected against the entrance of water?

Are weatherproofed cords and plugs provided for outdoor equipment?

Are wet floors and areas subject to flooding avoided for placement of electrical equipment?

Are protective pads or platforms provided for people to stand on who use or vend from machines?

Are service cords long enough to eliminate the need for extension cords?

Are all switches, junction boxes, and outlets covered?

Does all equipment with cord and plug connections have grounded connections—either three-pronged plugs or pigtail adapters?

Lighting

Is lighting adequate in all areas?

Are light fixtures, bulbs, tubes, and so on, protected with screen guards?

Is proper heat-proof lighting provided over cooking areas, in vent hoods, and so on?

Hot Water Heating

Are safety devices, such as temperature and pressure relief valves, or energy cutoffs, provided to prevent explosion of pressurized water heating systems?

Do safety valves meet the standards of the American Standards Association or the American Society of Mechanical Engineers?

Exhibit 12.5　Accident prevention checklist (continued)

Is hot water temperature properly controlled in lavatories and sinks or are mixing faucets provided to prevent scalding?

Are backflow preventers installed wherever necessary?

Are overhead pipes or fixtures high enough to prevent head-bumping?

Receiving Area

Are employees instructed in correct opening, lifting, and storing methods for each item that is received?

Are adequate tools available for opening crates, barrels, cartons, and other containers?

Storage Areas

Is there sufficient space for storage of everything, with nothing stored on floors, in corridors or on stairways?

Are shelves located and constructed to prevent pinched fingers?

Are shelves adequate to bear the weight of the items stored?

Are heavy items stored on lower shelves and lighter materials above?

Is a safe ladder or step stool provided for reaching high shelves?

Are portable storage racks and stationary racks in safe condition—free from broken or bent shelves and standing solidly on legs?

Is there a safety device in the walk-in cooler to permit exit from the inside, and a light switch inside?

Is the refrigerant in the refrigerator nontoxic? (Check with repairperson.)

Hazardous Materials

Are toxic materials and hazardous substances properly stored and handled?

Are cylinders of explosive gas secured or strapped to prevent their falling or rolling?

Are combustible and flammable materials stored and handled properly?

Are compressed carbon dioxide tanks stored properly in a cool, dry, well-ventilated and fire-resistant area? Are they protected from falling over? Are pressure gauges on the tanks working?

Are cartons or other flammable materials stored far enough away from light bulbs and other sources of heat?

Waste Storage Area

Are garbage and waste containers constructed of leak-proof material?

Are garbage containers covered when not in use?

Are containers adequate in number and size?

Are containers cleaned frequently?

Are disposal area floors and surroundings kept clean and clear of refuse?

Is there a proper rack for holding garbage containers?

Are containers on dollies, or other wheeled units, to eliminate lifting by employees?

Food-Preparation Area

Are prepared foods properly protected from contamination from above?

Is adequate aisle space provided between equipment to allow reasonable work movement and traffic?

Is a nonsplintering, easily cleanable tamper provided for use with grinders?

Are hot pads, asbestos gloves, spatulas, or other equipment provided for use with stoves, ovens, and other hot equipment?

Are scabbards, sheaths, racks, or magnetic bars available for proper storage of knives and other sharp instruments?

Are machines properly guarded?

Do employees make use of tampers, hot pads, safe knife storage devices, and machine guards provided for their protection?

Are knives and other blades kept sharp?

Are employees properly instructed in the operation of machines, mixers, grinders, choppers, dishwashers, and so on?

Are cooking utensil handles always positioned so that they do not protrude over the edges of cooking units and into passageways?

If anything breaks near the food-preparation or service area, are workers trained to discard all food from the areas adjacent to the breakage to prevent contamination?

Are stoves, vent filters, and cooking areas properly cleaned to remove greases and flammable wastes?

Are mixers in safe operating condition? Are beaters properly maintained to avoid introducing bits of metal and other foreign particles into the food?

Are steam tables regularly maintained by competent personnel?

If the temperature of the kitchen is very high, are employees aware of the symptoms of heat strain?

Utensil-Washing Area

If conveyor units are used to move soiled items, are edges guarded to avoid catching people's fingers or clothing?

Are portable racks or bus trucks in safe operating condition—wheels and castors working, shelves firm?

Are dish racks kept off the floor to prevent people's tripping and falling over them?

Is there an adequate drainboard or other drying area so that employees do not pile pots and pans on the floor?

Are racks, hooks, and gloves provided so that dishwashers do not have to put their hands into sanitizing baths of hot water or chemicals?

Are drain plugs mechanically operated or provided with chains so that employees can drain sinks without placing hands in sanitizing hot water?

Transportation

Are vehicles used in transport of food supplies equipped with all recommended or required safety devices—lap and shoulder belts, neck restraints, and so on?

Are driver and occupants instructed in use of the safety features?

Is defensive driving instruction provided?

Are vehicles provided with a safety partition to prevent slipping or shifting of merchandise forward against the driver?

Are shelving, recessed storage racks, and straps used to secure cargo and prevent sliding, slipping, falling, or breakage?

Exhibit 12.6   First aid kit (Photograph courtesy of Zee Medical Company, Inc., Irvine, Calif.)

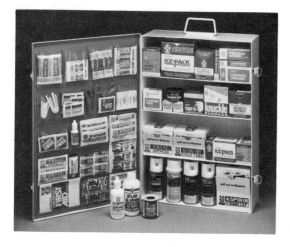

At least one employee trained in first aid should be present in the facility at all times. In addition, medical personnel must always be quickly accessible by phone. A foodservice establishment also should be equipped with a complete, sanitary, first-aid kit. Some states have laws specifying the supplies that must be included in this kit; in general the kit will contain individually wrapped sterile dressings, adhesive tape, slings, inflatable splints, scissors, aspirin, and soap (see Exhibit 12.6). Employers can subscribe to a first-aid service that inspects and restocks the kits.

Emergency action procedures should be included in the employee manual and in training information. Employees should know the policy for handling emergencies so that they may act on their own if necessary. The following procedures describe appropriate action in emergencies:

1. *Don't panic—remain calm.* This may seem simplistic, but it's worth noting that too often a common action is a *reaction* that delays help. Worse, panic is often catching.

2. Call for help when it is clearly necessary. Be as exact as you can when describing the emergency. Post emergency numbers—including your own— throughout the facility.

3. If waiting will worsen the extent of the injury or illness, provide what first aid you can.

4. Keep the person comfortable and quiet.

5. Keep people who are uninvolved away from the victim. Remember the adage, "If you're not part of the solution, you're part of the problem."

6. Keep a record of the incident. This should include the date, the victim's name, the nature of the injury or illness, who else was involved, what action by employees or bystanders was taken, and how quickly help arrived.

First Aid in Emergencies

Ideally, someone trained in first aid will be available in the facility at all times. Some injuries and illnesses do occur with some frequency in foodservice operations. It might be a good idea to provide first aid training through the Red Cross or a local hospital. Among the types of emergencies that may occur in a foodservice establishment are choking and heart attacks.

Choking

Your dining room is crowded and noisy. Your cashier is ringing up totals. Your service employees are going in and out of the kitchen with orders. Suddenly you notice a patron in the corner is turning blue. He is choking on a piece of food. What do you do? Hopefully, you or one of your employees will know what to do and act quickly. Minutes count in this type of emergency. Brain damage can occur in six minutes without oxygen.

Exhibit 12.7   First aid for choking victim
(Reprinted by permission of The American
Red Cross)

1

- **ASK: Are you choking?**
- If victim cannot breathe, cough, or speak…

2

- **Give the Heimlich Maneuver.**
- Stand behind the victim.
- Wrap your arms around the victim's waist.
- Make a fist with one hand. PLACE your FIST (thumbside) against the victim's stomach in the mid-line just ABOVE THE NAVEL AND WELL BELOW THE RIB MARGIN.
- Grasp your fist with your other hand.
- PRESS INTO STOMACH WITH A QUICK UPWARD THRUST.

3

- **Repeat thrust if necessary.**

IF VICTIM HAS BECOME UNCONSCIOUS:

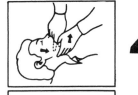

4

- **If a victim has become unconscious:**
- Sweep the mouth.

5

- Attempt rescue breathing.

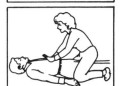

6

- Give 6-10 abdominal thrusts.
- Repeat Steps 4, 5, and 6 as necessary.

Choking is all too common in foodservice operations. People are talking, drinking, and eating fast, without properly chewing. Young children are particularly likely to have this type of emergency. If you are *sure* the victim is choking, the major stop-choking technique to use is called the Heimlich maneuver. The following procedures are for choking (see Exhibit 12.7):

1. *If* the victim can talk, cough, or breathe, don't interfere.
2. *If* the victim cannot talk, cough, or breathe, call for help. Even if first aid is given, the victim may still need help.
3. *If* the person is conscious, administer the Heimlich maneuver, which consists of manual thrusts to the abdomen, just under the rib cage.
4. *If* the victim is unconscious, he or she has probably stopped breathing. First, sweep the mouth with your finger to dislodge any foreign object. Next, attempt rescue breathing (see Exhibit 12.8). Follow this with 6 to 10 abdominal thrusts. Repeat this process as necessary.

Heart Attack

The heart attack outside the home is becoming increasingly common. If the heart stops, cardiopulmonary resuscitation (CPR) may be necessary to keep the victim alive until help arrives. You should have one or two people on the premises during all hours who have been trained in CPR. As with victims of any emergency, heart attack victims must be kept quiet and comfortable.

First-aid training, including such vital measures as cardiopulmonary resuscitation and treatment of a person choking on food, can be received from organizations such as local health departments, the American Red Cross,

some insurance companies, and local high schools and colleges.

Of course, it is important to remember where first aid ends and the practice of medicine begins. First aid is to be used in cases of minor injuries and critical emergencies requiring immediate attention. Prompt emergency first-aid attention can save lives and minimize injuries.

SUMMARY

The elimination of accidents and the pain and expense they cause is as much a part of the creation of a safe foodservice establishment as sanitation is. *Most accidents can be prevented.* The implementation of a well-designed accident-prevention program can significantly reduce the number of accidents and injuries in a foodservice operation.

An accident is an unexpected event resulting in injury, loss, or damage. Accidents are caused by people who either behave in unsafe ways or fail to adjust to unsafe conditions.

The most common employee accidents in foodservice establishments result in injuries such as sprains, strains, cuts, burns, bruises, and fractures. The nature of the equipment in a foodservice operation, and the type of work that is performed, contribute to the frequency of these injuries.

One of the most serious hazards in a foodservice facility is the danger of fire. Fires are all too frequent in the foodservice industry, and the cost of fire in lost lives, injuries, and financial loss makes fire prevention an absolute necessity.

Exhibit 12.8   First aid for unconscious victim (Reprinted by permission of The American Red Cross)

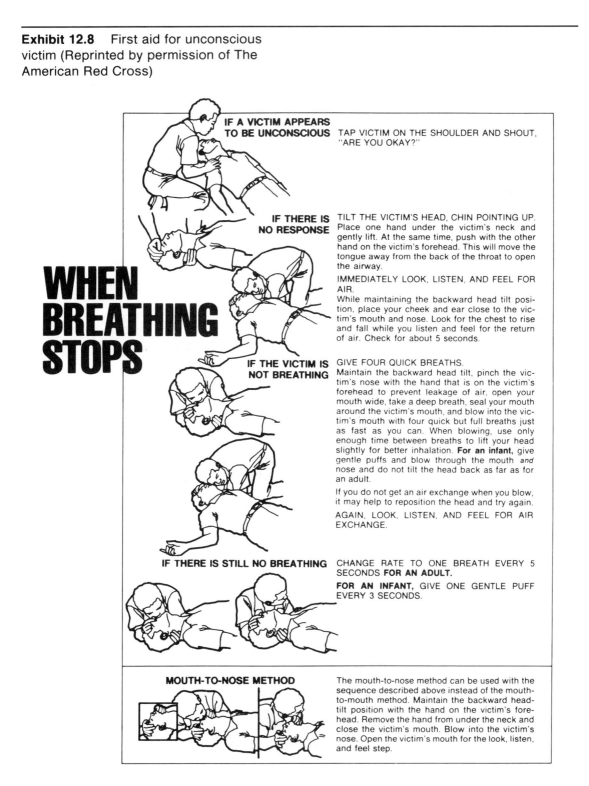

WHEN BREATHING STOPS

IF A VICTIM APPEARS TO BE UNCONSCIOUS TAP VICTIM ON THE SHOULDER AND SHOUT, "ARE YOU OKAY?"

IF THERE IS NO RESPONSE TILT THE VICTIM'S HEAD, CHIN POINTING UP. Place one hand under the victim's neck and gently lift. At the same time, push with the other hand on the victim's forehead. This will move the tongue away from the back of the throat to open the airway.

IMMEDIATELY LOOK, LISTEN, AND FEEL FOR AIR.
While maintaining the backward head tilt position, place your cheek and ear close to the victim's mouth and nose. Look for the chest to rise and fall while you listen and feel for the return of air. Check for about 5 seconds.

IF THE VICTIM IS NOT BREATHING GIVE FOUR QUICK BREATHS.
Maintain the backward head tilt, pinch the victim's nose with the hand that is on the victim's forehead to prevent leakage of air, open your mouth wide, take a deep breath, seal your mouth around the victim's mouth, and blow into the victim's mouth with four quick but full breaths just as fast as you can. When blowing, use only enough time between breaths to lift your head slightly for better inhalation. **For an infant,** give gentle puffs and blow through the mouth *and* nose and do not tilt the head back as far as for an adult.

If you do not get an air exchange when you blow, it may help to reposition the head and try again.

AGAIN, LOOK, LISTEN, AND FEEL FOR AIR EXCHANGE.

IF THERE IS STILL NO BREATHING CHANGE RATE TO ONE BREATH EVERY 5 SECONDS **FOR AN ADULT.**

FOR AN INFANT, GIVE ONE GENTLE PUFF EVERY 3 SECONDS.

MOUTH-TO-NOSE METHOD The mouth-to-nose method can be used with the sequence described above instead of the mouth-to-mouth method. Maintain the backward head-tilt position with the hand on the victim's forehead. Remove the hand from under the neck and close the victim's mouth. Blow into the victim's nose. Open the victim's mouth for the look, listen, and feel step.

The foodservice manager must develop an effective accident-prevention program, based on a thorough understanding of the needs of his or her own establishment. The program should include correction of existing physical hazards, the training of employees in safe practices, and constant supervision to see that unsafe conditions do not develop and that employees are working safely.

Training in first aid should be a vital part of a foodservice safety program. An employee trained in first aid should be available at all times. First-aid training should include CPR, stop-choking techniques, and artificial respiration.

A CASE IN POINT

The fire started in the kitchen of the Caravan County Mental Health Center. The fat in the fryers burst into flame when old grease and dirt dripped down from the hood. The fire caught one of the cooks literally by the throat and his tie was on fire. Another employee threw water on the cook and then threw it on the grease fire, which roared even worse than before. The manager evacuated the facility, hoping that someone else would see what was happening and call the fire department.

What safety factors were not observed here?
In the rescue attempt, what mistakes were made?
What steps should the manager take to improve safety and deal better with emergencies?

STUDY QUESTIONS

1. What do sanitation and accident prevention have in common?
2. List three indirect costs of accidents.
3. What steps are included in a good accident-prevention program?
4. What is an accident?
5. What is the most important cause of accidents?
6. Are sharp knives more dangerous than dull ones? Why or why not?
7. What is the most common cause of accidental fires in foodservice establishments?
8. What is meant by the *flash point* of fat or oil?
9. How is poor housekeeping related to the danger of fire?
10. How can the foodservice manager gain a complete understanding of the hazards in his or her own facility?
11. What should be done about physical hazards that are impossible to eliminate?
12. What is the safety significance of a spring switch on dangerous equipment?
13. Should the foodservice worker wait until the fire extinguisher has failed to put out a blaze before calling the fire department? Why or why not?
14. What steps should be taken if a patron is choking on a piece of food?
15. How do OSHA regulations affect employee safety?

MORE ON THE SUBJECT

NATIONAL RESTAURANT ASSOCIATION. *Fire Protection and Fire Prevention.* National Restaurant Association, 150 North Michigan Avenue, Chicago, Illinois 60601. This pamphlet completely covers the subject of foodservice fires, including protection devices, prevention and protection programs, and fire insurance. Included is a comprehensive self-inspection checklist.

U.S. DEPARTMENT OF HEALTH AND HUMAN SERVICES, Public Health Service, Centers for Disease Control, National Institute for Occupational Safety and Health. *Health and Safety Guide for Eating and Drinking Places.* DHEW Publication No. (NIOSH) 76–163. May 1976. This guide is geared toward helping the foodservice operator comply with the Occupational Safety and Health Act of 1970. It provides some health and safety guidelines, warns of some frequently violated OSHA regulations, and includes a safety checklist.

ANSWER TO A CASE IN POINT

Fat is a very volatile substance and safety is an essential consideration in its use. First, the temperature of the fat was probably too high. A hood over the frying operation needs to be cleaned regularly. Ties and other items of loose clothing should never be worn in food preparation areas. Not only may they catch fire from sources of heat, but they may become caught in other equipment, causing injuries.

Water and grease do not mix. While using water on the cook's tie may have served the purpose, applying water to the burning fat itself was a disastrous move. A Class B fire extinguisher should always be located near the frying area in a food service.

Obviously the fire department should have been called as soon as the fire began.

The manager should begin by going through the operation using the Accident Prevention Checklist described in this chapter.

The manager should implement a safety training program for employees that includes first aid.

Finally, the manager should prepare for emergencies by preparing an action plan listing the steps to be taken, posting emergency numbers, and preparing employees for potential emergencies through training, including first aid techniques.

13
Employee Sanitation Training

Training is teaching workers how to do a job properly. The purpose of sanitation training is to provide workers with the skills necessary to use sanitary procedures in their jobs in order to keep food safe. Employee training is an important factor in any operation's "bottom line."

The foodservice manager must necessarily be interested in the "bottom line" of the profit-and-loss statement. Therein lies one key indicator of the success and future prospects of the food service—and of the manager. In evaluating any facet of the business, then, the manager's first question will be, "How does this item contribute to my profits?"

The impact of some features of the operation are easy to measure and to record—like customer counts and check averages on one side and the costs of food and supplies on the other. But other factors are much more difficult to pin down. One of these elusive factors is the very real benefit derived from sanitation training.

The cost of training workers in safe and sanitary practices is quite clear—training requires measurable amounts of time away from regular tasks for both workers and trainers, or perhaps even the employment of specialists in training. Slides, films, books, posters—the cost of any item used in training can be readily figured. The costs of *not* training workers in sanitation, however, may be even more costly. Customer complaints, low scores on health inspections, spoiled foods that must be thrown out, and poor employee morale are very costly. The costs measured in negative public relations alone can be reflected in the bottom line. Good sanitation training can have a positive impact on the financial statement in the long run. But where is the return on the investment in sanitation training?

This question can be answered with a series of others. What is the cost of an outbreak of foodborne illness? How much loss is sustained by an establishment that is forced to close until it meets local health standards? How much do frequent sanitation violations damage a food service's reputation? How many customers never return to a restaurant where they have found hair in their food, or filth in the restroom, or have become sick after a visit? The *avoidance* of these costs is one benefit of an effective employee sanitation training program.

Another benefit of sanitation training for workers is that it saves wear and tear on the manager. The final responsibility for sanitation rests with the foodservice manager, but if employees are not familiar with sanitation and do not know how to avoid the dangers of contamination, the manager's job of protecting the food is impossible. The single largest source of food contaminants is the human being; imagine trying to hover over each and every human being in the establishment to personally prevent them from contaminating the food! Sanitation training for all workers allows the manager to take some time out for other matters, like operating the foodservice establishment.

Employee morale and job pride are other important benefits of sanitation training. Most people want to do their jobs right. Once trained in sanitation procedures and properly supervised, the payoff in good sanitation and in employee pride is a *dual* benefit.

A final and equally important benefit of sanitation training is customer appreciation, which may be reflected directly in the bottom line. Customers who know that management cares about them and their business, enough to train employees in all aspects of their jobs, are likely to return.

In order to derive these benefits from the training investment, the training must be effective. The program must be carefully thought out, well executed, and continually reinforced and evaluated. In this chapter, then, we will discuss

- Training as a management function
- Analyzing training needs for sanitation

- Planning, execution, and reinforcement of the training program
- Evaluation of the success of the training effort

CLOSING THE TRAINING GAP

All foodservice managers (and, unfortunately, all too many customers) are aware that the industry has a higher rate of employee turnover than many other industries. Turnover at lower worker levels approaches 80 percent in some establishments. Compounding this problem is a history of difficulties in recruiting competent and motivated workers.

The National Restaurant Association estimates that 225,000 new non-management employees must be hired each year of the next decade to keep pace with growth and replacement demands. The expanding, eating-out pattern of Americans—influenced by the ever-increasing mobility of our society, a shorter work week, more women wage earners, and a steady rise in the general standard of living—is fully expected to continue. This means that more people must be served good, wholesome food by personnel trained to the task.

At the operating level of the individual restaurant or other food service, where all non-school training ultimately must be done, the task of ensuring that all employees are fully conversant with the fundamentals of sanitation falls directly on the manager. The weight of the responsibility for seeing that all employees consistently observe safe practices in performing their jobs also rests squarely on the manager's shoulders. Needless to say, the manager's burden is not made lighter by high turnover rates, large numbers of new employees, and the need to keep pace with ever-growing customer requirements. Even with experienced personnel who have not had formal instruction in sanitation methods, where does the manager start? Several training methods are commonly used in the foodservice field.

Sometimes the new recruit is simply assigned to the employee being replaced or to some other person in the same work area. Thus, a new cook's helper would be assigned to follow a cook through the daily routine. A new bussing attendant might be told to help out a waiter. This one-on-one, or *magic apron,* system so widely found in foodservice establishments seems almost a calculated effort to guarantee that errors of the past will continue into the future. The new employee picks up the old worker's bad habits along with the good and has no basis for differentiating sanitary practices from unsanitary ones.

Although on-the-job training is very effective in some situations, it is not well suited for sanitation training. A basic familiarity with the concepts of sanitation, as well as with the safe practices required in the performance of the job, must be part of every employee's orientation.

On the other hand, the manager—possibly spurred on by a recent contamination incident, an anticipated sanitary inspection, or personal concern—might undertake a *crash training program.* But crash programs are rarely carefully planned and, though sometimes useful in the short run, are usually short-lived. Initial enthusiasm soon wanes, the materials and equipment are put away, and the training is forgotten. Continuous turnover soon produces new employees who have not undergone sanitation training, and even experienced workers cannot be expected to absorb all the necessary sanitation knowledge in one dose. What is needed is a well-planned, continuous, training and reinforcement program.

The ideal method for dealing with training needs is to set up a year-round training program. Initial training of new employees followed up by continual monitoring of progress is the best approach when it comes to teaching sanitation. The reason for this is simple: it is important to develop good habits early. Follow-up is needed to ensure the application of

Exhibit 13.1   Steps in planning a sanitation training program

Determining the Subject to Be Taught
Establishing Objectives
Choosing the Method of Training
Selecting an Instructor
Scheduling Training Sessions
Selecting the Training Area
Preparing for Training

sanitation knowledge and to decide if any re-training may be necessary. Training of employees already on the job should also be a priority.

Some large foodservice operations do set up a training department and hire a training director. Foodservice trainers have even established their own professional association, the Council of Hotel and Restaurant Trainers (CHART), and sanitation training has been high on their conference agenda. Although this may be ideal, sanitation can be taught well by foodservice managers or supervisors—once some basic facts about training are known.

In most foodservice operations professional restaurateurs rather than professional trainers must normally conduct the sanitation training. In this case, an interested member or representative of management—trained in foodservice sanitation—should personally conduct the course, thus providing a real and visible commitment to the program. The management-trainer must set up and conduct the training program and monitor and encourage employee progress after the training is completed. This responsibility for the on-the-job performance of workers after training, emphasizes management interest in individual achievement, and underlines the real importance of the principles and practices that are taught.

PLANNING A TRAINING PROGRAM

It is one thing to recognize that sanitation training *can* make a difference—in employee turnover, in productivity levels, in job performance, and in employee morale. It is quite another thing to implement a successful and continuous sanitation training program amid the other demands on a manager's time and attention.

How does a manager turn the truisms about training into reality? The following sections of the chapter present information on organizing available tools and techniques into a sanitation training program.

Training will not take place unless it is organized into a program. Random bull sessions, emergency instructions to a new employee about the proper use of a piece of equipment, or casual comments about a worker's sanitary habits do not constitute a training program. *Rather, a training program is a structured sequence of information and activities that lead, step-by-step, to learning.* A training program must be *planned* if learning is to be accomplished (see Exhibit 13.1). Planning itself involves a number of steps.

Exhibit 13.2   Learning flow

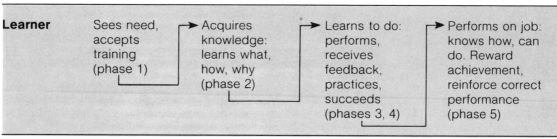

| Learner | Sees need, accepts training (phase 1) | → | Acquires knowledge: learns what, how, why (phase 2) | → | Learns to do: performs, receives feedback, practices, succeeds (phases 3, 4) | → | Performs on job: knows how, can do. Reward achievement, reinforce correct performance (phase 5) |

Key: Learning flow ⎯⎯⎯⎯→

Supervision in the Hospitality Industry by Jack E. Miller and Mary Porter. Copyright © 1985 by Jack E. Miller and Mary Porter. Reprinted by permission of John Wiley & Sons, Inc.

The Training Process

For knowledge to be applied on the job it must be *learned*. Training is really a two-way process. It requires that information be given by one person, the trainer, and transferred by the learner into applied skills. Two people need to be involved in the activity. The trainer must be *knowledgeable* and *prepared* and the learner must be prepared and *motivated*. The learner must also be encouraged and given feedback. Finally, *follow-up* by the trainer or supervisor is necessary to ensure compliance with sanitation procedures.

Learning is a process that must include some acknowledgement of each individual's learning skills and background. Different people learn at different rates. It is for this reason that one-on-one training may be best for teaching foodservice sanitation. Whatever the rate of learning, training is best keyed into the learning process itself. Training should be done in steps that include practice and positive feedback. Educator Jack Miller breaks this learning process down into four phases (see Exhibit 13.2).

Both the trainer and the trainee must be prepared for training. The trainer, of course, *must be knowledgeable about proper sanitation procedures and the reasons behind them.*

Once the basic knowledge is there, successful training is based on the interpersonal skills and preparation of the trainer.

Successful trainers and teachers seem to have a number of characteristics in common. They motivate by generating interest in the subject, are able to give information and ideas using a variety of techniques, plan and organize the instruction effectively, and are skillful in evaluating trainee progress.

Determining the Subject to Be Taught

The first step in setting up a training program is to determine the subject matter. The subject areas should be classified into ones that all employees need to know and into others that are unique to each job.

The *fundamentals* of sanitation should be stressed for *all new employees,* preferably before they undertake their job assignments. What are the sanitation fundamentals? At a minimum, they are as follows:

1. The importance of sanitation in preventing foodborne disease

2. Personal sanitary practices that every employee should follow before coming to work and during work

Exhibit 13.3   Task-breakdown for service employees

Sanitation-related Tasks for Service Employees
Teach by demonstration/practice personal hygiene

Hold cups and utensils by handles.
Carry multiple glasses on trays.
Hold glasses and dishes by bottoms.
Avoid stacking of dishes.
Scoop ice with plastic or stainless steel scoop.
Dispense rolls and bread and other such foods with tongs.
Wash hands after potential contamination.

3. Food protection, including basic information on proper foodhandling procedures
4. Sanitation of facilities and equipment, including special cleaning and sanitizing required in particular areas
5. Pest control, particularly the practices necessary to eliminate cockroaches, flies, and other insects, as well as rats, mice, and other vermin
6. Habits and practices that promote on-the-job safety and that help prevent accidents

After the general fundamentals are given, specific sanitation procedures related to each person's job should be provided. Sanitation job-related tasks should be broken down into teachable units. For instance, task analysis for service employees would identify procedures for the sanitary service of food (see Exhibit 13.3).

Establishing Objectives

The second step in setting up a training program is to determine the program's objectives. To undertake training without first defining expected outcomes and hoped-for benefits is foolhardy and nonproductive.

It is worth mentioning that training objectives must be compatible with larger management goals. One of these overall management goals is certainly the serving of sanitary and wholesome food, which is where training in sanitation comes in.

Setting up objectives starts with a planning team made up of a representative of management, representatives from the group of people to be trained, and the trainees' supervisors. This team analyzes the problem (What training needs to be done?), suggests a solution (How can it be accomplished?), and evaluates the present skills and abilities of the people who are to receive the training. The statement and selection of training objectives are also affected by cost factors (How much will this training program cost?) and time considerations (How long will this training take?). This identification of training needs is a major step in preparing a training program.

The planning team should draw up objectives that fit the needs of their particular food-service operation and their particular group of trainees. For example, though each employee in a foodservice operation should receive some training in sanitation, it would be wasteful to train at too technical a level, or to provide specific kinds of training, for those who will never

Exhibit 13.4   Sample sanitation objectives for a cook

After sanitation training, the cook will be able to	
General	Recognize the problem of foodborne illness Practice good personal hygiene to avoid contaminating food Use sanitation procedures for the safe handling of food Practice waste management and cleanliness to avoid pest problems Observe rules for cleaning and sanitizing of equipment and facility
Specific	Implement procedures during preparation that will protect the sanitation safety and quality of foods Observe the time-and-temperature rule during all phases of food preparation Exercise sanitation quality control by checking FIFO dates and by using other means of observation

use it. Different planning teams should be assigned to set training objectives for each job category in the establishment. If any substitutions are to be made between employees, the objectives should include both jobs.

Once objectives have been discussed and decided upon, they should be clearly stated (in writing) in a behavioral format. Behavioral objectives define what the trainee will be able to do on completion of training. Insistence on objectives stated in behavioral terms is critical to successful sanitation training, since employee performance is the purpose and measure of training. Further, by tying training to performance, it is possible to determine the success or failure of a particular training method or of a whole training program. When preparing objectives for a *particular task,* the words used should be behavioral words. For example, words like *implement* or *operate,* rather than *understand* or *appreciate.* Exhibit 13.4 shows sample sanitation objectives for a cook.

New employees, especially those with no prior work experience in foodservice operations, can well be considered as a separate job category in setting objectives for sanitation training.

Choosing the Method of Training

Methods of training can be divided into two types: one-on-one and group training. Which type to use for teaching sanitation will depend on how many people need to be taught, on cost, and most importantly, on how the subjects are best learned by the trainees.

One-on-One Training

Training one or two persons at a time is fairly common in the foodservice industry. This type of training has a number of advantages.

1. It allows for the special needs of the person being trained. Training can be tailor-made to suit the particular situation and the employee's job.

2. It can take place on the job or wherever else is convenient. It does not require a special location.
3. It provides for immediate feedback and enables the trainer to check employee progress.
4. It can be made interesting because it involves the trainee directly. One-on-one training is best done when a new employee needs to be trained or one or two present employees need retraining.

There are disadvantages. One-on-one training can be costly, in both time and money. The time spent by a manager or supervisor is usually time spent away from other management functions.

Group Training

If more than one employee requires sanitation training, holding group sessions may be an alternative to one-on-one training. The advantages are that a uniform program can be adapted and used for all training needs. Group training can include lectures, discussions, even role-playing sessions and use of filmstrips or other visual aids—all of which can be valuable in teaching sanitation.

One disadvantage of group training is its lack of personalized instruction. Also, trainees may have to learn more information than they actually need for their jobs. This is because group sessions must usually meet the overall needs of the workers, not specialized job needs. Another disadvantage is that unless various techniques are used to make group sessions interesting, they can be dull.

Applied Training

A variety of techniques for providing new information may be used with both methods. Classroom teaching may include lecturing, presenting audiovisual materials, discussions,

and role playing. One-on-one teaching can include demonstrations, practice, and a question-and-answer period. Both techniques should include follow-up.

The training method should be related to the behavior that is desired. If the manager wants a worker to manually sanitize a dish, the best option could be to demonstrate the process and have the worker perform the task. Demonstration allows for feedback. The employee can practice and explain the key points of a task while performing it; plus the trainer can check the worker's progress. Perhaps the manager could provide a diagram as a *learning* aid. However, if the manager wants workers to recognize the connection between the time-and-temperature principle and foodborne illness, the trainer might present a slide show that includes diagrams of bacterial growth and a brief lecture on the everyday hazards to safe food. Training should be as *applicable* and as *job-related* as possible. If some sanitation theory is necessary, it should be related to practical outcomes of sanitation training.

For many operations a mix of both training methods is useful. Such a program could combine general sanitation training with subjects relevant to a particular job. A sample sanitation-training session for service employees might include the following:

1. A slide presentation or film on foodborne illnesses and foodhandling hazards that contribute to them, which is followed by discussion
2. Demonstrations of sanitary procedures for serving foods and beverages
3. Practice by workers of various techniques
4. Individual instruction of foodhandling techniques; follow-up and reinforcement on the job.

Choosing Training Materials

It may be possible for an especially gifted instructor to use words alone to describe the operation of a dishwasher, the setting of a table, or the fundamentals of foodservice sanitation. However, the mere fact that words have been spoken certainly does not guarantee that anything has been learned. Even words that impart their message may not be enough. Additional instructional aids—written texts, drawings, charts, graphs, mock-ups, films, audiotapes, videotapes, slides, and transparencies—can raise the odds considerably in favor of training effectiveness. If these training aids are supported by trainee participation, actual exercises, and on-the-job experience, the odds in favor of effective training go up even higher.

Proper use of training materials saves time, adds interest, helps trainees to learn and remember what they've learned, and of course, makes the trainer's job easier.

In the choice of materials for sanitation training, the manager or trainer should be guided by the four A's. To be most useful, training materials must be

1. *Accurate.* They should be factual, up-to-date, complete, and in an understandable form.
2. *Appropriate.* They should be suitable for the purpose they are to serve and—most important—for the trainees who are to use them. Language levels, reading levels, and difficulty levels must be considered and matched to the trainees. It is also useful to consider whether the materials are suited to the abilities of the trainer who will conduct the program. Can the instructor use the materials successfully?
3. *Attractive.* All teachers, and probably all parents, know that one cannot teach anything to people without first gaining their attention. In subjects that do not generally have a wide appeal (and sanitation is one of these), it is often necessary to go to great lengths to make information exciting and interesting and—what is often most difficult—to make it memorable.
4. *Authenticated.* Training materials should bear the seal of an identifiable authority in the field.

No one kind of training media can do the job effectively for all trainees at all levels. Many companies have developed employee handbooks that are distributed to new workers and from which workers are expected to glean the necessary information. They are far from adequate for sanitation training but can be useful in other aspects of orientation and as a guide to company policy.

Audiovisual programs and aids, ranging from motion pictures to sound filmstrips and slides, are increasingly used for training in the industry. However, the trainer cannot expect an audiovisual presentation to be a total training program or the learner to be motivated solely by a film. Rather, the trainer should introduce each showing with a statement of objectives and expectations and discuss the presentation's content as it applies to the particular operation and to the employees involved.

In addition to audiovisual aids, *practical demonstrations* can be used to further bring home the subject matter to employees. Demonstrations are vital to the teaching of many sanitation procedures. They have the added plus of allowing the worker to actually do the task. They also provide a basis for feedback by the trainer.

Finally, a short examination should be given, scored by the trainee or trainer, and indicated problem areas should be clarified through discussion. Signs, posters, bulletin boards, and pay-envelope stuffers can serve as reminders or refreshers associated with sanitation training and proper sanitation practices.

Selecting an Instructor

Instructors should be selected for their knowledge of the subject of sanitation, their familiarity with the organization's sanitation problems, their skills in human relations, and their ability to help others learn.

The decision on "Who shall train?" is influenced by where the training takes place—on-site in the foodservice establishment itself or in a formal classroom situation at some separate location. An on-the-job location is typical of most sanitation training for those below the managerial level. This location allows for ample demonstration of equipment as well as providing opportunities to relate instruction to the specific needs of a particular foodservice operation.

1. *The manager.* The manager knows the operation best and is ultimately responsible for the sanitation level of the food and the premises.
2. *The trainees' immediate supervisor.* Many times this person is the logical choice as trainer because of the working relationship between employees and supervisor and because of the possibility for immediate on-the-job feedback.
3. *Staff trainer.* In large foodservice companies, a training professional is often available to provide sanitation instruction.
4. *Representative of the health department.* The local sanitarian and the health educator are possible candidates for instructors in sanitation training. The district sanitarians of the state health department will usually assist in setting up training sessions if their schedule allows.

Very often, the most successful training is a result of the combination of these resource persons, with one person acting as the senior instructor and other outside instructors called in to present special concepts or to provide a change of instructional pace.

It is important that the trainer be familiar with the daily routine of the people to be trained, so that the principles of sanitation can be presented in concrete form in situations that are sure to arise as the trainees perform their regular jobs. If the manager, or a member of the staff, is conducting the training, there should be no trouble in tying sanitation to the workers' normal tasks.

Scheduling Training Sessions

The difficulty of finding a time and place for training in a busy foodservice establishment is often given as an excuse for the lack of a training program. Obviously, special steps must be taken (and can be taken) if management is truly committed to training and is cognizant of the benefits that can be derived from a regularly scheduled program.

Scheduling sanitation training for foodservice employees is essentially a matter of deciding priorities. Who should be trained first? Should it be a new employee, or an employee being given new responsibilities? Should it be a group of employees, such as waitresses who have never received formal training in sanitation? Or should it be all members of the staff, to call renewed attention to general health and safety rules?

Probably it should be all of these, and a master training program with blocked-out time scheduling can be useful in showing both the company's and the manager's commitment and the application of the program to all employees. Both initial training and retraining should be included in the program.

Special attention can be given to priority situations—a large group of new employees, an opening of a new restaurant, a reopening after remodeling, or special preparations for banquet business or for a convention group. Adaptations such as these, however, should only be made after a master plan has been developed.

Training sessions should not be too long. The ideal length is probably about 45 minutes, but successful training sessions have lasted as long as an hour and a half.

Notices should indicate the date, time, and place of each session, the subject, the persons who are to receive the training, and the trainer who will conduct the session. The manager should make sure that announcements are posted where they will be readily seen, that everyone concerned is aware of management's commitment to sanitation training, and that company resources are involved. The trainees should also know that each session will begin on time and that unnecessary absences will not be tolerated.

Selecting the Training Area

Training should be conducted in an atmosphere in which employees feel at ease. There is normally no need for special training rooms. In most foodservice operations, an employee lounge, an executive office, part of a storage room, or a separate section of the dining room not in use can serve adequately. Part of the training should include practice, and employee work stations may also be used as training areas. If the manager or trainer conducts training sessions during slow periods or before the operation opens, there will be time to use different areas.

The training area should be of an appropriate size for the group to be trained—in particular it should not be crowded. There should be a place for all participants to write. Seating should be adequate and comfortable, and arranged so as to encourage the exchange of information in open discussion. If projectors, sound equipment, or other electrical equipment are to be used, the room must have enough electrical outlets to accommodate the equipment.

Giving the Training

In any training it is important to take the simplest route possible. Complex training methods may only make for perplexed workers. For the best results, keep the training simple. The following steps break the process down into simple, manageable units:

1. Tell workers what they're going to be taught and show them how and why.
2. Teach them.
3. Demonstrate.
4. Allow for questions.
5. Let them practice.
6. Praise and offer constructive criticism.
7. Review.

Now that you as the manager know what sanitation objectives are to be taught, have prepared objectives, have put up notices about the sessions, and have selected a training area, you're all set—right? Wrong.

Both the trainer and the trainees must be *prepared*. For training to be successful the trainer must know the information and be comfortable with any questions workers might have. Secondly, the trainer must know *how to properly train employees*. Finally, the trainees themselves must be prepared.

Trainer Preparation

For you, the trainer, the first step is to get complete control of the material you wish to teach—that is, sanitation. If you are uncertain of your subject matter, you will communicate this fact to your trainees, and they will have cause to doubt the accuracy of what you are saying.

Once you have command of your topic, the hard part is getting it across to the people you wish to train. The most important factor to consider in preparing a training session is the character of the group to be trained. If the material to be taught is not tailored to the needs of the workers—if it is too abstract to be relevant to their daily activities, if it is too complicated, or if it is presented in a way that fails to arouse their interest—they simply will not learn sanitation.

Before training, it is a good idea to take an honest look at yourself as a trainer. How skilled are you at getting information across? Do your employees strain to hear you, ask you to speak up, or ask so many questions when you're done that you know they didn't understand what you just said? If so, don't despair. Training employees in any aspect of their jobs usually requires some skills that are not developed overnight. The following are suggestions for developing communication skills and conducting successful training sessions:

1. Above all, be prepared. Be sure you know the sanitation practices and the reasons they are important. You should have chosen which training techniques are best and know your presentation well. Make sure the room is ready and that any visual aids or tools are in working order. Sometimes it is the little things that can make or break a training session.

2. During any presentation maintain eye contact with the listeners.

3. Make sure you keep your delivery as conversational and informal as possible.

4. Vary the tone of your voice for emphasis. A monotone is deadly. Also, speak at a moderate rate.

5. Use simple language. Unnecessary technical terms will only cause listeners to tune out. Be sure you are speaking on their wavelength.

6. Treat all questions and comments made by the workers seriously. Show that you value their opinions and suggestions and that you appreciate questions and do not consider them interruptions or evidence of stupidity.

7. Try to avoid doing all the talking. Ask questions. Let trainees approach a point by allowing them to put it in their own words. Give trainees time to answer questions.

8. Don't overwhelm workers with information in one sitting. Only give employees the amount of information you think they can handle. Try to look for cues that may indicate the workers are not picking up the information. If necessary, go over the subject again. (If one training method is not working, you may need to revise your technique.)

9. Keep the sessions short. Even if you have succeeded in interesting the employees in the subject of sanitation, it is very easy to lose their attention. One of the most effective methods of boring your trainees is to allow the session to run too long without a break. It is pointless to continue to talk to a class of trainees after the scheduled end of the session, unless it is obvious that they are so wrapped up in the topic being discussed that they do not notice the time. In most cases, attention drops off sharply as soon as it appears that the session is liable to run late. It is better to schedule another session than to alienate your trainees by running overtime.

10. Keep the training as related as possible to sanitation and the workers' jobs. If the range of subjects is too broad, people might not learn the procedures they need to know.

Motivating the Trainees

In addition to establishing a relationship between the material you are teaching and the workers' actual jobs, you must also find a way to motivate the group to want to learn what you have to teach. Many workers will find sanitation to be a less than stimulating topic. It is the job of the trainer to capture and keep the attention of the group and to get them to remember the material. One common method of accomplishing this feat is through the use of entertaining training materials.

A second way to motivate workers to learn is to make each one feel that you are talking to him or to her individually and that you have a real interest in whether the needs of each member of the group are being met and in what they have to say.

A third and very effective method of interesting workers in sanitation training is to employ a style of training that maximizes employee participation. Whether it is some form of learning-by-doing, conferences, role-playing, or dialog, a style that will get trainees active in self-training is essential to success.

EVALUATING TRAINING OUTCOMES

The stem of the word "evaluate" is "value." The word "evaluate" means, dictionaries tell us, "to ascertain the value of" or "to appraise carefully." For the foodservice manager the process of evaluating sanitation training for employees is particularly important because it takes the manager directly to the payoff—the tangible results, or lack of them, on the job. It forces an examination of the benefits of training to the trained employee and to the foodservice operation and balances these benefits against the cost of the training in time and in dollars.

Attaining Objectives

The first step in evaluating training begins before training is initiated. The manager or trainer should have already determined training needs by answering the following questions: "What training does the employee need to perform the duties of the assigned job?" "What training is needed to help the employee develop in the job?" The answers provide a list of training objectives. Converted to a training schedule, these objectives also help ensure that all employees receive necessary training without duplication.

What do training objectives have to do with evaluation? The relationship is clear. When you know what the training objectives are, you know what the outcomes—the end results—should be. You have a standard against which to measure results and to assign a value.

The second phase of training evaluation takes place during training and after employees have been trained. This phase requires that the manager or trainer answer two more questions. The first is "Did the training produce results on the job?" The second is "If intended results were not produced, why not?" Failure to ask (and to answer) these questions means that the manager will never know if the training was effective, whether knowledge was learned but never applied, or whether knowledge was learned but applied incorrectly.

Measuring Outcomes

With some oversimplification, there are two basic approaches available to a manager in placing a value on training. Evaluation works best when both approaches are used. The first approach is through the use of tests and measurements, both during and after training and on the job. The second approach incorporates training evaluation in day-to-day operations by making it a continuing part of each manager's and supervisor's job.

Evaluation through Objective Measurement

Objective measurement of individual progress can involve a variety of testing tools. Written and oral quizzes and examinations, used as either formal or informal classroom activities, can be valuable in demonstrating employee knowledge of the content of individual training sessions as well as of entire training programs.

Formal methods of measurement also help keep the trainer informed on how well the teaching objectives of a session or a program are being met. The results of tests can give the trainer a good idea if what is being taught is above, below, or at the learning and interest level of the trainees.

To be most useful, tests should be integrated into training programs as learning aids, whether in the form of paper-and-pencil examinations or trainee demonstrations of performance followed by group discussion. Tests should not be treated as threats to trainees at any time. In this connection, research by learning-theory psychologists has consistently stressed the importance of providing trainees with test results at the earliest practicable opportunity after the test. In fact, telling a trainee how well he or she performed, and doing so immediately after the test, can actually improve the trainee's performance.

Evaluation through Performance

The true measure of training in sanitation is the ability of foodservice employees to do their assigned tasks in the work situation. In this sense, evaluating training outcomes at work is part of employee evaluation and thus can well be considered a part of the responsibilities of each work supervisor and manager. When standards of achievement have been set before training and are mutually understood by both workers and supervisors, progress can be assessed by looking at individual achievements as measured against those standards.

If sanitation procedures are being followed, both the practices themselves and the outcomes are generally observable: for example, if the manager or supervisor wants to see if the FIFO rule is being used, he or she need only check the dates on the food items. Adherence to the time-and-temperature rule may be slightly less observable, however, and the supervisor may have to be very alert for problems by making sure that employees are using thermometers and by making regular checks of the temperature of food items. Supervision is a natural follow-up to training.

Positive feedback is a part of any learning experience. It indicates to the worker that he or she has been able to pick up the information and apply it. Generous praise can help reinforce workers' attitudes about their job. If they see that management *values* their best effort, they will be less tempted to slouch off.

Each trainee should receive some recognition when training is completed, preferably as soon as possible after the end of the training. Awards and certificates are commonly used, but the form of recognition should be matched to the situation. In any case, the recognition should come from the management, and its presentation should clearly indicate that the manager is genuinely interested in the trainee's progress.

The supervisor, in the kitchen or in the front of the house, can arrange work so that an employee's new knowledge and skill can be used and observed. The supervisor has a direct person-to-person contact with each employee, a relationship shared by no one else. A supervisor knows firsthand the training needs and successes. Having identified a need, having arranged for training, and having helped the employee put his or her knowledge to work, the supervisor can then watch for the results. If the need is met, a success is chalked up. If positive results are not achieved or only partly achieved, the supervisor can ask "Why?" Then, assuming the operation's management system so provides, the supervisor can report the facts and recommend further action.

Employee turnover data, absenteeism and tardiness reports, and productivity-rate information have also been found valuable in measuring the outcomes of training. Finally, guest complaint-reports (or lack of them) and customer-return rates (of failure thereof) can often be tied directly to the quality of sanitation training. The astute manager uses all sources of such information to evaluate the worth of what training dollars can buy.

SUMMARY

One of the foodservice manager's most important responsibilities is to train employees in the principles and practices of foodservice sanitation. Since food service in the broadest sense is a public industry, only through effective training can the manager protect the public from foodborne illness.

The special "people problems" of the industry—arising from growth demands and patterns, high employee-turnover rates, and the fact that most training must be done at the level of the individual restaurant or operation—make sanitation training a difficult and yet a continuous need. Year-round training programs on an individual basis for both new and experienced employees are essentially a public-service requirement placed on the foodservice industry.

The benefits accruing from a properly designed and conducted training program are demonstrable in very practical and measurable terms—dollars. Progressive restaurants and foodservice companies are recognizing these benefits on an increasing scale. Full-time or part-time training director positions are being established in practically all major multi-unit companies, in many medium-sized companies, and increasingly in smaller companies interested in future growth. Foodservice sanitation training must be a common denominator in the job descriptions of all these positions.

Training involves a number of steps, but the bottom line should be workers who can perform sanitary procedures to keep food safe. Whoever trains the workers, whatever techniques are used, and wherever sanitation is taught, employees should recognize the importance of proper food handling procedures. Positive feedback is an important aspect of any training program.

Two methods are generally used to evaluate the outcome of training. The most typical in the foodservice industry is evaluation of the employee on the job. Written tests or quizzes may also be used.

A CASE IN POINT

Paul has two employees that must be trained in sanitation. One is an experienced cook who Paul wants to retrain. The other is an inexperienced waitress.

Which method of training should be used for each person?
What techniques do you suggest for getting sanitary procedures across to these two?
What type of evaluation do you think would be best in each situation?

STUDY QUESTIONS

1. Why should a foodservice operation invest in a year-round program of sanitation training?

2. What defects are associated with the ''magic apron'' and ''crash'' methods of sanitation training?

3. According to the text, what is the definition of a ''training program''?

4. What are two training methods mentioned in the text and the advantages and disadvantages of each?

5. Why should training objectives be written in behavioral terms?

6. What should be considered the core content of a sanitation training program for all foodservice workers?

7. What are some interpersonal skills that trainers might develop to improve their presentations?

8. List four guidelines for choosing sanitation training materials.

9. What information should be included in a notice announcing a training session?

10. Describe the physical requirements for a room in which a training session will be held.

11. Why should a trainer be familiar with the daily routine of those who are being trained?

12. Name three methods for motivating trainees.

13. How are training objectives related to training evaluation?

14. What two approaches are available to a manager in evaluating the outcomes of sanitation training?

MORE ON THE SUBJECT

MAGER, ROBERT F. *Preparing Instructional Objectives*. Belmont, Ca.: Fearon Publishers, 1964, 136 pages. This is a must for every trainer and a cornerstone book in educational technology. In easily understood and interesting language, the book demonstrates how to define teaching objectives, how to state them clearly, and how to describe criteria by which to measure success. Also *Developing Vocational Instruction*. 1967, 83 pages. This book provides direct information on vocational training methods and plans.

MILLER, JACK E. and MARY PORTER. *Supervision in the Hospitality Industry*. New York, N.Y.: John Wiley & Sons, 1985, 347 pages. Chapter 6 discusses the various types of training conducted in hospitality operations. Job instruction training is broken down into phases and information on developing a plan is included.

PLUNKETT, W. RICHARD. *Supervision: The Direction of People at Work*. Dubuque, Ia.: Wm. C. Brown Publishers, 1983, 370 pages. Chapter 12 on training is a thorough survey of training, including the principles of motivation and reinforcement.

ANSWER TO A CASE IN POINT

One-on-one training is probably best for both employees. The reason: they require slightly different knowledge as far as their jobs go. They both might benefit by a slide presentation on the hazards to safe food. Since the cook has to have more information on foodhandling techniques, a step-by-step training program that includes actual practice is probably best in that situation. The waitress would also benefit from step-by-step training.

On-the-job evaluation is probably best for these two employees. Written tests would not really give the manager a true measure of their progress.

14

Dealing with Sanitation and Safety Regulations and Standards

If at this point you are a bit overawed by the demands of foodservice sanitation, be reassured. You are certainly not alone in the battle against food contaminants. Many people and organizations are trying to help and guide you.

In this chapter we will briefly examine the two basic systems of guidance and control that operate in our society to protect the sanitary quality of food. These two systems are

- The official system of regulatory and advisory controls administered by agencies of government
- The unofficial system of voluntary controls observed by industry, trade associations, and professional groups

Every facet of a foodservice facility is inspected, evaluated, or regulated in one way or another by government and trade organizations. Some foodservice operators view much of this interest in their affairs as unwarranted intrusion, but that attitude is a narrow one. No matter how capable the operator is, he or she cannot guarantee wholesome food at competitive prices without outside help.

It is wise to recognize the constructive guidance that regulatory and advisory organizations offer and consider how to use that guidance to realize the greatest public and private benefit. It may seem burdensome to have inspectors scrutinizing every area of an establishment, but the receptive and cooperative operator will discover that inspectors can offer practical solutions to vexing problems. The foodservice manager who tries to be cooperative will appreciate the value of regulatory and advisory agencies and resolutely seek to understand the help they offer.

GOVERNMENT REGULATION OF THE FOOD INDUSTRY

Government long ago became interested in assuring the sanitary quality of food. The first health ordinances in the Western world were adopted more than 400 years ago, and the nation's first health officer was appointed when the United States was still a group of British holdings. Today government control is exercised at three levels: federal, state, and county or municipal.

Federal Regulatory Agencies

The large majority of federal laws about food have no direct bearing on the average foodservice operator. Federal standards for foodservice sanitation are, however, often reflected in state and local regulations. Moreover, the federal government works to safeguard the sanitary quality of many food products that are purchased by a foodservice establishment. The federal agencies of most interest to the foodservice operator are described in the following section.

Food and Drug Administration (FDA)

The Food and Drug Administration is a major entity of the U.S. Department of Health and Human Services, Public Health Service. Within the FDA, the Center for Food Safety and Applied Nutrition, Retail Food Protection Branch has the responsibility for designing programs involved in promoting the quality and safety of foods for retail sale. The many functions of the branch include developing model ordinances and codes and promoting their adoption by state and local health departments. The Model Food Service Sanitation Ordinance is contained in the *Food Service Sanitation Manual* published by the FDA. This document is revised periodically to reflect developments in the foodservice industry and in the field of sanitation. *Applied Foodservice Sanitation* is consistent with the regulations and standards of the FDA sanitation manual. The FDA also provides a survey service to state and local health departments to help them standardize their inspection and administrative procedures.

The FDA also enforces mandatory provisions of the laws and regulations relating to foodservice operations on interstate carriers. Planes, boats, trains, buses, and their commissaries are inspected by the FDA.

Another important job of the FDA, which is shared in part by the U.S. Department of Agriculture, is the inspection of food-processing plants to ensure adherence to standards of purity and wholesomeness and compliance with labeling requirements. The milk industry is cooperatively regulated by the FDA and state agencies. The National Shellfish Safety Program is a cooperative effort between the FDA and the shellfish industry and state agencies to ensure a sanitary shellfish supply.

The FDA also maintains a list of food additives. This list is available to foodservice managers on request.

U.S. Department of Agriculture (USDA)

The U.S. Department of Agriculture is responsible for the inspection and grading of meat, meat products, poultry, dairy products, eggs and egg products, and fruits and vegetables shipped across state boundaries. It does this through the Food Safety and Quality Service agency. These functions of the USDA are described in chapter 4 of this book.

U.S. Centers for Disease Control

The U.S. Centers for Disease Control, located in Atlanta, Georgia, are a field agency of the Public Health Service. The centers investigate outbreaks of foodborne illness, study the causes and control of disease, regularly publish statistical data, and provide educational services in the field of sanitation.

Other Federal Programs

Several other agencies of the national government play lesser roles in the control of food quality.

The Environmental Protection Agency (EPA). The EPA sets standards for air and water quality and regulates the use of pesticides and the handling of wastes.

The National Marine Fisheries Service. The National Marine Fisheries Service of the U.S. Department of Commerce develops noncompulsory standards for the sanitary quality of fishing waters and for safe processing methods.

State and Local Regulations

The laws that affect the foodservice operator most meaningfully on a day-to-day basis are those enforced by state and local health authorities. These agencies create detailed regulations and conduct inspections to ensure compliance.

From state to state and from city to city the regulations vary in language, coverage, and manner of enforcement. The organization and scope of the monitoring agency will vary also, depending on the locality. In a large city, the enforcement agency will probably be a local one. In a small municipality and in rural areas, a county or state health department will have jurisdiction over implementation of health codes. In any case, the manager has a duty to be familiar with the applicable laws and with the enforcement system in effect. Some health departments issue guidelines on foodservice sanitation that explain the law in simple terms.

Regardless of differences in wording, regulations in any state or locality have the same intent: to protect the dining public from foodborne illness. Thus, the mission of the public health officer is not so different from that of the sanitation-minded foodservice manager. Both the officer and the manager are eager to protect people by protecting food from contamination and by preventing the growth of microorganisms that may succeed in getting into food.

Many state and local ordinances are patterned after the Model Food Service Sanitation Ordinance recommended by the federal Food and Drug Administration. The following list of the main provisions of that ordinance will illustrate the range of interests of all levels of government:

1. Food Care: Supplies, protection, storage, preparation, display and service, transportation
2. Personnel: Health, personal cleanliness, clothing, practices
3. Equipment and Utensils: Materials, design, and fabrication, equipment installation and location
4. Cleaning, Sanitization, and Storage of Equipment and Utensils
5. Sanitary Facilities and Controls: Water supply, sewage, plumbing, toilet facilities, lavatory facilities, garbage and refuse, insect and rodent control
6. Construction and Maintenance of Physical Facilities: Floors, walls and ceilings, cleaning facilities, lighting, ventilation, dressing rooms and locker areas, poisonous materials
7. Mobile Units
8. Temporary Units
9. Compliance Procedures: Issuance and suspension of permits
10. Examination and Condemnation of Food

Foodservice Inspections

To the foodservice manager, the law is most directly represented by an official with a clipboard—the sanitarian. Although the sanitarian differs from the manager in point of view, he or she is a professional in the field of sanitation as well as a representative of the state or local health service.

The inspection process may begin even before a foodservice facility is built. Many jurisdictions require advance review of plans and specifications for new construction or extensive remodeling. This procedure guarantees that applicable codes will be met, and thereby benefits the manager as well as the community. Correcting an error after construction is completed may prove costly and delay the opening of the establishment.

Once the foodservice building is completed, an initial inspection visit can be expected prior to issuance of a permit. Several agencies may be involved in the visit. For example, if liquor is to be served, both the state liquor control authority and the local health authority may visit the establishment. If the facility is to process foods for interstate shipment, the Food and Drug Administration and the U.S. Department of Agriculture may become involved in the authorization procedure.

After a food service has opened, inspections may occur anywhere from once a month to once a year. The FDA recommends that inspections be held at least every six months. The exact frequency will be influenced by such factors as the workload of the local agency and the severity of the violations found during the previous inspections. The inspections may be held at any time.

In most instances, the health officer will complete an inspection report that must be signed by the owner, manager, or a designated representative. A copy of the report is given to the foodservice facility. Exhibit 14.1 shows the form suggested by the FDA for use by local health departments. Note the relative weight given to each kind of violation. The operation receives a "score" after any weighted violations are subtracted from 100.

Although a sanitation inspection is a cause for concern, it need not be a cause for panic. If the food service's sanitation standards are consistent with or exceed the local laws, a routine inspection will be just that. A good sanitation program and trained employees should

Exhibit 14.1 Food Service Establishment Inspection Report form (Source: The Food and Drug Administration)

DEPARTMENT OF HEALTH, EDUCATION AND WELFARE
PUBLIC HEALTH SERVICE — FOOD AND DRUG ADMINISTRATION

Food Service Establishment Inspection Report

PURPOSE
Regular 29-1
Follow-up 2
Complaint 3
Investigation 4
Other 5

Based on an inspection this day, the items circled below identify the violations in operations or facilities which must be corrected by the next routine inspection or such shorter period of time as may be specified in writing by the regulatory authority. Failure to comply with any time limits for corrections specified in this notice may result in cessation of your Food Service operations.

OWNER NAME

ESTABLISHMENT NAME

ADDRESS

ZIP CODE

EST. I.D. (1-10)	COUNTY	DIST.	EST. NO.	CENSUS TRACT 11-13	SANIT. CODE 14-16	17-22	YR.	MO.	DAY	TRAVEL TIME 23-25	INSPEC. TIME 26-28

ITEM NO. | WT. COL.

FOOD

*01	Source; sound condition, no spoilage	5	30
02	Original container; properly labeled	1	31

FOOD PROTECTION

*03	Potentially hazardous food meets temperature requirements during storage, preparation, display, service, transportation	5	32
*04	Facilities to maintain product temperature	4	33
05	Thermometers provided and conspicuous	1	34
06	Potentially hazardous food properly thawed	2	35
*07	Unwrapped and potentially hazardous food not re-served	4	36
08	Food protection during storage, preparation, display, service, transportation	2	37
09	Handling of food (ice) minimized	2	38
10	In use, food (ice) dispensing utensils properly stored	1	39

PERSONNEL

*11	Personnel with infections restricted	5	40
*12	Hands washed and clean, good hygienic practices	5	41
13	Clean clothes, hair restraints	1	42

FOOD EQUIPMENT & UTENSILS

14	Food (ice) contact surfaces: designed, constructed, maintained, installed, located	2	43
15	Non-food contact surfaces: designed, constructed, maintained, installed, located	1	44
16	Dishwashing facilities: designed, constructed, maintained, installed, located, operated	2	45
17	Accurate thermometers, chemical test kits provided, gauge cock (1/4'' IPS valve)	1	46
18	Pre-flushed, scraped, soaked	1	47
19	Wash, rinse water: clean, proper temperature	2	48
*20	Sanitization rinse: clean, temperature, concentration, exposure time; equipment, utensils sanitized	4	49
21	Wiping cloths: clean, use restricted	1	50
22	Food-Contact surfaces of equipment and utensils clean, free of abrasives, detergents	2	51
23	Non-food contact surfaces of equipment and utensils clean	1	52
24	Storage, handling of clean equipment/utensils	1	53
25	Single-service articles, storage, dispensing	1	54
26	No re-use of single service articles	2	55

WATER

*27	Water source, safe: hot & cold under pressure	5	56

SEWAGE

*28	Sewage and waste water disposal	4	57

PLUMBING

29	Installed, maintained	1	58
*30	Cross connection, back siphonage, backflow	5	59

TOILET & HANDWASHING FACILITIES

*31	Number, convenient, accessible, designed, installed	4	60
32	Toilet rooms enclosed, self-closing doors; fixtures, good repair, clean; hand cleanser, sanitary towels/hand-drying devices provided, proper waste receptacles	2	61

GARBAGE & REFUSE DISPOSAL

33	Containers or receptacles, covered: adequate number insect/rodent proof, frequency, clean	2	62
34	Outside storage area enclosures properly constructed, clean; controlled incineration	1	63

INSECT, RODENT, ANIMAL CONTROL

*35	Presence of insects/rodents—outer openings protected, no birds, turtles, other animals	4	64

FLOORS, WALLS & CEILINGS

36	Floors, constructed, drained, clean, good repair, covering installation, dustless cleaning methods	1	65
37	Walls, ceiling, attached equipment: constructed, good repair, clean, surfaces, dustless cleaning methods	1	66

LIGHTING

38	Lighting provided as required, fixtures shielded	1	67

VENTILATION

39	Rooms and equipment—vented as required	1	68

DRESSING ROOMS

40	Rooms, area, lockers provided, located, used	1	69

OTHER OPERATIONS

*41	Toxic items properly stored, labeled, used	5	70
42	Premises maintained free of litter, unnecessary articles, cleaning maintenance equipment properly stored. Authorized personnel	1	71
43	Complete separation from living/sleeping quarters. Laundry	1	72
44	Clean, soiled linen properly stored	1	73

Received by: name _____
title _____

Inspected by: name _____

FOLLOW-UP	RATING SCORE 75-77	ACTION
Yes 74-1	100 less weight of items violated →	Change 78-C
No 2		Delete . . . . D

*Critical Items Requiring Immediate Attention.   Remarks on back (80-1)

FORM FDA 2420 (2/79)   PREVIOUS EDITION MAY BE USED   USE REVERSE FOR REMARKS

result in good inspection reports. The following tips will enable managers and operators to get the most out of sanitation inspections.

1. Ask for identification. Many sanitarians will volunteer their credentials.

2. Always remember, the inspector is not the enemy. Most sanitarians expect some defensiveness and even resentment from foodservice operators. Unfortunately, too often they get these two responses, as well as evasiveness, from operators and employees alike. Creating an adversary relationship where none exists is counter-productive to your role as a sanitation-conscious operator.

3. Cooperate. Answer all of the sanitarian's questions to the best of your ability. Instruct employees to do the same. Be polite. Say you wish to accompany the inspector. This will demonstrate your concern, and you can see your operation as the sanitarian sees it.

4. Keep the relationship professional. The sanitarian is not in the operation to sample your soup—although he may check to see if it is hot. Don't offer food or drink before an inspection. In some areas this may be construed as bribery.

5. Be ready to provide records. The sanitarian may request records, including employee files. You may ask why they are needed. Be sure you keep records of pesticide use in the facility and of any recent remodeling or equipment purchases.

6. Discuss any violations with the sanitarian. The inspection report is not just another piece of bureaucratic paperwork to be forgotten and discarded. You should study it closely and any violations noted should be discussed in detail with the sanitarian.

The intelligent manager will want to know the exact nature of the violation. It should be remembered that the sanitarian sees many foodservice operations and can offer advice on correcting any violations, on employee training, and provide general information on improving foodservice sanitation. The sanitarian who merely finds fault but does not suggest solutions is hardly achieving effective enforcement of the law and protection of the consumer.

7. Follow-up. You can expect a copy of the report. Go over it carefully. Then take it with you through your facility. Have the violations been corrected or only temporarily so? Were violations the result of employee carelessness or poor supervision? If so, have the problems been corrected? You may have a more objective view of how the sanitarian saw your operation when you start to notice some so-called "hidden" violations. These may include low hot-water pressure, crevices in storage areas, and incorrect handling of food during service.

It is essential that violations discovered by sanitarians be corrected promptly. Failure to do so may make the owner subject to a fine and unfavorable publicity. When violations are of an extreme nature, the establishment may be closed.

The extent of inspection coverage and the areas of greatest and least emphasis will vary between localities and even among individual sanitarians. Some are most concerned with refrigeration temperatures; others may concentrate on the general physical appearance of the facility. One sanitarian may examine dishwashing procedure in detail, and another may give primary attention to the personal hygiene of workers.

It is a waste of energy trying to guess beforehand what the sanitarian will examine. It is far better for the manager to know that the operation is sanitary rather than to worry about what the health officer will find. The manager who is serious about protecting customers will see to it that all areas of the facility meet high standards of sanitation.

Every foodservice manager should have a copy of the local foodservice sanitation ordinance, as well as copies of regulations and standards. Between inspections managers should look at ways to cooperate with the health department to make the facility and food products as sanitary as possible. A passing score on an inspection report rarely means there's no room for improvement. Some of the more dangerous time-and-temperature violations are difficult to identify in a routine foodservice inspection. The foodservice manager has the primary responsibility for patron safety irregardless of the unit sanitation score. The health department may offer information and/or training for employees, interpretations and advice on ordinances, and various materials on sanitation.

The choice, then, is between positive *action* and negative *apprehension,* and the self-reliant manager will no doubt choose the former. In chapter 15 we discuss self-inspection procedures to be used by the foodservice operator. Surely self-inspection, followed by any necessary corrective action, is the best preparation for a visit from the health department.

Inspection After an Outbreak

If an outbreak of foodborne illness is suspected as having come from a particular food service, the health department will usually investigate it. This may include interviewing employees, excluding ill employees from food preparation areas, requiring employees to have physicals, isolating and laboratory testing of food items, and in some cases, closing the establishment.

The best approach in dealing with an outbreak is for the manager to be solely in charge of working with the health department. Full cooperation is important. Most health officers do not want to close an establishment unless it is absolutely necessary. They generally recognize the economic implications of such a move. However, their most important concern is the public health of the community.

A cooperative attitude on management's part can help prevent drastic action. Belligerence or evasiveness only demonstrate to health officials that management is not to be trusted with the public's health. A positive approach is always a plus when it comes to dealing with health officials. (Chapter 15 discusses how to deal with a customer who complains of a foodborne illness.) If samples are requested, the manager may want to take a split-sample and have it independently analyzed.

In the final analysis, the success of standards, laws, and enforcement by government will depend upon the extent to which government agencies consider the practicalities of the foodservice operations. The foodservice industry can most effectively protect the consumer, with least disruption and minimal cost, by working in close cooperation with government agencies. It is for these reasons that the Energy and Technical Services Committee of the National Restaurant Association has urged establishment of joint food-protection councils in state and local health jurisdictions. Several such councils are already in existence and are actively cooperating with health departments in formulating regulations, operating training programs, and solving enforcement problems.

VOLUNTARY CONTROLS WITHIN THE INDUSTRY

Probably few segments of U.S. industry have devoted as much effort to policing themselves as have food, food service, and associated enterprises. Scientific and professional societies, manufacturing and marketing firms, and trade associations have energetically pursued programs designed to raise the standards of the industry through research, education, and cooperation with government. The overall results in the area of sanitation have included the following:

- An increased understanding of foodborne illness and its prevention
- Improvements in the design of equipment and facilities for greater cleanability, effectiveness, and reliability
- Assistance in maintaining the sanitary quality of foods during processing, shipment, storage, and service
- Efforts to make foodservice laws uniform throughout the nation, and to give them practical applicability

Relevant Organizations

While countless organizations have contributed to these endeavors, those having the greatest relevance for the foodservice operator are discussed in the remainder of this chapter.

The American Public Health Association (APHA)

The American Public Health Association is an umbrella organization representing doctors, nurses, and sanitarians concerned with public health. The Food Protection Committee of the APHA serves as a forum for professionals in public health and establishes policies and standards for food sanitation on a broad base.

The National Environmental Health Association (NEHA); The International Association of Milk, Food, and Environmental Sanitarians; The National Society of Professional Sanitarians

NEHA is an organization of environmentalists and sanitarians, including those responsible for food inspection services and for establishing environmental health programs. The International Association of Milk, Food, and Environmental Sanitarians was a pioneer in the highly successful U.S. milk sanitation program. These two organizations and the National Society of Professional Sanitarians are composed of sanitarians concerned with environmental health protection policies at the national, state, and local levels. The organizations promote professional standards, recommend legislative policy, and sponsor uniform enforcement procedures.

The National Sanitation Foundation (NSF)

A nonprofit research and testing organization, the National Sanitation Foundation evaluates foodservice equipment and materials. NSF also publishes widely accepted standards for equipment design, construction, and installation. Manufacturers can request NSF to evaluate their equipment. The NSF seal appears on equipment that has been approved by the organization.

The National Sanitation Foundation's approach to determining the suitability of individual units of equipment for use in a food service exemplifies the kind of progress that can be achieved through voluntary programs on the part of the foodservice industry.

The National Pest Control Association

The National Pest Control Association, the organization of pest control operators throughout the nation, provides guidelines for pest-prevention programs.

The Association of Food and Drug Officials

The Association of Food and Drug Officials develops food sanitation codes and encourages food protection through the adoption of uniform legislation and enforcement.

The Frozen Food Industry Coordinating Committee

The Frozen Food Industry Coordinating Committee has developed the *Code of Recommended Practices for the Handling of Frozen Food,* which describes procedures to be used from the processing stage to retail food service.

The Educational Foundation of the National Restaurant Association

A not-for-profit educational foundation, the Educational Foundation of the National Restaurant Association, formerly the National Institute for the Foodservice Industry, provides educational services to the industry, including professional courses for foodservice managers and workers. The Educational Foundation promotes sanitation in the foodservice industry through its certification course, *Applied Foodservice Sanitation,* and offers other foodservice programs as well.

The Food Research Institute

The Food Research Institute is a nonprofit organization that conducts research into the causes and prevention of food contamination and foodborne illness. It works to benefit both food processors and foodservice operators by setting maximum permissible levels of microorganisms, chemicals, and chemical additives in food.

The National Restaurant Association (NRA)

The National Restaurant Association is the national trade association for retail and institutional foodservice establishments. Through its Energy and Technical Services Committee, the NRA promotes food sanitation in cooperation with government, scientific, commercial, and educational institutions.

SUMMARY

Public and private organizations and agencies can offer valuable assistance to the foodservice manager in the fight against foodborne contaminants. It is up to the manager to make use of the help that is available.

Government at all levels recommends standards and administers controls that affect the foodservice operator directly or indirectly. Many federal regulations do not apply directly to retail food service; nonetheless the model ordinance developed by the Food and Drug Administration serves as a pattern for a large number of state and local regulations. In addition, federal authorities regulate the purity and safeness of foods in interstate commerce.

While state and local health codes vary throughout the nation, virtually all of them contain provisions governing food safeness; personal hygiene; sanitary facilities, equipment, and utensils; safe operating practices; and enforcement procedures. To the foodservice manager the most visible representative of the law is the local sanitarian. One highly effective way to prepare for visits from the health officer is to institute a rigorous program of self-inspection. A positive approach to dealing with public health officials is always best.

Professional and trade organizations in the fields of food service and public health study business activities, investigate sanitation problems, and recommend standards for foodservice practices, equipment, and facilities. Professional associations also develop educational programs in sanitation and conduct research into the causes and prevention of foodborne illness.

A CASE IN POINT

The sanitarian inspector was standing there with his clipboard and Jerry was in a panic. He was short two employees and the dishwasher was not functioning properly. The hot water was not anywhere near 180°F (82.2°C) for the final rinse. In addition, the garbage containers were overflowing. Jerry told the sanitarian to wait a few minutes and went back to empty the garbage. That done, Jerry told the inspector to go ahead but that the place was busy and would he hurry. "I've got a business to run," he said.

Jerry forgot about the sanitarian until he came over with the report. Jerry was appalled at the score. The operation had passed but barely. The sanitarian said that there was room for improvement. He said that the dishwasher had to be repaired immediately. He also pointed out that he noticed several problems with personnel hygiene and foodhandling practices. The inspector asked if Jerry had any questions, and said he would be happy to discuss the report with him. Jerry said no because he had "work to do."

How could Jerry have prevented a low score?
How should Jerry have dealt with the sanitarian?

STUDY QUESTIONS

1. What are the two basic systems of guidance and control that work to guarantee the sanitary quality of food in this country?
2. Briefly describe the functions of the Food and Drug Administration with regard to food protection.
3. What government body is responsible for inspecting and grading meat and poultry shipped across state lines?
4. What level of government is more likely to directly affect foodservice operations— federal or local?
5. What is the best way to prepare for a visit from the public health inspector?
6. What are the possible consequences of failure to correct violations found by an inspector?
7. What management information can be gained from a visit by the health officer?

MORE ON THE SUBJECT

SCHULTZ, H. W. *Food Law Handbook.* Westport, Connecticut: AVI Publishing Company, Inc., 1981, 662 pages. This handbook is a comprehensive reference on the various laws affecting food production and distribution in the United States.

SHERRY, JOHN E. H. *Legal Aspects of Foodservice Management.* Chicago: The National Institute for the Foodservice Industry, 1984, 334 pages. Chapter 2 contains information on the various regulatory agencies that affect foodservice operations and the related implications for managers.

U.S. DEPARTMENT OF HEALTH AND HUMAN SERVICES, Food and Drug Administration. *Food Service Sanitation Manual.* Washington, D.C., 1976. The manual contains the recommended ordinance for foodservice sanitation.

ANSWER TO A CASE IN POINT

An ongoing sanitation program is the best way to prevent a low score on an inspection report. A program that includes worker training should be an ongoing part of running a food service.

Jerry should not have been so quick in dealing with the sanitarian. Such an attitude might indicate a lack of management interest in sanitation. It could also cause the inspector to wonder if management has something to hide.

Jerry should have used the sanitarian to his advantage. He could have sat down with the sanitarian and discussed the problem areas and received advice on how to handle them.

15
Managing a Sanitary and Safe Food Service

As manager of a foodservice establishment, it is your responsibility to see that the food served to your customers is safe and wholesome. Managing a sanitary food service is as important to the success of an operation as controlling costs and advertising. Sanitation must be a continual priority in day-to-day operations. Managers who concern themselves with sanitation only during a crisis will find it impossible to keep up with even the most minimum health requirements. Managers need to integrate sanitation supervision into other duties so that it becomes an integral part of their jobs. Once a good sanitation program is in place, most managers will find they have fewer crises and better patron counts.

You cannot do the entire job of purchasing, storing, preparing, holding, serving, and cleaning without help. You must be able to get your employees to do these jobs for you, as thoroughly and as well as you would do them yourself. This, after all, is the definition of management: "Getting things done through people."

THE CONTROL POINTS

The overall goal of a sanitation program is to control the handling of food from purchase to service to ensure its safety. Much of this book has been devoted to steps taken to prevent sanitation hazards. These steps include hiring safe foodhandlers, purchasing and maintaining equipment, and purchasing, storing, preparing, and serving safe food (see Exhibit 15.1). The goal is to ensure that safe food remains safe right up until it is eaten.

The manager has a number of factors within his or her control that can ensure a sanitary operation and safe food. These control points include the following:

- Hiring foodhandlers. Job applicants must be observed for the physical signs of health problems and for poor hygiene habits.

- Purchasing and maintaining equipment. Equipment and facilities must be designed and maintained with sanitation in mind.
- Purchasing food. Food must be purchased from safe sources and checked immediately on receipt.
- Storing food. Food to be stored for any period of time must be kept at the proper temperature and humidity. The FIFO rule must be observed.
- Preparing food. Food should be prepared as close to serving time as possible. The cardinal rule of time and temperature must be observed.
- Serving food. Proper handling of utensils and food items is required during service. Foods for self-service must be displayed so that contamination by patrons is avoided (see Exhibit 15.1).

The foodservice manager has control over each of these factors. How much control is exercised depends on the skills and attitudes of the manager. The manager who knows what the sanitation hazards are, develops a sanitation program to prevent contamination, and hires and trains workers is three-fourths of the way to ensuring safe food. The final factor in any sanitation program is *evaluating the results*.

Evaluating results is a part of any management operation. So it is with sanitation. Few people know the facility and the employees as well as the foodservice manager. Even the health inspector will not know every potential hazard in the operation as well as management. Evaluating the sanitation program, including procedures and employee progress, is a vital part of keeping food safe.

Many methods are available to gather information on the success of sanitation efforts. You can watch the sanitation activities in progress as your employees carry them out. You can ask them about their jobs. You can survey the physical results of their efforts. Or you can

Exhibit 15.1   Management control factors

Operational Steps	Control Factors	Foodhandling Steps	Control Factors
Hiring personnel	Health Personal hygiene Habits Training	*Purchasing*	Supplier Government aids
		Receiving	Temperature Packaging Labeling Dating
Purchasing and maintaining equipment	Cleanability Pest control Maintenance		
		Storage	Temperature Humidity Length of storage Stock rotation
		Preparation	Time/temperature Sanitary handling
		Service	Sanitary handling of utensils and food Protection of self-service foods

go to your most important source of information—and your most difficult critics—your guests.

In this chapter, then, we will talk about the following:

- Supervision and employee feedback: monitoring the actions and practices of your employees and getting information from employees on sanitation.
- Self-inspection: examining your own operation at each control point in order to detect defects in sanitation.

- Customer-inspection: tuning in to the reaction of your guests regarding the sanitation level of your establishment.

SUPERVISION AND EMPLOYEE FEEDBACK

The manager's responsibility for a safe food service doesn't end when a trained employee is assigned to do a job. A manager must continue to make certain, through regular, on-the-spot observation, that tasks are being properly performed. Every aspect of the operation deserves the manager's personal attention, even though workers have proven reliable and official sanitation inspections have been favorable.

Employees should be made to feel not that they are being graded or spied upon but that their work is important. It should be made clear to them that the boss is interested in what they do and how they do it and is receptive to new and better ideas. The difference here is between a manager demonstrating a genuine interest in operating a thriving business and an employee thinking, "Look out, the boss is checking up on me again." If problems are discovered, the employee should be *shown* how to correct them. Discipline alone is not going to change worker actions.

Supervision is made much easier if employees are motivated to do a good job. Much of this motivation should be accomplished during training, but the way employees are treated on the job will also have a telling effect on their morale. Treat your employees as fully contributing members of the foodservice team, and the chances are good that their actions will fall in line with this treatment.

Employees can be valuable sources of information when it comes to sanitation. They may observe things during their jobs that do not seem quite right; yet they may not tell the management for one reason or another. Managers should encourage constructive feedback from employees who perform sanitation-related tasks or are directly involved in the preparation and service of food.

The best way to get information from employees is during employee meetings. Encourage employees to let you know if they have noticed problems with equipment, pest problems, or ways sanitation could be improved. Their answers could be enlightening. You may discover that the reason the sanitizing solution isn't working is because it isn't dispensing properly into the machine or that the delivery people bring the poultry in when there is no one available to check it immediately.

Encouraging employees to speak up about sanitation does several things. First of all, it demonstrates management's interest in sanitation. Secondly, it increases the employees' participation in sanitation activities and can help morale. Lastly, it can provide the manager with information to solve a sanitation problem.

SELF-INSPECTION

Another way in which you will be able to tell whether sanitation efforts have borne fruit is whether you can pass your local health department's inspection. But you cannot rely on these infrequent visits to monitor the day-to-day success of your attempts to prevent contamination. You must develop a system for continually and systematically checking on all phases of your operation to assure yourself that unsafe conditions do not arise despite all your efforts. The best way is through regular self-inspection.

Self-inspection must be thorough to be valuable. A quick run through the facility is not sufficient. A pocket thermometer should be carried for spot checking food temperatures, FIFO dates should be examined, and equipment checked for cleanliness. Remember, outward appearances do not tell the whole story. *Close, regular* inspection is the best route.

Who Should Inspect?

Self-inspection should be a regularly recurring task performed by trained personnel who are thoroughly familiar with the establishment's overall operation. In-house inspection should not be a hit-or-miss affair or scheduled only for when the manager or supervisor has nothing else to do. The following people should be authorized to conduct inspections:

1. Yourself as owner/operator or manager
2. Supervisors of various departments (Departmental inspections can then be pooled to provide an overall picture)

3. Sanitation consultants hired especially to contribute an informed, objective view

What Should Be Inspected?

A self-inspection program should cover the following areas:

1. Personal hygiene of foodhandlers and servers
2. Foodhandling practices
3. Receiving areas
4. Food storage areas
5. Food preparation areas and equipment
6. Food holding equipment
7. Food transportation equipment
8. Warewashing and storage areas
9. Lobby, dining rooms, and serving areas
10. Customer restrooms
11. Employee facilities
12. Storage areas for supplies and equipment
13. Inside and outside garbage and trash storage and disposal areas
14. Boiler rooms and mechanical operating equipment; utilities installation

Self-inspection should cover the layout of the entire facility and include a check of procedures for the storage, preparation, and service of food. Special attention should be given to areas both inside and outside that might harbor pests.

When Should Self-Inspection Occur?

Self-inspection that is a regular part of a management routine is the most valuable. The manager should categorize the areas and sanitation practices into an inspection schedule that is flexible. Self-inspection should be conducted as often as necessary to identify and solve sanitation problems. If certain areas of your establishment are constantly found to violate sanitation standards, they should be inspected more often until corrective measures have brought about an end to the problem.

The food preparation procedures should be observed as often as possible *during* busy periods because this is when sanitation problems are likely to occur. Storage areas should be checked regularly to ensure that food is being held at proper temperatures. Employees should be observed every day for signs of illness or poor personal hygiene.

When conditions are found that do not measure up to sanitation expectations, steps should be taken to remedy the situation as soon as possible—immediately if the problem results in direct food contamination. These steps may be as simple as replacing worn scrub brushes or defrosting the refrigerator; or more complicated measures such as emergency training sessions may be required.

Discuss the results of your inspection with your employees to alert them to problems and ask for their suggestions regarding improvements.

Developing a Sanitation Checklist

So many small but important details should be reviewed in the process of your sanitation self-inspections that it would be easy to overlook some. The manager of even a small food service may find it desirable to make inspections on the basis of a written checklist.

Checklists for facility-wide inspections can be obtained from a variety of sources, including national, state, and local public health departments. To be most helpful, however, your checklist should cover your particular establishment in detail. It should be compatible with your local foodservice sanitation regulations. It should also be organized so that you can conduct either full-scale inspections or spot-checks of problem areas.

Exhibit 15.2   Sanitation self-inspection checklist

Personal Safeness

Do any food handlers have infected burns, cuts, boils?

Do any food handlers have acute respiratory illness?

Do any food handlers have infections or contagious illness transmittable through foods?

Are food handlers wearing clean outer garments?

Are food handlers free of body odors?

Are food handlers' hands clean—washed at start of work day and as frequently as necessary?

Are food handlers wearing hats, caps or hairnets, or other effective hair restraints?

Are food handlers observed picking nose or pimples, scratching head or face?

Are food handlers observed smoking or eating in food preparation or serving areas?

Are fingernails of food handlers short and clean?

Are instances of spitting in sinks, on floor, or in disposal area observed?

Are food servers seen to cough in hands?

Are food handlers wearing rings (other than plain band), dangling bracelets, wristwatches, etc., while preparing or handling food?

Are cooks' wiping cloths used to wipe off perspiration on face used for no additional purpose?

Have all employees been instructed on minimum sanitation and food protection requirements?

Food-Handling Practices

Is food, in pans or containers, on floor?

Are perishable or potentially hazardous foods being held at room temperature?

Are fruits and vegetables thoroughly washed prior to preparation and serving?

Are food warmers, steam tables and bains-marie used to reheat prepared foods?

Are frozen foods being properly thawed under refrigeration or under cold running water or cooked directly from frozen state?

Are raw, and cooked or ready-to-serve foods being prepared on the same cutting board without washing and sanitizing the board between changed use?

"Sanitation Self-Inspection Program for Food Service Operators." Copyright 1983 by the National Restaurant Association. Reprinted by permission.

The National Restaurant Association publishes a guide to developing your own sanitation checklist. This publication is called *Sanitation Self-Inspection Program for Food Service Operators* and is designed so that the checklists can be removed and copied for repeated use. (For information on obtaining this publication, see "More on the Subject" at the end of this chapter.)

In the guidelines accompanying its checklist, the National Restaurant Association recommends that you keep your self-inspection sheets on file. Copies can then be furnished to local regulatory agencies as a token of your interest in sanitation. This cooperative action will encourage them to regard your establishment

Are hands being used to pick up rolls, bread, butter pats, ice, or other food to be served?

Are waitresses or bus boys handling place settings and serving food without washing hands after wiping tables and bussing soiled dishes?

Are food servers touching food-contact surfaces of plates, tumblers, cups, and silverware when setting table or serving customer?

Is floor being swept while food is exposed, being served, or when customers are eating?

Food and Supplies Receiving

Is food inspected immediately upon receipt for spoilage or infestation?

Is perishable food moved promptly to refrigeration?

Are unattended perishable food deliveries on loading dock or dolly?

Are non-food supplies checked for infestation?

Are empty shipping containers and packing removed to disposal area promptly?

Is receiving area free of food particles and debris?

Is floor of receiving area clean?

Are packages dated upon receipt to assure "First-in–First-out" use?

Are shellfish packages identified with processor or packer's name and number?

Dry Stores

Is all food stored at least six inches off the floor—on the shelves, racks, or platforms?

Is the floor clean and free from spilled food?

Are shelves high enough off floor to permit cleaning underneath, or is area beneath shelf enclosed to preclude accumulation of soil?

Are shelves away from wall to permit ventilation and discourage nesting of insects and rodents?

Have empty cartons and trash been removed?

Are canned goods removed from cartons for shelving to maximum extent practicable?

Are food storage shelves clean and free of dust and debris?

Are food supplies stored in a manner to ensure "First-in–First-out" use?

Is storeroom dry—free from dampness?

in a favorable light. Agency representatives may also be able to identify your special problems on the basis of these inspection sheets and to assist you in finding solutions. The self-inspection records will also be useful as evidence of your active sanitation program in case you are confronted by representatives from the news media or consumer groups. They can also be useful in the event of a legal problem.

The series of questions in Exhibit 15.2 is reprinted from the NRA's *Sanitation Self-Inspection Program for Food Service Operators*. Use these questions to inventory your own operation and to develop your own sanitation checklist.

Exhibit 15.2   Sanitation self-inspection checklist (continued)

Are non-food supplies stored separately from food stock?

Are all toxic materials, including pesticides, conspicuously labeled and used from original containers only?

Are pesticides separately stored in a well-marked cabinet?

Is there evidence of insects or rodents?

Is there evidence of misuse or spillage of insecticides or rodenticides?

Are bulk foods (sugar, flour), if no longer stored in original package, now stored in a covered container with identifying name?

Are food containers stored under exposed or unprotected sewer or water lines, or close to "sweating" walls?

Are most frequently needed items on lower shelves and near entrance?

Are heavy packages stored on lower shelves?

Refrigerator Storage

Are refrigerators equipped with accurate thermometers?

Are refrigerators maintaining potentially hazardous foods at temperatures of 45°F (7.2°C) or lower?

Are refrigerators clean and free from mold and objectionable odors?

Is all potentially hazardous food, not in actual preparation or hot holding, stored under refrigeration?

Is all food being stored off the floor of walk-in refrigerators?

Are foods stored on shelves spaced to provide for adequate air circulation and is shelving free of linings that retard circulation?

Are panned raw or cooked foods, on shelves, covered to prevent contamination?

Are cooked foods such as ground meat, stew, dressing, or gravy not stored in large-quantity containers?

Are foods stored in a manner to permit "First-in–First-out" use?

Is proper cleaning and maintenance being conducted?

Are any spoiled foods present?

Are raw foods stored separately from cooked foods?

Are shelves high enough from the floor to permit cleaning underneath?

Are shelves free from food husks, leaves, wrappings, or debris?

Are cooked foods or other products removed from original containers stored in clean, sanitized, covered containers and identified?

Are dairy products stored separately from strong-odored foods?

Are fish stored apart from other food products?

Are there sufficient refrigerator facilities to handle normal delivery schedules?

Is there sufficient space in the refrigerators to permit good air circulation around the stored food?

Is there awareness that ice used for cooling food will not be used for human consumption?

Are solid cuts of meat (except quarters and sides) covered in storage and placed to allow circulation of cool air?

Freezer Storage

Are freezer storage units operating?

Do all boxes or cabinets have accurate thermometers?

Are freezer storage units maintaining an interior temperature of 0°F (−17.7°C) or lower?

Is warewashing equipment cleaned after each day's use to remove chemicals, food particles, soil, and debris?

Are jets and nozzles cleaned of food particles and other obstructions and contaminants?

Are cleaned and sanitized wares and utensils stored off the floor and in a clean, dry location?

Is improper toweling of tableware and utensils observed?

Employee Facilities

Are employees' facilities clean, dry, and free from odor?

Is there a sufficient supply of soap, towels, and tissues for employee needs?

Is all sanitary equipment operational and in good repair?

Are proper receptacles available for waste materials?

Are these receptacles emptied frequently?

Are soiled cooks' aprons, whites, and other soiled clothing improperly stored in lockers or left in the facilities?

Are containers provided for employees' soiled uniforms?

Is unwrapped food stored in lockers or left in employee facilities?

Is there evidence of rodents or insects in the facilities?

Storage Rooms for Supplies and Equipment

Are storage facilities for supplies and equipment clean, dry, and free of trash and debris?

Are storage facilities free of empty cartons and wrappings, which might provide nesting for rodents?

Are supplies stored in a neat and orderly manner?

Are supplies stored off the floor and away from walls to permit access for cleaning and to prevent harborage of rodents and roaches?

Is perishable or unpackaged food present?

Are containers of pesticides in marked cabinet and apart from detergents and other chemicals?

Is there evidence of rodents or insects?

Are single-service articles stored at least six inches off the floor, in closed containers, and not placed under exposed sewer or water lines?

Are utensils, single-service items, or food equipment stored in toilets or vestibules?

Garbage and Trash Storage and Disposal Areas

Is area generally clean and orderly, free of spilled food and liquids?

Is floor, platform, or ground surface free from spilled particles of food and constructed of nonabsorbent material such as concrete or asphalt?

Is area free from objectionable odor?

Are spilled food particles and litter present in front of incinerator, dumpsters, etc.?

Are trash and garbage containers clean on the outside?

If can liners are not in use, are all garbage containers closed with tight-fitting covers?

Is trash confined in orderly fashion or in suitable containers?

Is there an accumulation of trash or garbage because of infrequent pick-up?

Are there puddles of wash water and food particles and liquids?

Exhibit 15.2   Sanitation self-inspection checklist (continued)

Is there any evidence of rats, rat holes or nests in the vicinity of the disposal area?

Are empty garbage and refuse containers washed prior to being returned for use?

Is mop water properly disposed of as sewage?

Are drain plugs in place on those containers designed with drains?

Are hot water, brushes, and detergent or steam provided for washing containers?

Is room constructed of easily cleanable nonabsorbent material?

Mechanical Rooms

Are boiler rooms, compressor rooms, and other utility rooms clean, dry, and free of foods, soiled or greasy utensils, and food preparation equipment?

Are they free of soiled linen and rags, empty containers and cartons, trash and debris?

Is there evidence of rodents and insects?

Is adequate ventilation provided?

Entryways, Exits, and Exterior Areas

Are entryways clear of trash and debris?

Are doors and screen doors tight fitting to prevent entry of insects and rodents?

Is there any evidence of rat holes or entry points near or into the building?

Are there wet spots or pools, or high grass or weeds, which could form breeding spots for insects?

Is the rear area, parking lot, or surrounding area free of litter, trash, and debris?

Do noxious birds nest or roost in ledges or eaves of the establishment?

Vehicles Used for Transporting Food

Is the cargo area of the vehicle thoroughly clean and free from dirt and debris?

Has all food in containers been removed for proper disposal or storage?

Is potentially hazardous food being carried at proper temperatures of heat or cold?

Is food being carried in adequately insulated containers?

Are all food spills on shelving or floor washed from the vehicle after each use?

Is there any evidence of insect infestation of the vehicle body?

Restrooms

Are customer restrooms clean, dry, light, well ventilated, and free from odor?

Is all sanitary equipment operating satisfactorily?

Is there a satisfactory supply of soap, tissues, towels or a hand drying device?

Are waste containers covered, kept clean, and emptied frequently?

Is there adequate hot and cold water, tempered by means of a mixing valve or combination faucet?

Is there any sign of rodents or insects?

Are toilet doors solid, self-closing, and in good working order?

Entrance and Foyer or Waiting Room

Is the entryway and waiting room clean and attractive?

Is it free from litter?

Are chairs and benches clean and are lamps and fixtures clean and free from dust?

Are posters and printed materials clean and neatly racked or posted?

Does the customer's final view of your establishment convey the image of cleanliness and freshness?

General Cleanliness of Dining Area

Is the floor dirty or littered, particularly with food particles and napkins?

Are there crumbs or spilled liquid on chairs or benches?

Are menus food-marked or worn and dirty, and are condiment containers unclean?

Are table linens food-marked? Are they tattered or torn?

Is tableware cracked, chipped, streaked, or food-soiled or silverware thumb-marked or food-soiled?

Are soiled dish trays left near customer tables?

Are insect sprays being used when food is exposed or customers are present?

Is floor being swept while food is exposed or being served or when customers are eating?

Is adequate lighting available for cleaning?

Cleanliness of Service Personnel

Are waitress uniforms wrinkled or soiled?

Are service personnel using strong or offensive perfume or smelling of body odor?

Are servers sniffing, coughing, or rubbing or wiping nose?

Do servers handle drinking glasses by their tops or silverware by their blades, tines, or bowls?

Are servers using effective hair restraints?

Do cooks and servers smoke in view of customers?

Do servers handle rolls, butter, ice, etc., by hand in filling dishes and water glasses?

Do employees scratch head, face, or body in view of customers?

Do servers touch food with thumb or fingers when serving plated food?

Sensory Factors

Is dining area too hot or cold for customer comfort?

Is heat and steam from serving line unpleasant for customers (and the servers)?

Is light in dining room too bright and glary?

Is light too dim, so that customer has difficulty seeing the menu and food and tableware?

Is clatter of warewashing offensive to the customer?

Is removal of soiled tableware noisy?

Does odor of the kitchen greet the customer entering the dining area?

Is there an "old grease" odor in the dining room or exhausted to the street or parking area?

Is spoiled food disposed of promptly to prevent obnoxious odor?

THE "GUESTRONOMICS" OF SAFE FOOD

In most industries you have to pay for surveys on what the customer thinks of your products and services. You, the foodservice manager, are lucky. Your surveys are free of charge, and if you are attentive, you can get results almost immediately.

Each time you welcome customers into your establishment you are inviting them to inspect your operation. You are asking, directly or indirectly, what they think of the quality of the food, the decor, the conduct of your personnel, and—most important for our purposes in this book—the sanitation standards achieved.

It is of course important that the customer approve of the taste and appearance of the food, and of the service. But, you may ask, what do the customers know about sanitation? If you ran an unsanitary kitchen that looked spanking clean, would the customers know the difference? Why should you trust a stranger as a guide to foodservice sanitation?

The customers may have an incomplete understanding of sanitation, but in reacting to your establishment, they can reveal a number of valuable things about its sanitary character.

That is the premise we urge you to examine: that the customer usually has at least an intuitive sense of sanitary conditions in a food service, and that the manager can identify many shortcomings in sanitation by viewing the facility as a customer would and by carefully evaluating customer reactions.

Put Yourself in the Customer's Place

No matter how exacting you make your self-inspection standards, your toughest critic will still be the customer. It is your customer's opinion, in the last analysis, that really counts. But how do you get the customer to give you that opinion?

One way is to assume the role of the customer yourself. If you have owned, managed, or worked in a foodservice establishment for any length of time, you have probably become accustomed to its shortcomings. But you will remain sensitive to its failings if you compel yourself to keep a customer's-eye view. It is no easy psychological trick to put yourself in another's shoes, but it will pay you to try.

Play the game this way. Tell yourself, "This is not my place. I have come here to get a meal, and they had better give me my money's worth." Forget about all the difficulties you are having with suppliers, the staff, and the landlord. You are the Royal Customer, and these are not your concerns.

Outside Impressions

Your impressions as a customer start even before you enter the establishment. If the parking lot, sidewalk, shrubbery, and entryway are free of litter, you will get a good feeling about the interior even before you see it. If the reverse is true, you may begin to doubt the cleanliness of the entire operation. As a manager-customer, you may also wonder whether the litter hides insect colonies and rodents waiting for an opportunity to enter.

Now sniff the air. Subtle cooking odors are acceptable, even appetizing. But noxious clouds of smoke and oily vapors from the exhaust vents are not. In addition to being hard on the neighbors and in violation of air-pollution ordinances, accumulations of grease in the vents may provide breeding and feeding sites for insects as well as a fire hazard.

Inside Impressions

Assume that all is well outdoors, so that when you step into the establishment your eyes, ears, and nostrils are fully sensitive to all the telltales, good and bad. Some of these indicators will relate more to aesthetics than to sanitation, but you, the customer, will not make a conscious distinction. Grimy posters in the entryway do not bear directly on food safeness, but they will have their effect on the customer. Cigarette butts and litter in the corners of the waiting room and rips and tears in the upholstery, however, are patently unaesthetic *and* unsanitary.

Surveying the Dining Room

Now you enter the dining room. The first sound that assaults your ears is the noise of tableware being dumped into washbins. Such clatter hardly contributes to pleasant dining. It also does violence to the sanitary setting. Chipped, cracked dishes and glassware are difficult to clean, unsafe, and provide numerous tiny refuges for bacteria.

Still fresh from the outdoors, you detect an unpleasant odor only partly masked by food aromas. As a patron, you suspect that decaying food particles and scraps—hardly the hallmarks of a clean establishment—that have collected in and around chairs, benches, booths, and tables may be the cause of the smell. As a manager-sanitarian, you also realize that bacteria may be multiplying rapidly in the decomposing food. Many common microorganisms produce characteristic odors. You will also be aware that the same conditions that produce unpleasant bacterial odors also can provide breeding sites for insects and vermin, and that these creatures in turn can produce malodorous conditions.

Dark, damp, and uncleaned crevices in dining and service areas are highly vulnerable to insect invasion. The problem is especially acute around bussing stations and service areas subject to frequent food spills. Bar and fountain areas are also susceptible to invasion because of high moisture conditions.

With the smell still in your nostrils, your first reaction may be to order someone to apply deodorant, disinfectant, or pesticide in the suspect areas. Further reflection should tell you that covering up the odor or destroying bacteria and insects is only a temporary solution.

Instead, get to the root of the problem. Why are food and excess moisture collecting? Perhaps because of poor work habits on the part of busy employees who splash and spill as they rush through their tasks. Or there may be a leak in a water or drain line. It may be that the equipment and facilities are constructed or positioned so as to make them difficult to clean, or in such a way as to make it hard for employees to work around them without mishaps.

Next, survey the dining room as a whole. Dusty drapes, streaked or grimy windows, smudged or cracked walls, cob-webbed ceilings, loose floor tiles, or a heavily soiled carpet should make you feel a bit uneasy about the wholesomeness of the food. The customers might overlook those failings in their homes, but they are much less tolerant when eating out.

Inspecting the Set-Up

All through the dining room there have been situations and events that caused you, the manager-turned-customer, to question the attention given by your staff to sanitation standards. Now look at your own table.

Is the linen freshly laundered and free of stains? Is your menu card finger-marked and greasy? Are the sugar, salt, and pepper containers streaked, spotted, or caked with bits of food? Are salad dressings, cream, and condiments left out on the table? Are the table and chairs and the floor clear of dust, litter, and food scraps? Are water glasses and tableware streaked, spotted, or caked with bits of food?

Evaluating Serving Personnel

Try to evaluate your personnel as the customer would. The waiter and the busboy may be the only visible members of the foodservice staff. If the busboy has a clean uniform and is well groomed, you feel reassured. If he is slovenly and rude, you feel quite the opposite.

You spy a waitress taking a cigarette break in a corner of the dining room. As a patron you might worry about ashes in the food. As a sanitarian you would also be concerned that she could transfer micro-organisms from mouth to cigarette, to hands, to food. If a waiter coughs or sneezes over food, your reactions as a manager-sanitarian and as a customer pretty well coincide. Your confidence in the food service will similarly be shaken if the waitress touches food or food-contact surfaces.

Grading the Restrooms

Now it is time to examine one of the most sensitive areas of a food service—the restroom. As a manager, you know that careless patrons often defeat the most sincere efforts to keep restrooms clean. As a customer, you may not be very indulgent about management's problems with other patrons. However endless and thankless the task may seem, restroom sanitation is an absolute must. So take a look.

Is everything working? Is there soap in the dispenser and not on the counters or the floor? Do the toilet doors latch as they are supposed to? And most of all, is everything shining clean and odor-free? If not, your restrooms may be your competition's best asset.

The Customer Acts

Posing as a customer is a valuable way of obtaining information about your establishment, but if you really want the cold, hard truth, you must get it from the customers themselves. This quest for information is not always easy. Customers do not feel it to be their responsibility to tell you how to improve your restaurant, nor are they interested in hearing your excuses. Many customers are too timid to voice their complaints; others just don't want to get involved.

If you are open for business, you are promising the customer a wholesome meal in clean, pleasant surroundings. If you do not make good on this promise, your customers will simply take their health, tastebuds, and pocketbooks elsewhere, usually without a word to tell you why.

If this "silent treatment" occurs, how can you tell when your customers are dissatisfied? By closely—but discreetly!—watching them for the many unspoken signs of displeasure.

For example, there is a small group of people who will always wipe their tableware with their napkins when they sit down in a restaurant, no matter how clean the items are. But if you see your guests doing so, you cannot assume that they are doing it out of habit. It may be that the dishwashing machine is not doing its job, and the customers are trying to wipe away the visible evidence. Any time customers ask for tableware replacements—because a cup bears lipstick marks or bits of food are stuck to a fork—there is reason to check on dishwashing procedures and equipment. In this case, "clean" and "sanitary" are one and the same. If the souvenirs of a previous meal have not been removed from the serving ware, the same may be true of harmful bacteria, which could easily have been deposited at the same time.

When a customer asks to be seated elsewhere because of a draft, that person may be overly sensitive to temperature changes, or the ventilation system may not be operating properly. Drafty conditions can raise dust and contaminate unprotected foods. One serious food poisoning incident was traced to bowls of pudding set out to cool in a drafty, dusty corridor. Too *little* air movement can be just as bad, since it may promote bacterial growth and insect infestation.

A plate of food left untouched can mean a number of things, and it may well be a sanitation danger signal. Possibly it was a case of overestimation of capacity, or perhaps your customer wanted to experiment with a new dish and lost gustatory courage after it arrived. But it may also be that the food had an off taste, indicating spoilage or worse, or that it included an unwelcome hair or insect fragment, indicating unsafe foodhandling. Similarly, the couple who ordered an expensive meal may rush through it because they are running late for the theater, or they may have found the surroundings so unappetizing that they wanted to put the experience behind them as quickly as possible.

Food sent back to the kitchen is another sign that your sanitation guard may be down. When a customer asks the waiter to heat up the soup, that should tell you that safe—as well as savory—holding temperatures are not being maintained.

It is a curious trait of some patrons to reserve negative comments until they are at a safe distance. All through the meal they give you no reason to suspect that anything is amiss, perhaps because they find it too embarrassing to complain. They pay their bills and then, in voices meant to be overheard, they tell each other, "The food was okay, but that washroom was disgusting!" or "I couldn't see the cockroaches for the flies!" The manager who usually stands near the cash register might well move closer to the revolving doors for an uncensored critique of the establishment.

Handling Customer Complaints

No matter how faithfully you adhere to the principles of sanitation, some sorry day the regrettable will probably happen. A customer will be served glass in a salad, or the proverbial fly in the soup, or may even become the victim of foodborne illness. The manager's reaction to such an incident can mean the difference between an unpleasant but valuable lesson and a costly lawsuit.

A customer who believes his or her health has been imperiled by your operation has the right to take you to court. Your objective is to avoid that problem, as well as to regain the customer's goodwill and patronage. And the first step in doing so is to realize that the customer may indeed have a legitimate grievance and can provide helpful information. Too many foodservice operators assume at the outset that the customer's complaint is unjustified.

Your legal responsibilities and liability may vary from place to place and from incident to incident, but if contaminants have found their way into a customer's food, whether or not illness has resulted, you have an ethical obligation to be concerned, and you must show this concern to the customer. Treating an angry customer as a crank is a sure way to escalate the seriousness of the situation. Take the customer's problem seriously and take the opportunity to elicit information that can help you.

1. Demonstrate a genuine interest in the customer's complaint and assure him or her that you and your staff make every effort to provide safe and wholesome food.

2. Offer to assist the customer in any way that you can. Your own sincerity and professional attitude will do much to relieve the customer's resentment and to avoid liability. At the same time be cautious. Be careful that you don't *accept* or *admit* liability before all the facts are known.

3. Determine how the contamination occurred. Use your powers of investigation and observation. An incident of foodborne illness is a high price to pay for an education, but once you've paid it, don't ignore the lesson. How did the stew spoil? Was the refrigerator working properly? Did the cook leave the stew to sit out while he or

she prepared another dish? Was the cook ill? Was there a leak over the preparation table? How did the glass or the fly get into the food? Perhaps an unprotected light fixture is located too close to food preparation areas, and a bulb was shattered in an accident. The back-of-the-house windows and doors may not be adequately screened to prevent the entry of insects. Find the source of the problem and you will be better able to prevent a repetition.

4. Question the customer. Did the food taste spoiled or not quite right? Did the customer take the food home first and wait to eat it? Did the customer eat somewhere else? Did he or she observe the server and notice anything that may have contaminated the food? The customer may provide some valuable information about your facility, your employees, and your food preparation. Also, by questioning the customer closely you may both discover it was not your food at all but something else.

5. Take corrective action. Once you have the information you need, don't delay. Do what you have to do in order to prevent another incident.

6. Finally, don't be complacent because you get few complaints. Most customers won't tell you when something is wrong. They simply do not come back.

Again, don't assume that all is well with your establishment just because no one has told you about a stomach upset after eating your food. Eternal vigilance is the price of high sanitary standards. It is also the price you must pay for peace of mind—the assurance that no one is going to become ill as a result of having been your guest.

SUMMARY

Achieving good sanitation in a food service requires you, as the manager, to exert control at each critical stage in an operation in order to ensure proper practices and evaluate the results.

Supervision of employees' tasks must be constant but at the same time tactful. The task of sanitation supervision can be made much simpler if your staff is motivated to participate actively in the sanitation effort.

The results of your sanitation program can be monitored through frequent self-inspections. The use of detailed checklists, such as the one published by the National Restaurant Association (see Exhibit 15.2), can make this task easier and more systematic. Self-inspection will indicate your areas of weakness before the arrival of the health inspector and enable you to pinpoint those items needing more attention.

Sanitation checklists can be kept on file to use in demonstrating to health officials, the mass media, and the law your active approach to the prevention of foodborne illness.

As the manager of a foodservice operation, you may come to know it so well that you no longer notice its failings. Compelling yourself to see it as a customer does can open your eyes to many possible shortcomings.

Customers are generally reluctant to complain about unsatisfactory conditions. To find out how your customers feel about your operation, you must watch for such telltale clues as hurried dinners, uneaten food, and the wiping of tableware on napkins to warn you when all is not right.

In the event of an actual complaint, whether major or minor, from a customer, the manager's attitude is all-important. Give the complaint your serious attention, and try to locate the cause of the problem so that you can avoid its repetition.

A CASE IN POINT

First the customer sent back some perfectly good soup, saying it was cold. Then she came up to the cafeteria manager and said she saw a cockroach at the salad bar. The manager laughed and asked if the cockroach preferred Italian or French dressing. The customer was clearly disgusted by this approach and left in a huff, but not before pointing out to the manager that one of the line servers smelled as if he hadn't washed in weeks. She also said that she was going to say something to the health department.

How could this incident have been handled?

STUDY QUESTIONS

1. What are three basic steps in evaluating the success of a sanitation program?
2. What are the foodservice control points over which a manager has control?
3. How often should self-inspection for sanitation occur?
4. Who should conduct sanitation self-inspections?
5. Describe how you would develop a sanitation checklist for your facility.
6. How does customer-inspection aid you in your sanitation program?
7. Since most customers are not experts in the rules of sanitation, why should they be considered reliable sources of information on the sanitation level of your establishment?
8. Why is putting yourself in the customer's shoes and evaluating your operation from that standpoint so difficult?
9. What should you do if a customer complains about unpleasant odors?
10. What should you do if a customer complains about sanitation?
11. Why are chipped, cracked dishes a hazard?
12. When are customers most likely to voice their dissatisfaction with a foodservice establishment?

MORE ON THE SUBJECT

NATIONAL RESTAURANT ASSOCIATION. *Sanitation Self-Inspection Program for Food Service Operators.* Washington, D.C., 1983. 32 pages. This publication provides guidelines for a sanitation and safe-foodhandling self-inspection program and contains a complete set of check-sheets covering the various areas of a commercial foodservice operation.

ANSWER TO A CASE IN POINT

The manager should have taken the customer's complaints more seriously. He could have double-checked the soup for temperature (perhaps the holding equipment for the soup was not working properly) and there should not have been pests near the salad bar—or anywhere else in the establishment. Also, the customer may have been correct about the line server.

The manager's laughter was probably offensive to the customer, who was serious about what she was saying. The attitude told her that the manager just didn't care. A better approach might have been to question the customer, thank her for her comments, provide her with a fresh bowl of *hot* soup, promise to look into her complaints—and then do so.

Glossary

Abrasive Cleaner containing a scouring agent, usually finely ground feldspar or silica used for cleaning some sinks, rusty metals, or badly soiled floors. Abrasives may mar some surfaces.

Accident An unintended happening resulting in injury or damage.

Acid A substance with a pH less than 7.

Additive Any substance added to foods that may become a component or affect the characteristics of a food. Such substances may be hazardous under certain conditions.

Aerobic Able to live and reproduce only in the presence of free oxygen.

Air door Ventilation unit consisting of outgoing air that can help keep out flying insects if used around doors and windows.

Air gap An unobstructed, vertical distance through the free atmosphere separating the outlet of a potable water supply from the flood-level rim of a potentially contaminated receptacle (see Backflow).

Alkali A substance with a pH of more than 7.

Amino acids Organic compounds that make up proteins.

Anaerobic Able to live and reproduce in the absence of free oxygen.

Anticoagulant An agent that prevents blood from clotting. When used in multiple-dose rodenticides, it causes rodents to die of internal bleeding.

Antiseptic An agent that stops the growth of micro-organisms in or on the body.

Bacillary dysentery A highly infectious disease caused by consumption of *Shigella* bacteria. Also called shigellosis.

Bacilli Rod-shaped bacteria.

Bacillus cereus Rod-shaped, spore-forming bacterium. The cause of bacillus cereus food poisoning.

Backflow The flow of water or other substances into the distributing pipes of a potable water supply from any unintended source.

Back-siphonage A plumbing hazard. The reverse flow of water as a result of negative pressure in the potable water system.

Bacteria Single-celled organisms, usually classified as the simplest of plants.

Bactericide An agent that kills vegetative bacteria, but not necessarily spore forms.

Bacteriostat An agent that inhibits the growth of bacteria in the presence of moisture but does not necessarily kill them.

Baits Multiple-dose, anticoagulent pesticides mixed with pest-attracting food and left where rodents will find them.

Biological hazard Danger to food from disease-causing micro-organisms and poisonous plants and fish.

Blast freezers Freezers that can bring unfrozen foods to the frozen state. Also called *plate freezers*.

Botulism Intoxication resulting from consumption of botulinum toxin produced by the *Clostridium botulinum* bacterium.

Budding A form of asexual reproduction typical of yeasts, in which a new individual arises as an outgrowth of an older individual.

Carrier An individual who harbors an infectious agent in his or her body, and can transmit it to others, but exhibits no symptoms of disease.

Celsius Temperature scale related to Fahrenheit scale by the formula $5/9$ ($°$Fahrenheit $- 32°$) $= °$Celsius.

Chalaza Spiral bands of a thickened substance in the white of an egg.

Chemical hazard Danger to food safety posed by chemical substances, especially pesticides; food additives; and toxic metals.

Clean Free of visible soil.

Cleanability Capability of being exposed for inspection or cleaning without difficulty. Construction allowing soil to be removed effectively by normal cleaning methods.

Cleaning The physical removal of soil from a surface.

Clean-in-place A technique for treating equipment designed so that food-contact surfaces are not readily removable. Cleaning and sanitizing is done by circulating solutions throughout the item.

Clostridium botulinum A rod-shaped, spore-forming, anaerobic bacterium that produces a powerful toxin responsible for causing botulism.

Clostridium perfringens A rod-shaped, spore-forming, anaerobic bacterium that causes foodborne illness in humans.

Cocci Spherically shaped bacteria.

Colony A cluster of micro-organisms, visible to the naked eye, growing on or in a solid medium.

Communicable Capable of being transmitted, directly or indirectly, from one human being to another.

Compressor In a refrigeration unit, the component that compresses air to provide energy to run the refrigerator. A high-capacity compressor is required in foodservice refrigerators.

Contact insecticide An agent that penetrates the body wall or legs of an insect to kill it.

Contagious Capable of being transmitted by contact.

Contamination The unintended presence of harmful substances or organisms, especially in food.

Coving Molding with a concave face; installed to soften a floor–wall angle for ease of cleaning.

Cross-connection Any physical link between two otherwise separate piping systems, one containing potable water and the other containing potentially contaminated substances.

Cross-contamination The transfer of harmful micro-organisms from one food to another by means of a nonfood surface such as utensils, equipment, or human hands.

Cry-o-vac aging A process of aging meats in a plastic bag. A method of vacuum-packaging.

Danger zone The temperature range between $45°$ and $140°$F ($7.2°$ and $60°$C) within which most bacteria experience their best growth and reproduction.

Dead-man control A handle on a machine designed so that the machine will automatically stop if the operator's hand releases the handle.

Decline phase The phase of bacterial growth following the stationary phase, in which the rate of death within the colony exceeds the rate of reproduction and the number of living cells begins to decrease.

Detergent A cleaning agent: especially any of numerous synthetic organic compounds that are chemically different from soaps but share many of the cleaning properties of soap.

Diplococci Spherically shaped bacteria arranged in pairs.

Disinfectant An agent that kills the growing forms, but not necessarily the spores, of micro-organisms; especially for use on inanimate surfaces.

Encyst To form a capsule or resistant cover around a parasite.

Enzyme An organic substance that promotes the chemical processes of life without being altered or destroyed in these processes.

Facultative Able to grow and reproduce with or without the presence of free oxygen.

Fahrenheit A temperature scale related to Celsius by the formula $(9/5 \times °\text{Celsius}) + 32°$ $= °\text{Fahrenheit}$.

Fermentation Anaerobic oxidation of compounds by enzyme action of micro-organisms, used in such industrial processes as the production of alcohol and cheese.

FIFO "First In, First Out": a stock-rotation rule for the storage of food.

Fission A method of asexual reproduction, found among micro-organisms, in which the individual splits into two or more parts, each of which becomes a complete individual.

Flagella Relatively long, whiplike appendages on some bacterial cells, serving as organs of locomotion.

Flash point The temperature at which hot fat will burst into flame; varies with the type of fat.

Food Any substance intended for use or for sale in whole or in part for human consumption, including ice and water.

Foodborne illness Disease or injury occurring as a result of consumption of contaminated food.

Food-contact surface Any surface of equipment or utensils with which food normally comes in contact, or from which food may drain, drip, or splash back onto surfaces normally in contact with food.

Food poisoning A general term for intoxication or infection caused by consumption of contaminated food.

Food shields Barriers of either clear plastic or glass placed between self-service foods and patrons to prevent contamination.

Footcandle A unit of illumination equal to one lumen per square foot.

Fungi A group of single-celled or filamentous plants that lack chlorophyll and are made up of nucleated cells, including molds, yeasts, and mushrooms.

Galvanized Coated with zinc.

Gastrointestinal The stomach and the intestinal tract.

Germ A general term for micro-organisms, particularly pathogens.

Germicide An agent that kills germs but not spores. Same as disinfectant.

Germination The sprouting, or beginning of development, of a spore or seed.

Hard water Water with relatively large amounts of mineral salts dissolved in it.

Hepatitis Inflammation of the liver caused by a virus found in infected people and some raw shellfish. Usually transmitted by consumption of water or food contaminated with the virus.

Hermetically sealed container A container designed to prevent the entry of micro-organisms and to maintain the sterility of its contents, as a home-canning jar.

Host An animal or plant on or in which another organism lives and nourishes itself.

Hygiene Practices necessary for establishing and maintaining good health.

Hygrometer An instrument for measuring the humidity of the atmosphere.

Hyphae The filaments or threads composing the vegetative body of a fungus.

Incubation period The phase in the course of an infection between the invasion of the host by the pathogen and the appearance of the symptoms of illness.

Infection Disease caused by invasion of a host by living, pathogenic organisms, which multiply within the body.

Infestation Occupation or invasion by parasites other than bacteria.

Intoxication Disease caused by consumption of poisons, which may be chemical, naturally occurring in food, or produced by pathogenic micro-organisms.

Iodophor A bactericide made up of iodine and a surface-active agent, which releases iodine when dissolved in water.

Irradiation Use of radiation in processing foods.

Laceration A wound made by tearing the skin.

Lag phase The period of bacterial growth following transfer to a new environment, when adaptation to new conditions takes place and there is little or no increase in the number of cells in the colony.

Larva An immature, usually wormlike, self-supporting form of any animal that must undergo fundamental changes in form and size before reaching adulthood.

Log phase The period of bacterial growth following the lag phase, when multiplication rate is constant and rapid and the number of cells in the colony increases exponentially.

Medium Any nutritive substance on or in which micro-organisms can grow and reproduce.

Mesophilic Able to grow best at moderate temperatures, approximately in the range of 60° to 110°F (15.6° to 43.3°C).

Metabolism The sum of chemical and physical processes by which an organism derives energy from food.

Micro- Prefix denoting small size.

Microbe A general term for microscopic organisms, particularly pathogens.

Micron A unit of length equal to one-millionth of a meter.

Micro-organisms Forms of life that can be seen only with the aid of a microscope, including bacteria, viruses, yeasts, algae, and single-celled animals.

Mold Any of various fungi composed of hyphae and forming colonies having the appearance of wooly growths.

Monosodium glutamate A chemical substance used as a flavor enhancer. May cause allergic reactions in some people.

Neutral Having a chemical composition that is neither acidic nor alkaline, with a pH of 7.

Nucleus The major organ in most plant and animal cells, which contains the chromosomes and functions in metabolism, growth, and reproduction.

Organic Pertaining to or derived from an organism. Organic chemical compounds contain carbon and hydrogen, with or without oxygen and other elements.

Organism An individual living thing.

Outbreak The development of foodborne illness by two or more people who have eaten a common food that is shown by laboratory analysis to be the source of the illness. One case of botulism qualifies as an outbreak.

Parasite An organism that lives on or in another organism (host) of a different species, from which it derives nutrients and shelter.

Pasteurization A process that kills most pathogenic bacteria in food and retards the growth of others with minimal chemical change by heating the food to a specific temperature for a definite length of time.

Pathogen Any disease-producing agent, usually a living organism.

Pathogenic Capable of producing disease.

Perishable Food subject to quick decay or spoilage, except under proper conditions.

Personal hygiene Individual cleanliness and habits that contribute to healthful conditions.

pH A measure of the acidity or alkalinity of solutions; pH 7 is neutral, under 7 is acidic, and 7 to 14 is alkaline.

Physical hazard A danger to food from particles or fragments of items that are not supposed to be in food, such as glass or bits of tableware.

Porosity The extent to which a substance is permeable, or can absorb liquids.

Potable Suitable or safe for drinking.

Potable water Water that is fit to drink.

Potentially hazardous food Any food that consists in whole or in part of milk or milk products, eggs, meat, poultry, fish, shellfish, edible crustacea, or other ingredients, in a form capable of supporting rapid growth of infectious or toxicogenic micro-organisms.

Precipitate A deposit of insoluble substance resulting from chemical or physical changes in a solution.

Protein Any of a group of complex organic compounds made up of amino acids, which are the essential constituents of living cells.

Protozoan Single-celled animal.

Psittacosis Pneumonia and generalized infection transmitted to man by certain types of birds.

Psychrophilic Able to grow best at relatively low temperatures, approximately in the range of 32° to 45°F (0° to 7.2°C).

Quaternary ammonium The main ingredient in many noncorrosive, chemical, sanitizing formulations.

Quats Quaternary ammonium compounds.

Rancidity A condition caused by the oxidation or breaking down of fats and fatty acids, responsible for much meat spoilage.

Reconstituted Dehydrated food products recombined with water or other liquids.

Repellant A chemical that will keep insects away from a specific area but will not kill them.

Replication Duplication by exact copying of a molecular model.

Reservoir An alternate host or passive carrier of a pathogenic organism.

Residual spray A contact insecticide, which when applied to a surface leaves a deposit that can kill insects.

Resiliency Ability to withstand shock without permanent deformation or rupture; used to classify floor materials.

Salmonella Facultative, rod-shaped, nonspore-forming bacteria that can cause salmonellosis if it contaminates food eaten by humans.

Salmonellosis Infection caused by consumption of food containing certain species of *Salmonella*.

Sanitary Free of disease-causing organisms and other harmful substances.

Sanitation The creation and maintenance of conditions favorable to good health.

Sanitization The reduction of the number of pathogenic micro-organisms on a surface to levels accepted as safe by regulatory authorities.

Saponify To convert fats into soap and glycerol by heating with alkalies.

Scale Buildup of lime deposits on some foodservice equipment resulting from magnesium, calcium, and iron ions in the water (water hardness). An acid cleaner is recommended for removal.

Sealed A surface that is free of cracks or other openings that permit the entry or passage of moisture.

Shelf life Length of time a product can be stored.

Shellfish According to the FDA, this includes oysters, clams, and mussels.

Shigella Rod-shaped bacteria that cause bacillary dysentery, or shigellosis, in humans.

Shigellosis Bacillary dysentery.

Single-service articles Cups, containers, lids, closures, plates, knives, forks, spoons, stirrers, paddles, straws, napkins, wrapping materials, toothpicks, and similar articles intended for one-time, one-person use and then discarded.

Sneeze guards See Food shields.

Soap A compound of fatty acids and alkalies that has cleaning properties.

Space spray A contact insecticide that, when discharged into the air, drifts for several minutes to kill flying insects.

Spirilla Spiral- or comma-shaped bacteria.

Spoilage Damage to the edible quality of food through improper handling, contamination, or natural processes of aging or enzyme action.

Spore An inactive, resistant, resting, or reproductive body that can produce a new vegetative individual in a favorable environment.

Staphylococci Spherically shaped bacteria in masses or bunches.

Staphylococcus aureus A species of staphylococcus responsible for a type of food intoxication.

Stationary phase The period of bacterial growth following the log phase, in which the number of bacterial cells remains more or less constant, as cells compete for space and nourishment.

Sterile Free from all living organisms, especially micro-organisms.

Streptococci Spherically shaped bacteria arranged in chains of cells.

Sulfiting agents Chemical substances used to preserve a variety of food items; especially fruits and vegetables.

Surfactant A surface-active substance; one that reduces the surface tension of water.

Temporary foodservice establishment One that operates in one location for a period of not more than 14 days consecutively and in conjunction with a single event or celebration.

Thermophilic Able to grow best at relatively high temperatures, approximately in the range of 110° to 130°F (43.3° to 54.4°C).

Toxic Poisonous.

Toxicogenic Capable of producing poisons.

Toxin A poison. Specifically, a poison produced by a living organism.

Trichinella spiralis A parasitic worm whose larvae may be found encysted in the muscles of pigs, bears, rats, and humans and which causes trichinosis.

Trichinosis Disease resulting from the consumption of live *Trichinella spiralis* larvae in improperly cooked meat.

Vacuum-packaging A process of aging meat in a transparent, sealed bag. This process will preserve food quality over a period of time, if proper sanitary practices are met.

Vegetative Involved in nutrition and growth, as opposed to reproduction.

Vermin Animals obnoxious to humans, especially small, numerous, hard-to-control animals such as rats, mice, and various insects.

Virus Any of a large group of infectious agents, lacking independent metabolism and requiring a living host in order to reproduce, consisting of DNA or RNA in a protein shell.

Water activity Expression of amount of moisture available to aid bacterial growth.

Yeast A general term for single-celled fungi that reproduce by budding.

Index